WHAT IF . . .?
Toward Excellence
in Reasoning

▲WHAT IF...?

▼Toward Excellence in Reasoning

Jaakko Hintikka
Boston University

James Bachman
Valparaiso University

Mayfield Publishing Company
Mountain View, California
London • Toronto

Library of Congress Cataloging-in-Publication Data

Hintikka, Jaakko, 1929–
    What if— ? : toward excellence in reasoning / Jaakko Hintikka, James Bachman.
    p.   cm.
    Includes index.
    ISBN 0-87484-964-0
    1. Reasoning. 2. Critical thinking. I. Bachman, James, 1946–. II. Title.
BC177.H56   1991
160—dc20   90-44120
                                                                                                           CIP

Manufactured in the United States of America
10 9 8 7 6 5 4 3 2

Mayfield Publishing Company
1240 Villa Street
Mountain View, California

Sponsoring editor, James Bull; managing editor, Linda Toy; copy editor, Lauren Root; text and cover designer, Paula Goldstein; cover art, *Study 82* by John Casado. The text was set in 10/12 Palatino by ExecuStaff and printed on 50# Finch Opaque at Malloy Lithographing, Inc.

Credits: Pages 21–27/Reprinted from 'The Meno' in PROTAGORAS AND MENO by Plato, translated by W. K. C. Guthrie (Penguin Classics, 1956), copyright © W. K. C. Guthrie, 1956. Pages 166–167/ Reprinted from Richard Robinson, PLATO'S EARLIER DIALECTIC, 2nd ed. 1953) pages 7–8. Copyright © 1953 by Richard Robinson. Pages 176–177/Reprinted from Dick Francis, HOT MONEY, published by Michael Joseph, Ltd. and Pan Books, Ltd. 1988. Pages 203–204/Reprinted from FER-DE-LANCE by Rex Stout, Bantam, 1983, by permission of the estate of Rex Stout. Pages 224–225/Reprinted with permission of Macmillan Publishing Company from THE ART OF CROSS-EXAMINATION by Francis Wellman. Copyright 1936 by Macmillan Publishing Company; copyright renewed © 1964 by Ethel Wellman. Pages 317–319/Reprinted from J. H. Phillips, J. K. Bowen, FORENSIC SCIENCE AND THE EXPERT WITNESS, The Law Book Co., Ltd., Sydney, 1985, pp. 3–5. Pages 331–332/From THE EVIDENCE NEVER LIES by Alfred Allan Lewis with Herbert Leon MacDonell. Copyright © 1984 by Alfred Allan Lewis and Herbert Leon MacDonell. Reprinted by permission of Henry Holt and Company, Inc.

▲ C O N T E N T S
▼

v

PART TWO

Logical Inferences in Detail   81

PART THREE

Interrogative Moves in Detail   159

PART FOUR

Advanced Topics in Interrogative Reasoning   235

Conclusion   359

Appendixes, Glossary, and Index

▲ P R E F A C E
▼

"They can send me to college but they can't make me think!" So reads a bumper sticker on a student's car. The slogan refutes itself since it took some thought both to create and to appreciate the quip. The problem is not so much to make people think, but to enable and encourage them to think well. That is the goal of this book.

Many college and university courses aim at improving students' reasoning. The recorded history of recommendations for achieving this goal stretches back to Aristotle. We venture adding to this history because for several years Jaakko Hintikka and various associates have been developing a comprehensive theory for understanding the nature of reasoning that sheds new light on how students may be encouraged and enabled to achieve creatively disciplined reasoning skills. This theory, the interrogative approach to inquiry, makes it possible to integrate deductive logic and informal reasoning into a unified whole. Its core is what is known as the interrogative model of reasoning.

The Interrogative Model of Reasoning

The interrogative model, which is used consistently throughout the book, offers a uniform framework for studying and teaching both formal logic and argumentation theory, including the analysis, evaluation, and construction of arguments in ordinary English. As in the old Socratic method, reasoning is cast in the form of a sequence of questions and answers, interspersed with logical (i.e., deductive) inferences.

The interrogative model distinguishes *definitory rules,* which are concerned with reasoning correctly, from *strategic rules,* which tell how to reason effectively. The former define what is admissible in reasoning, while the latter show students how to make creative use of what is allowed by the definitory rules. Strategic rules thus serve as signposts on the way to excellence in reasoning. By stressing strategic rules this text stays focused on the pursuit of excellence in reasoning.

In the interrogative model all inferences are required to be deductive. This eliminates the problem that an *inference* might introduce an element of uncertainty. Thus all inferences are strictly truth preserving.

The effect is to locate problems with uncertainty in the process of discovering and gathering information rather than in the inference process. The interrogative model can then deploy many different insights to develop strategies for coping with uncertainty about the information available to the reasoner. The Instructor's Manual directs interested readers to a bibliography of the original research on the interrogative model.

The text introduces fundamental notions of deductive logic in the early pages of Chapter 1, but the usual terminology of deductive logic is not introduced until the beginning of Part Two (Chapter 5). Our experience has been that students more easily grasp the fundamental nature of valid deductive inference if we postpone the traditional terminology. We find that too many students think they already know what the terms "valid" and "deductive" mean. By employing the less familiar phrase "logical inference," we are able to focus on learning the nature of inference rather than unlearning ideas carried over from everyday use of the traditional terminology.

In Parts Two and Four we face the perennial problem of moving back and forth between everyday English and the formal notation of logicians. We consider it important to face the realities of the problem and acknowledge that no cut-and-dried rules can be formulated (on the beginning student's level, at least) which would be adequate to this task of translation.

Sooner or later, therefore, we must appeal to the students' semantical intuitions, and it is best to appeal to the intuitions that are likely to be strongest and most sure. Our strategy is this: In order to apply the formal rules of interrogative games, it typically suffices to focus on the main logical operator of the statement in question. Accordingly, the formal rules can be applied directly to an English sentence as soon as one identifies its main connective or quantifier—that is, knows whether the statement is a negation, or a conjunction, or a disjunction, or a conditional, or a universal statement, or an existential statement. The ability to make this identification is part and parcel of the ability to understand the statement in the first place. The strategy of focusing on the main logical operator in the sentence frees the students from having to engage in wholesale translation from English into formal notation.

Organization and Special Features

A step-by-step approach ensures that students master each phase of the interrogative model before moving to the next phase. All important definitions are highlighted in boxes, and key concepts are reviewed at frequent intervals. Dozens of exercise sets are provided throughout the text. Half of these are solved and/or discussed in the back of the book. These exercises are marked by a caret (▸).

Literary and scientific examples are provided throughout the text. Selections ranging from Plato's *Meno* to Isaac Newton to several Sherlock Holmes stories illustrate the interrogative model at work. Many examples from legal contexts are also included.

Part One (Chapters 1–4) gives an overview of the interrogative model of reasoning and its use in the analysis and construction of arguments. In Part One we attempt to keep technical terminology and apparatus to a minimum. In Part Two (Chapters 5–9) deductive logical inference is studied in detail through a flexible system of statement (propositional) logic that is designed to help students integrate deductive inference with the other aspects of reasoning. There is opportunity for considerable work with a formal system, but the connections with everyday English are always near at hand. We do not recommend lingering over statement logic and have therefore kept exercises to a minimum. Appendixes A and C, however, contain additional exercises and insights for those who wish to devote more time to the study of formal logic.

Part Three (Chapters 10–13) presents rules and strategies for introducing information into an argument or inquiry and for assessing the reliability of the information that is introduced. Because the book focuses on how one can reason correctly and effectively, the traditional fallacies are not stressed. Nevertheless, interesting insights into some of the most significant informal fallacies are provided in this part. Those who seek more discussion of the traditional fallacies in the light of the interrogative model are invited to turn to Appendix C.

The interrogative model encourages repeated examination of argument sketches, especially toward the end of Part One and in Part Three, as students become more and more skilled in various aspects of argument analysis, construction, and evaluation. Appendix A contains a large number of argument sketches suitable for illustrating many different features of arguments. We call these "sketches" because the interrogative model emphasizes how important it is to learn how to spot and "fill in" the gaps typically found in everyday reasoning.

Argument construction and the writing of argumentative essays are covered in detail in Parts One and Three. The goal is to help students learn not only how to analyze and evaluate arguments but also how to construct their own and to present them in essay form.

Parts One, Two, and Three complete the examination of the basic elements of reasoning as understood through the interrogative model. Part Four moves on to consider more advanced topics. Chapters 14 and 15 introduce the basics of first-order predicate logic. The tools acquired in these chapters are then employed in subsequent chapters to help students understand more deeply the structure of information seeking through questions. By now students can be expected to have sufficient understanding to appreciate one of the most significant insights of the interrogative model: that parallels between the questioning process and deductive reasoning make it possible to learn new strategies for questioning from proven strategies for deductive reasoning. Chapter 18 examines these strategic parallels. Chapters 19 and 20 offer further discussions of the nature of scientific reasoning and of definability and identifiability.

A complete glossary of terms is provided to help students learn and remember new vocabulary. The entries are all cross-referenced to the more extensive discussions in the text itself. An index provides another convenient tool for finding and exploring topics covered in the text.

Appendix B discusses several recreational questioning games. These games give students insight into the interrogative model and provide the possibility of applying the model in a recreational context.

Appendix C puts the main traditional fallacies into historical and theoretical perspective. Students are not encouraged simply to learn fallacies by rote, but rather to understand what it is about reasoning that makes certain fallacies tempting. Students also come to understand why what is a fallacy in one context may be an important consideration for reasoning in another.

The Instructor's Manual includes theoretical background, teaching tips for each chapter, sample examinations, additional exercise sets, and answers to exercises not solved in the back of the text.

Acknowledgments

The authors are grateful to many people for their help on this project. The Department of Philosophy at Florida State University and its chair, Alan Mabe, made many crucial resources available. The Council for Instruction of Florida State University provided a grant to support some of the early work. Richard Baepler, Philip Gilbertson, and Kenneth Klein of Valparaiso University in Indiana freed James Bachman to devote considerable time and resources to the project. It will perhaps not surprise Lutherans, but it may surprise others that the Florida–Georgia District of the Lutheran Church–Missouri Synod, through people like Lloyd Behnken, Erdmann Frenk, and Thomas Zehnder, also provided substantial resources for this project. Thanks are also owed to Dean N. Patricia Scheer of Neuchatel.

Steve Harris has worked closely with Jaakko Hintikka for a number of years, and he contributed many exercises as well as insight into how topics might best be presented. Staff persons in the Department of Philosophy at Florida State University, Laura Behr, Florene Ball, Cathy Butler, and Roxane Fletcher were all most patient with the uncounted writings and rewritings. Laura VanMiller of Valparaiso University also provided much help. We owe thanks also to staff persons at Boston University and at the University of Helsinki.

Several semesters of students at Florida State University and at Valparaiso University helped us refine our adaptation of a complex theory to the needs of undergraduate students. Our editors, Jim Bull, Linda Toy, and Lauren Root, and the staff of Mayfield Publishing Company have been most patient and helpful. We also owe thanks to the following reviewers for their many helpful suggestions: Lenore Langsdorf, Southern Illinois University at Carbondale; Frank Wilson, Bucknell University; Nelson Pole, Cleveland State University; Deborah Hansen Soles, Wichita State University; and Anita Silvers, San Francisco State University.

PART ONE

Introduction to
the Interrogative
Model of Reasoning

▲1
▼

Inquiry as Inquiry

To be able to reason well, to be able to construct good arguments and to analyze and evaluate arguments effectively, one has to know what reasoning is. But the nature of reasoning and thinking is a profound philosophical problem to which one cannot expect an easy answer. Fortunately, for the purpose of learning how to reason well, rather than try to formulate an answer that would satisfy a professional philosopher, it suffices to grasp some useful guidelines. In fact, finding some examples of good reasoning will take us a long way in our efforts to understand it.

Useful examples occur in many different contexts. For instance, imagine that you are a TV producer or advertising executive who has been given the task of depicting on TV examples of good thinking (reasoning). You have been asked to present your client as a "thinking man's and thinking woman's company." How would you do that? What is your conception of effective thinking? Pondering this problem may help you to clarify your own ideas.

1.1   Think About It: What If . . . ?

Describe a TV commercial which depicts employees of a company involved in creative or effective thinking. Then explain why you think your commercial succeeds in getting the idea of effective thinking across to the viewers—why you think it serves as an illustration of good thinking.

Not long ago a major computer company asked its advertising agency to create a commercial showing employees engaged in effective thinking. The ad agency's problem was to convey such a concept to TV viewers. Their solution shows a young professional in various nonprofessional activities. Suddenly he or she stops, stands or sits still for a while, goes to a computer, works on it for a while, and then calls his or her boss, saying, "I just thought of it. *What if . . . ?*"

The relevant features of these commercials are fairly obvious. First, the employee of the company appears to have been given a serious professional problem. This problem occupies, perhaps only subconsciously, his or her mind even outside regular office hours. Second, the hero or heroine of the commercial is shown coming upon a way of approaching—perhaps even solving—the problem. How? By asking, "What if . . . ?" that is to say, *by raising a new question.*

The idea of effective thinking, or reasoning, on which the commercial is based is clear. Reasoning is a goal-directed activity. The goal may be to solve a problem, and the means of solving the problem is *by posing suitable questions.* The answers to these questions are ultimately expected to yield the solution or otherwise help to reach the desired goal.

1.2   Inquiry as Inquiry

This text can be thought of as taking a clue from the commercials just described. It is calculated to teach you to reason better by assuming that *reasoning is a process of questioning or interrogation.* Thus, we will often speak of the reasoning process as **rational inquiry.** That great authority on the English language, the *Oxford English Dictionary* (colloquially known as the *OED*), defines one sense of *inquiry* as "the action of seeking . . . for truth, knowledge, or information about something; search, research, investigation, examination." Another sense is defined in the *OED* as "the action of asking or questioning; interrogation." In this book we show how rational inquiry in the first sense is inquiry also in the second sense, that is, an activity of questioning.

▲

Inquiry: (1) The action of seeking for truth, knowledge, or information about something; search, research, investigation, examination. (2) The action of asking or questioning; interrogation.

1.3   Correct Methods and Effective Strategies

Our approach to the study of reasoning focuses, as noted above, on *inquiry as inquiry,* that is, on inquiry as a questioning process. Another word for questioning is *interrogation.* We shall often speak of this approach as the **interrogative approach to rational inquiry.** Soon you will begin learning the basic ingredients of the interrogative approach, but first we need to alert you to two different kinds of skills you will need to develop.

The first skill involves learning and using correct methods for reasoning. One can formulate various rules for reasoning that simply show how to do things correctly, how to avoid mistakes: In this book these are called the **definitory rules** of reasoning. The early parts of the book emphasize these rules. The other skill, however, involves building effective **strategies** for reasoning upon the definitory rules. It is necessary, but not sufficient, that we observe the definitory rules. To achieve genuine excellence in inquiry it is also important to learn strategic principles that can guide us into creative and effective use of the definitory rules of reasoning. The understanding of inquiry as a questioning process helps develop effective strategies for reasoning.

— ▲

Rational Inquiry: Inquiry pursued with attention both to correct methods (definitory rules) and effective strategies in reasoning.

Interrogative Approach to Inquiry: The approach that stresses the importance of questioning in rational inquiry.

1.4   Excellence in Reasoning

Understanding rational inquiry as a process of questioning provides us with two immediate clues about *excellence in reasoning.* First, we recognize that we need to study the whole process of questioning very closely. To aid in this task there exists a theory of questioning processes (question-answer sequences). You will not have to learn all the details of this theory, simply the framework it offers by which you can train yourself to become a better reasoner and to achieve excellence in constructing, analyzing, and evaluating arguments. That framework you will find explained later in the book.

The notion of *inquiry as inquiry* also tells us that excellence in reasoning requires an active imagination. We cannot think that reasoning is merely a passive thing that goes on in our heads. Instead, *the good reasoner must actively and imaginatively formulate questions* to make progress in his or her inquiry.

It is not at first sight clear, however, that successful reasoning can always (or at least in a wide range of interesting cases) be dealt with as a questioning process. It is therefore in order to consider a few examples. The rest of this chapter presents famous cases of reasoning which illustrate it as a questioning process. But we begin with an opportunity for you to examine a piece of your own reasoning.

△▼ IN-CLASS EXERCISE

In this course on excellence in rational inquiry, we will be examining many examples of reasoning processes. In this assignment you are asked to examine some of your own reasoning. Please write on *both* parts of the assignment.

1. Briefly describe the main lines of thought that have led you to register for this course. Do not worry if you now think that some of your reasons were ill-advised. Simply describe what you have been thinking. What do you expect to get out of this course?

2. In the light of the list of thought-starter questions below, briefly construct at least two additional lines of thought that might support your decision to register for the course. (One purpose of this exercise is to provide information so that we can shape the course as much as possible to meet the needs and interests of the students. It will help if you indicate the main benefits you hope to gain from the course.)

   Thought Starters: (These are *not* questions to be answered. They are simply meant to get you started on the second part of the exercise. You are free also to pursue matters not mentioned in this list.)

   a. Could this course help you to improve your reading and writing skills?
   b. Where are reasoning skills needed anyway?
   c. Does your favorite aunt teach philosophy?
   d. Are you looking for help with standardized tests like the Graduate Record Exam, the Medical College Acceptance Test, the Graduate Management Admissions Test, or the Law School Admissions Test?
   e. Is Finland your homeland?
   f. What do you think about arguments over politics, religion, business practices, and so forth?
   g. What are you likely to major in?
   h. Who is Sir Arthur Conan Doyle?
   i. Are you in a preprofessional program such as premed or prelaw?
   j. Who was Aristotle?
   k. Are you a business major?
   l. Are you interested in foreign policy and military strategy?
   m. Did this course just happen to fit your schedule?
   n. Do you enjoy math?
   o. Are you interested in logical puzzles?
   p. Have you discussed this course with other students?

q. Do you enjoy studying science?

r. What is philosophy anyway?

1.5 Case One: The Curious Incident of the Dog in the Nighttime

This first case is not formulated as a question-answer sequence. It is from the detective story "Silver Blaze" by Sir Arthur Conan Doyle and features the famous fictional detective Sherlock Holmes. (If you have not read it, you might want to read the whole story. It is included in many different anthologies, one of which is *The Complete Sherlock Holmes*, Vol. 1 [New York: Doubleday, 1905], pp. 335–350. We will return to other episodes from this story later in the book.)

The story is supposed to take place in England around 1890. The famous racing horse Silver Blaze has been stolen from its stable in the middle of the night and has not been found. Its trainer, the stable master, also disappeared during the night, and was found in the heath in the morning, killed by a mighty blow. All sorts of suspects crop up, but everybody is quite in the dark as to what happened during the fateful night until Holmes gets into the act.

"Is there any point to which you would wish to draw my attention?" [asks the inspector of Sherlock Holmes].

"To the curious incident of the dog in the night-time."

"The dog did nothing in the night-time."

"That was the curious incident," remarked Sherlock Holmes.

What is Holmes doing? *He is actually asking three questions.* Was there a watchdog in the stables? Yes, we have all been told earlier that there was. Did it bark during the night, including the time when the horse was stolen? No, it never woke the stable lads in the loft. Now who is it that a trained watchdog does not bark at in the middle of the night? His master, the stable master, of course. Hence it must have been the stable master himself who stole the horse. . . . "Elementary, my dear Watson," Holmes says on this kind of occasion.

1.6 Asking the Right Questions

In the case study just presented we can see clearly how an interesting line of reasoning amounts to a question-answer sequence. It is especially striking to note that the answers to Holmes's questions are quite obvious as soon as the relevant

question is raised. Hence the force of Sherlock Holmes's reasoning is due entirely to his *actively imagining and asking the right questions.* The others knew what he knew but failed to ask the key questions. Later we shall examine what it is about Holmes's questions that lends them their capacity to prompt an interesting and even surprising conclusion.

1.7   Making Logical Inferences

Some additional comments on the first case study are in order. First, the brief passage quoted above is an example of something we shall encounter all the time in the study of human reasoning. Both oral and written reports of a line of reasoning are very often *abbreviated sketches* of what is actually going on. We will need to use our imaginations to spell out effectively and fairly the whole train of thought the reasoner intends us to consider. A line of reasoning is often called an *argument.* (Note that in the study of reasoning the word *argument* is not used in the sense of "quarrel.") We will call the process of spelling out an argument sketch **argument analysis.**

For example, when Sherlock Holmes's train of thought is delineated as it was above, something else is found there besides three questions and the answers to them—that is, the conclusion (indicated by the words, "Hence it must have been the stable master himself who stole the horse"). This conclusion was not obtained as new information answering another question but, rather, by combining the earlier answers. The conclusion does not in any obvious way add new information to the three answers. It instead spells out what the three earlier answers reveal.

Such a step of reasoning will be called an **inference** or, more explicitly, a **logical inference.** The output of a step of inference is called its **conclusion** and what it relies on (what it results from) is called its **premises.** In the Sherlock Holmes story the premises "the watchdog did not bark at anyone" and "the only person a watchdog does not bark at is its master" led to the conclusion: The stable master was the thief. The inference was a step from the two earlier answers (premises) to the conclusion. So we see that in the questioning process we also have to include steps other than question-answer pairs, namely, logical inferences. See Sections 1.9, 3.3, and 14.11 for examples of increasingly more detailed analyses of the first case study.

Much more must be said and learned about questions and about logical inferences. For now, a few brief reminders and definitions are provided, followed by some examples and exercises.

▲

Questions: A crucial part of reasoning. Having the imagination to ask the right question is often the key to excellence in reasoning.

Argument Sketch: An oral or written report of a line of reasoning. Lines of reasoning are typically reported in a compressed, abbreviated form. (In the study of reasoning "argument" does not mean "quarrel.")

Argument Analysis: To study fairly and effectively a report of a line of reasoning, one must learn how to make explicit all the questions and inferences actually involved in the reasoning. This process is called argument analysis.

Infer: To conclude something on the basis of information that is known or assumed to be true.

Inference: The process of inferring; something that is inferred; a conclusion; something derived from other information by reasoning. (Note that *an inference is not simply a statement*. It is a statement that has been derived from other information by reasoning. Sometimes "inference" refers to the whole process of reasoning that led to the conclusion and sometimes the word simply refers to the conclusion itself. Do not let this confuse you.)

Premise(s): The information that serves as the basis for an inference step.

Conclusion: The statement of what has been derived from the premises.

Logical Inference: An inference in which the conclusion cannot possibly be imagined to be false while the premises are all together imagined to be true. (The meaning of "imagining" here is very wide-ranging. In testing whether an inference is a logical inference, we are free to imagine situations that do not conform to the way things are in our actual world.)

In Chapter 5 we will learn that logical inferences are also called "valid deductive" inferences. There are still other kinds of inference, but we do not need to concern ourselves about them until later in the book. In fact, it is a helpful feature of the interrogative approach to inquiry that logical inferences are all that we essentially need. It is very important that you learn precisely what is required for an inference to be a *logical* inference.

Illustrations of Inferences

In each of the following examples the inference is the "move" from statements 1 and 2 to statement 3. The first two statements are functioning as premises and the third is functioning as the conclusion. In each example the suggestion is being made that a process of reasoning leads us to accept the conclusion on the basis of the premises. The main thing to understand now is the difference between premises and conclusions and what an inference is supposed to be. For future reference you might review the definition of *logical inference* and ask yourself why each of these inferences can also be called a logical (valid deductive) inference.

Example A

1. If you eat your peas, then you get dessert.
2. You eat your peas.
3. You get dessert.

Example B

1. Anyone who has broken the law deserves to be punished.
2. Bad Bart has broken the law.
3. Bad Bart deserves to be punished.

Example C

1. Either you are for us or against us.
2. If you were for us, you would not help the other side.
3. You are against us.

(Illustrations A and B are logical inferences as they stand. Illustration C is an inference but it is not a *logical* inference in its present form. It could, however, become one if one more premise were added to it. Try to understand why it is not, as it stands, a logical inference.)

△▼ EXERCISE 1-A

▶ 1. What additional premise will turn example C into a logical inference? The process of supplying the additional premise illustrates how *argument analysis* spells out what may be intended in an *argument sketch*.

2. For each of the following passages, indicate which expression(s) act as the premise(s) and which is the conclusion. Use your understanding of what an inference is to decide what are premises and what are conclusions. You may, however, note that certain familiar words seem to be used to indicate or highlight the premises or the conclusion. Make a list of these words and be prepared to discuss this matter of "indicator words" in class.

   After you have identified the premises and conclusion, try to understand whether (and if so why and if not why not) any of these inferences might qualify to be a *logical* inference. If an inference is not a logical inference, consider whether adding another premise might turn it into one. Be sure you understand what it is about any logical inference that makes it a *logical* inference. We will examine this matter of logical inferences again in Chapter 2 and in close detail in Part 2. It is an important element of interrogative inquiry.

   a. If there were intelligent life on other planets, we would have received messages from them by now. But we have received no such messages. So there is no intelligent life on other planets.

   ▶ b. One way to stop the greenhouse effect is to protect the rainforests of the world. We must stop the greenhouse effect. Therefore, the rainforests must be protected.

c. If the Loch Ness monster existed there would be scientific proof of its existence. So the monster does not exist, because there is no proof of its existence.

▸ d. The car must be out of gas. That is the only thing which could account for the way it stopped so suddenly.

e. All great forms of art have generated controversy in their own time. Since rap music is extremely controversial, it follows that rap music is a great art form.

▸ f. No Christians are polytheists, because no Lutherans are polytheists and all Lutherans are Christians.

g. All oaks are deciduous trees. Hence, some deciduous trees are not conifers, because some oaks are not conifers.

▸ h. A number is even only if it is divisible by two. Some prime numbers are not even numbers. Therefore, some prime numbers are not divisible by two.

▸ i. A number is even if it is divisible by two. Some prime numbers are not even numbers. Therefore, some prime numbers are not divisible by two.

▸ j. It's going to be a very good election, since we have three people running.

k. Only students will go to Daytona Beach. Sharon is a student, therefore she will go.

▸ l. All students will go to Daytona Beach. Sharon is a student, therefore she will go.

m. Frank is eligible because he is a Floridian and only Floridians are eligible.

▸ n. Vermicelli is fattening, as pasta always is.

[handwritten margin note: All oaks are deciduous trees. Some oaks are not conifers. Hence, some deciduous trees are not conifers]

1.8 Two Kinds of Steps in Rational Inquiry

Looking back at Sections 1.6 and 1.7, we find that our first case study illustrates two main ingredients in rational inquiry. If we break a line of reasoning (a rational inquiry) down into its simpler steps, we find that some steps are questioning, or interrogative, steps and others are logical inference steps. Interrogative steps bring in new information, whereas logical inference steps spell out the information which is contained in some of the earlier steps of the process.

It is important to notice that *interrogative steps are not always expressed as actual questions.* In "Silver Blaze" Sherlock Holmes is asking crucial questions about the watchdog, but they are expressed in indicative sentence form. We call such steps "interrogative steps" because it is helpful to analyze them as actual questions. Whenever new information is being brought into the inquiry, we will analyze what is happening in terms of questions and answers. Notice carefully that the important thing is not whether we see a question mark but *whether we see new information coming into the inquiry.* If we do, we have what we are calling an interrogative step.

It is also important to recognize that *logical inference steps are sometimes expressed in the form of questions.* We must learn, however, to recognize when questions are actually an invitation to draw a logical inference. Whenever a step spells out information already contained in earlier steps, we will analyze that step as a logical inference, even if it is in the form of a question.

_ ▲ _____

Information: That which makes it possible to eliminate from an inquiry certain alternative situations that otherwise might have been thought possible.

New Information: Information that was not previously available in any way for use in a given inquiry. (New information will always be analyzed as coming into the inquiry by way of an interrogative step.)

Interrogative Step: A step in an inquiry which brings in new information. Interrogative steps are not always phrased as questions, but they can always be analyzed as though a question has been asked.

Previous Information: Information which was already available in some way in previous steps of an inquiry but which may require a logical inference in order to show exactly what alternative situations are being eliminated. (Whenever a step spells out previously available information, the step will always be analyzed as a logical inference step.)

Logical Inference Step: A step which spells out some of the information that is already contained in previous steps of an inquiry. Logical inference steps are sometimes phrased as questions, but if the step does not bring in new information, it should not be analyzed as an interrogative step. The basic test for a logical inference step is that it cannot possibly be imagined to be false while the previous steps on which it is based are imagined to be true.

_____

Illustration   If you were trying to help your brother keep his checkbook in order, the following discussion might occur: What was your balance after check number 350? It was $426.32. OK, how much was check number 351? It was $25. Well, that leaves $401.32. Check 352? $57.88. What does that leave? And so on.

Information about the original balance after check number 350 is new information that comes into the reasoning through an interrogative step. Information about the amount of check number 351 is also new and again comes from an interrogative step. You do not need, however, to ask what the balance is after check number 351, because an understanding of the rules of checking account amounts and of subtraction suffices to guarantee that the balance will be $401.32. This is a logical inference step. The amount of check number 352 comes from an interrogative step. The question "What does that leave?" might make you think that new information is being sought, but you should see that it can be answered through a logical inference. Even if your brother makes an error in the subtraction and gives you the wrong answer, you are in a position to get the right answer from the previous information.

△▼ EXERCISE 1-B

For each of the following sets of sentences, indicate whether the last sentence adds new information or whether it instead simply spells out or makes explicit information already contained in the earlier sentences. What we are asking is whether the last sentence represents an interrogative move or a logical inference move.

1. a. All whales are mammals.
   b. There are whales.
   c. Some mammals are whales.

▶ 2. a. Many people are losing their jobs.
   b. Unemployment is rising.

3. a. The hottest days in history have all been in August.
   b. Today is a day in August.
   c. Today is among the hottest days in history.

▶ 4. a. All periods of low unemployment are accompanied by higher-than-average inflation.
   b. When inflation rises, interest rates also rise.
   c. Rising interest rates lead to a slowdown in the housing industry.
   d. If our unemployment level continues to drop, then the housing industry will eventually slow down.

5. a. There are more classes offered than students in any one class.
   b. No class is empty.
   c. Two classes have the same number of students.

▶ 6. a. Each time it rains, the TV stops working.
   b. The rain causes the TV to stop working.

7. a. The team loses if Louie does not pitch.
   b. Louie pitches.
   c. The team does not lose.

▶ 8. a. The team loses only if Louie does not pitch.
   b. Louie pitches.
   c. The team does not lose.

9. a. Scurvy always occurs when there is a deficiency of ascorbic acid in the human body.
   b. Deficiency of ascorbic acid in the human body necessarily gives rise to scurvy.

Logical Inference Moves and Information

A technical point should be briefly mentioned at this point. In a number of ways logical inference moves increase the information available in an inquiry. In particular, they delineate for us what the alternatives are that have been eliminated by the information currently available. Logical inference moves take complex information and work on it in such a way that the information becomes clearly available in our inquiry. In this sense they also increase the information at our disposal. Thus, we should not think that logical inference moves are unimportant.

1.9   Argument Analysis

Returning to Sherlock Holmes's "curious incident," we discover that when the character of the logical inference it contains is fully spelled out, this logical inference step is actually an abbreviation of several more basic steps of inference. These steps can be detailed as follows.

1. There was a watchdog in the stable during the night. (Interrogative step)

2. The watchdog did not bark at anyone. (Interrogative step)

3. Hence the watchdog did not bark at the thief. (Logical inference step from statement 2)

4. The only person any watchdog does not bark at is its master. (Interrogative step)

5. Hence the only person the watchdog [in the stable] could not have barked at was its master, the stable master. (Logical inference step from statement 4)

6. Hence the thief was the stable master. (Logical inference step from statements 3 and 5)

We can see from 1.6 that what first looked like a simple inference was in reality the end point of a longer process involving at least three interrogative steps and three separate logical inference steps. This may lead you to ask what the basic types of logical inference are (or at least what some of them are) that we in fact rely on in our everyday reasoning. This question will be discussed in detail in Part 2. For now prepare to practice some of your new skills in *argument analysis*.

▲

Argument Analysis: The process of discovering and listing the basic, simpler interrogative and logical inference steps that are found in a complex everyday inquiry. As most complex inquiries are reported in a compressed and abbreviated way, imagination and ingenuity are often required to supply the steps that are not explicitly stated in the reported sketch of the inquiry. (*Analysis* is a word from the Greek language that originally meant "to take something apart.")

Illustration of an Argument Analysis   Consider the argument contained in the following passage.

> Do you want to raise the academic standards at your college or university? Make sure that you have a successful football team! If you do, students will flock to your university. You can admit more students who are more highly qualified and hence raise academic standards.

The following is a possible analysis of this argument.

1.   If a college or university has a successful football team, more students will apply to it than before. [This can be analyzed as an answer to a question, i.e., an interrogative step that introduces new information not already present in the argument.]

2.   If more students apply to a college or university, it can have a more highly qualified student body. [This is actually a complicated step which relies partly on some tacit, i.e., unspoken, new information and partly on making logical inferences.] We might fill in the reasoning this way:

2.1. If more students apply to a college or university, there will be a correspondingly larger number of more highly qualified applicants. [This is new information that is involved in statement 2 and that is being tacitly added to the inquiry. Here we are informed that, among the additional applicants, there will be roughly the same proportion of highly qualified applicants as there were among the original applicants. Whenever new information is added, it is possible for us to wonder whether the information is accurate or reliable. For now we will not worry about that problem.]

2.2. If a larger number of more highly qualified students apply to a school, then it can raise its admission standards. [This is some more new information that the arguer is assuming you will naturally bring into the argument. You and the arguer both will likely do this without even giving it much conscious thought.]

2.3. If a school raises admission standards, it will have more students who are more highly qualified. [This too is information that is new to the argument, but it seems so obvious that the arguer did not explicitly mention it. Now, if you put statements 2.1, 2.2, and 2.3 all together, you can make a logical inference that gives you statement 2.]

3.   If a university has a more highly qualified student body, it can raise its academic standards. [This is one more piece of new information that can be analyzed as being brought into the argument by an interrogative step.]

4.   If a university has a successful football team, it can raise its academic standards. [Logical inference step from statements 1, 2 and 3.]

The above example shows that what looks like a fairly simple argument can turn out to depend on several tacit answers not explicitly mentioned in the reported sketch of the argument. The example also shows why it is important to analyze an argument so as to bring out in an explicit way information involved in the reasoning. For when this information is brought out into the open, we are in a better position to criticize the argument than we might have been.

One might, for instance, wonder whether the tacit information in 2.1 is true. Even if more students do apply, does that mean there will be "a correspondingly larger number of more highly qualified applicants"? Perhaps the increase in applications will come from students who are very interested in football but less so in academics. Similar questions can be asked about the other interrogative steps uncovered by the process of argument analysis. One of the primary practical purposes for learning argument analysis is that it puts us in a position better to *evaluate* arguments in everyday life.

△▼ EXERCISE 1-C

Try to produce an analysis of each of the following short arguments.

1. The guilty party is either Smith or Jones. The fingerprints on the murder weapon left by the perpetrator of the sinister act indicate that the scoundrel was left-handed. But because Smith is right-handed, she cannot be the murderer. So the crime was committed by Jones.

▶ 2. Given the challenges facing our nation in the years to come, our next president must be a person of courage and strength, with a proven capacity for leadership. Who possesses these essential traits? Ask any member of Congress, and he or she will tell you that Representative Hardin fills the bill.

3. If you are to pass the class, you must learn how to analyze arguments. In order to learn techniques of argument analysis, you must successfully complete all of the exercises. Therefore, if you are to pass the class, you must analyze this argument.

▶ 4. One thing that is clear from the anonymous letter is that the author is extremely shy, and no matter what other character traits Bob Bravado may have, he certainly lacks shyness. So the letter must not have been written by Bob.

5. The cat must have eaten the cheese. It was there this morning. No one was in the house, and when I returned from work the refrigerator door was slightly ajar. Besides, Felicia was happier than normal when she greeted me at the front door this evening.

▶ 6. No one who loves America would ever burn the flag. But flag burnings have been a part of the demonstrations of many groups, including some Vietnam veteran organizations. Are we really obligated to protect the freedom of expression of those who obviously do not love this country? Of course not. So the demonstrations of such groups do not warrant constitutional protection.

7. It is clear that the proposed gas tax hike is a good idea. Anyone who has tried to cross town during rush hour can see that our community desperately needs to improve its roads, and there just isn't enough money to accomplish this given existing revenue sources. The trivial increase in the cost of gas is a small price to pay for the benefit of congestion-free roads. Besides, those who end up paying the extra money are the ones who have the most to gain. So

not only would this tax solve a serious problem facing most members of the community, it is fair as well.

1.10 Is Logic the Key to Reasoning?

logos

logike: art of logic

Our recipe for good reasoning thus far is rather simple: *well-chosen questions interspersed with logical inferences based on the answers to the questions.* It will help you to appreciate this answer if we raise the question: What other recipes have been suggested?

To this question there exists a time-honored answer which at first sight looks quite different from ours. This competing answer identifies the art of reasoning with the science of logic. The answer is even codified in the ordinary use of words like "logic," "deduction," and so forth. Good reasoning is according to this view called "logical" reasoning, and what is accomplished by such reasoning is called "inferences" or "deductions." You have perhaps read about the brilliant "deductions" of real or fictional detectives. Moreover, and most importantly, such logical inferences are supposed to give rise to substantial new results.

What are we to say of the claims of logic to be the science (or perhaps the art) of good reasoning? Several things can be said. First, a curious ambiguity marks such expressions as "inference," "logic," and "deduction." When we spoke of logical inference steps (as distinguished from interrogative steps) of inquiry, we used this term in a narrow sense. (Recall the definition of *logical inference* given in Section 1.7.) In this sense, which is what you normally find in philosophy books, steps of logical inference do not bring any new information into the inquiry or argument but merely serve to spell out the information already available or to combine several previously obtained items of information. In this sense, only steps 3, 5, and 6 of Sherlock Holmes's line of reasoning outlined in Section 1.9 are logical inferences.

Sherlock Holmes and Logic

However, there is also a much broader sense to words such as *logic, inference, and deduction.* In this sense, Holmes's entire line of thought would be called a "deduction." More generally, most good reasoning can be called "logical inference" in this broad sense of the crucial words. We shall call this the "Sherlock Holmes" sense of words such as "logic," "deduction," and "inference." And Sherlock Holmes does indeed use such terms in the "Sherlock Holmes" sense. For example: Conan Doyle lets a character in one of the Sherlock Holmes stories describe the great fictional detective's method as follows:

> "From a drop of water," said the writer [Sherlock Holmes], "a logician could infer the possibility of an Atlantic or a Niagara without having seen or heard

of one or the other. So all life is a great chain, the nature of which is known whenever we are shown a single link of it. Like all other arts, the Science of Deduction and Analysis is one which can only be acquired by long and patient study, nor is life long enough to allow any mortal to attain the highest possible perfection in it. Before turning to these moral and mental aspects of the matter which present the greatest difficulties, let the inquirer begin by mastering more elementary problems. Let him, on meeting a fellow-mortal, learn at a glance to distinguish the history of the man, and the trade or profession to which he belongs. Puerile as such an exercise may seem, it sharpens the faculties of observation, and teaches one where to look and what to look for. By a man's finger-nails, by his coat-sleeve, by his boot, by trouser-knees, by the callosities of his forefinger and thumb, by his expression, by his shirt-cuffs—by each of these things a man's calling is plainly revealed. That all united should fail to enlighten the competent inquirer in any case is almost inconceivable." (From "A Study in Scarlet," in *The Complete Sherlock Holmes*, Vol. 1 [New York: Doubleday, 1905], p. 23.)

As you read this passage, you will see that Holmes's "inferences" and "deductions" include a liberal use of his "faculties of observation." But, in making an observation, an inquirer is not simply restructuring information that he or she has already acquired. Observation is unmistakably a way of bringing new information into one's inquiry. Hence information from observation cannot be included among logical inferences or deductions in a philosopher's narrow sense of these words.

But if the terms "logic," "inference," and "deduction" are used in their wider, "Sherlock Holmes" sense, there is no incompatibility between our claims that good reasoning is a matter of judicious questioning, combined with intelligent use of logic in its narrow sense, and the traditional answer according to which good reasoning is "logical" reasoning. In fact, the difference between our answer to the question of the nature of good reasoning and the traditional answer is to a considerable extent not a substantial disagreement but only a verbal one. For, as the "Curious Incident of the Dog in the Nighttime" illustrates, much of what is traditionally called "deduction" or "inference" in reality involves crucially an interrogative step or even several interrogative steps. Even though Holmes's line of thought was not expressed by means of explicit questions, it unmistakably involved such questions.

Hence there is conflict between our answer and the traditional one to the question of the recipe for good reasoning only if in the traditional answer the word *logic* is taken in its narrow, technical sense.

1.11   Review and Reminders

It is important to understand certain basic things about the role of logic in reasoning. First, you have to *understand the distinction between interrogative steps and logical inference steps in inquiry* and to begin to learn to distinguish the two in actual arguments. This is not easy, for the two kinds of steps usually are not distinguished from each other in arguments expressed in ordinary language.

Second, you need to understand that inquiries and arguments are usually reported in a compressed and abbreviated way. We are beginning to learn skills in *argument analysis* that enable us to spell out in detail what is intended in a given argument sketch.

Third, you should recognize the difference between the narrower sense of logic and deduction and the traditional, wider sense (the "Sherlock Holmes" sense). What has to be kept in mind is that we shall usually restrict the crucial terms logic, deduction, and inference to their narrow sense in which logical inferences or deductions do not introduce any new information into the argument. But we shall sometimes also interpret logical inferences or deductions in the wider "Sherlock Holmes" sense as a mixture of interrogative steps and logical inference steps. This is the basic idea of our *inquiry as inquiry* approach to reasoning.

This section leaves us with a problem to which we shall return in Part 4. What is it that makes it natural to extend such terms as *logic* and *deduction* to cover all reasoning, not just what we shall in this book usually restrict them to?

△▼ THINK ABOUT IT

Examine which sense of "logic" or "deduction"—the narrow or the "Sherlock Holmes" sense—is exemplified in the following passages.

The Barber of Shave-ville: Assume that you already know that the village barber shaves all and only those men in the village who do not shave themselves. Then you also know that the village barber is a woman or does not live in the village. For if the barber were a man living in the village, would he shave himself? By the initial assumption, the barber would shave himself only if he did *not* shave himself, which is impossible. Think about how this little exercise proceeds and try to explain which sense of "logic" is exemplified in this case.

Newton's Apple: One of the most widely told anecdotes about actual scientific discoveries (creative thinking in science) concerns the way the great English physicist Isaac Newton (1642–1727) came to discover his law of gravitation.

The law states that any two bodies attract each other with a force which is proportional to their masses and inversely proportional to the square of their distance. The detailed form of the law does not matter here. By means of this law Newton was able to explain the behavior of falling bodies on earth, the motions of planets around the sun, and the motion of the moon around the earth.

The anecdote has sometimes been dismissed as nonhistorical. However, a contemporary of Newton reports that the story was told by Newton himself. The following reports are all from *The Newton Handbook* by Derek Gjertsen (London, 1986), pp. 29–31.

> The weather being warm, we [the narrator and Newton] went into the garden and drank tea, under the shade of some apple trees, only he and myself. Amidst other discourses, he [Newton] told me, he was just in the same situation, as

when formerly, the notion of gravitation came into his mind. It was occasioned by the fall of an apple, he said in a contemplative mood.

Can Newton's story of his discovery be interpreted as a description of part of a questioning process? Does it follow the same pattern as the "What if" example (Section 1.1) or the "Silver Blaze" case (Section 1.5)? If so, how? If not, why not?

Contemporary accounts of "Newton's apple" do in fact mention questions. The quoted account continues as follows.

Why should that apple always descend perpendicularly to the ground, thought he to himself. Why should it not go sideways or upwards, but constantly to the earth's centre?

Another account mentions another question:

Whilst he [Newton] was musing in a garden it came into his thought that the power of gravity (which brought an apple from the tree to the ground) was not limited to a certain distance from the earth but that the power must extend much further. . . . Why not as high as the moon, said he to himself.

1.12   Case Two: Meno's Slave Boy

This case is taken from the dialogue *Meno* by the great ancient Greek philosopher **Plato** (ca. 427–347 B.C.E.). Meno is one of the two main characters in the dialogue; the other one is **Socrates** (ca. 469–399 B.C.E.), the philosopher known for his method of questioning.

▲

Socrates: Socrates (ca. 469–399 B.C.E.) was the first of the three most famous ancient Greek philosophers. (The other two are Plato and Aristotle.) He was a stonemason in Athens. During the early part of his life (469–430 B.C.E.) Athens was the foremost political, military, scientific, and cultural center in Greece. During the last part of Socrates's life (429–399 B.C.E.), Athens was engaged in a long and demoralizing war with the city of Sparta. Athens lost the war in 404 B.C.E., and in the aftermath of recriminations Socrates was found guilty of being some kind of religious innovator and of corrupting the youth. At the age of seventy he was executed by the Athenians.

Plato: Plato (ca. 427–347 B.C.E.) was forty years younger than Socrates. As a young man he was profoundly influenced by Socrates's ways of inquiring about important questions in life. Plato was also deeply troubled by the events of the war between Athens and Sparta and by the trial and execution of Socrates. He devoted his life to philosophy, and he established the Academy, one of the first colleges or universities in Western history.

Socrates left no written works, but Plato left a large number, and in his writings he tells us much about Socrates. Plato is the author of the *Meno*, in which he makes Socrates the central character. The *Meno* is an extremely important early work in philosophy.

Aristotle: Sorry, you will have to wait until Chapter 3.

There is much more in the passage from the *Meno* than you are prepared to grasp at this point. We include the passage now, however, because it is a classic example of the use of a questioning method in reasoning. The dialogue also illustrates how logical inference moves are sometimes phrased as questions. Do not try at this point to determine which moves are interrogative, but do try to identify several of the logical inference moves. In Part 4 we shall refer back to this case for a deeper understanding of what is going on.

In the famous scene to be quoted, Socrates puts questions to Meno's slave boy, who has had little formal education. Socrates's purpose is to show how the slave boy can be made to discover things no one has taught him. This is to be done merely by putting suitable questions to him, apparently without imparting any new facts. Socrates calls this process of creating apparently new knowledge by means of questions "recollection." This term, and the philosophical theory connected with it, do not concern us here. Our purpose is *to see how logical inference steps are at work.* Socrates is asking questions, but most of them require the slave boy to draw a logical inference. (This translation of *Meno* [82A–85E] is by W. K. C. Guthrie in *Plato's Meno with Essays,* edited by M. Brown [Indianapolis, IN: Macmillan/Bobbs Merrill, 1971], pp. 33–42.)

MENO: If you can in any way make clear to me that what you say is true, please do.

SOCRATES: It isn't an easy thing, but still I should like to do what I can since you ask me. I see you have a large number of retainers here. Call one of them, anyone you like, and I will use him to demonstrate it to you.

MENO: Certainly. (*To a slave boy.*) Come here.

SOCRATES: He is a Greek and speaks our language.

MENO: Indeed yes—born and bred in the house.

SOCRATES: Listen carefully then, and see whether it seems to you that he is learning from me or simply being reminded.

MENO: I will.

SOCRATES: Now boy, you know that a square is a figure like this?
(*Socrates begins to draw figures in the sand at his feet. He points to the square ABCD.*)

BOY: Yes.

SOCRATES: It has all these four sides equal?

BOY: Yes.

SOCRATES: And these lines which go through the middle of it are also equal (*The lines EF, GH*)?

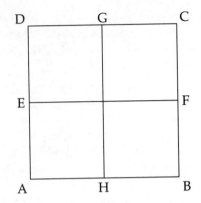

BOY: Yes.

SOCRATES: Such a figure could be either larger or smaller, could it not?

BOY: Yes.

SOCRATES: Now if this side is two feet long, and this side the same, how many feet will the whole be? Put it this way. If it were two feet in this direction and only one in that, must not the area be two feet taken once?

BOY: Yes.

SOCRATES: But since it is two feet this way also, does it not become twice two feet?

BOY: Yes.

SOCRATES: And how many feet is twice two? Work it out and tell me.

BOY: Four.

SOCRATES: Now could one draw another figure double the size of this, but similar, that is, with all its sides equal like this one?

BOY: Yes.

SOCRATES: How many feet will its area be?

BOY: Eight.

SOCRATES: Now then, try to tell me how long each of its sides will be. The present figure has a side of two feet. What will the side of the double-sized one be?

BOY: It will be double, Socrates, obviously.

SOCRATES: You see, Meno, that I am not teaching him anything, only asking. Now he thinks he knows the length of the side of the eight-feet square.

MENO: Yes.

SOCRATES: But does he?

MENO: Certainly not.

SOCRATES: He thinks it is twice the length of the other.

MENO: Yes.

SOCRATES: Now watch how he recollects things in order—the proper way to recollect.

You say that the side of double length produces the double-sized figure? Like this I mean, not long this way and short that. It must be equal on all sides like the first figure, only twice its size, that is eight feet. Think a moment whether you still expect to get it from doubling the side.

BOY: Yes, I do.

SOCRATES: Well now, shall we have a line double the length of the original side (*AB*) if we add another the same length at this end (*BJ*)?

BOY: Yes.

SOCRATES: It is on this line then, according to you, that we shall make the eight-feet square, by taking four of the same length?

BOY: Yes.

SOCRATES: Let us draw in four equal lines (*i.e., counting AJ, and adding JK, KL, and LA made complete by drawing in its second half LD*), using the first as a base. Does this not give us what you call the eight-feet figure?

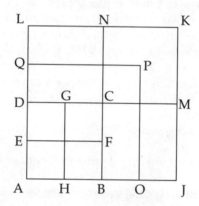

BOY: Certainly.

SOCRATES: But does it contain these four squares, each equal to the original four-feet one?

(*Socrates has drawn in the lines CM, CN to complete the squares that he wishes to point out.*)

BOY: Yes.

SOCRATES: How big is it then? Won't it be four times as big?

BOY: Of course.

SOCRATES: And is four times the same as twice?

BOY: Of course not.

SOCRATES: So doubling the side has given us not a double but a fourfold figure?

BOY: True.

SOCRATES: And four times four are sixteen, are they not?

BOY: Yes.

SOCRATES: Then how big is the side of the eight-feet figure? This one has given us four times the original area, hasn't it?

BOY: Yes.

SOCRATES: And a side half the length gave us a square of four feet?

BOY: Yes.

SOCRATES: Good. And isn't a square of eight feet double this one and half that?

BOY: Yes.

SOCRATES: Will it not have a side greater than this one but less than that?

BOY: I think it will.

SOCRATES: Right. Always answer what you think. Now tell me: was not this side two feet long, and this one four?

BOY: Yes.

SOCRATES: Then the side of the eight-feet figure must be longer than two feet but shorter than four?

BOY: It must.

SOCRATES: Try to say how long you think it is.

BOY: Three feet.

SOCRATES: If so, shall we add half of this bit (*BO, half of BJ*) and make it three feet? Here are two, and this is one, and on this side similarly we have two plus one; and here is the figure you want.
(*Socrates completes the square AOPQ.*)

BOY: Yes.

SOCRATES: If it is three feet this way and three that, will the whole area be three times three feet?

BOY: It looks like it.

SOCRATES: And that is how many?

BOY: Nine.

SOCRATES: Whereas the square double our first square had to be how many?

BOY: Eight.

SOCRATES: But we haven't yet got the square of eight feet, even from a three-feet side?

BOY: No.

SOCRATES: Then what length will give it? Try to tell us exactly. If you don't want to count it up, just show us on the diagram.

BOY: It's no use, Socrates, I just don't know.

SOCRATES: Observe, Meno, the stage he has reached on the path of recollection. At the beginning he did not know the side of the square of eight feet. Nor indeed does he know it now, but then he thought he knew it and answered boldly, as was appropriate—he felt no perplexity. Now however he does feel perplexed. Not only does he not know the answer; he doesn't even think he knows.

MENO: Quite true.

SOCRATES: Isn't he in a better position now in relation to what he didn't know?

MENO: I admit that too.

SOCRATES: So in perplexing him and numbing him like the sting-ray, have we done him any harm?

MENO: I think not.

SOCRATES: In fact we have helped him to some extent toward finding out the right answer, for now not only is he ignorant of it but he will be quite glad to look for it. Up to now, he thought he could speak well and fluently, on many occasions and before large audiences, on the subject of a square double the size of a given square, maintaining that it must have a side of double the length.

MENO: No doubt.

SOCRATES: Do you suppose then that he would have attempted to look for, or learn, what he thought he knew (though he did not), before he was thrown into perplexity, became aware of his ignorance, and felt a desire to know?

MENO: No.

SOCRATES: Then the numbing process was good for him?

MENO: I agree.

SOCRATES: Now notice what, starting from this state of perplexity, he will discover by seeking the truth in company with me, though I simply ask him questions without teaching him. Be ready to catch me if I give him any instruction or explanation instead of simply interrogating him on his own opinions.

(*Socrates here rubs out the previous figures and starts again.*)

Tell me, boy, is not this our square of four feet (ABCD)? You understand?

BOY: Yes.

SOCRATES: Now we can add another equal to it like this (BFEC)?

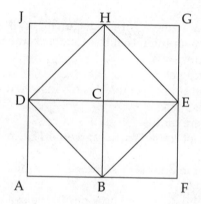

BOY: Yes.

SOCRATES: And a third here, equal to each of the others (CEGH)?

BOY: Yes.

SOCRATES: And then we can fill in this one in the corner (DCHJ)?

BOY: Yes.

SOCRATES: Then here we have four equal squares?

BOY: Yes.

SOCRATES: And how many times the size of the first square is the whole?

BOY: Four times.

SOCRATES: And we want one double the size. You remember?

BOY: Yes.

SOCRATES: Now does this line going from corner to corner cut each of these squares in half?

BOY: Yes.

SOCRATES: And these are four equal lines enclosing this area (*BEHD*)?

BOY: They are.

SOCRATES: Now think. How big is this area?

BOY: I don't understand.

SOCRATES: Here are four squares. Has not each line cut off the inner half of each of them?

BOY: Yes.

SOCRATES: And how many such halves are there in this figure (*BEHD*)?

BOY: Four.

SOCRATES: And how many in this one (*ABCD*)?

BOY: Two.

SOCRATES: And what is the relation of four to two?

BOY: Double.

SOCRATES: How big is the figure then?

BOY: Eight feet.

SOCRATES: On what base?

BOY: This one.

SOCRATES: The line which goes from corner to corner of the square of four feet?

BOY: Yes.

SOCRATES: The technical name for it is "diagonal"; so if we use that name, it is your personal opinion that the square on the diagonal of the original square is double its area.

BOY: That is so, Socrates.

SOCRATES: What do you think, Meno? Has he answered with any opinions that were not his own?

MENO: No, they were all his.

SOCRATES: Yet he did not know, as we agreed a few minutes ago.

MENO: True.

SOCRATES: But these opinions were somewhere in him, were they not?

MENO: Yes.

SOCRATES: So a man who does not know has in himself true opinions on a subject without having knowledge.

MENO: It would appear so.

SOCRATES: At present these opinions, being newly aroused, have a dream-like quality. But if the same questions are put to him on many occasions and in different ways, you can see that in the end he will have a knowledge on the subject as accurate as anybody's.

MENO: Probably.

SOCRATES: This knowledge will not come from teaching but from questioning. He will recover it for himself.

MENO: Yes.

SOCRATES: And the spontaneous recovery of knowledge that is in him is recollection, isn't it?

MENO: Yes.

SOCRATES: Either then he has at some time acquired the knowledge which he now has, or he has always possessed it. If he always possessed it, he must always have known; if on the other hand he acquired it at some previous time, it cannot have been in this life, unless somebody has taught him geometry. He will behave in the same way with all geometrical knowledge, and every other subject. Has anyone taught him all these? You ought to know, especially as he has been brought up in your household.

MENO: Yes, I know that no one ever taught him.

SOCRATES: And has he these opinions, or hasn't he?

MENO: It seems we can't deny it.

1.13 Comments on the Slave Boy Case

Unlike our example from Conan Doyle, Socrates's conversation with Meno's slave boy is already in the form of a question-answer sequence. It illustrates, first of all, the same point as "The Curious Incident of the Dog in the Nighttime." It illustrates the fact that by asking suitable questions one can arrive at interesting and unexpected information. In this case, the ultimate conclusion of the argument is a geometrical theorem, whereas Sherlock Holmes's conclusion was a factual truth.

Another difference is that in Socrates's argument no distinction is made between questioning steps and logical inferences. What happens is that what in reality are logical inferences are presented as the slave boy's answers to Socrates's questions.

The most important difference between our two main cases is the following. The three questions Sherlock Holmes asks bring in information he initially did not have. In contrast, Socrates claims that the slave boy's answers represent knowledge which the slave boy in some sense had always possessed. Yet even this difference is not complete. Some of the slave boy's answers are not in reality logical inferences from premises that have been stated in the course of the discussion. Socrates is appealing also to the slave boy's tacit knowledge of geometric relationships.

For instance, the inference that by doubling the side of a square one quadruples the area is strictly speaking not a logical inference from what the speakers actually say in the dialogue. It also depends on tacit geometric knowledge which is brought to bear on the figure Socrates has drawn. Thus, part of what Socrates accomplishes by his questions is to activate the slave boy's tacit knowledge. More will be said about tacit knowledge in Part 3.

In a similar way, one of Holmes's questions did not concern the particular facts of the case, but rather the kind of knowledge we all tacitly have. ("Now who is it that a trained watchdog does not bark at in the middle of the night?") Hence, the two examples are not completely dissimilar, and the slave boy's answers do after all bring new information into the argument.

What lends a special flavor to our example from Plato is that Socrates is doing the slave boy's job for him. As we saw, Socrates in effect helps the slave boy draw the logical inferences by putting suitable questions to him. Moreover, all of Socrates's questions to the slave boy are such that the slave boy might have asked them himself on his own. (There is one important exception to this statement. Can you spot what it is? Could just anybody have seen the relationships introduced by the diagonal?)

What, then, is Socrates's essential role in the famous conversation? The answer is clear: Socrates is the one who chooses the questions. And, as we have seen, *it is the choice of questions that makes or breaks a line of reasoning.*

In a sense, it is the slave boy who works out the argument. He is the one who gains insight through the process. Socrates undoubtedly knew ahead of time the geometric truth to which he led the slave boy. The slave boy could even have raised most of the questions himself. What Socrates is doing by his wise choice of questions is thus opening the doors to possibilities of reasoning which were there in the slave boy right from the beginning. Socrates's skill in doing so has made him a model for all teachers of reasoning, and indeed for all teachers, ever since.

△▼ THINK ABOUT IT

Find three examples of logical inference steps in the slave boy's answers.

.2

Interrogative Games:
The Structure of
the Reasoning Process

We have seen that reasoning can be thought of as a process of inquiry which involves interrogative steps and steps of logical inference. Now we have to examine the structure of this reasoning process in greater detail. We shall do this by describing a set of rules for carrying out and for evaluating an inquiry. These rules are said to define the *interrogative model of inquiry*. This model will serve as a framework for spelling out, explaining, and practicing good reasoning. Note that *reasoning*, *reasoning process*, *argument*, *inquiry*, and *rational inquiry* will all be used as names for what we are studying.

2.1 Some Simplifying Assumptions

For the time being, we shall make a few simplifying assumptions. The way they can be removed will be discussed later.

1. First, we shall assume that the reasoner is carrying on her or his inquiry alone, not in cooperation with others. We shall refer to the reasoner as the **inquirer.**

2. Second, we shall usually speak as though only one source of answers is used for interrogative steps. To have a neutral name for this source, we shall call it the **oracle.** In real life the inquirer typically consults several sources of answers in the course of the inquiry. For many purposes, however, the multiple sources can all be treated as if they were one and the same oracle. Often the differences between oracles do not matter.

3. Third, and most importantly, we shall assume for the time being that in interrogative steps *the oracle's answers are all true,* and are known by the inquirer to be true. This is obviously a strong assumption, and we will need to learn how to do without it later.

The Inquirer(s): Our name for the person(s) who are pursuing a rational inquiry.

The Oracle(s): Our name for the source(s) of answers to questions asked in interrogative steps. (In the early chapters of the book, it is assumed that the oracle is infallible and always gives true answers.)

2.2 Rational Inquiry as a Questioning Game

In order to spell out the structure of inquiry, interpreted as a questioning process, it is useful to think of it as a game played between the inquirer and the oracle. This is in keeping with historical precedent. In ancient Greece, in Plato's Academy, the Socratic questioning method was practiced as a game for purposes of training in reasoning. Later we shall find that this game approach is helpful for other reasons as well.

These questioning processes will be called **interrogative games.** What were earlier called *steps of reasoning* can now also be called **moves** in an interrogative game. (At this point you may be interested to read about recreational questioning games in Appendix B.)

Interrogative Game: A way to make an explicit description of the interrogative model of rational inquiry.

Interrogative Move: Another name for interrogative steps in reasoning. (We will also continue to use the word *step* and sometimes use the word *questioning* rather than *interrogative,* as in *questioning move* or *questioning step.*)

Logical Inference Move: Another name for logical inference steps in reasoning. (We may also occasionally shorten this to *inference move, inference step, logical move,* or *logical step.* In each case we mean a logical inference step as described in Chapter 1.)

By using as playful a term as *game* to refer to the process of rational inquiry, we are not trying to belittle the seriousness of reasoning processes. Rather, we are following the example of scientific students of decision making. These scholars have found it useful to consider many different types of decision-making processes as games. There actually exists a mathematical theory called *game theory,* which was founded by the brilliant mathematician John von Neumann (1903–1957). This theory can serve as a tool for many different kinds of decisions.

Such "games," like interrogative games, can involve a human opponent as, for instance, in military decisions, competitive business operations, or courtroom litigation. Other games, however, can involve an "opponent" who serves merely as a source of information but does not play an active role in the process. In such cases, students of decision making often speak of "games against nature." Our point in saying that the oracle is a "player" in an interrogative game is not that there is an adversarial relationship between the inquirer and the oracle. Rather, we are highlighting the fact that the oracle answers the inquirer's questions independently of the inquirer. This might be experienced by a human inquirer as a source of frustration from time to time, but it does not mean that an interrogative game is always a competitive one.

Thus, interrogative games of the kind considered here need not always involve a conflict of interests. Games are not always competitive. For example, the games of golf and bowling are structured in such a way that there is no need for a human opponent. A person can simply play to see how well he or she happens to do. People involved in community emergency preparedness often work cooperatively together in mock emergency "games" to test how well they are likely to perform in a real emergency. Cooperative games exist alongside competitive games. The main point is that the art of reasoning well can now be thought of as a skill in playing interrogative games.

In order to play a game, we must know its structure and rules. Now what is the structure of an interrogative game and what are its rules? In many respects this whole book is devoted to answering this question. Following is a rudimentary description of a simplified form of interrogative game.

2.3 Definitory vs. Strategic Rules

Games are usually played according to a set of rules. Actually, two very different kinds of rules are involved in most games. In Chapter 1 (Section 1.3) we briefly mentioned definitory rules of reasoning. **Definitory rules define the basic moves in the game.** They tell us what is and what is not admissible in a game. Following them, however, *does not in the least guarantee that you play the game well*, it only assures that you are playing the game correctly. For example, in a board game like chess or monopoly, the definitory rules tell you when and how you may move the different pieces. These rules do not tell you how to move the pieces in such a way as to make you successful against your opponent. The definitory rules for bowling are not very complicated, but much practice is required in order to achieve high scores.

Rules that tell you how to play a game well can be called **strategic rules** or **strategic principles.** They are usually much more difficult to formulate and learn than are the definitory rules. Strategic rules have to take into account your overall goal, your opponent's goals and tendencies, your own strengths and weaknesses. Strategic rules must also take into account the entire course of the game, not just particular moves one by one. In many games successful players follow strategic principles which they themselves are not clearly aware of. Strategic rules often have to be learned and developed by practicing the game in question and reflecting on how one plays the game.

Examples In baseball virtually every manager places the fastest player in the lineup in the first position in the batting order. Why? The definitory rules of baseball do not require this, but doing so is recognized to be good strategy in most instances.

In football most coaches elect to punt on fourth down and twenty. As the few exceptions to the contrary illustrate, this is not required by the rules of the game. However, as experience has shown, ignoring this advice is often bad strategy.

It should be clear that we must first study the definitory rules of a game before we can go very far in examining the strategic rules. We have to learn how a game is structured and how it is played before we study how to play it successfully. Discussion of interrogative games must therefore begin with the definitory rules of the game of reasoning and ours will do so in this and the next few chapters.

The danger always exists, however, that definitory rules command attention to the detriment of strategic rules. In fact, many books and courses on reasoning emphasize definitory rules disproportionately. One learns logical inference rules, inductive inference rules, and rules about mistakes (called fallacies) in following the definitory rules. Eventually the student gets the impression that good reasoning is mainly a matter of avoiding mistakes. But we have already seen that this is not in any way the main feature of good reasoning.

In the Sherlock Holmes story "Silver Blaze," the local investigator, Inspector Gregory, is described as "an extremely competent officer." He makes no mistakes in his logic. Yet he does not achieve success in solving the mystery. Sherlock Holmes says this is because he lacks imagination. Imagination plays a large role in the strategic rules of reasoning.

In this book we wish to help develop your imagination and your abilities to reason well. Therefore, although many of the following pages now introduce you to the details of the definitory rules of reasoning, we want to alert you that all this is preparation for the far more important adventure of learning how to reason creatively and well.

___ ▲ _____

Definitory Rules: The rules which define and describe how to play a game correctly.

Strategic Rules: The rules which give insight into how to play a game successfully and well.

△▼ EXERCISE 2-A

On the basis of what you learned in Sections 1.7 and 1.8 of Chapter 1 indicate which of the following are logical inference moves. Explain clearly in each case why you think your choice is or is not a logical inference move.

▶ 1. Mark is in the kitchen with Dinah.
    Therefore, someone's in the kitchen with Dinah.

   2. Sue finished the test and Bob did not.
    Therefore, Bob did not finish the test.

▶ 3. Sue finished the test or Bob finished the test.
    Therefore, if Sue finished the test then Bob did not.
    (Watch out for two different possible meanings of *or*.)

   4. If no one is at the bus stop, then the bus has already come.
    Therefore, if someone is at the bus stop, the bus has not yet come.

▶ 5. Everyone who uses Supradent has sex appeal. Someone uses Supradent.
    Therefore, someone has sex appeal.

   6. All ants are insects, and all ants have six legs.
    Therefore, all insects have six legs.

▶ 7. She is a college student.
    Therefore, she is always tired.

   8. You will be inducted if you are qualified, and you are qualified.
    So, you will be inducted.

▶ 9. You will be inducted only if you are qualified, and you are qualified.
    So, you will be inducted.

   10. Unless she pays me (and she won't), I can't pay you.
    Therefore, I can't pay you.

▶ 11. On the island of knights and knaves, knights always tell the truth and knaves always lie, and everybody on the island is either a knight or a knave. An islander says, "If I am a knight, I will tell you that I am."
    Therefore, he is a knight.

△▼ **EXERCISE 2-B**

Give three examples of sources of information that may play the role of the oracle in everyday processes of reasoning. What oracles do you consult in everyday life? Are these sources of information infallible? If a source is not infallible how might this affect the processes of reasoning that rely upon them?

△▼ **EXERCISE 2-C**

Give an example of a game in which one might have complete mastery of the definitory rules and yet be a poor player.

2.4   Structure and Definitory Rules of Simple Interrogative Games

The Initial Situation

There are two players, the inquirer and the oracle. In the initial situation, the players may be given one or more initial premises. **Initial premise(s)** are statements which both of the players have agreed in the beginning to take to be true. There may be more than one initial premise, and there can be games with no initial premise. In some applications, the initial premise is the theory on the basis of which the inquirer is conducting his or her inquiry. (In the study of reasoning the word "theory" means an organized statement of a body of information. In this context "theory" does *not* mean "a conjecture or guess.")

Note that sometimes you could just as easily think of the initial premises as a set of already answered interrogative steps and already performed logical inference steps. The point is that all of this initial information is given and structured prior to the actual work of the inquiry. In many of the simpler examples some students will treat the initial information as initial premises; others are just as likely to begin right away with interrogative moves and logical inference moves. Either approach is well within the basic structure of the interrogative model of inquiry.

It is important to realize that *any initial premise is to be an explicitly acknowledged one.* For instance, when the inquirer is a scientist, the initial premise of his or her inquiry might be a theory on which the inquirer is relying. Tacit (unspoken or unacknowledged) assumptions must not be included in the initial premises but must be brought into the inquiry by means of a questioning process.

In the initial situation the players are also given an **ultimate conclusion.** The ultimate conclusion is the statement the inquirer is trying to show to be true. The inquirer makes interrogative moves and logical inference moves in an attempt to show the truth of the conclusion. The oracle provides answers to the inquirer's questions, but it is also the oracle's job to see if there is any way, despite the work the inquirer is doing, to imagine the ultimate conclusion false. The inquirer's work is not successful until all ways of imagining the ultimate conclusion false have been blocked.

Note: this is the very reason to be able to think IN PRINCIPLE

For purposes of simplicity, we are also assuming that the players are aware of what the ultimate conclusion of the game is right from the beginning. We are also going to assume that there is just one ultimate conclusion being sought in the inquiry. In real-life applications the ultimate conclusion sometimes comes as a surprise even to the inquirer himself or herself. In real life there may also be more than one ultimate conclusion to the inquiry.

What the interrogative model is designed to do is, among other things, to help us evaluate reasoning processes. For the purpose of such evaluation we need to know, at least in hindsight, what the inquiry was trying to establish. For this reason, we are including the ultimate conclusion as part of the initial situation. The ultimate conclusion defines the goal the inquiry is trying to reach.

Later we shall extend the interrogative model to situations in which the inquirer is trying to answer a question, for instance, a yes/no question, rather than to prove a foregone conclusion. In such situations, the inquirer of course is not aware from the beginning what the answer will be. Still, the inquirer must know what the question is that the entire inquiry is intended to answer.

▲

Initial Premise(s): Explicitly acknowledged information that is available right at the beginning of an inquiry. (Remember that in Chapter 1 [Section 1.7] we defined *premise* as "the information that serves as the basis for an inference step." Initial premise[s] are one source of material for future logical inference steps.)

Ultimate Conclusion: The goal of the inquiry, what the inquirer is trying to establish. (Remember that in Chapter 1 [Section 1.7] we defined *conclusion* as "the statement of what has been derived from the premises." The ultimate conclusion is what the inquirer is hoping finally to derive from the entire inquiry.)

A Bookkeeping Method   Before explaining what the rules of the interrogative games are like, it is useful to agree on a simple method of "scorekeeping" in these games. This is a kind of double-entry bookkeeping method, sometimes known as the method of semantical tables (or, as it was originally called by a French term, of semantical *tableaux*). It is a double-entry bookkeeping method in the sense that it uses one side to indicate what is true, or is assumed to be true, and it uses the other side for what we hope to show to be true. We will call this the **table method.**

Thus in the beginning of the interrogative game the "scoreboard" looks like this:

Premises, Answers, and What Follows from Them	Conclusion
1. An Initial Premise 2. Possibly Another 3. Possibly Another 4.	Ultimate Conclusion

The rules of the game explain how such a table grows as moves are made in the game.

Two Different Kinds of Moves

As discussed previously, there are two kinds of moves in the interrogative games, *interrogative* moves and *logical inference* moves. At each stage of the game, the inquirer is free to choose which kind of move is to be performed next. These are the only two types of move possible.

Interrogative Moves   In an interrogative move, the inquirer addresses a question to the oracle. The oracle will, in the right situation, give an answer to the question. The inquirer may then use this answer in the rest of the argument. We shall examine later what makes for a "right situation" in which a question can be asked and when it is that the oracle will answer it.

In our tables we will number each move. Interrogative moves are always put in the *left side* of our tables. After the number we will write in the information that has been obtained from the interrogative move. We will also write *IM* to indicate that an interrogative move has been made. Whenever an interrogative move is made, it is a good practice to indicate the presumed source of the answer right after the obtained information has been written in. As shown in Parts 3 and 4 it can also be important to refer back to the place in the table where the presupposition of the interrogative move has been established.

Logical Inference Moves   In a logical inference move, two different things may happen, depending on which side of an interrogative table we are dealing with. Interrogative moves are always put on the left side, but logical inference moves can take place on either side. In practice, we will be concentrating most of the time on the left side of our tables.

Left-Side Logical Inference Moves

The basic idea is that the players have agreed that the initial premise information at the top of the left side of the table is true. The goal for all left-side moves is to preserve truth, that is, never to introduce any falsehoods. This idea will guide us in formulating the logical inference rules. (If you keep this idea of truth preservation in mind, you can soon learn how to formulate logical inference rules by yourself.)

A logical inference move in the left side of a table will be one that leads from the agreed initial premise(s) and other previous moves in the left side of the table to another statement that must be agreed to be true on the basis of the preceding information in the table that has already been agreed to be true. The inquirer is allowed only to make logical inference moves that lead from statements that are already agreed to be true to another statement that must now also be agreed to be true.

This notion of a logical inference move will be further developed in Part 2. The following examples will illustrate what has been discussed so far.

Example One   Assume that the following statement is in the left side of a table and has been agreed to be true:

1. Tom broke into the apartment and Dick broke into the apartment.

Now if statement 1 is agreed to be true, then obviously the two simpler statements in it must also be agreed to be true. These simpler statements are:

2. Tom broke into the apartment.

and

3. Dick broke into the apartment.

In this situation, statement 2 can be put as a new line in the left side of the table based on the agreed truth of statement 1, and so can statement 3. In other words, statement 2 can be added by a logical inference move based on statement 1, and so can statement 3.

This can be represented schematically as follows ("LI" stands for "logical inference move"):

Premises, Answers, and What Follows from Them	*Conclusion*
1. *T* (initial premise)	*C* (ultimate conclusion)
2.	
3. *S1* and *S2* (already given info)	
4.	
5. *S1* (LI from 3)	
6. *S2* (LI from 3)	

There could, of course, have been many steps between 1 and 3, and many steps between 3 and 5. The point is that line 5 can be added to the left side of the table whenever a line like line 3 is already present in the left side. Similarly, line 6 can also be added by a logical inference move. Notice how the information is written as a new numbered line on the left side, and a brief explanation is given of where the information came from after the statement of the information. Whenever a logical inference is being made, it is standard practice to indicate what the previous line or lines are upon which the inference is based. (Note also that the uppercase letter *T* is often used to indicate the initial premises. This is because in scientific inquiries the initial premises often consist in some theory that is being used in the inquiry. "Theory" in this context does not mean "opinion" or "guess." It instead indicates a systematic arrangement of information that has been agreed upon as a beginning basis for a given inquiry.)

What justifies a logical inference move is precisely the connection between the truth of the statements we are dealing with: If the first statement(s) are agreed to be true, then the statements obtained by a logical inference move must also be agreed to be true. This relates directly to the definition of logical inference in Chapter 1 (Sections 1.7 and 1.8). There it was stipulated that a logical inference involves a step that cannot be imagined false if the preceding steps on which it is based are imagined to be true.

In Parts 2 and 4 we will give a number of more detailed rules as to when a statement or a number of statements can be added to the left side of a table by a logical inference move. These rules all help to define what is possible in the game of reasoning.

In the example about breaking into the apartment, the logical inference from statement 1 to statement 3 may appear trivial to you. Yet there are circumstances in which even such a trivial-looking logical inference can be important. For instance, let us assume that a breaking and entering by Tom and Dick is a felony crime and that in the course of that felony Tom commits a murder. In many states or provinces Dick will also be guilty of that murder because he was involved in the breaking and entering. Thus the logical inference from statement 1 to statement 3, combined with the rules about felony crimes, might cost Dick his liberty or even his life.

Example Two   In this next example we shall proceed the other way around and give you the rule first. The rule indicated schematically in the following table is known as the *substitutivity of identity*. (Remember that "LI" stands for "logical inference move" and "IM" stands for "interrogative move.")

Premises, Answers, and What Follows from Them	Conclusion
1. *T* (initial premise)	*C* (ultimate conclusion)
2.	
3. *S*[*a*] (IM)	
4.	
5. *a* is identical with *b* (IM)	
6. *S*[*b*] (LI from 3 and 5)	

Here $S[a]$ is to be thought of as a statement about a. $S[b]$ is the same statement applied to b. Thus, what the rule of the substitutivity of identity says is that, if the players have agreed that a statement about a is true and have also agreed that b is the same entity as a, then they might as well agree that the same statement is true about b.

Again, this may seem utterly trivial. But consider the following illustration a novelist has kindly constructed for us. The scene takes place in a mansion in the French countryside. The lord of the manor is entertaining a number of guests, including the narrator. At one point, the narrator is talking to the priest, who has served the parish for a while. Reflectively, the priest says, "Strange things can happen in one's life. Can you imagine, my first confessant had a murder on his conscience." In the next moment the lord of the manor shows up and says, "I am glad to see that you two have met. You know, a long time ago I happened to be our good abbe's very first confessant."

Lesson: Beware of the force of the rule of the substitutivity of identity! More importantly, try to understand how logical inference moves work on the left side of our tables. Here is how the illustration of the substitutivity rule would look in a table:

Premises, Answers, and What Follows from Them	Conclusion
1. The priest's first confessant confessed that he was a murderer. (IM) 2. The lord of the manor was the priest's first confessant. (IM) 3. The lord of the manor confessed that he was a murderer. (LI from 1 and 2)	. . . .

Summary of Left-Side Logical Inference Moves   The basic concept of logical inference moves on the left side is simple. Whenever a new statement must be accepted as true on the basis of what has already been agreed to be true on the left side, the new statement can be added to the left side.

It is important to keep in mind the connection between the notions of truth and falsity, on the one hand, and logical inference, on the other, that emerged in the course of the discussion. This will be discussed in much more detail in Part 2, but we briefly state the ideas here. The essence of acceptable logical inference moves on the left side is that they preserve truth. If the previous information on which the move is based is true, then the statement obtained by a logical inference move must also be true.

But notice carefully that the logical inference move does not itself say anything about the truth of the previous information on the left side. The players have agreed to take the premises to be true, and we assume that we are getting true answers to questions. But the information might actually be false. If the previous information happens in fact to be false, then an acceptable logical inference move cannot assure us that we have added a true statement to the left side.

But notice also that if we recognize that a new statement added by an acceptable logical inference move happens to be false, this tells us something. If the newly added statement is false, then at least one of the previous pieces of information on which it is based must also be false. For if all the previous information were true, the new statement would have to be true, since an acceptable logical inference move preserves truth.

Right-Side Logical Inference Moves

What happens on the right side of our tables is a reverse image of what happens on the left, as far as logical inference moves are concerned. It will help in grasping this notion to think that the oracle's role is to keep the inquirer honest in the attempt to establish the ultimate conclusion. The oracle gives true answers for the left side of the table, but if there is any way to imagine the ultimate conclusion on the right side of the table false, the oracle will point that out. The oracle then can be thought of as trying to show that the conclusion statement could be false despite everything agreed to be true on the left side of the table.

This will mean that logical inferences on the right side work in a reverse way as compared with logical inferences on the left side. **On the right side we must think of logical inference moves as falsity-preserving.** The idea is this. In order to help the oracle with its side of the game, everything in the right side of the interrogative table must initially be able to be imagined as being false. So, if a logical inference step can show that some other statement must be imagined to be false when the preceding statements in the right side are imagined to be false, then that new statement may be added to the right side.

This is a reverse image of what happens in the left side. On the left side the inquirer is writing true statements which can be logically inferred from the statements already present on that side, or the inquirer is writing new information that is imagined to be true from answers to interrogative moves. On the right side are entered statements which can be logically inferred to be false on the basis of statements already being imagined false on that side.

To avoid confusion, in the early stages of our study we will focus mainly on the left side of tables. We will deal with complicated right sides only after we have got a good grasp of left-side logical inference moves. Here are a couple illustrations of right-side logical inferences:

Take as an ultimate conclusion the statement

1. Sandra is taller than either Mary or Jack or Nancy.

In order to imagine this statement false, it is necessary for the oracle also to be able to imagine the following three statements all to be false at the same time:

2. Sandra is taller than Mary.

3. Sandra is taller than Jack.

and

4. Sandra is taller than Nancy.

On the right side of a logical table in which statement 1 is the ultimate conclusion, we could go on to write statements 2, 3, and 4 as further specifications of what the oracle must try to imagine to be false.

Take as an ultimate conclusion the statement

1. Some students are more than twenty-five years old.

To imagine this statement false it is necessary for us to be able to imagine quite a few other statements to be false. For example, if someone says that

2. Jill is a student and she is twenty-seven,

we will have to be able to imagine that false in order to be able to imagine the ultimate conclusion false. Numerous other statements like this one would all have to be able to be imagined false in order for the oracle to imagine statement 1 to be false.

△▼ EXERCISE 2-D

▶ Our definition of logical inference in Sections 1.7 and 1.8 of Chapter 1 is designed specifically for left-side logical inference moves. Try to give a similar but "reverse image" definition for right-side logical inference moves.

△▼ EXERCISE 2-E

In the following treat the given statement as an ultimate conclusion. Write down other statements that must also be false, if we are trying to imagine the ultimate conclusion to be false.

▶ 1. Some insects have eight legs.
  2. Either Marge or Jack is a native of California.
▶ 3. Some number is larger than 1,000,000.

In the following cases write *one* statement whose falsehood would be enough to show the falsehood of the ultimate conclusion.

  4. Harriet helps Harold, and they succeed.
▶ 5. Neither Marge nor Jack is a native of California.
  6. Retired U.S. presidents are always well respected.

The Problem of Subtables

One other point needs to be made about logical inference moves. Sometimes logical inference moves split a side of a table into two or more subordinate lines of thought. Consider this example:

Premises, Interrogative Steps, and Logical Inferences	Conclusion
1. Either Sue or Sam will help. (premise) 2.	. . . .

In this example the first premise tells us that help will come from either Sue or Sam, but it doesn't tell us for sure which one will help. If we had other information, we might be able to figure out which of the two will help, but at this point we don't have that information. One way to start reasoning from line 1 of the table would be to split the left side of the table into two paths. In one path we would assume that Sue will help and in the other that Sam will. Then, as other information is provided from interrogative moves, we could see if the one assumption or the other (or possibly both) turns out to be true.

When the left side of a table splits like this, we have to keep track of the alternative **paths** for truth that have been introduced into the table. All of the paths have to be dealt with if the overall inquiry is to succeed. What this requires will be explained in the next section.

Summary of the Two Different Kinds of Moves   What happens in the course of an interrogative game is that the inquirer starts from the initial situation with the initial premise(s) on the left side and the ultimate conclusion on the right. The inquirer then builds up an interrogative table step by step. If the inquirer performs an interrogative move and receives an answer, then this answer is added as a truth to the left side. In a logical inference move, a statement is added either to the left or to the right side along the lines indicated above.

Closure of an Interrogative Table

But when does the work of building an interrogative table come to an end? When does the inquirer or the oracle succeed? An interrogative game comes to a positive end (or, as we might put it, the inquirer wins) if and only if the table is completely closed. What *closed* means involves two different issues: **path closure** and **closure of the entire table.** Path closure occurs under one of two possible conditions:

1. Two statements that cannot be imagined both together to be true occur in the same path on the left side. The path in which they occur together is said to be *closed* and does not need to be considered any further.

2. Two statements that cannot be imagined both together to be false occur in the same path on the right side. The path in which they occur together is said to be *closed* and does not need to be considered any further.

Closure of the entire table takes place as follows: Any path which is not already closed is called an *open* path. Compare all open paths on the left side of the table with all open paths on the right side. If, for every pairing of left and right open paths, an identically matching whole line is found to occur in both paths, the *entire table* is said to be *closed*.

The most important case here is closure of the entire table. That this is a correct description of a successful conclusion of an interrogative inquiry can be seen from what was said earlier. On the left side the inquirer is writing truths. These truths are initial premises (agreed to be true for the purpose of the inquiry), the oracle's answers (assumed for now to be true) to the inquirer's questions or they come from truth-preserving logical inference moves. On the right side the oracle is trying to defend the possibility of imagining the ultimate conclusion to be false. But if closure of the entire table occurs, then the truth of the ultimate conclusion or something that leads to its truth has appeared in the left side. This means that the oracle's answers along with the players' agreement on the truth of the initial premise(s) has forced the oracle to see that the ultimate conclusion is true.

The interrogative game can be thought of as an exercise in bridge building. What the inquirer hopes is that a series of truths on the left side can make contact with one of the statements that the oracle is trying to imagine false. The inquirer's bridge is completed precisely when the two sides meet, that is, when the same statement occurs on both sides. (If the table has split into several paths, it is necessary that bridges be built from every open path on the left side to every open path on the right side. In this way the oracle will be left with no ways in which to imagine the ultimate conclusion false while imagining the lines on the left side of the table to be true.)

Illustration   **Closure of an Entire Table**

Premises, Interrogative Steps, and Logical Inferences	Conclusion
1. Pam and Paul play poker. (premise) 2. Poker is a card game. (premise) 3. Pam plays poker. (LI from 1) 4. Paul plays poker. (LI from 1) 5. Paul plays a card game. (LI from 2 and 4) Table is entirely closed.	Paul plays a card game.

This is the main kind of closure in which we are interested. The work on the left side of the table has established the truth of the ultimate conclusion. We say the entire table is closed to indicate that the inquirer's work is completed.

Path closure, on the other hand, indicates that a particular path is finished, but it may or may not show that an entire table is closed.

Consider, first, path closure on the left side. If two statements that cannot both together be true occur among the statements the inquirer has been led to write in a path on the left side, that path can no longer be considered one in which all the lines on the left side of the table can be imagined to be true.

We can see the importance of this by expanding the illustration about Sue and Sam helping.

Illustration   **Path Closure and Entire Table Closure**

Premises, Interrogative Steps, and Logical Inferences	Conclusion
1. Either Sue or Sam will help. (premise)	Sue will help.
2. Sam will not help. (premise)	
3. Sue will help. │ Sam will help.	(Line 3 is LI from 1.)
Table is entirely closed. │ Path closed.	

In this illustration two paths opened on the left side in line 3 on the basis of line 1, but the path that assumed that "Sam will help" also contained line 2, which asserted that "Sam will not help." These two statements cannot both be true together, so that path is closed. Meanwhile, the other open path on the left side contains the statement "Sue will help." This statement is identical to the ultimate conclusion on the right side, so the whole table closes by the process of bridge building between the open path on the left and the open path on the right.

Path closure on the left side of a table can also arise if the players happen to agree on initial premises which turn out not to be able to be imagined all together true at the same time. In such a situation the initial premises are said to be *inconsistent* with each other. It can also happen that the oracle might give an answer in an interrogative move that ends up being inconsistent with the previous information.

Following is an illustration of a table that contains inconsistent premises.

Illustration   **Path Closure When Premises Are Inconsistent**

Premises, Interrogative Steps, and Logical Inferences	Conclusion
1. Pam and Paul play poker. (premise)	Paul and Pam are good friends.
2. Poker is a card game. (premise)	
3. Paul doesn't play cards. (premise) ·	
4. Pam plays poker. (LI from 1)	
5. Paul plays poker. (LI from 1)	
6. Paul plays cards. (LI from 2 and 5)	
Path (and Table!) is closed. (Line 3 is the denial of line 6.)	

In this example the inquirer's work is done and in a sense the oracle has been defeated. The oracle is trying to show that when all the lines on the left side are imagined to be true the conclusion can still be imagined to be false. The oracle "fails" in this case because it turns out to be impossible to imagine all the lines on the left side true at the same time. Line 3 is the denial of line 6; there is no way for them both to be true at the same time. The path closes and, since there are no other open paths on the left side, the whole table is closed. In this example it looks like the inquirer wins by a fishy default. The problem of inconsistent premises requires careful study, and we will return to it in Part 2.

Path closure on the right side of a table is similar to path closure on the left side. On the right side the paths contain statements that the oracle is trying to imagine to be false. Thus, if two statements that cannot both together be imagined false appear in a path, then that path is no longer of use to the oracle and the inquirer can permanently close it. Sometimes the ultimate conclusion itself turns out to be a special kind of statement that simply cannot be imagined false. We need to spend some time thinking about the meaning of *or* in order to get an illustration of the issues raised by path closure on the right side of a table.

In English we can mean two related but different things when we say "or." For example, in an earlier exercise we used the statement "Sue finished the test or Bob finished the test." In everyday English this statement will be true if Sue finishes the test and Bob does not. It will also be true if Bob finishes the test and Sue does not. The statement will be false if Sue and Bob both fail to finish. However, in everyday English we sometimes intend to say that the statement would be false also if both of them finish, and sometimes we allow that the statement would be true if both of them finish. The first possibility is called the "exclusive" use of *or* and the other is called the "inclusive" use.

As will be explained in Part 2, logicians usually choose to treat *or* as inclusive unless it is explicitly said to be exclusive. They do this because their strategy is to take the less informative reading of a word like *or* unless they have reason to do otherwise. In this way they hope to avoid reading more into a statement than was originally intended. Throughout this book we will intend the less informative, "inclusive" use of *or* unless we specifically say otherwise.

Note that this discussion of *or* provides an illustration of the distinction between definitory and strategic rules. There would be nothing *incorrect* about choosing to have a definitory rule that takes *or* to be exclusive rather than inclusive, but it would likely be a less effective strategy for pursuing the game of reasoning.

With these thoughts about *or* in mind we can figure out what is required in order to imagine an inclusive "or" statement to be false. Think again about the example "Sue finished the test or Bob finished the test." Using the inclusive sense of *or*, we have three ways for the statement to be true (Sue finishes and not Bob, or Bob finishes and not Sue, or both Sue and Bob finish) and only one way for it to be false. The only way for it to be false is for both Sue and Bob not to finish. This gives us the interesting result that if we have an "or" statement, it can be imagined false only by imagining *both* of its sides to be false. Now we are ready to look at an example of path closure on the right side of a table.

Illustration **Path Closure on the Right Side of a Table**

Premises, Interrogative Steps, and Logical Inferences	Conclusion
1.	1. Either the glass is empty or it is not empty.
2.	2. The glass is empty. (LI from 1)
3.	3. The glass is not empty. (LI from 1)
4.	Path (and Table!) is closed. (Line 3 is the denial of line 2.)
5.	
6.	

In this illustration all the action takes place on the right side. There is no need for anything on the left side. Remember that on the right side the oracle is trying to imagine the conclusion statement to be false. In this case the conclusion statement is an "or" statement, and we have seen that an "or" statement can be false only if both sides of the *or* can be imagined false. This explains the logical inference steps taken in lines 2 and 3 of the table. In order to imagine the falsity of the conclusion, the oracle must also be prepared to imagine the falsity of lines 2 and 3, because these are the two sides of the *or* in line 1.

Line 3, however, is the denial of line 2. It's going to be impossible to imagine both line 2 and line 3 false at the same time. This means that it is impossible to imagine line 1 false. And this means that the oracle has been "defeated" in the interrogative game. The inquirer does not need to do any work on the left side of the table, because the ultimate conclusion is a statement that cannot possibly be made false. Because there are no other open paths on the right side, the entire table is closed. Table closure is the indication that the inquirer has been successful.

___ ▲ _____

Path Closure:

1. When two statements that cannot be imagined both together to be true occur in the same path on the left side of a table, the path in which they occur together is said to be *closed* and does not need to be considered any further.

2. When two statements that cannot be imagined both together to be false occur in the same path on the right side of a table, the path in which they occur together is said to be *closed* and does not need to be considered any further.

Open Path: Any path which is not closed is called an *open* path.

Table Closure: Compare all open paths on the left side of the table with all open paths on the right side. If, for every pairing of left and right open paths, an identically matching whole line is found to occur in both paths, the entire table is said to be *closed*. Closure indicates that there is no way to imagine the conclusion false while imagining the lines on the left side of the table to be true.

Unclosed Tables

It may happen that, after a finite number of moves, the inquirer's attempt to construct a closed interrogative table fails. It can happen that a line of reasoning does not lead to table closure. In order to recognize such a situation, you must have a complete list of game rules, and we are not in a position yet to study these.

However, should you perceive that a table is not able to be closed, you know that your inquiry has been unsuccessful. In this case you must either admit defeat or (better) try to devise new questions that will help you find a way to close all attempts at imagining your conclusion to be false. Alternatively, you can also consider revising your conclusion.

Go on now to Chapter 3 and learn how to use the table method for detailed argument analysis. You will then be able to use the table method to analyze the arguments you studied in Exercise 1-C at the end of Section 1.9 of Chapter 1 and to analyze many others as well.

.3

Interrogative
Argument Analysis

Already in Chapter 1 (Section 1.9) you were encouraged to begin trying your hand at argument analysis. This is such an important practical skill that we wanted you to get started with it right away. Now, however, you are in a position to get a much more systematic grasp of it. (Remember that we are using the word "argument" as a convenient name for what can also be called "reasoning," "reasoning process," "inquiry," or "rational inquiry.")

In Chapter 1 we gave a brief description of argument analysis. In this chapter we will examine in close detail what this involves.

▲

Argument Analysis: The process of discovering and listing the basic interrogative and logical inference steps found in a complex everyday inquiry.

You may be wondering why argument analysis is so important. It is an essential skill in the reasoning process because it provides the foundation for **argument construction** and **argument evaluation.**

___▲_____

Argument Construction: The process of discovering and formulating the questions and logical inferences that create a rational inquiry. Skills in argument construction are closely related to skills in argument analysis. The ability to analyze the argument that one is constructing helps keep the construction process on a good foundation.

Argument Evaluation: The process of checking an argument for definitory correctness, for strategic excellence, and for closure of the argument table. Skills in argument evaluation are closely related to skills in argument analysis. The ability to analyze an argument provides a foundation for the evaluative tasks.

After concentrating on argument analysis in this chapter, we will turn to argument construction in the next. As you learn skills in analysis and construction you will gradually find yourself better able to evaluate arguments. We will not, however, systematically study argument evaluation until we have tackled Parts 2 and 3 of the book.

3.1 Argument Analysis and Interrogative Tables

In Chapter 2 you learned all the basic elements involved in interrogative tables. These elements are the primary building blocks of an argument or inquiry. Argument analysis involves identifying these elements in an oral or written sketch of an inquiry and arranging them in proper order in an interrogative table.

The following questions should call to mind the main elements of an interrogative table.

1. Who are the players in this "game" of inquiry? That is, who is doing the inquiring and what oracles are available?

2. What was the initial situation? That is, what were the initial premise(s) and the ultimate conclusion?

3. Which are the different steps in the argument?

4. Which steps should be considered answers to questions and which steps should be considered logical inferences? You will often find that there are steps which are initially difficult to classify either as answers or as logical inferences.

5. For each interrogative step, what is the (often unspoken) question it is supposed to be answering, and what is the source of the answer?

6. Should some of the answers to questions be thought of as results of a subordinate, more detailed reasoning process?

7. For each logical inference, from what earlier statements is it supposed to follow?

8. Which steps of inference should be considered as ultimate conclusions of a more detailed series of inferences? We will find in the examples and exercises that what looks like a simple inference is often really the output of a number of shorter inferential steps.

9. Does the interrogative table close? Has the inquirer been successful?

The explicit report of the details of a given reasoning process does not always enable you to answer all of the questions above. Remember that in Chapter 1 we noted that oral and written reports of arguments are best thought of as sketches for arguments. Argument analysis requires that we creatively imagine what the inquirer would do if challenged to fill in the missing details.

This will often mean that a sketch of an argument may result in more than one possible analysis. But it is by searching for the basic elements of the argument and arranging them in an interrogative table that you will be able to achieve sufficient understanding of the argument to be able to begin to evaluate its significance.

The skills of argument analysis can be acquired only through practice, that is, through examples and exercises. Accordingly, we provide now a number of these by means of which you can begin your training.

Illustration of the Table Method

Following is an illustration of the application of the interrogative table method to an everyday argument.

Argument

There is no justification for the astronomical salaries paid to professional athletes these days. Even players who might never find their way into a game earn six-figure salaries, whereas there is not one elementary school teacher in the entire country who earns anywhere near this amount. Are the services rendered by a professional jock really of greater value to the country than an effective school teacher? Of course not. But what other standard for determining salaries is superior to one based upon the worth of the job performed? So unless one is willing to grant that elementary school teachers deserve more money than back-up athletes are currently being paid, a suggestion no one can take seriously, one cannot escape the conclusion that these athletes should be earning less.

Table Analysis

Premises, Interrogative Moves, and Logical Inference Moves	Conclusion
1. Athletes frequently earn more than teachers. (premise or IM)	1. Athletes are overpaid.
2. The job performed by athletes is of less value than that performed by teachers. (premise or IM)	*less value to whom.*
3. Persons should be paid in proportion to the value of the work performed. (premise or IM)	
4. School teachers should earn more than athletes. (LI from 2 and 3)	
5. School teachers should not earn as much as athletes currently earn. (IM)	
6. Athletes are overpaid. (LI from 1, 4, and 5)	

We may consider lines 1–3 in the table to be initial premises or, alternatively, to be answers to questions put to various oracles. Line 4 follows by means of a logical inference step from lines 2 and 3. Line 5 can be considered an answer to a question put to an oracle. Line 6 follows by means of a logical inference step from lines 1, 4, and 5. The table is closed; i.e., the conclusion appears in the open path on the left side of the table and also in the open path on the right side. If we assume that the initial premises and all answers to questions are true, then the inquiry has been successful. We said in Chapter 2 that for the time being we would assume that all premises and answers are true. We recognize, of course, that not everyone will agree with the answers and information given in the above example.

△▼ EXERCISE 3-A

Indicate the kinds of sources of information which might serve as oracles for statements 1–3 and 5 above. Are you willing to accept this information as true? Can you imagine some information that would lead toward an opposite conclusion to the one given? We shall return to these questions in an exercise in Chapter 4.

△▼ EXERCISE 3-B

Label the left-hand lines of the following tables according to whether the line is an IM or an LI. If you claim that a line is the result of an interrogative move, indicate a possible source of information for the answer. If you claim that a statement is the result of a logical inference step, indicate the line(s) from which it follows.

As you look for logical inferences, you may need to supply some background or "between the lines" information. The more carefully you test for a logical inference, the more likely it is that you will need to fill in between the lines so that a genuine logical inference appears. We will learn more about this as we go on. The second exercise is more difficult in this respect than the first.

1.

Premises, Interrogative Moves, and Logical Inference Moves	Conclusion
1. Children should be allowed to attend school unless their presence poses a threat to either the normal operation of the school or to the health of any other individuals present. ▶ 2. The AIDS virus cannot be transmitted to others at school by students with the virus. 3. Students with the AIDS virus are otherwise like other students. ▶ 4. No special medical precautions need to be taken because of these students. 5. No other special allowances need to be made for these students. ▶ 6. These students do not pose a health threat to others at school. 7. These students do not pose a threat to the normal functioning of the school. ▶ 8. Children with AIDS should be allowed to attend school.	1. Children with AIDS should be allowed to attend school.

2.

Premises, Interrogative Moves, and Logical Inference Moves	Conclusion
1. One of the factors relevant to the determination of the value of a work of art is its success in stimulating others. ▶ 2. Perhaps the best measure of this success is the influence it exerts on other artists.	1. It may be impossible to evaluate adequately the greatness of a work of art in its own time.

3. Truly powerful art has not a conscious influence, but a subconscious or tacit effect on other artists.

▶ 4. Often, however, this influence, while significant, may be relatively subtle and hard to detect at first.

5. Sometimes it takes years for this influence to be recognized by critics and other artists.

▶ 6. Thus it may be impossible to evaluate adequately the greatness of a work of art in its own time.

3.2   Facts, Ma'am, Just the Facts

It is important to realize and to keep in mind what kinds of statements are entered into an interrogative table as bookkeeping lines. Here the best advice may be Sergeant Friday's line in the old TV series *Dragnet:* "Facts, Ma'am, just the facts." In other words, when you are constructing an argument, enter into your table only statements pertaining to the subject matter of your argument. Only such statements can be used as a basis of a logical inference.

For example, *do not* preface your line by "The inquirer believes" or "I believe" or "It seems to me," or even by "The oracle answers" or "The witness said." From the fact that you or the inquirer think something, the only conclusion that can be drawn is that you think so. You may be wrong, hence nothing follows with certainty about the facts of the case.

Later we shall see that it will be a good idea to keep in mind what you think of the reliability of different answers. However, such comments do not belong in the table. They will affect your strategies, not the particular moves you make.

Also, it does not help to write on the left-hand side "X says that . . . " where X is the oracle. If X had not been acknowledged as the oracle right from the beginning, you would not be addressing questions to X in the first place. What you should write into your argument table is simply the information the oracle gives, not the comment that the oracle said it. It *is* a good idea to indicate in parentheses who or what the oracle (the source of answers) is each time an interrogative move is made. But those indications are not parts of the actual information to be used in the rest of the inquiry.

What is being urged here is not merely that all the entries in a line of reasoning be statements. They must indeed be statements, but they must also be statements about facts or information relevant to the case.

△▼ **EXERCISE 3-C**

Analyze the following arguments by means of the table method. Identify any initial premises and the ultimate conclusion. Try to list the different steps in the reasoning and to show which are interrogative steps and which are logical inference steps. Supply any important missing steps. Indicate for each line in your table whether it is an initial premise, an answer to a question, or the result of a logical inference step from earlier lines. Discuss whether the table closes or not.

▶ 1. Joe either escaped out the window or through the vent in the ceiling. But he did not escape out the window, because if he had there would be footprints underneath it outside, and no footprints could be found. Therefore, Joe escaped through the vent in the ceiling.

2. If either of them were on time, one of them would have answered the phone. But I called, and no one answered. So both of them were late.

▶ 3. The president either knew about the stock deal, or she did not. If she did, then she allowed unethical and perhaps illegal practices to continue unchecked. If she did not, then she was ignorant of important aspects of the work-related activities of her executives. In either case, she was neglectful of her responsibilities. Thus, we ought to find a new chief executive for the firm.

4. Return to the argument analyses that you did for Exercise 1-C at the end of Section 1.9 of Chapter 1. Put analyses for numbers 1 through 5 into interrogative table form, and discuss whether the tables close.

3.3   Difficulties in Distinguishing Moves

Argument analysis requires that we clearly distinguish between questioning (interrogative) moves and logical inference moves. This, however, is not easy, because in everyday reports of arguments the two kinds of moves are not always carefully distinguished. Here are several points to keep in mind as you approach the problem of distinguishing the two kinds of moves.

First, as we have already noted, the difference is not usually indicated verbally in actual arguments. For instance, in Chapter 1 in "The Curious Incident of the Dog in the Nighttime," what were in fact Holmes's questions were not indicated by a question mark. Conversely, in the *Meno* example, what were clearly conclusions of logical inferences were obtained as answers to questions.

Second, what looks like an answer to a question—for instance, an observation or perception—may turn out to be the result of an inquiry involving logical inferences as well as questions. This can be illustrated by another example from Sherlock Holmes. In this case we listen in on Holmes's reasoning about how he "perceived" that Dr. Watson had been to Afghanistan. The very same conclusion is said by Sherlock Holmes to have been reached by deduction (inference move) and by observation (interrogative move). This passage reports the occasion when Dr. Watson meets Sherlock Holmes for the first time. The good doctor tells the story himself:

> "Dr. Watson, Mr. Sherlock Holmes," said Stamford, introducing us.
>
> "How are you?" he said cordially, gripping my hand with a strength for which I should hardly have given him credit. "You have been in Afghanistan, I perceive."
>
> "How on earth did you know that?" I asked in astonishment.
>
> "Never mind," said he, chuckling to himself.

Later, Holmes explains how he "perceived" where Watson had come from.

> "You appeared to be surprised when I told you, on our first meeting, that you had come from Afghanistan."
>
> "You were told, no doubt."
>
> "Nothing of the sort. I *knew* you came from Afghanistan. From long habit the train of thoughts ran so swiftly through my mind that I arrived at the conclusion without being conscious of intermediate steps. There were such steps, however. The train of reasoning ran: 'Here is a gentleman of a medical type, but with the air of a military man. Clearly an army doctor then. He has just come from the tropics, for his face is dark, and that is not the natural tint of his skin, for his wrists are fair. He has undergone hardship and sickness, as his haggard face says clearly. His left arm has been injured. He holds it in a stiff and unnatural manner. Where in the tropics could an English army doctor have seen much hardship and got his arm wounded? Clearly in Afghanistan.' The whole train of thought did not occupy a second. I then remarked that you came from Afghanistan, and you were astonished." (From Sir Arthur Conan Doyle's "A Study in Scarlet," in *The Complete Sherlock Holmes*, Vol. 1 [New York: Doubleday, 1905], p. 24.)

This example illustrates how difficult argument analysis can be. What first might look like an answer to an observational question ("I perceive") turns out to require a longer argument ("train of thought") involving several answers and several logical inferences.

△▼ EXERCISE 3-D

Analyze a portion of Holmes's "train of thought" above as a series of interrogative and logical inference steps.

It can be difficult to distinguish between interrogative and logical inference moves. Yet the distinction is very real. It can even play a role in ordinary life. You have perhaps seen scenes in courtroom dramas where a lawyer puts a question in cross-examination and the opposing lawyer says, "Objection! The question calls for an inference." Typically, such an objection is sustained. An eyewitness is expected to report the answers he or she got to questions put to the witness's immediate environment, that is, what the witness saw or heard. The witness's replies to questions must not be based, partly or wholly, on inferences.

To understand the distinction, it might be helpful to see how it first developed. The distinction, and the very notion of logical inference, originated from the Socratic questioning games, illustrated by the example from Plato's *Meno* in Chapter 1. The famous Greek philosopher **Aristotle** (384–322 B.C.E.) studied philosophy with Plato at the Academy in Athens where questioning games were used as a central part of intellectual training.

Later Aristotle tried to systematize a set of rules for such questioning procedures. He was especially interested in the rules that guide a questioner's choice of strategy and tactics. In these questioning exercises, all steps were phrased as questioning steps.

What Aristotle noticed was that answers to certain questions could be predicted on the basis of the earlier steps of the game. Such answers were independent of what the answerer knew or believed. Recognizing questions with such predictable answers is, of course, a tremendous help in planning one's questioning strategy. (We shall ourselves emphasize the importance of strategy selection in later chapters.)

Now, such predictable answers are precisely the ones which can be logically inferred from the earlier answers together with the initial premise(s). In beginning to study them systematically, **Aristotle became the founder of the science of logic.**

Because such unavoidable answers do not depend on the answerer but only on the inquirer's choice of the question, it is helpful to consider them as steps of an essentially different kind from ordinary answers, which depend on the answerer. Thus, we now call answers to these kinds of questions logical inferences, and we no longer treat them as questions.

— ▲ _____

Aristotle: Aristotle (384–322 B.C.E.) came from Macedonia in northern Greece. At the age of seventeen he became a student in Plato's Academy in Athens. He stayed on for twenty years, becoming a teacher at the Academy. After Plato's death Aristotle traveled, pursued marine biological research, tutored Alexander of Macedon who came to be known as Alexander the Great, and eventually founded his own school, the Lyceum, in Athens. Sometimes he and his followers are called "peripatetics" (i.e., "walkers") because they are supposed to have conducted much of their reasoning while walking about in the school gardens. Aristotle, Plato, and Socrates are among the greatest philosophers in the Western tradition.

_____

We have seen that what looks like an interrogative step may actually be a lengthy line of reasoning which involves inferences, and that what looks like a logical inference step may likewise be a sequence of several moves, some of which involve questions. Hence the distinction between interrogative and logical inference moves is applicable only when the argument or inquiry one is studying is analyzed (taken apart) into its basic steps (steps that need not be analyzed any further). The distinction cannot always be made in unanalyzed arguments.

For this reason, among others, in analyzing a given argument it is especially important to search for the basic steps of the argument. An example is offered once again by Holmes's "curious incident," which on a closer scrutiny turns out to involve many more steps than first meet the eye.

Analyzing "The Curious Incident"

It is interesting to see what the interrogative table might look like for "The Curious Incident of the Dog in the Nighttime." Fortunately, in this case all the action takes place on the left side, which therefore is the only one that needs to be represented here. Just remember that the ultimate conclusion on the right side is "The thief was the stable master."

The left side of the table might be built up by the inquirer (Sherlock Holmes) in the following way, step by step. The first thing to notice is that there is no initial premise. The factual information on the left side is all gained from interrogative moves.

Left Side of the Table

Answers and What Follows from Them

---

1.   (Was there at least one watchdog in the stable?)
     Yes. (IM; Source: stable boys.)
2.   Call one of the dogs *d*. (LI from 1)
2a. *d* was in the stables. (LI from 1)
2b. *d* is a watchdog. (LI from 1)
3.   (Did any of the watchdogs in the stables bark at the thief?)
     No. (IM; Source: stable boys)
4.   *d* did not bark at the thief. (LI from 2 and 3)
5.   (Who is it that a watchdog does not bark at?)
     Its master. (IM; Source: common knowledge)
6.   The thief whom *d* did not bark at was *d*'s master. (LI from 5, 4 and 2b)
7.   (Who is *d*'s master?)
     The stable master. (IM; Source: stable boys)
8.   The thief was the stable master. (LI from 6 and 7)

Here statement 8 is the ultimate conclusion which now occurs on both sides of the interrogative table, thus closing it. So Sherlock Holmes's apparently simple "deduction" turns out to involve at least eight steps. Furthermore, we must eventually learn how to analyze the logical inference moves of this "game" into several smaller moves. (We shall return to this analysis in Part 4.)

You may wonder why we had to pick out one of the watchdogs for special attention. The reason is that only in this way can we hope to reach the truly basic steps of the argument. As we said in the preceding section, it is necessary to get to the basic steps for a complete analysis.

3.4 Further Perspective

In pursuing an argument analysis, it is helpful to think about the attitude one must adopt. Analysis prepares us to be able to evaluate the work done by some inquirer, but analysis is not itself the time for evaluation. Therefore, our attitude during analysis is one of *sympathetically* trying to put the best construction on the materials that are to be found in the inquiry. This entails several consequences:

1. We try to determine and indicate the sources of information found in the initial premises and in the interrogative moves, but, during analysis, we accept the information as reliable despite our own thoughts about its reliability.

2. As we go further into the table, we expect that the inquirer intends us to see inference links between earlier information and what is being said in a given line. This is not always the case, but we should be as alert as possible to discovering inference links that the inquirer may have had in mind.

3. Our method requires that we try to turn all inferences into *logical* inferences. This will usually mean that we must look "between the lines" for the tacit information needed to make the inferences strong enough to be logical inferences. This "between the lines" information is often brought into the table by means of interrogative moves, though logical inference moves may also be needed to get the information into usable shape. Often the source of the information is "common knowledge" or "background information" that the inquirer could reasonably have expected us to have in mind.

4. It is not easy to know how detailed we should be in making this between-the-lines information explicit. You need, however, to be sufficiently explicit about such information so that it is clear to you and to other reasonably intelligent observers that you have the materials needed to defend the correctness of the logical inferences. Much will depend upon how important the argument is. The more important it is, the more carefully we will need to work at making the inferences logical inferences.

5. Sometimes you will be bringing in between-the-lines information with which you yourself do not agree, but you should try to present this information as favorably as possible for the sake of the original argument. During analysis we are trying to see the argument or inquiry in its best possible light. There will be plenty of time during argument evaluation to expose all that is wrong with the argument.

6. During analysis we try to the best of our ability to supply what is needed to bring the inquiry to a successful ultimate conclusion. This will not always be possible, and it is not finally our job to do major, creative work that the inquirer failed to do. Still, if we are interested in the subject matter and in truth about it, the harder we work at analysis, the better prepared we are to succeed where the inquirer may have failed.

Another reason it is useful to analyze an argument sympathetically, even when you ultimately want to criticize it, is the following: If you can show that there is something wrong with the argument even when analyzing it in the most favorable light, then your criticism is more telling than it would have been if you had based your criticism on an unfavorable analysis.

We are now ready to try a more complicated example. Consider the following argument, or line of thought. This has been freely constructed for our purposes, but it does represent a line of thought put forward by some law enforcement officials.

> The war on drugs cannot be won by trying to restrict the influx of drugs into the United States. It is impossible to prevent totally the smuggling of controlled substances, as was shown by the United States's experience with prohibition of alcohol. Suppose now that by a major effort the government manages to cut down the flow of drugs into the country by 15 percent. What will happen? The major drug suppliers are in their business for money. If they have 15 percent less to sell, they still want the same profit. Hence they will raise the street price by 15 percent. In order to get that money, the drug addicts will commit correspondingly more crimes. Consequently, the situation will actually get worse, not better.

How are we to analyze such an argument? We use our table method. For the most part we will be concentrating on what is happening on the left side of the table. In what follows we will briefly indicate the ultimate conclusion, which should go on the right side. Then everything else is happening on the left side of the table. For convenience, we are not actually drawing a table.

The first sentence seems to state the ultimate conclusion the inquirer is trying to reach. One way to emphasize a sentence in English is to place it at the beginning of a paragraph. When no other words are indicating the conclusion, this is one of the ways people point to what they are trying to establish. Thus, this first statement is not a starting point for the argument; rather it is the goal, the conclusion the inquirer will try to establish. That statement can be put on the right side of the table analysis.

The second statement in the example sets up a two-branched movement on the left side of the argument table. The first step of the argument could be something like this:

1. Restricting the influx of drugs into the United States will be achieved either totally or partially.

With this statement in mind the inquirer splits the line of thought into two paths based on the "either/or" of statement 1. One of the two paths runs somewhat as follows:

2. The experience of prohibition of alcohol in the United States shows that it is impossible to prevent totally the illegal importation of controlled substances.

3. Illegal drugs are controlled substances.

4. Hence, it is impossible to prevent totally the illegal importation of drugs.

Here statement 4 is a logical inference from statements 2 and 3. Statement 3 is an obvious truth. It can be thought of as an answer to the question "Are illegal drugs controlled substances?" The answer is in this case provided by the meanings of the terms "controlled substances" and "illegal drugs." The answer to the question might be thought of as coming from a dictionary or a code of law.

Where does statement 2 come from? There are no earlier steps of the argument from which 2 might be logically inferred. Hence, it must also be an answer to a question. (If you think you also see in it a logical inference, you are correct. This compressed statement brings in a complex of new information and logical inferences about that information. At our level of analysis, we simply treat the line as an answer to a question.) The source of information for answering a question about the experience of prohibition of alcohol in the United States would likely be knowledge of American history. The inquirer is assuming either that you know this bit of history or that you will trust what he or she is telling you.

Statements 2, 3, and 4 push the first path of the argument as far as it can go. Statement 1 had said that restricting the influx of drugs into the United States will be achieved either totally or partially. This first path seeks to eliminate the possibility of totally restricting the influx of drugs. This permanently closes off this path; we no longer need to consider it.

To show this exactly in terms of our definition of path closure in Chapter 2 (Section 2.4), we would say that this path on the left side also contains statement 1a.

1a. It is possible to prevent totally the illegal importation of drugs.

This statement is one part of the either/or in statement 1. Statement 4 is the denial of statement 1a. Therefore, a statement and its denial have appeared in this path of the table. That closes the path, and we can turn our attention to the other path. There will not be need again to come back to this path.

So the inquirer turns to the other path, the possibility that a partial (but perhaps substantial) restriction of the influx of drugs might be achieved. (Remember that we are still on the left side of the table. We have pushed one path to closure, and now we are looking at the other path.) In this path the argument proceeds as follows:

5. The major drug suppliers are in this illegal business to make money.

This statement is not a logical inference from earlier statements. Hence it must be an answer to a question. Where does this information come from? As so often happens in real life, it is not clear who or what is the source of the information in statement 5. Is it common-sense knowledge about human motivation that the inquirer is relying on? Or has he or she consulted studies of the actual manners and morals of drug lords? Fortunately, for our analysis of the structure of the argument, it is not necessary for us to be able to determine how the inquirer got the information. We will worry about that problem later when we come to argument evaluation.

A crucial statement in the argument is

6. The restriction of the influx of drugs into the United States can only be partial.

Statement 6 is a logical inference from statements 1 and 4. It states what is left over after the other half of the either/or has led to a dead end.

From 5 and 6 it is inferred that

7. The drug suppliers would raise the price of drugs by an appropriate amount to preserve their previous profit levels.

This step should really be broken down into several. If the argument were spelled out fully, it would have to acknowledge that the inquirer is assuming that from statement 5 it follows that

5a. The major drug suppliers would not let their profits drop.

The inquirer is making another assumption as well:

6a. If the drug suppliers have less to sell, they must raise their prices to maintain the same profit levels.

Statement 6a is tricky, but we will treat it for now as an interrogative step. We can think that this information about the connection between supply of goods, prices, and profit levels has been provided by some suitable source of information.

These additional statements help spell out a little more clearly how statements 5 and 6 lead to statement 7. This line of thought proceeds further as follows:

8. When the major suppliers' prices are raised, the street price goes up correspondingly.

9. Addicts will buy drugs regardless of the price.

10. The only source of money for the addicts is crime.

11. The average yield of any one crime committed by an addict is roughly constant.

We leave it to you to think through how statements 8 through 11 all involve interrogative moves. Line 8 is a little tricky, like 6a, but the others are clearly bringing in new information.

From statements 8 and 9 it follows logically that

12. The addicts will need more money for their habit.

From statements 10, 11, and 12 it follows that

13. The addicts will commit more crimes.

To get from statement 13 to the desired ultimate conclusion the inquirer needs an assumption to the effect that an increased number of crimes committed by addicts means that "the war on drugs" is not being won. Let us make this interrogative move line 14:

14. An increased number of crimes committed by addicts means that the war on drugs is not being won.

The source of information for line 14 would seem to involve answers to the question: What would winning the war on drugs amount to? Different people might answer that question differently. What the inquirer needs is our agreement that an increased number of crimes committed by addicts means that the war is not being won.

From statements 13 and 14 it follows logically that

15. The war on drugs is not being won.

This is almost the ultimate conclusion. We now look back to lines 1, 4, and 15 to see how the inquirer handled the two possibilities about total or possible restriction of the influx of drugs, and we can see that it follows logically that

16. The war on drugs cannot be won by trying to restrict the influx of drugs into the United States.

Because this is the ultimate conclusion, we have closure of our table by left-to-right bridge, which means that structurally the argument appears to be successful. It does *not* mean, however, that we are necessarily satisfied with the answers provided in the various interrogative moves. It is also possible that we may be suspicious about one or another of the logical inference moves. If we *do* accept all the answers and all the logical inferences, it looks as though we are forced to accept the ultimate conclusion.

The important thing to see is that argument analysis has put us in a position to evaluate more closely the interrogative and logical inference moves made in the argument. Parts 2 and 3 of the book will discuss in greater detail how to evaluate interrogative and logical inference moves.

Here, as in the Sherlock Holmes example, relatively straightforward answers to appropriate questions lead to a surprising conclusion. As in "The Curious Incident of the Dog in the Nighttime," our main interest in the argument does not currently lie in its infallibility or persuasiveness, but rather in studying how such an argument is constructed and how it can be analyzed.

This relatively simple-looking example turns out to have a much greater complexity than first meets the eye. In particular, more questions are tacitly asked and answered than one might at first suspect. This demonstrates how our interrogative analysis can serve to bring out at least some of the hidden assumptions and moves that are typically present in an ordinary, everyday argument sketch. This, in turn, opens up more ways of evaluating and criticizing an argument.

△▼ EXERCISE 3-E

Analyze the following arguments by means of the table method. Identify any initial premises and the ultimate conclusion. Try to list the different steps in the reasoning and to show which are interrogative steps and which are logical inference steps. Supply any important missing steps. Indicate for each line in your table whether it is an initial premise, an answer to a question, or the result of a logical inference from earlier lines. Discuss whether the table closes or not.

▶ 1. Civilization will prosper only if it learns to respect nature, and this requires at least a knowledge of nature. Today, the only source of this knowledge for civilization as a whole comes from zoos and botanical gardens, by means of which the knowledge which engenders respect may be conveyed to the population at large. Thus, the continued prosperity of civilization itself is tied to these islands of nature, which we too easily dismiss as merely a diversion from the "serious business" of civilized life.

▶ 2. Are there moral absolutes? If there were, either the moral beliefs of our culture or the moral beliefs of other cultures must be mistaken. But who is to say which are wrong? From this it follows that there can be no moral absolutes.

3. The more you study, the more you know. The more you know, the more you forget. So, the more you study the more you forget.

4. The most important thing you can teach your children is self-respect. But this can only be done by setting a good example. Therefore, parents lacking self-respect are unable to perform this vital role for their children.

5. How long can humans of the coming century expect to live? Science promises surprising answers to this question. The health sciences are continuing the revolution which began over the last three decades. Advances are being made on two fronts. Not only have methods for diagnosing and treating illness undergone dramatic improvement over this span, important steps are being made in the direction of preventive medicine also. We are just now beginning to recognize the true significance of lifestyle for overall health. Nutrition, exercise, and the dangers associated with habits such as drinking and smoking are now seen to be major factors in determining not just the quality of life, but its duration as well. And there is every reason to expect these health trends to continue well into the next century. This tremendous progress in the health sciences has led many experts to conclude that life expectancies of 100 years or more await the children of tomorrow.

6. Find a report of some inquiry or a newspaper editorial or commentary on some issue. Alternatively, your instructor may assign a piece for analysis. Analyze the piece by determining what the initial premises are, what the conclusion is, and what the main logical inference and questioning moves are. Discuss whether the table closes.

7. Return to the argument analyses that you did for Exercise 1-C at the end of Section 1.9 of Chapter 1. Put your analysis for number 7 into interrogative table form, and discuss whether the table closes.

▶ 8. Many more argument sketches suitable for analysis can be found in Appendix A. You may wish to practice your skills on some of these, or your instructor may assign some. The arguments in the appendix will also be used for more advanced assignments in later chapters.

3.5   Irrelevant Material in Argument Sketches

You are well on the way to learning a powerful set of methods for analyzing real-life inquiries and arguments. In your analyses you will regularly encounter two problems. One is that the oral or written report of an argument will nearly always *omit important moves that are essential to the success of the argument.* The other is that the formulation will very often *include material that is not actually part of the argument.*

The first of these two problems has already been tackled in Chapter 1 and in this chapter and will continue to be discussed in a variety of ways throughout the book. Learning how to recognize omissions and to fill in missing moves is a skill to which we will devote much attention.

The second problem also requires due consideration, but as you learn the interrogative method, you will become practiced at recognizing and eliminating material that is not actually part of an argument. For example, we are learning how to recognize interrogative moves. In an interrogative move an oracle gives an answer to a question, and information is provided that may be helpful to the inquiry.

Quite often, however, the real-life sketch of an argument will also tell us that the oracle feels very strongly about the issue or that the oracle is absolutely convinced of the truth of its answer. Or, again, the inquirer will let it be known that she or he is impressed by the answer, or perhaps disgusted with it, or saddened, or whatever. The inquirer might say that he or she is convinced that you would agree with what is being said.

Such comments may be interesting or entertaining and they may give us clues as to what the inquirer is hoping to accomplish, but they do not provide information that actually belongs to any of the moves of the argument. The only information belonging in a table analysis of an argument is information that is actually relevant to the ultimate conclusion the inquirer is seeking to establish.

The arguer may be using emotion-laden words to provoke you to feel strongly with him or her in favor of the conclusion. Argument analysis, however, looks at the information that is being provided and the logical inferences that can legitimately be drawn. Strong feelings have a place, but our emotions and our reasoning should not work at cross purposes with each other.

Illustration   An inquirer might say,

> It is unthinkable that Americans should be asked to pay higher taxes so that do-gooder officials in our bloated federal government can squander it on aid to foreign countries.

This single sentence requires careful analysis to determine what would actually go into an interrogative table and what would not. It is best first to try to determine what the ultimate conclusion is that the inquirer is trying to establish. It appears that, in this case, the inquirer is trying to show that

Ultimate Conclusion: American tax dollars should not be spent on foreign aid.

When we rewrite the conclusion, we try to put it in as straightforward a way as possible. In this case the use of the word *squander* in the original argument tells us more what the inquirer thinks is happening with the money than what the actual conclusion is.

Next we try to identify any explicit initial premises. In this case we might be misled by the phrase: "It is unthinkable that . . ." This phrase in some cases might introduce premise information that will be used to support the ultimate conclusion. In this case, however, the phrase is mainly telling us that the inquirer feels very strongly about the conclusion. She or he considers it to be so well founded that no one could think otherwise. Our job, however, is to check whether the conclusion is, after all, so well established. Therefore, we ignore the report of how the inquirer feels.

Through use of words like *bloated, do-gooder,* and *squander,* the inquirer *is* making several claims. Our job is to state these claims in a straightforward way. We might be tempted to think of these claims as initial premises, but because so much is implied rather than stated in the few words of the argument, it is better to treat them as answers to questions. One way to state the inquirer's claims would be the following:

Interrogative Move: How efficient is the federal government in using American tax dollars? Answer: It is not efficient; it squanders money; it is bloated.

Interrogative Move: What is one way by which federal officials squander American tax dollars? Answer: They give the money away to foreign countries.

Interrogative Move: Why do they give money away to foreign countries? Answer: They want to "do good."

Interrogative Move: What's wrong with doing good and why does it amount to squandering money? Answer: Nothing is wrong with doing good, but in this case no good is done and the money is wasted.

Notice how this interrogative approach to the argument tries to get at possibly relevant information the inquirer had in mind when she or he used words like *bloated, do-gooder,* and *squander.* This is done so that the information can be looked at in the clear light of careful thinking. Each of the answers given in the interrogative moves above deserves some careful thought and criticism. Notice also how this approach tones down the emotion that is found in the original statement of the argument. We recognize that the inquirer feels strongly about the issue, but in analyzing the argument we want to examine and assess the key pieces of information.

If we were to analyze this argument completely, a number of other steps would have to be added as well. The important message at this stage is that *the interrogative approach to arguments requires that we try, step by step, to sift out the relevant information in a straightforward way.* We try to get at the actual information involved in strong or emotional words, so that we can assess the claims that are being made. We set aside information concerning how strongly the inquirer feels about his or her work.

△▼ EXERCISE 3-F

Complete an interrogative table analysis of the preceding example.

△▼ EXERCISE 3-G

Provide an interrogative table analysis for the following arguments. Work carefully to provide a straightforward reconstruction of the actual information that may be relevant to the ultimate conclusion.

▶ 1. If it's not broken, don't fix it. This is sage advice every child learns, but which evidently has escaped the wizards at city hall. They have adopted a proposal to "streamline" the building permit process, a process which I as a builder can tell you works just fine now. Why don't they exert some of this nervous energy addressing the real problems of this community? This proposal is a bad idea.

2. One of the most talked about crises facing industrialized nations today is the crisis of the family. The traditional, nuclear family, once the foundation and strength of our society, is an endangered species. On virtually every front the forces of "progress" are taking their toll on perhaps the most important institution in history. Whether it is "progress" in the guise of equality of the sexes, sexual and reproductive technology, economic advancement, or secular humanism, the victim is the family. At some stage, we must ask ourselves how high a price we are willing to pay for this "progress." Are drug addiction, crime, a climbing suicide rate among children, and lives of quiet desperation for millions a price worth paying for a VCR, easy sex, and bossy broads? Of course not. It is time we took a good, hard look at "progress," before we find that we have advanced all the way to the Stone Age.

3. Try to find an example in your school newspaper or some other source of an argument that includes a high percentage of irrelevant material. Provide a straightforward table analysis of the argument. Alternatively, your instructor may assign a piece for analysis.

4. Return to the argument analyses that you did for Exercise 1-C at the end of Section 1.9 of Chapter 1. Put your analysis for number 6 into interrogative table form.

3.6 The Importance of Argument Analysis

What you have learned in this chapter has consequences for the way you ought to look at the arguments you come across in real life. Such arguments may be presented by lawyers or judges, by the writers of newspaper editorials or of letters to the editor, by a business executive or a consultant, by a scientist or a philosopher, a pastor or a college teacher, to mention only a few possibilities.

When you read or hear an argument, what should you do? The same as we have done in this chapter: *look for the ultimate conclusion and any initial premises, and distinguish the interrogative steps from logical inferences.* When they are not explicitly indicated, you have to drag them out into the open. Usually you will find that the argument involves much more than first meets the eye.

If you practice these skills, you will find that they put you in a position to assess much more carefully the advice that others give you and the conclusions that others are trying to get you to accept. You will also find that you are better able to construct arguments and inquiries of your own. In the next chapter we turn our attention to this matter of constructing arguments.

4

Argument Construction
and Argumentative Essays

Now that you have begun to develop skills in argument analysis, we can go on to relate these skills to argument construction. Many times in life it is important to be able to construct arguments that support conclusions which may be important to you. Perhaps you are inquiring into what career to pursue or what area to major in. Perhaps you are uncertain which political candidate to support, or someone has challenged you to explain why you support a particular governmental policy. Perhaps you want to persuade a friend to join or not to join a fraternity or sorority. Perhaps you need to decide what car or house to buy.

It may also happen that people ask you to put your arguments into writing. The campus newspaper might appreciate an article defending your position on the proposed hike in student fees. Mom or Dad may want a letter explaining your latest change in major. (Why would anyone take a course in philosophy?!) A composition teacher might assign an argumentative essay. And if a decision is really important to you, it can help to put your thinking into writing.

The ability to construct arguments is important in all of these cases. Here again is a brief description of argument construction:

_ ▲ _____

> **Argument Construction:** The process of discovering and formulating the questions and logical inferences that create a rational inquiry. Skills in argument construction are closely related to skills in argument analysis. The ability to analyze the argument that one is constructing helps keep the construction process on a good foundation.

On the basis of your skills in argument analysis you can begin to expand your understanding of argument construction.

4.1 Argument Construction

In argument analysis we take an inquiry or argument that has already been set forth in everyday language, and we seek to take it apart into its basic interrogative and logical inference steps. Argument construction involves discovering and formulating the questions and logical inference moves that together create a rational inquiry.

In ordinary life we are constantly constructing arguments, but we often develop them with little critical care and attention to detail. In this book you will be learning how to use the insights of the interrogative model to help you more carefully and effectively discover, develop, and create arguments.

Argument construction involves three interrelated activities:

Step 1: You will often begin by discovering and formulating brief statements of main ideas and materials for your argument or inquiry.

Step 2: Then you will proceed to develop your argument by analyzing the ideas and materials from step 1, using the skills in argument analysis that you have been learning in the preceding chapters.

Step 3: After step 2 you will usually be in a position to begin to see clearly what the ultimate conclusion is that you may wish to argue for and to select some key premises, interrogative moves, and logical inference moves that are relevant to establishing your ultimate conclusion. You will also often see many places in your argument where you need more information (answers to questions) or more careful working out of your logical inferences. If necessary you can return to step 1 to ask some more questions and/or gather additional rough statements of argument materials that now seem needed. Then you can return again to step 2 to subject the materials to further, careful analysis. Finally, you can return again to step 3 to examine how well your own argument table is developing.

You will likely find yourself working through these three steps in several cycles as you develop and polish your argument. You have already learned many skills for steps 2 and 3, that is, analyzing the materials you have assembled for your argument and analyzing your own attempts to take the materials and put them into your own argument table. In the rest of the book we will learn many other specific insights into the skills of argument analysis and will also learn more about evaluating arguments in step 3. For example, you will study why it is important not to think only move by move as you construct an argument. Instead, you should seek to formulate an overall plan for putting different moves together so as to form a well-connected line of reasoning that leads to a closed interrogative table.

For now we should discuss step 1 in more detail. There are many ways to gather materials for an inquiry. First, if you are working on a topic with which you are already familiar, there may be a number of facts about it already known to you. Some of these could likely serve as initial-premise information for the argument you are going to be constructing. Second, if you are familiar with the topic, you may already have some idea what the ultimate conclusion is that you think you can argue for, or at least what the overall question is that you will be trying to answer in your inquiry. Third, you may also already know what some of the main inference moves are that are needed to connect your initial premises with your ultimate conclusion. Fourth, you may also have an idea about some specific questions that will need to be answered in interrogative moves before the whole picture of the argument can be filled in. Fifth, you can consider what sources of information, what oracles, seem most likely to be able to provide you with answers to your questions.

Sixth, most of the time our inquiries are concerned with problems that have been of interest to many people. Another way to gather material, then, is to study what others have said about the topic into which you wish to inquire. Your skills in argument analysis will enable you to identify what sort of initial premises, interrogative moves, and logical inference moves are to be found in the material you have gathered from the work of others. Notice how step 1 of argument construction—gathering materials—flows naturally into step 2—interrogative table analysis of the materials you have gathered.

We may compare our three-step approach to argument construction with what happens in a jury trial. Each of the opposing attorneys has the task of constructing an argument she or he can use to persuade the jury to adopt the desired ultimate conclusion about the trial. The actual argument must be presented during the trial, but in order to construct such an argument, each attorney must usually gather a large amount of information and subject it to careful analysis. Much of this work takes place prior to the actual trial.

Notice that it is not only necessary to gather information; it is also necessary to take it apart to find out how it may best be reassembled (often in new ways) to produce the argument needed in the trial. Gathering, analyzing, and assembling are the three steps of argument construction we are studying. Here is another example:

You might be inquiring into what model of compact disc player to buy and how much to pay for it. In step 1 of argument construction you may find that you already know some basic facts about compact disc technology. You also know that your main question involves choosing a satisfactory model and price. You may also have some specific questions in mind that you think need to be answered about various models. You can probably think of a number of helpful "oracles" who can answer some of your questions.

Turning from what you yourself already have in mind, you may discover that friends can provide information about why they chose a particular model. Salespersons will be happy to tell you about the superior features of the models they sell. Consumer magazines may report on strengths and weaknesses of various models and also on comparative prices. As you gather information you will probably find that you have sketches for several different possible arguments.

In step 2 of argument construction you use the skills of argument analysis to take apart the various sketches you gathered in step 1. This will enable you at step 3 to try to see for yourself if the information you have gathered and analyzed can be reassembled into an argument (a series of interrogative moves and logical inference moves) that leads in one direction rather than another. If you have enough information you think is reliable, you will end up with an argument of your own that leads to a decision whether to buy and what model and how much to pay. If, on the other hand, you find that you have not yet gathered sufficient information, you will want to return to steps 1 and 2 to try to gather more information and deepen your analysis.

Notice that, even if it is necessary to return to step 1, you will return with a more focused understanding than you had when you first began to gather the information. The analysis you do in step 2, and the table construction you attempt in step 3 using the results of your analysis, will focus your attention on the gaps in your information. The second time around you should be able to ask more specific questions of your friend, of a salesperson, or of a consumer magazine. You may also have a more focused understanding of what it is that you think is most important. Once you have gained more information, you can again return to step 2 to see precisely what you have learned and to step 3 to discover whether you can complete your argument and make your decision.

One important problem as yet unaddressed is likely to come up as you work at argument construction: You are likely to find that your sources of information, your oracles, disagree with each other. Different sources may provide materials that could support opposite decisions. In Part 3 of the book we shall study this problem in much more detail. You are, however, already practiced in coping with disagreements among sources of information. You do not believe everything a salesperson, a magazine, or even a friend tells you. You know how to use information from one source to assess how reliable information from another may be. You know that it is important to consider not only what people say but why they say it.

In step 3 of argument construction you study the results of the analyses you carried out in step 2. It is at this point that you must make some judgments about which information is likely to be most reliable and which sources of information might be able to help you further with your decision. You must also, of course, make sure that the inferences involved in the inquiry are *logical* inferences. In Part 2 of the book we will study in much more detail how to assess inferences, and in Part 3 we will study useful strategies for assessing the reliability of information. In Part 4 you will learn how to search for the most effective questions to ask as we construct our arguments. For now, here is a brief summary of our approach to argument construction.

▲

Argument Construction: Argument construction involves three interrelated activities:

Step 1: Gathering argument materials.
Step 2: Using interrogative tables to analyze the information that has been gathered.
Step 3: Assembling the materials into one's own interrogative argument table.

The three steps can be repeated as needed until a satisfactory argument emerges.

4.2 A More Detailed Example of Argument Analysis

Because argument analysis is so central to our study of reasoning, we provide one more detailed example. *Deliberative arguments* are often interesting and important in everyday life. A deliberative argument is one in which you have set a goal for yourself and are trying to determine what you must do in order to reach it.

The way to analyze a deliberative argument in strict table form is to write as the initial premise on the left side of the table a statement that says you will reach your goal. In deliberative arguments the initial premise does not express a known fact but rather the goal you hope to attain. Ultimate conclusions which can be established by imagining this initial premise to be true will then tell you what you must do to reach your goal.

For an example of a deliberative argument we offer the following exposition, which we suspect is similar to the argument some of you used in choosing to take this course and read this book. We shall first sketch the argument in ordinary English and then show how it can be analyzed in the form of an interrogative table. We number the sentences in order to make the discussion of the argument easier.

(1) I want to get into the law school of my choice. (2) To be admitted I need a high score on the LSAT exam. (3) How can I get a high score on the exam? Either by being a naturally good test taker or else by training for the exam. (4) But I am not a naturally good test taker. (5) Hence, I must train for the exam. (6) I can

do that in two ways—either by taking a commercial LSAT preparation course or by taking a college or university course which prepares me for the exam. (7) If I took a commercial test preparation course, I would have to pay for it. (8) But I cannot pay for it, because I don't have the money. (9) Hence, I must take a regular college or university course which prepares me for the LSAT exam. (10) Only a course in reasoning and critical thinking will prepare me for the exam. (11) So, I will take this course.

An analysis of this argument could proceed as follows. Only the left side of the table is written out. The right side contains the ultimate conclusion: "I will take this course."

1. I will be admitted to the law school of my choice. (This is the initial premise for this deliberative argument. It is a statement of the inquirer's goal. In this case the inquirer is the oracle providing information about her or his goal.)

2.1. No one is admitted to the law school I have chosen without a high score on the LSAT exam. (This is clearly an interrogative move. But who or what is the oracle? In argument analysis it is important to try to identify the source of the information in premises and interrogative moves. In this case the admissions office of the law school might be the oracle, or perhaps an adviser at the inquirer's college or university might be, or maybe simply the inquirer's own fatalistic—but perhaps ill-founded—opinion that the LSAT score is the key to admission.)

2.2. I will not be admitted to the law school of my choice without a high score on the LSAT exam. (This is clearly a logical inference from line 2.1.)

3. If I am going to get a high score on the LSAT exam, I am either a naturally good test taker or else I will train for the LSAT exam. (This was phrased as a question in the original sketch of the argument, and it is in fact an interrogative move. The oracle in this move is general background information about what it takes to achieve a high score on the LSAT exam.)

4. I am not a naturally good test taker. (Another interrogative move. The oracle in this case is the inquirer's own knowledge about his or her performance on standardized exams.)

5. I will train for the LSAT exam. (This is a logical inference from lines 3 and 4.)

6.1. One can train for the LSAT exam in two ways: Either one takes a commercial LSAT preparatory course or else a course at one's own college or university which prepares one for the test. (In this interrogative move it is not completely clear where this information is supposed to come from. General background knowledge may be involved, or perhaps advice from some counselor. Note that you might very well wonder whether this information exhausts all the possibilities for preparation.)

6.2. I can train for the LSAT exam in two ways: Either I take a commercial LSAT preparatory course or else a course at my own college or university which prepares me for the test. (A logical inference from line 6.1.)

6.3. I will either take a commercial LSAT preparatory course or else a course at my own college or university which prepares me for the test. (This is a logical inference from lines 5 and 6.2.)

7.1. If I take a commercial LSAT preparatory course, someone will have to pay for it. (This can be considered a logical inference based on the meaning of "commercial.")

7.2. If I take a commercial LSAT preparatory course, no one else will pay for it for me. (This is an answer to an unspoken question concerning my situation.)

7.3. If I take a commercial LSAT preparatory course, I will have to pay for it. (This is a logical inference from lines 7.1 and 7.2.)

8.1. I will not be able to pay for a commercial LSAT preparatory course. (Interrogative move. The oracle here is likely to be the inquirer's budget and bank balance.)

8.2. I will not take a commercial LSAT preparatory course. (A logical inference from lines 7.3 and 8.1.)

9. I will take a course at my own college or university which prepares me for the test. (A logical inference from 6.3 and 8.2.)

10. Only a course in reasoning and critical thinking prepares me for the test. (An interrogative move. Once again, it is not clear where this answer to a tacit [unspoken] question comes from. Teachers of a course like the one you are taking and authors of a book like this one would perhaps be likely to give such an answer!)

11. I will take a course in reasoning and critical thinking. (A logical inference from lines 9 and 10.)

Because line 11 is a statement of the ultimate conclusion which appears on the right side, the whole table is closed and the inquirer has successfully established the conclusion. (We recognize, of course, that if any of the answers in any of the interrogative moves turns out to be unreliable, then the conclusion is likely to be unreliable as well.)

Discussion

The preceding example illustrates several issues. First, as we have often seen, a simple-looking argument may turn out to be more complicated than it appears. The effort to analyze an argument exposes some of its hidden complexities. We also see here again the difference between logical inference moves and interrogative moves.

Second, this example can bring to our attention that not all the information an inquirer needs is likely to be available at the beginning of the construction of an argument. When the inquirer first began to consider whether to take a course in reasoning and critical thinking, she or he may not have known how important the LSAT exam is to the chosen law school. Information on the cost of commercial preparatory courses may also have been lacking. More information about reasoning and critical thinking courses may have been needed. Thus letters or phone calls or visits to advisers may have been required to get the appropriate information.

Third, even though we are not yet directly discussing the evaluation of arguments, it can already be seen that the identification of the interrogative moves and of the different oracles consulted in an argument is vitally important for such evaluation. For instance, in line 2.1 it makes a difference what oracle was consulted. It may not be strictly true that the law school the inquirer chose always requires high LSAT scores. There may be exceptions. An applicant may be able to prove that she or he is a good law school prospect in other ways. Some schools give careful attention to aspects of a student's performance not reflected in the LSAT. A student whose scores are rather low might be able to convince a good law school that his success in student government activities demonstrates his fitness to study law.

The information in line 2.1 will be more or less reliable depending upon the reliability of the oracle. If the oracle is the admissions officer for the law school, then the reliability of line 2.1 may be much stronger than if the oracle were, say, the inquirer's roommate.

Of course, even if line 2.1 is unreliable this does not show that the decision to take a course in reasoning and critical thinking is wrong. It may be that the skills needed to be successful in other ways than on the LSAT are the very skills you are learning in this course! However, if line 2.1 is called into question, the original argument will likely have to be rebuilt in different ways.

Our readiness to call into question some of the information used in an argument may lead us in the end to stronger arguments and possibly to different conclusions. Argument analysis puts us in a position to see where further thought may be needed. This is why argument analysis is so important both for argument construction and for argument evaluation.

△▼ EXERCISE 4-A

Construct an argument on one of the following topics.

▶ 1. Construct an argument for or against the continued commercial use of nuclear power. As oracles, consider scientific sources, economic sources, governmental sources, and historical sources of information.

2. Construct an argument for the purchase of a major item, such as a car. Your oracle should have access to information concerning your needs and preferences, as well as financial and other constraints, not to mention relevant information concerning the various competing versions of the item in question.

3. Construct an argument which has as its conclusion the identification of a mechanical or electrical problem with an appliance or machine. Assume that you have access to information resulting from observation and various tests you may perform on the object in question.

4. Return to Section 3.1 of Chapter 3. There you studied an argument about athletes' salaries that led to a rather predictable conclusion. Use the techniques of argument construction to try to develop an argument leading to a rather different conclusion about salaries. This will require looking for new questions to ask about the topic.

5. Choose an argument sketch or a group of sketches from Appendix A and use the material to get you started on the construction of your own argument on the topic.

4.3 Argumentative Essays

The key to putting an argument into written form is to have a well-organized argument. Thus, it is of utmost importance to develop your skills in argument construction. Arguments are not, however, usually expressed in table form in everyday life, so you must learn how to put them into normal English prose. One way of doing this is through writing an *argumentative essay*.

The three steps of argument construction can be carried over into your preparation for an argumentative essay. First, you determine what the problem is and you begin to gather information and argument sketches that are relevant to the problem. You may already have information that is useful for the essay. Usually your problem will be something many other people have also studied. So you can read what they have to say about it, or you can interview people who may be able to provide helpful materials.

Because you will be writing your argumentative essay on the basis of the information you are gathering, it is helpful if you put this information into some kind of written form. At this stage the information does not need to be well organized, but writing the information and argument sketches down will help you get your own thinking going. You may find yourself also sketching out your own versions of possible arguments on the topic.

The idea here is that as you read and do your research you should always have something in mind that you are looking for. In this way you will read actively rather than passively. Keep a pen or pencil or personal computer handy and make your mind use it. People use many different techniques from underlining to notebooks to note cards to computers. The important thing is to make the mind work while the eyes and ears are scanning.

Once you have gathered some information, you can begin to analyze it by using interrogative tables. This is step 2 of argument construction. In step 3, on the basis of the material you have gathered and analyzed, you will begin to see where you think the information could lead, that is, what conclusion or solution to the problem you might decide to argue for. You can begin to construct your own argument table. You will also likely see various gaps in the material you have assembled.

Many college students are weakest on this part of essay writing. They are good at gathering information, but they are tempted mainly to report what others have said rather than to analyze what has been said so that they can reshape it into work of their own. If your teachers fault you for merely reporting rather than arguing, the problem is likely to be that you only carry out step 1 of argument construction. You fail to go on to the more important task of taking the information apart in step 2 and putting it back together in step 3 in a structured argument of your own. The skills of argument analysis that you have been learning can help you once and for all get beyond reporting the information and arguments of others to constructing arguments of your own.

More than likely you will have to go round the cycle of gathering information, analyzing it, and reassembling it several times before you are sufficiently prepared to produce your finished argument. After each cycle you should stop at step 3 to assess what you have learned up to that point and to decide what parts of the material need renewed attention when you return to steps 1 and 2.

In the preceding section we discussed the problem that sources of information may provide conflicting or unreliable information. One of your tasks will be to decide what sources of information seem best for you to rely on for material for your own argument. Here you can appreciate the importance of crediting your sources. Others cannot fully evaluate your conclusions if they lack information about the sources you have consulted. How such crediting of sources is done differs from discipline to discipline (and from college professor to college professor). The important point is that crediting of sources is an integral part of constructing an argument. Crediting of sources is also, of course, a matter of intellectual honesty.

Perhaps you can see more clearly now the difference between using a source of information in your own argument and simply reporting what a source says. If you take apart the argument sketches that you derive from your sources and then put them together into your own argument, you will be using some of the information your sources have provided, *not* simply reporting what they say. Instead, you will be critically examining and extracting information to construct your own argument.

Writing the Argumentative Essay

Once you have finished constructing an argument, you will have in front of you your own sequence of premises, interrogative moves, and logical inference moves that lead to an ultimate conclusion. This will serve as the outline for your essay. You now present the argument in paragraph form.

You can begin the essay with a brief statement of the problem you are addressing, and you will usually also indicate the ultimate conclusion for which you will be arguing. (Some people like to keep the reader in suspense as to where the argument will come out, but in most cases readers appreciate knowing from the beginning where you are trying to lead them.) If the argument is long or complicated, it would be a good idea to give the reader a brief preview of the key steps in the argument that will be being discussed. Note that you will not mention *all* the steps at this point but only those that are likely to be the most important.

After introducing the argument in this way, you are ready to present the initial premises (if there are any). In addition to identifying your premises, you should also explain at the beginning of the argument why you think these are significant points upon which people can agree. If the premises are not likely to find wide agreement, then it is especially important that you show your awareness of this fact and that you explain why you nevertheless are asking the reader to come along with you on the basis of these premises. You may need also to discuss the source(s) (oracles) upon which you are relying for the premise information.

Next you can present the various interrogative steps and logical inference steps in your argument. The order of steps in your table outline will guide you for the order in which to present the material, but you will sometimes find that a related series of steps can be presented more effectively in slightly different order. Also, if your table contains more than one path, you will probably want to follow one all the way to its end and then go on to the next.

As you present the interrogative moves, you will also want to indicate the sources of information on which you are relying and perhaps discuss why you think they are reliable. You may also want to discuss contrary information that you are not using because you think it is less reliable than the information you have used. Some of the interrogative moves are likely to be more controversial than others. Focus your energy on defending the moves that are most likely to be challenged by the reader.

Many of the logical inferences may need little comment, but it is essential that you double-check them so that they are in fact logical inferences. It is true that in many cases you can rely on the reader to supply common background information that makes an inference a logical inference. It would be impractical for you to include such information in tedious detail in your essay. However, in cases where it is not easy to see how a step follows from preceding information, you will want to make clear to the reader how the inference works.

If you constructed your table carefully, discussion of the interrogative and logical inference steps will lead you in an orderly way to the ultimate conclusion. Once you have reached the conclusion, you have essentially finished. If the essay has been rather long or complicated, you may wish to provide the reader with a summary of the key moves that were made in the argument and a brief statement of how they led up to the conclusion.

There are, of course, many other skills needed for good writing. You need to be able to use English in ways appropriate to and expected by your readers. You need to be careful in choice of words and in finding refreshing turns of phrase. These sorts of skills are learned by practice; probably you have had instruction and practice in them over a number of years.

Our focus has been on the problem of constructing a good, well-organized argument. If your thinking is well organized, your expression of it in written form is likely to be clear and to the point. You are more likely to find appropriate words and phrases that effectively express your meaning.

Once you have completed your essay, read it out loud to yourself. It is surprising how many annoying little errors can be caught in this way. How much better for you to catch them than for your reader to! You might also prevail on a friend or roommate to listen to the essay or to read it. This too can help you catch errors. Furthermore, others who read the essay will perhaps be able to point out to you places where you have omitted an important step in the reasoning or where your writing is unclear and hard to follow. Of course, if you prevail on others to help you in this way, you should be prepared to help them too. In fact, helping others better their writing is another means to practice and strengthen your own.

If you work hard at constructing an argument table that stands up to analysis and if you stay focused on presenting the steps of that argument as they lead to the ultimate conclusion, you will be able to produce an essay that is well focused and well argued. You will be able to avoid such problems as aimlessly reporting information on the topic or getting sidetracked into irrelevancy.

Nevertheless, none of us is born being able to write such an essay. It requires much practice. Skills in this area are so important that you would be wise to choose courses that give you plenty of opportunity to practice argument construction and argumentative writing.

Occasionally you may be assigned the task of writing an argumentative essay for which you are supposed to choose your own topic. This can be frustrating, because it is surprisingly hard to decide what to write on when given such an open-ended assignment. In such a case you might be helped by browsing through the many different argument sketches that are given in Appendix A of this book. One or another of these may get you started on a topic that catches your interest.

Note on Term Paper Assignments

In many cases term paper assignments in your other courses can fruitfully be approached as occasions for writing an argumentative essay. Even if your instructor does not tell you to argue for some particular conclusion, you will more likely be able to focus your writing in an effective way if you try to argue for some particular ultimate conclusion or to solve a well-formulated problem.

Most instructors want evidence that you can go beyond gathering information and reporting other people's arguments. They are likely to want to see whether you can intelligently construct arguments using the material dealt with in the course. Even if your instructor does not explicitly ask you to construct an argument, you are likely to write a crisper paper (and receive a better grade!) if you treat your term paper assignment as an exercise in argument construction and in the writing of an argumentative essay.

The famous British historian Lord Acton advised his fellow historians: "Study problems, not periods." The same advice, suitably generalized, can be given to students writing term papers: *Don't tell a story; argue for a conclusion.*

△▼ **EXERCISE 4-B**

Take an argument table you constructed in Exercise 4-A and write an argumentative essay based on that table.

△▼ **EXERCISE 4-C**

Choose an argument sketch from the list compiled in Appendix A and use it to get started on the construction of an argument table and the writing of an essay based on the table.

4.4   Reaching a Milestone

We have defined and illustrated what an interrogative game is and we have argued that it captures what is involved in the reasoning process. You have practiced analyzing and constructing arguments. If you have understood what happens in an interrogative table analysis, you have understood what reasoning and argumentation are about. We have in a sense accomplished the main purpose of the entire book.

We have, however, postponed careful study of many features of interrogative games to later chapters. Fortunately or unfortunately, defining these games does not yet finish the business of this course. Several reasons explain why we have to push further.

First, we have not systematically examined the definitory rules of logical inference. Nor have we systematically studied the definitory rules for interrogative moves. Parts 2 and 3 of the book are dedicated to these tasks. As you work with the detailed rules of the interrogative games, you will develop a much firmer understanding of what is going on in the reasoning process.

Second, even after you have learned the definitory rules of the interrogative games, another task still confronts you. Knowing the defining rules of chess does not make you a good chess player nor does knowing the defining rules of basketball make you an outstanding coach. You still must learn how to play the game well. The same holds for the "game" of reasoning. Accordingly, after the definitory rules of the interrogative games have been thoroughly explained, we shall go on to discuss the strategies you must know to become an effective reasoner and arguer. Discussions of strategy will appear in all three of the remaining parts of the book.

PART △ TWO
▽

Logical Inferences in Detail

.5

Deductive Logic
and Its Role in Reasoning

In Part 1 you were introduced to the important distinction between definitory and
strategic rules of rational inquiry. We also explained the difference between interrogative moves and logical inference moves in interrogative inquiry. Now you will
examine more closely some of the definitory rules of logical inference moves.

It is important to remind ourselves that although definitory rules are necessary to good reasoning, they are not sufficient. After studying the basic definitory
aspects of logical inference moves, you will learn something about the strategies
that make for excellence in logical inference.

5.1 The Nature of Logical Inferences

The division of labor involved in the distinction between interrogative steps and
steps of logical inference depends on the fact that answers to questions (results

of interrogative steps) introduce new information into an argument, whereas in a logical inference the arguer processes the information she or he already possesses. A logical inference spells out information the arguer, or inquirer, has managed to acquire. Often, a logical inference serves to combine different items of information, to "add our admissions together" as Socrates used to say. The example of the first confessant given in Chapter 2 (Section 2.4) illustrates such "adding two and two together."

From this basic idea several things are seen at once. One is that *a step of logical inference cannot be taken independently of the particular situation in which the inquirer finds himself or herself at the time.* A logical inference always requires earlier statements (sometimes only one earlier statement). These are the statements whose information is spelled out or combined by the logical inference. As we learned in Chapter 1 (Section 1.7), they are called the "premises" of the inference. The output of a logical inference is called its "conclusion." Thus, a logical inference cannot be represented by a single statement. *It always involves a transition from an earlier statement (or statements) to a new one.*

It may be useful for you at this time to review the examples of inferences and Exercises 1-A and 1-B given in Chapter 1 (Sections 1.7 and 1.8).

Because logical inferences do not introduce new information into a line of inquiry, you might be tempted to think they are somehow easy or trivial. This impression is mistaken, however. It may be very difficult to find a chain of logical inferences leading to the desired ultimate conclusion, even though this conclusion can in fact be reached by means of such a chain. The ultimate conclusion may even be surprising. The example of the "Barber of Shave-ville" presented in Chapter 1 (Section 1.11) may convey to you a sense of how unexpected ultimate conclusions of chains of logical inferences can sometimes be. The sad (or exhilarating) fact is that it is not always possible to give mechanical rules for the best possible logical inferences. The reasons for this are given in Chapter 14 in the section on "undecidability." The exercises at the end of that chapter may convince you that finding purely logical arguments is not always easy.

5.2   Truth Preservation

The fact that a logical inference does not bring in new information suggests a further characteristic: **A correct logical inference preserves truth.** Suppose that an inquirer has managed to ascertain the truth of a number of statements, call them S_1, $S_2, \ldots, S_k$. They are entered into the left side of a logical table. Suppose that the inquirer draws a correct logical inference from these statements, call it C. Must C also be true? This chapter will examine in detail how it is in the nature of a correct logical inference that C must indeed be true. This is a most important feature of logical inference: Logical inferences must be and in fact are truth-preserving.

5.3   Deductive Logic

Rules of inference found in philosophy books are not all truth-preserving. The truth-preserving rules of logical inference are known as **deductive** rules. The central part of logic which deals with truth-preserving inference is known as **deductive logic.** All students of rational inference agree that it is necessary to give some attention to the rules of deductive logic.

In Chapter 1 (Section 1.10) you met the term "deduction" as one of the words often used in a wide "Sherlock Holmes" sense about reasoning in general. Here we propose to use the term in a much narrower sense. It will designate only steps that do not introduce new factual information into the reasoning process.

▲

Deductive Logical Inference: An inference which introduces no new information and which is truth-preserving. The word "deductive" simply specifies further what has been called "logical inference" up to this point. In the interrogative model of rational inquiry, the only type of inference needed is deductive inference. If you have understood what is meant by "logical inferences," then you understand what we mean by "deduction." The literal meaning of the word suggests that the information found in the premises of an inference will be "drawn out" and made explicit.

5.4   Inductive Logic

We have already seen in Part 1 and now again in this chapter that deductive inferences are the only kind of inference needed in the interrogative model of inquiry. Nevertheless, in addition to rules of deductive inference, you will often find in logic books rules for another kind of inference, which can be called "nondeductive." An important type of nondeductive inference is often called **inductive inference.**

Typically, inductive inferences are illustrated by reasoning that proceeds from premise statements about a number of particular cases to a general conclusion about all similar cases that have been or will be.

For example, a doctor might observe a number of patients who all have similar symptoms and who all suffer from a vitamin-C deficiency. On the basis of these particular cases, the doctor might inductively infer the conclusion that all patients who have the same symptoms suffer the same vitamin-C deficiency. The doctor might think that the next time she or he sees a patient with those symptoms, that patient will definitely be suffering from vitamin-C deficiency.

No one would disagree with the fact that inductive inferences can lead from true premises to true conclusions. The important point to notice, however, is that, *because inductive inferences introduce new information into the reasoning, they are not infallibly truth-preserving.*

To continue with our medical example, it is imaginable that the doctor might have been right about the patients she or he had observed, so that the premises of the inductive inference are true. Yet it is also imaginable that the doctor might well be wrong about what happens in general, so that the conclusion of the inductive inference would be false. In other cases the same symptoms might have a cause different from vitamin-C deficiency. In other words, inductive inferences are not always truth-preserving.

This example also shows that inductive inferences introduce new information into the inquiry. The hoped-for conclusion was that all patients with certain symptoms suffer from vitamin-C deficiency. This conclusion excludes certain imaginable and possible situations *not* excluded by the actual premise information. We can easily imagine that in some cases in which patients have the same symptoms, they nevertheless are not suffering from vitamin-C deficiency. In order to exclude this imaginable situation, we would need more information than is given by the premises. Hence, the conclusion of an inductive inference brings into the inquiry information that was not contained in its premises. This brings us back to the most important point about inductive inferences: Because inductive inferences introduce new information into the reasoning, they are not infallibly truth-preserving.

△▼ EXERCISE 5-A

Determine for each of the following inferences whether it is deductive or nondeductive. Be prepared to explain and defend your answer.

1. I have been sniffling all day. Therefore, I have caught a cold.
2. Tom is taller than Bob but shorter than Jan. Therefore, Bob is shorter than Jan.
▶ 3. Today is Monday. Therefore, tomorrow is Tuesday.
4. Banning the private ownership of firearms will decrease the number of murders in this country. Therefore, the private ownership of firearms should be prohibited.
▶ 5. Most senators are rich. Therefore, Senator Stanton is rich.
6. Socrates is a duck. Therefore, Socrates is a bird.
▶ 7. If the reports of the witnesses are true, then either UFOs exist or the Air Force is responsible for the airborne phenomena. The witnesses are telling the truth, and the Air Force is not responsible. Therefore, UFOs exist.

If R, then U ~ A

5.5   Why Is Truth Preservation So Important?

Why are we making such an issue about truth preservation? Because we want to be able to pinpoint and effectively handle the places in our inquiries where new information enters the argument. If some of our inferences are truth-preserving and introduce no new information while other inferences introduce new information and fail to preserve truth, then many opportunities for confusion will arise.

In the interrogative model of inquiry we guard against these confusions by *requiring that all inferences be truth-preserving and that new information only be introduced by interrogative moves.*

For this reason, the interrogative model of inquiry focuses its attention on deductive logical inferences rather than on inductive inferences. Only after we have become well practiced in interrogative inquiry will we return to the problem of inductive inference in Part 4. Whenever we refer to "inference" or "inference step" we will always mean *deductive logical inference*.

An Interrogative Approach to the Vitamin-C Deficiency Example

The following discussion of the case of the doctor studying the effects of vitamin-C deficiency on his patients will illustrate how the interrogative model of inquiry uses only deductive inferences and interrogative moves. The doctor concluded that anyone with a certain set of symptoms must be suffering from the same vitamin-C deficiency. We have seen that analyzing this reasoning in terms of inductive inference allows for the possibility of inferences which need not be truth-preserving. How else might we analyze the doctor's reasoning in a way that avoids this problem?

The interrogative model could approach this case as follows: Take as initial premises that certain of the doctor's patients all suffer from vitamin-C deficiency and that they all exhibit the same basic set of symptoms. The doctor now asks what might be responsible for such symptoms. A source of information—perhaps background knowledge on related maladies—offers the answer that only dietary factors could be. The doctor now asks what dietary abnormalities his patients share. This time the oracle might be clinical tests the doctor performs, which yield the answer that the only dietary peculiarity to be found in the patients is the uniform vitamin-C deficiency.

Now from the initial premises and the two answers provided in response to questions put to sources of information, it follows deductively that a vitamin-C deficiency is responsible for these symptoms in the doctor's patients. (You might benefit from sketching out the interrogative table analysis up to this point.)

The doctor, however, also wants to be able to assert the more general conclusion that vitamin-C deficiency is responsible for the particular set of symptoms in *any* and *all* patients who have them. The inductive approach allowed the doctor to make an inference from the individual cases to the general case. But we noticed, and people who use the inductive approach also recognize, that inductive inferences are not truth-preserving.

Because of this fact, the interrogative approach requires that the doctor now frame appropriate additional questions that will bring in new information. The goal is to find reliable information that will permit a truth-preserving, logical deductive inference to establish the general conclusion.

You have learned that new information enables an inquirer to eliminate alternatives. The main alternative creating trouble for the doctor is that other factors besides vitamin-C deficiency might also be the cause of the symptoms in some patients. We have assumed that some reliable source of information has already told the doctor that only dietary factors are involved in producing such symptoms. If the doctor wants to establish that vitamin-C deficiency is the only factor involved in every case, she or he will need to ask questions about other possible dietary factors. What is needed is reliable information that rules out the other possible alternatives.

We will not at this point pursue the doctor's reasoning any further. The point to be made is that the interrogative model is pointing us in the proper direction for analyzing and improving the reasoning. The key to analysis and improvement is not to focus on inductive inference, but rather to look for the questions that need to be asked to strengthen or generalize the conclusion. In many cases the further questions and answers concern the uniformity of the phenomena to be accounted for. In the interrogative model many inferences that are typically said to be "inductive" are treated as *deductive* inferences based on answers to tacit questions concerning the uniformity of the phenomena in question.

The uncertainty surrounding the doctor's reasoning has not mysteriously disappeared; there are still many difficulties in the way of establishing the general conclusion. But now their source has been focused in one main part of interrogative reasoning, that is, in the interrogative steps. Rather than worrying that one of the inference steps might be responsible for the uncertainty, we now see clearly that the key to progress lies in finding reliable answers to appropriately chosen questions. Throughout the book we will be learning more and more how to find the appropriate questions needed in our inquiries and how to test the reliability of the answers we receive.

5.6   The Importance of Deductive Logical Inference

At first sight, it might seem that the study of deductive logic deals only with a small part of actual reasoning processes. New information is brought in by interrogative steps. Logical inferences, which are the deductive steps, serve to combine and spell out the information you already have available to you. Interrogative steps seem clearly more important than the logical inference steps. Yet the interrogative approach to reasoning will soon show that deductive logical inference is more important in reasoning than you might think. One important strength of the interrogative approach is that it explains why knowledge of deductive logic is an important key to helping you reason more effectively.

Within the interrogative approach we shall discover that deductive logic helps us in several areas. First, it turns out that learning how to be creatively effective in deductive logic involves some of the same skills needed for creative effectiveness in everyday reasoning. Second, even though deductive steps do not in themselves seem to bring anything substantially new into an argument, they often help us (as we shall see) get into the right position to ask the key questions that will move the reasoning ahead. Third, suitable deductive inferences can sometimes lead to more interesting conclusions than you would first expect. For instance, much of Socrates's argument in the *Meno* slaveboy example can be considered deductive, and yet the argument led to an unexpected ultimate conclusion.

In Part 2 and again in Part 4 we shall examine the basics of deductive logic. Some of you will find deductive logic to be a source of wonderful puzzles. Others are likely to become impatient and wonder how this can be of any help in everyday reasoning. Our goal will be to learn enough deductive logic so that those who enjoy it can go further on their own or in other courses, while those who find it less than amusing will have gained sufficient grasp to help them with everyday reasoning.

We have already learned some important terms for the ingredients of the interrogative model. Now we will relate some of these terms to deductive logic.

5.7   Statements

Deductive logic is concerned only with sentences which are being used to say something that is either true or false. We will call such sentences **statements**. (They are also sometimes called "propositions.") The following sentences would be ordinarily used as statements:

1. "Orel Hersheiser is a Los Angeles Dodger."
2. "Atlanta is north of Orlando."
3. "Asking questions is an important part of reasoning."
4. "Ronald MacDonald was the fortieth president of the United States."
5. "St. Paul wrote the New Testament 'Letter to the Ephesians.' "

A sentence does not have to be true to be a statement. "Ronald MacDonald was the fortieth president of the United States" is a statement. Furthermore, we do not have to know whether a sentence is true or false for it to be a statement. "St. Paul wrote the New Testament 'Letter to the Ephesians' " is a statement even though scholars argue about whether it is true or not.

The following sentences would not ordinarily be used as statements:

6. "Do your homework."
7. "Does Orel Hersheiser live in Atlanta?"
8. "Who was St. Paul?"
9. "Why am I reading this?"

In each of these cases it is difficult to see how the sentence might be true or false. These sentences can be used to do important work, but they do not usually function as statements.

Often the grammatical form of the sentence gives good clues as to whether it will be used as a statement. So-called indicative sentences are usually used to make statements. Questions, imperatives, and exclamations are not usually used to make statements. There are, however, exceptions. If you are in doubt as to whether a sentence is a statement, a good test will be for you simply to ask, "Is this sentence being used to say something which is true or false?" If so, it is probably functioning as a statement and could become involved in the study of deductive logic.

Because statements are sentences which are true or false, we can ask whether they are true or not. "Orel Hersheiser is a Los Angeles Dodger" is true at the time of this writing. "Ronald MacDonald was the fortieth president of the United States" is false. We do not always know whether a particular statement is true or false, but we do know that it is one or the other. "St. Paul wrote the New Testament 'Letter to the Ephesians'" is certainly either true or false.

Even when we do not know whether a statement is true or false, it is still possible to ask important questions about what would be the case if it were true and what would be the case if it were false. Deductive logic does not usually ask whether a statement actually happens to be true or false but rather what happens to a group of related statements when some are taken to be true. Perhaps you can see that this is part of why deductive logic requires an *active imagination*. We need to imagine what would be the case if some statement were taken to be true and what would be the case if it were taken to be false.

— ▲ _____

> **Statement:** A sentence used to say something that is true or false. A statement usually serves to convey information to a hearer or reader. It is not necessary to know whether the statement is actually true or false, only that it is one or the other. Another word sometimes used for such sentences is "proposition."

△▼ EXERCISE 5-B

▸ From the exercises you did in Part 1, find one example of a question used as a statement and one example of a question not used as a statement. Justify your choices.

5.8   Premises and Conclusions

We have already encountered the terms "premise" and "conclusion" in Chapters 1 and 2. In deductive logic we are concerned with how the truth and falsity of statements relate to each other. Often we are interested to study what the assumed truth of a given statement or group of statements can tell us about the truth or falsity of another statement or group of statements. The given statements which are imagined to be true are usually called premises. We often want to study whether another statement or group of statements can be false even if the premise(s) are imagined to be true. These other statement(s) which we are trying to imagine false are usually called the conclusion(s).

— ▲ _____

Premises: In Chapter 1 (Section 1.7) *premise* was defined as "the information serving as the basis for an inference step." Now is added the idea that in deductive inferences premises are those statements currently imagined to be true.

Conclusion: In Chapter 1 (Section 1.7) *conclusion* was defined as "the statement of what has been derived from the premises." Now is added the idea that in deductive inferences conclusions are those statements which we are currently trying to imagine false while we imagine the related premises to be true. The goal is to find that it is impossible to imagine the conclusion false while imagining the premises true. Then we know we have a successful, truth-preserving, deductive logical inference.

△▼ EXERCISE 5-C

For each of the following, indicate which statements act as premises and which acts as a conclusion.

1. Money is not important for happiness, for the best things in life are free.
2. The new Spitfire is the best new car value on the market. No other car can match the Spitfire's level of luxury, reliability, and price.
▸ 3. While records keep falling in many track events, there is reason to believe that the two-hour marathon is a feat which may not be accomplished in this century. Precious little improvement in marathon times has been made in the recent past, and physiological evidence suggests that such a time for the marathon is at the limits of human capabilities.
▸ 4. In these days of mass-media politics, anyone successful enough to run for president must lack the ethical qualifications to serve well in that capacity. Unless substantial campaign reform changes this fact, we are destined to have less-than-great leaders.

5.9   Validity Is Different from Truth

By means of the terms "premise" and "conclusion," we can express the characteristic feature of deductive inferences. A *valid* deductive inference has the following property: The assumption that the premises are true forces us to admit that the conclusion will be true as well. (Note that sometimes there is only one premise statement, and sometimes there is more than one conclusion statement.) **Validity and its opposite, invalidity, involve the relation between the premises and the conclusion,** and the relation can be studied independently of whether the premises and the conclusion happen in fact to be true or not. Truth and validity are closely related to each other, but you must learn carefully to distinguish between them.

▲
_____

Valid Inference: A deductive inference in which the relation between the premise(s) and the conclusion(s) is such that it is *impossible* to imagine the conclusion to be false while imagining all the premise(s) to be true at the same time.

Invalid Inference: An inference in which it remains possible to imagine a way for the conclusion to be false while imagining all the premise(s) to be true at the same time.

_____

Valid deductive inferences are truth-preserving, and this allows us to make three important observations. First, we see why **deductive logic is directly applicable only to statements.** Only statements are true or false, and deductive logic concerns itself with what happens when premise statements are imagined to be true.

Second, we can also see how deductive inferences do their job in interrogative inquiry. We are, in such an inquiry, trying to write truths that lead to the ultimate conclusion. For this purpose it is especially helpful if we can use steps that are known always to lead to new lines that are true so long as they are based on previous material that is true. Valid deductive inferences have this feature.

A Test for Validity and Invalidity

Third, the characterization just given suggests a way of studying the question whether a deductive inference is possible in a given case. What we can do is try to imagine a situation in which the premise statement(s) are all true at the same time but in which at least one conclusion statement is false. If we can imagine such a situation, we have to say that the relationship between the premise(s) and the conclusion(s) is *invalid*. If we can show that such a situation is impossible to imagine, then we say that the relationship between the premise(s) and the conclusion(s) is *valid*.

As we saw in Part 1, this thought experiment can be viewed as a game. In playing this game it is important to realize that in deductive logic we are not simply interested in how things actually are in the world as we know it. *The study of valid and invalid relationships requires that we wonder about what could happen if the world were different than we know it to be.* Thus, the thought experiments we perform in logic are free of the fetters of how things actually are. This makes the "game" more complicated (and for some of us more interesting).

From what has been said it follows that the validity of an inference tells very little about the truth or falsity of its premises and its conclusion. The premises of a valid inference can be true or false, and so can its conclusion. Only one thing is crucial: In a valid inference it is impossible to imagine the conclusion to be false when all the premises together are imagined to be true.

Two Illustrations

For an illustration, let the following statements be our premises:

p1. Either you are more than five years old or the temperature in Indianapolis is 130 degrees Fahrenheit.

p2. You are not more than five years old.

In our actual world the first premise is a bit difficult to interpret, but it probably could be understood to be true. The second of these premises, however, is most likely false about the people reading this chapter. Still, we have decided to take these statements to be premises, and this means that we will try to imagine a situation in which *both* statements are true at the same time. Try it. Perhaps in class you can see who has the more entertaining imagination in doing this.

Okay, now let the following statement be our conclusion statement:

c1. The temperature in Indianapolis is 130 degrees Fahrenheit.

Again, in our actual world, this conclusion is most likely false. But we have decided to study how this statement will relate to the premises when we imagine the premises both to be true. If we imagine the premises both to be true, is there any way to think that the conclusion could still be false? Try it. Discuss the possibilities with the class or a friend. It looks as though we cannot in any way imagine the conclusion to be false, given that we are imagining the premises to be true. So, the relationship between these premises and this conclusion is not invalid. It is a valid relationship.

Let us make a couple changes to give a second illustration:

p1. Either you are more than five years old or the temperature in Indianapolis is less than 130 degrees Fahrenheit.

p2. You are more than five years old.

All we have done is added *less than* to the second part of the first premise and removed *not* from the second premise. In our actual world both of these premises are now most likely true. Here is a slightly changed conclusion for us to study:

c1. The temperature in Indianapolis is less than 130 degrees Fahrenheit.

In our actual world this conclusion statement is also most likely true, so both the premises and the conclusion seem likely to be true in the actual world. Does this mean that the relationship between premises and conclusion is valid? No. *The game of deductive logic requires that we think not only about the way things actually are but also that we imagine other possibilities.* In this case we claim that it is possible for us to imagine that the premises are true while still imagining that the conclusion is false. Talk about this in your class or with your roommate. Exercise your imagination. If we are right, then it is possible to imagine a situation in which the premises are true but the conclusion is false. If so, then the relationship between the premises and the conclusion is, according to the rules of our game, invalid.

Another Example   Consider the following argument: In nonindustrialized nations overpopulation is a serious problem, which must be addressed. It is clear, as demonstrated in some of these nations, that compulsory restriction of family size is an effective way to deal with this crisis. Therefore, this practice ought to be adopted in countries suffering from overpopulation.

This is not a valid deductive argument. In this case it is clearly possible to imagine the premises true and the conclusion false. One may grant that overpopulation is a serious problem in these countries and that compulsory restriction of family size would solve the problem. But it could still be false that this practice ought to be adopted.

Imagine, for example, that this proposal was not the only one which could solve the problem. Perhaps incentives for *voluntary* restriction of family size would also work. This possibility might have every advantage found in the original proposal, without the disadvantage of coercion. One might then argue that a conclusion different from the proposed conclusion is more appropriate.

Notice that it may be false in the actual world that any alternatives such as the one just imagined exist. This makes no difference to our testing for validity. The important point as far as a determination of validity is concerned is that it *is* possible to imagine there are alternatives like this one. This imaginable possibility is enough to render the argument invalid.

In testing for validity we are free to disregard all known facts of biology or physics or psychology or anything else. If we can consistently imagine an alternative situation in which the conclusion is false while the premises are true, then we have shown invalidity.

△▼ EXERCISE 5-D

Return now to Exercise 5-C at the end of Section 5.8. Test each inference for validity. For each inference ask yourself if it is possible to imagine the premises to be true and the conclusion false. If so, indicate in some detail what the world would have to be like in order for this to be the case. If not, explain why it is impossible to imagine the conclusion false while imagining the premises true. This will tell you which of the inferences are valid and which invalid.

5.10   Deduction and Imagination

This business of imagining other situations may at first seem crazy. Some of you will welcome it just because it makes the puzzles of deductive logic richly interesting. All of us, however, should welcome this aspect of deductive logic, because this is the part that most meaningfully connects us with everyday reasoning. We have already been studying how everyday reasoning asks "What if . . . ?" This requires imagination and the willingness to wonder if things might be different than we first thought. Good thinking does not get very far by cataloging what in the actual world we currently think is true or false. Good thinking advances by asking "What if . . . ?" as we try to expand our knowledge. Deductive logic can give us useful practice in asking "What if . . . ?" as we look at the relationships between premises and conclusions.

A famous mathematician and logician by the name of David Hilbert (1862–1943) once spoke about a student who gave up studying advanced mathematics and mathematical logic to become a novelist. Hilbert's comment was that the poor soul did not have enough imagination to do mathematical research!

5.11   Summary

In summary, an *invalid* relationship will be one in which we can imagine a way for all the premise statements to be true at the same time while at least one of the conclusion statements is false. This is called imagining a **counterexample** to the inference. If we can imagine a counterexample, then the relationship between premises and conclusion is said to be invalid. A *valid* relationship will be one in which we can show that there is no way for the premise statements to be true while a conclusion statement is false. This is to say that no counterexample is possible.

— ▲

Counterexample: An imaginable scenario or situation in which the premise(s) all turn out to be true while the conclusion turns out to be false.

Notice carefully that **it is statements that are true or false. A statement will not usually be said to be valid or invalid. The words** *valid* **and** *invalid* **will usually be applied only to the relationship between premises and conclusions.** More importantly, because the relationship between premises and conclusions has to do with some statements being true and others being false, it will not make much sense to say that the *relationship itself* is true or false. This explains the need for the special words *valid* and *invalid*.

In traditional approaches to deductive logic, this game of seeing how premises relate to conclusions is said to be about "arguments" or "inferences" or "deductions." And premises are often said to be "evidence" or "reasons" or "grounds" for conclusions. It will help for now, however, if you focus on the meanings we have given for *statement, premise, conclusion, invalid,* and *valid.* Everything we need to do can be thought of in terms of a puzzle or game in which we are trying to discover whether the relationship between the premise(s) and conclusion(s) is invalid or valid. We can understand talk about arguments, inferences, evidence, reasons, grounds, and so forth, in terms of our fundamental understanding of deductive logical inferences and the role they play with interrogative moves in rational inquiry.

△▼ EXERCISE 5-E

Determine whether or not a counterexample exists for each of the following.

1. I parked my car last night where I always park it. No one asked to borrow it. Conclusion: My car was stolen.

▶ 2. The mayor should be reelected only if she is honest. The mayor is honest. Conclusion: The mayor should be reelected.

3. Tom believes in Santa Claus. Conclusion: Tom has at least one false belief.

▶ 4. Tom believes that he has at least one false belief. Conclusion: At least one of Tom's beliefs is not true.   *valid — Reflexivity*

▶ 5. If person A is B's friend, then B is A's friend, no matter who A and B are. Everyone is a friend to himself or herself. Conclusion: At least two people at the party have the same number of friends present.

[margin handwritten notes:]
R⊃H | R
H |
FALLACY OF
AFFIRMING
CONSEQUENT

5.12 Deductive Logic and Interrogative Game Tables

We conclude this chapter by examining the role played by deductive logic in the interrogative model of inquiry. In Part 1 we learned how to construct interrogative game tables. In the interrogative model all new information enters the left side of the table either in the initial premises or through interrogative moves. Deductive logic is not involved in how we get the initial premises or in any particular interrogative move.

Instead, on the left side of our tables deductive logical inferences take the information that has been brought into the table and draw out of it that part of the information that moves us closer to our ultimate conclusion. Deductive logical inferences also help us relate pieces of information that originally came into the table in unrelated moves.

In Chapter 2 we learned that logical inferences need to be truth-preserving. You should now see that valid deductive logical inferences are definitely truth-preserving. The whole point of searching for counterexamples is in trying to see whether the premises absolutely force acceptance of the conclusion. Thus, any particular logical inference step involves adding a new true line to the left side of the table on the basis of the earlier lines that force this line to be a true statement. The newly added line is the "conclusion" based on the earlier lines, which are the "premises" of that particular logical inference.

The left side of interrogative tables is supposed to consist of agreed-upon initial premise lines, followed by a mixture of true answers to questions and true logical inference conclusion lines based on earlier lines. (Remember that in these early chapters we are assuming that the oracle always tells the truth.) If the sequence of lines on the left side of the table eventually includes the ultimate conclusion, then we have a closed table. (See Chapter 2, Section 2.4.) This means that the entire inquiry has been successful.

Notice that a closed table also means there is a valid relationship between the lines on the left side and the ultimate conclusion on the right side. This is so because the appearance of the ultimate conclusion in the sequence of lines on the left side means there is no way to imagine the ultimate conclusion false while also imagining all the left-side lines to be true.

For the time being we are postponing any detailed discussion of what happens when the left side splits into paths, but the idea remains the same. Each path on the left side represents one way to imagine a series of lines to be true and to check this series of lines against the ultimate conclusion. If there has been branching, it will be necessary to attend to all the paths before we can say that the ultimate conclusion is validly connected to all the lines on the left side of the table. For the time being we will keep problems with branching to a minimum.

You may also remember that in Chapter 2 (Section 2.4) we said a sequence of lines in a path will be closed if two statements that cannot together be imagined to be true appear together in the sequence. This is so because it now becomes impossible to construct a counterexample. A counterexample requires that all the premise lines be imagined true. But if two statements that cannot together be imagined to be true are both in the collection of premise lines, then there is no way to imagine all the premise lines to be true.

In this chapter we have not discussed how deductive logical inference works on the right side of our tables. This matter was briefly presented in Chapter 2 (Section 2.4) and will get plenty of attention in Chapter 8. For now we will keep nearly all of our work on the left side of our tables.

△▼ EXERCISE 5-F

▶ This set of exercises asks you to begin using all that you have learned in Part 1 as well as in this chapter. You should construct actual interrogative game tables. The argument sketches become increasingly complicated so that you will need to break the arguments down into smaller interrogative and logical inference steps. You should not simply look at the whole picture and seek one grand counterexample. Instead, try to construct a path or paths on the left side made up of interrogative moves and small logical inference moves which lead in a truth-preserving way from the premises to the conclusion. You will find that some background or between-the-lines information will also likely need to be provided.

1. You should play the lottery. After all, how can you win if you don't play?

2. The blue whale is the largest animal ever to live on the earth. Dinosaurs reached greater lengths than the blue whale, but no fossil has ever been found of a dinosaur weighing as much.

3. The flag and the bald eagle are America's most important symbols. Anyone can tell you that it is wrong to desecrate a nation's important symbols. How, then, can one deny that burning the American flag ought to be illegal? Obviously, burning the American flag constitutes the desecration of this precious symbol.

4. If all eligible voters participated in the election, the results could genuinely be said to reflect the will of the people. But these results do not reflect the people's will, as less than one half of those eligible voted.

5. All normal adults have a right to life. If you were to take a single brain cell from something with a right to life, the result would still have a right to life. So the right to life of adults does not depend upon the possession of a brain.

6. Although it is true that the sound systems of Discotech are the most prestigious available, this is not why you will find our systems in the homes of audiophiles. To true audiophiles, sound quality, not prestige, is the only relevant consideration when purchasing a sound system. They recognize the value which can only come from being the best. Discotech, we're playing your tune.

△▼ EXERCISE 5-G

The following two exercises, which are examples of standard logic puzzles, are more complicated but in some ways more simple than the preceding exercise. Nearly all the information needed to solve each puzzle is provided, but the logical inferences can be tricky to find. Often they depend on common background knowledge, but recognizing this is not always easy.

▶ 1. This first puzzle is sometimes called the "Smith-Jones-Robinson (SJR) Classic." Many puzzles like it exist, but this is the classic version. It is reported that in one group of 240 people trying it, only 6 came up with the solution. Many people, however, have solved it in five to ten minutes.

The puzzle begins as follows: On a train, Smith, Robinson, and Jones are the fireman, brakeperson, and engineer, but not necessarily respectively. Also aboard the train are three passengers who have the same names: To distinguish passengers from workers they are called Ms. Smith, Mr. Robinson, and Mrs. Jones. Who is the engineer?

It should be plain to you that there are three possible conclusions to put into the right side of the game table. What are they? The puzzle is asking which conclusion is the right one. You will have to experiment with the given information to determine which conclusion is validly connected to the given information.

For the purposes of this interrogative game the oracle can answer only the following questions directly:

a. Where does Mr. Robinson live? *Detroit*
b. Where does the brakeperson live? *1/2 b - Chi + Det*
c. How much does Mrs. Jones earn? *20,000*
d. How much does the brakeperson's nearest neighbor earn? *3x brake - exactly*
e. Who beats the fireman at billiards? *Smith*
f. Which passenger lives in Chicago?

Here are the answers the oracle will give you:

a. In Detroit.
b. Exactly halfway between Chicago and Detroit.
c. Exactly $20,000 per year.
d. The brakeperson's nearest neighbor is one of the passengers and he or she earns exactly three times as much as the brakeperson. (The oracle suggests that you note the word *exactly* very carefully.)
e. Smith (not Ms. Smith). (The oracle also points out that the fireman cannot be said to beat himself.)
f. The passenger whose name is the same as the brakeperson's.

Whatever common sense, everyday knowledge and mathematical knowledge you need can be introduced into the table by interrogative moves. Also, the initial description of the puzzle contains some information that can be introduced either as initial premises or as answers to questions.

Whenever you start to spell out in more detail what is involved in the information gained through interrogative moves, you should find that you are using some deductive logical inferences. These too should be entered into your table and noted at the appropriate places.

Solve the puzzle and put the solution into the form of an interrogative game. There is more than one technique for solving a puzzle like this. You may or may not want to think it through initially as an interrogative game, but after you have the solution, put it into this form.

Even if you fail to get a solution, do work at constructing a table. It is more important to learn how to make moves in an interrogative game than to get the correct solution to the puzzle.

As a further step in your analysis, examine one or two of the logical inference moves you made in the table. Explain whether and how these moves *validly* connect the preceding premises with the step you are examining.

▶ 2. Here is another "SJR" puzzle which can be treated in a similar way to the one above.

NOBODY LEAVE THE ROOM!

Smith has been found dead in the bar, his drink poisoned.

Four men, seated on a sofa and two armchairs in front of the fireplace (as shown above), are discussing the foul deed. Their names are Lee, Jones, Garcia, and Green. They are, not necessarily respectively, a mechanic, a restaurateur, a teacher, and a doctor.

1. The waiter pours a second glass of whiskey for Garcia and a second beer for Jones.

2. The mechanic looks up and, in the mirror over the fireplace, sees the door close as the waiter leaves the room. He then turns to speak to Green, next to him.

3. Neither Lee nor Jones has ever been married.

4. The restaurateur is a teetotaler. ~ doesn't drink

5. Lee, who is sitting in one of the armchairs, is the teacher's brother-in-law. The restaurateur is next to Lee on Lee's left.

Suddenly, a hand steals forward to put something in Garcia's whiskey as it sits on the table. It is the murderer. No one has left his seat, no one else is in the room, and Garcia is not suicidal. Who is the murderer? What is the profession of each man, and where is he sitting?

.6

Representing Statements

Interrogative inquiry consists of two kinds of steps: interrogative steps and logical inference steps. The last chapter gave an overview of the nature of logical inferences, and you learned that these steps should always be valid, deductive moves. In the rest of Part 2 we shall study a particular type. This will not exhaust the range of logical inferences that you will find yourself needing in your inquiries, but they do constitute singularly important and clear-cut kinds of deductive logical inferences.

One of the things we have discovered about the interrogative model in general and deductive logical inference in particular is that it requires an active imagination. In this and the following chapters we will try to make the imagining easier by studying a part of deductive logic called "statement logic." (Some people call this "propositional logic," because they use the term *proposition* for what we call a *statement*. This is also known as "truth-functional logic" for reasons which will be explained later in this chapter.) In this part of deductive logic we learn one of the simpler ways to analyze (i.e., take apart) complicated premise and conclusion statements into simpler statements. This makes the job of checking for validity and invalidity simpler and allows it to be more reliably handled.

6.1 Simplifying Complex Statements

In Chapter 5 (Section 5.9), when we were learning about validity and invalidity, we considered a couple of fairly easy examples. In analyzing these you were asked to imagine whether and how the premises might be true while the conclusion was false. In both cases we noted that the first premise statement probably gave you the most trouble. Here is one of those premises:

Either you are more than five years old or the temperature in Indianapolis is
     130 degrees Fahrenheit.

What you have to do here is consider two different simpler statements joined by the word *or*. The idea behind statement logic is to take apart complicated statements like this one into combinations of simpler statements.

Statements are complicated in many different ways. Here we are concerned with the role of words such as "not," "and," "or," and "if-then." Two different approaches will be used together in trying to isolate the simpler statements of a complex statement:

1. We will learn to look for the simpler statements that can be taken to be parts of a more complicated statement.
2. We will learn to keep an eye on how "not," "and," "or," "if-then," and their cousins are complicating a statement.

The first approach is the more fundamental. We look for the simpler statements that may be part of a more complicated statement. The essential point here is to remember that *even the simplest statement must be able to be formulated as a sentence that is true or false.* Here again is our complicated premise statement from Chapter 5:

Either you are more than five years old or the temperature in Indianapolis
     is 130 degrees Fahrenheit.

Included in this statement is the sentence

1. You are more than five years old.

This sentence passes the test for being a statement. There is also the sentence

2. The temperature in Indianapolis is 130 degrees Fahrenheit.

This too is a statement. So, we have two simpler statements, which are joined by the words "either . . . or." Neither of the simpler statements can be broken down any further without losing some information. You might be tempted to take "You are" as a simpler statement out of "You are more than five years old." You would be right that "You are" could be a statement, but there is no way to turn "more than five years old" into a statement by itself. It must be kept with "You are."

△▼ EXERCISE 6-A

Find the simpler statements and discuss how they are being connected to each other by logical words like "or," "and," and "if-then."

1. Either I was the brunt of a cruel joke, or my best friend wrecked my mother's car.
▶ 2. Joshua sat at the lake and counted the fish as they jumped in front of him.
3. Kim Nash, the first human to set foot on Mars, radioed her findings back to Earth.
▶ 4. We finished lunch and began to plan for the visit of the Prime Minister and her husband. *both* *Cannot break into two statements*
5. If you don't brush your teeth you'll get cavities.
▶ 6. Bo Jackson, the most successful multisport athlete since Jim Thorpe, promises to eclipse even that great athlete's achievements.
▶ 7. Only if you were truly interested in the ways of wisdom and enlightenment would the readings of the Grand Wazoo be of use to you.
8. The person who found the lost child was a Canadian.

6.2 Representing Simple Statements

Once we have isolated the simplest statements, we represent them by uppercase letters. The reason for doing this will be explained later. In our previous example we might let *A* represent "You are more than five years old." We could let *B* represent "The temperature in Indianapolis is 130 degrees Fahrenheit." Note carefully that italicized *uppercase letters are being used to represent whole statements, not just parts of statements*. In statement logic there is no way to use a letter to represent something like "the temperature in Indianapolis." An uppercase letter must represent a complete statement.

Here is a another example:

You and your brother are both more than five years old.

This is a statement, and it looks as though it includes two simpler statements, one of which is:

1. You are more than five years old.

and the other:

2. Your brother is more than five years old.

Both of the simpler sentences are statements. We could again represent "You are more than five years old" by *A*. And because we have already used *B* to represent a statement, we will take *C* to represent "Your brother is more than five years old." Remember that uppercase letters are always representing complete statements. The statements represented by *A* and *C* are, in this example, joined by "and." Notice that "both" often goes along with "and" to help make clear what "and" is doing. In a similar way "either" is often used with "or" to help make clear what "or" is doing.

You are perhaps observing that words like "and" and "or" can be a sign that we have a complicated statement which can be taken apart. This is our second way of approaching problems of simplifying complex statements. When we see little words like "not," "and," "or," and "if-then," we will check to see if they are joining some simpler statements. This approach can, however, be misleading, so it should always be used along with the first. The following example will show why:

You and your sister are a tennis doubles team.

Here we see "and" at work, and we might be tempted to think that two simpler statements are to be found in this case. We should, however, check what sort of simpler statements we could actually get. We might try

1. You are a tennis doubles team

and

2. Your sister is a tennis doubles team.

These two statements do not really make sense, and together they do not represent what the complex statement was saying. The secret is that "and" in this example is not linking two separate statements. Instead, it is linking two people—you and your sister—into a doubles team. Neither "you" nor "your sister" is a statement. So *and* is not always a reliable clue that we have a complicated statement which can be simplified.

Not, And, Or, and If-then

With these initial illustrations in mind we now go on to look more closely at how the little words "not," "and," "or," and "if-then" can be dealt with. Consider first how *not* complicates a statement:

John does not live in Florida.

This sentence is a statement because in normal use it could be true or false. It is also, however, somewhat complicated because two things are happening in it. We hear about John possibly being in Florida and we also hear that being denied. We could rewrite the statement this way:

It is not the case that John lives in Florida.

This looks rather clumsy, but we could agree to use the simple dash (–) as a sign for "It is not the case that." Then our new statement becomes

–(John lives in Florida.)

The statement is now a little simpler since the *not* has been put outside it in the sign – . If we represent "John lives in Florida" by an uppercase letter like *D*, we can now write

–*D*

There are many ways to say "it is not the case that" in English. Sometimes it is hard to decide whether to analyze a statement as containing " – ". For example, if we say "Nan failed her physical," that statement could be treated as a simple one, or it could be taken to say "Nan did not pass her physical." In cases like this it will not be important whether we treat the statement as containing " – ". What *will* be important in such cases is that we treat the same statement the same way each time we encounter it in a passage we are analyzing.

We have already seen that it is often helpful to isolate the *and*s and *or*s in our complex statements. Consider this statement:

John and Mary live in Florida.

Again, we have a statement because in normal use the sentence is either true or false. The statement is, however, complicated by the "and." We can show how the "and" is working by taking the two simpler statements individually and joining them by "and":

John lives in Florida and Mary lives in Florida.

This is complicated in its own way, but it has achieved the goal of disentangling the simpler statements from each other. Furthermore, we can agree now to replace *and* by & as follows:

John lives in Florida & Mary lives in Florida.

We have let *D* stand for "John lives in Florida," and we can let *E* stand for "Mary lives in Florida." This gives us

D & *E*

You will want also to note that words like "but," "although," "yet," "still," "however," "nevertheless," and a number of others can also function like *and* in the way they join statements together. In English we also have ways of using the comma and the semicolon to join statements the way "and" does. In all these cases, if the words or punctuation marks in a complex statement are showing that two (or possibly more) simple statements are all being asserted to be true together, then we can represent the simpler statements by uppercase letters and join them with &. You should remember, however, that, as we have seen, "and" has other functions in English than only to join statements together.

Here is another example with "or":

John or Mary lives in Florida.

We can uncomplicate the statement by writing two statements joined by *or:*

John lives in Florida or Mary lives in Florida.

We shall agree to replace *or* by ∨ as follows:

John lives in Florida ∨ Mary lives in Florida.

This then leads naturally to

> *D* ∨ *E*

In English we can also express "or" by the words "or else" and "unless." There are some complicated problems with understanding the precise meaning of *or* and we will come to these shortly. But we first have one more symbol to learn.

Another interesting and important way statements are complicated involves the use of the words "if" and "then." Consider the following statement:

If John lives in Florida, then Mary lives in California.

Two simpler statements are incorporated here:

1. John lives in Florida.

and

2. Mary lives in California.

As a first step toward simplifying the complicated statement, we can agree to use the symbol ⊃ to represent the "if-then" connecting the simpler statements. (The two words always work together, so only one symbol is needed.) The statement immediately following the *if* will be put to the left of the ⊃, and the other simpler statement will be put to the right of the ⊃. So we will write

John lives in Florida ⊃ Mary lives in California.

If we represent "Mary lives in California" by *F,* we get

> *D* ⊃ *F*

Notice that the words "if" and "then" do not belong in the simple statements. Rather, they indicate the way in which the simple statements are being put into relation with each other. Many times in English the word "then" is omitted. For example, "If Jack wins, I'll be surprised." In this case a comma marks the break between the two statements, but commas are often omitted as well. It is also possible to express the "if-then" relationship by putting the "if" part second in the sentence. For example, "Gordon will be pleased if Gail calls him." Note carefully that the simple statement following the "if" always goes to the left of the ⊃ regardless of the order of the simple statements in English. So, in this case, if *P* stands for "Gordon will be pleased" and *Q* stands for "Gail calls him," then our representation of the sentence would have to be *Q* ⊃ *P* and *not P* ⊃ *Q.*

In "if-then" statements it is of the greatest importance to keep straight which statement belongs on the left side of the symbol ⊃ and which belongs on the right. In the case of & and ∨ it makes no difference which statement goes on which side of the symbol, but with ⊃ the difference must be carefully noted.

"If-then" relationships can also be indicated in English by the phrase "only if." This phrase is the source of much confusion in people's thinking. We have said that the statement following the word "if" is the one that should go on the left side of the symbol ⊃. The phrase "only if" provides an exception to this rule. A proper representation of statements with "only if" requires that the statement following "only if" be put to the *right* of the symbol ⊃. For example, consider the statement

Harold will stay home only if Sharon calls him.

It is tempting to read this statement as though it were saying "If Sharon calls him, Harold will stay home." The reason for this is that the word "only" appears simply to be adding some emphasis. What is actually happening, however, is that the order of the "if-then" relationship is being reversed by the word. The correct representation of the statement is as follows (Let S stand for "Harold will stay home" and T stand for "Sharon calls him"):

$S \supset T$

Shortly we will discuss this matter in even more detail, but a simple piece of practical advice can be given. Whenever you see "only if" joining two statements, treat "only if" as though it were the word "then." This can remind you that the statement following "only if" belongs on the right side of the symbol ⊃.

Summary

Basic statements can be made simpler by substituting "if-then," "or," "and," and "not" with ⊃, ∨, &, and –, as appropriate. Usually two statements are required instead of one, but each of the new statements is simpler in that it does not contain one of these little words. Once we arrive at the simpler statements, we represent them by uppercase letters. **Note carefully that a different uppercase letter is used for each different statement and that the same uppercase letter is used to represent the same statement wherever it appears.**

We learn to simplify statements in this way to make our analysis of the relationship between premise(s) and conclusion(s) easier. The kind of deductive logic we are dealing with in this chapter is called statement logic (or propositional logic). It bears this name because in this kind of logic details inside a simple statement are ignored. For example, we forget about Florida and John and Mary and where they are living.

Remember that in deductive logic we are trying to imagine all the different things that might happen in the *relationship* between statements. In statement logic we condense "John does not live in Florida" to $-D$. Now our imagining becomes very easy. Because D is a statement, we only need imagine two possibilities. Either

D is true or *D* is false. You can probably see it coming that if *D* is imagined to be true, we'll be forced to think that –*D* is false. And if *D* is imagined to be false, you can work out what –*D* will be.

Perhaps you are wondering, however, what happened to good old John and Mary and Florida. Why are we leaving them behind? The answer is twofold. First, never fear, in more complicated deductive logic (in Part 4) we shall bring them back. But, more importantly, remember that in logic we are asking about the relationships between statements and not about their truth in the actual world. Remember that in this game we agree to let the premise statements be true and then we try to figure out whether we can imagine a way for the conclusion statement(s) to be false. The simple tricks we have just learned about statement logic will make this game rather easy to play.

△▼ EXERCISE 6-B

▶ Go back to the exercises in Section 6.1, and use the techniques of this section to represent each of the complex statements with letters and symbols.

6.3   Rules for Representing Statements

Let us sum up what we have seen and learn some rules for seeing how the truth and falsity of complex statements can be determined. Remember that any statement is either true or false. Because every statement is either true or false, logicians say that every statement has a *truth value*. All that is meant by this phrase is that *a true statement has the truth value* true *and a false statement has the truth value* false. There are many cases in which we may not know the actual truth values of a group of statements, but we can still learn important things by studying how the truth values of statements are related to each other through words like "not," "and," "or," and "if-then."

1. Uppercase letters in italics will represent statements. We will use a different uppercase letter for each different statement; we will use the same letter for each occurrence of the same statement.

2. We bring *not* out of our statements by using – as a symbol for "It is not the case that." We will follow the rule that if *A* is true, then –*A* is false. Also, if –*A* is true, then *A* is false. –*A* is called the **denial** (or **negation**) of *A*. So we are saying that **denial reverses the truth value of a statement.**

3. We will bring *and* out of our statements by using & as a symbol for *and*. We will follow the rule that if *A* is true and *B* is true, then *A* & *B* is also true. Also, if *A* & *B* is true, then *A* is true and *B* is true. Statements joined by & are called **conjunctions.** So we are saying that **conjunctions are true if and only if all components are true, and false if even one component is false.**

4. We will bring *or* out of our statements by using ∨ as a symbol for *or*. We will follow the rule that if either *A* is true or *B* is true or both are true, then *A* ∨ *B* is also true. Also, if *A* ∨ *B* is true, then either *A* or *B* or possibly both are true. Statements joined by ∨ are called **disjunctions.** So we are saying that **disjunctions are true if even one component is true, and false if and only if all components are false.**

This account of *or* makes a decision about the meaning of "or." In English we can mean two related but different things when we say "or." For example, in Chapter 2 (Section 2.4) we discussed the statement "Sue finished the test or Bob finished the test." In everyday English this sentence will be true if Sue finishes the test and Bob does not. It will also be true if Bob finishes the test and Sue does not. The sentence will be false if Sue and Bob both fail to finish. However, in everyday English we sometimes intend to say that the sentence would be *false* also if both of them finish, and sometimes we allow that the sentence would be *true* if both of them finish. The first possibility is called the **exclusive** use of *or* and the other, the **inclusive** use. Throughout this book we will follow the example of most logicians and treat *or* as "inclusive" unless there is specific information to show that the "exclusive" use is intended.

Logicians make this decision in favor of the inclusive use of *or* for a strategic reason. Both uses have their place and neither is necessarily incorrect. Inclusive use, however, is weaker in the sense that it makes fewer assumptions about what is being communicated in a disjunctive statement. Inclusive use captures all that is meant by the exclusive use except for the definite indication that not both of the statements in the disjunctive relationship can be true. Thus, the exclusive use provides more information. Logicians argue that it is strategically wiser to interpret all disjunctions as inclusive, because in this way we will avoid reading more into a disjunction than was originally intended. Admittedly, we may miss a further piece of information that was intended, but it seems wiser to risk missing that information than to risk assuming that the additional information is intended when often there is no way to tell.

A further note about "or": The words "or else" and "unless" can be treated as substitutes for "or." In these cases too there is a risk that we will miss an intended exclusive use of "or," but for many purposes it is sufficient to capture the main meaning of "unless" and "or else" by representing them with the symbol ∨.

5. We will bring "if-then" out of our statements by using ⊃ as a symbol for "if-then." The statement that immediately follows the "if" will be put to the left of the ⊃ and the other statement will be put to the right. (As we have seen "only if" can be represented with the ⊃. In a complex statement with "only if" the statement that follows "only if" is put to the right of the ⊃ and the other statement is put to the left.)

The rule for truth of an "if-then" statement is both complicated and controversial. In Appendix C "if-then" is discussed in more detail. In statement logic "if-then" statements are all treated as though they were like the following example. *Learn this example:* Suppose someone says that, in a particular game,

"If a player's foot touches the line, that player is out of bounds." How could you prove that this person has made a false statement about the rules? There is only one way for you to show that this statement of the rules is false. This would be to show that in the game a player's foot can touch the line and yet it is false that the player is out of bounds. In a similar way in statement logic we shall follow the rule that if A is true while B is false, then $A \supset B$ is false. In any other situation we will say that $A \supset B$ is true.

Statements joined by $\supset$ are called **conditionals.** The rule for truth and falsity of conditionals is troubling to many students when they notice that logicians are claiming that a conditional is true even when both components of it happen to be false. It can help to think again about the example above. Suppose it is false that during a play of the game a player's foot touches the line and also that it is false that the player is out of bounds. Nevertheless, the rule can still be true that "If a player's foot touches the line, that player is out of bounds." Notice that the rule can still be true also in the situation when the left component is false and the right component is true. It could happen that it is false that during a play of the game a player's foot touches the line and yet also true that the player is out of bounds (for some other reason). Thus, the only way to show that the statement of the rule is false is to have the left component be true while the right component is false.

The component statement to the left of the $\supset$ is called the **antecedent;** the statement to the right is called the **consequent.** So we are saying that **conditionals are true except in the case in which the antecedent (left component) is true while the consequent (right component) is false.** It is useful to notice that this means that in statement logic the conditional $A \supset B$ has the same rules for truth and falsity as the disjunction $-A \vee B$. $-A \vee B$ also is false only when A is true and B is false. You may want to discuss this in class.

In treating the conditional this way, logicians are once again making a strategic decision. They are looking at the many different ways in which "if-then" relationships are used in English and trying to settle on the weakest meaning so that the risk of reading too much into a complex statement is avoided. This will help you understand how it is turning out that conditionals can just as well be expressed as a disjunction (inclusive "or"). This way of treating "if-then" is sometimes called the "material conditional."

The material conditional can capture a large part of the meaning of many different English expressions. The phrases "in case," "provided that," "given that," and "on condition that" can each often be treated as though they function like *if* in a conditional. The conditional $A \supset B$ also captures part of the force of such English expressions as "A implies B" or "A entails B." However, sometimes they express valid inferential relation rather than material conditional.

The phrases **"sufficient condition"** and **"necessary condition"** provide another way to express conditional statements. "A is a sufficient condition for B" is represented by "If A then B." "A is a necessary condition for B" is expressed by "If B then A." In many cases the word "if" indicates a sufficient condition while the phrase "only if" indicates a necessary condition.

It can be seen from the preceding rules that denials, conjunctions, disjunctions, and conditionals can be thought of as complicated statements whose truth values are determined by the truth values of the simpler statements. The rules we have just formulated enable us to determine how denials, conjunctions, disjunctions, and conditionals will be true or false based on the truth values of the simpler statements which are their components. This feature of this kind of logic has given it the name **truth-functional logic:** The truth values of the complicated statements are said to be functions of (to depend on) the truth values of the simpler statements.

The above five rules for representing statements give us the basics for translating English into the formal symbols, and vice versa. The symbolic language of statement logic is called a "formal" language, because its purpose is to expose and make more clear the *form* of the relationships between statements. The content of the statements is hidden behind the uppercase letters that represent them, but the way in which the statements are related to each other is clearly shown by our special symbols.

We have been learning to look for special words that may indicate that simpler statements are being joined into more complex statements. This is what we called at the beginning of the chapter the second (and less reliable way) of learning how to represent statements in statement logic: keeping an eye on how "not," "and," "or," "if-then," and their cousins are complicating a statement. The first way remains more fundamental: looking for the simpler statements that can be taken to be parts of a more complicated statement.

The reason this first way is more fundamental is that English does not easily translate into the formal language we are developing. Natural languages like English make it possible for us to do and say many more things than can be captured in our simple formalisms. Thus, the presence or absence of words like "and," "or," "if-then," "not," and their cousins will not mechanically show us how to do a representation. In every case we must ask ourselves what precisely the English statement is saying and then try to see if we can restate all or a significant portion of the meaning with the simpler tools of our formal language.

The art of translating English into a formal language is actually quite difficult in many cases. In this chapter we are keeping the difficulties to a minimum. In the next two chapters we will work mainly with formulas that are already in symbolic form. This too will make matters simpler. Then, in Chapter 9, we will learn a technique for working back and forth between everyday English and the insights of statement logic. We do, however, in this chapter need to study a few more details of the art of translation.

6.4   Complex Statements Involving More Than One Operator

More and more complicated statements can be represented by our symbols. $-$, &, $\vee$, and $\supset$ are called logical "operators." Whenever there is more than one operator in a complex statement, it is necessary to determine which is the main operator. The **main operator** is the one that links all components of the statement together. It is the operator that governs a full line of symbols.

When statements are already represented in our formal symbols, it is relatively easy to find the main operator in a formula. Logicians usually make some standard agreements about how the symbols work, and they also make use of parentheses, brackets, and braces to help indicate how the symbols are related to each other and which is the main operator in the formula.

One of the agreements logicians usually make is that the symbol for denial (–) will apply to the smallest combination of statements permitted by the way the formula is put together. For example, if you have the formula –*A* & *B*, the denial will be taken to apply only to the statement *A*. If, however, you have the formula –(*A* & *B*), the parentheses indicate that the denial is meant to apply to the more complicated conjunctive statement inside the parentheses. This will mean that a formula like –(–*A* & *B*) will have to be given careful thought. The first denial symbol applies to the whole formula inside the parentheses. The second one, however, applies only to the statement represented by *A*.

Some students may be tempted to think that because one denial reverses truth value and two denials bring us back to the original truth value, we can usually drop double denials from our formulas. Note, however, that in the example –(–*A* & *B*) we do not have the denials operating on the same statements. The first denial applies to everything in the parentheses, but the second applies only to the statement *A*. Thus, it would be a mistake to think that (*A* & *B*) could be equivalent to –(–*A* & *B*).

On the other hand, if it is in fact the case that two denials are being applied to precisely the same part of a formula, then the double denial can be dropped. For example, ––(*A* & *B*) is equivalent to the simpler formula (*A* & *B*).

When more than one symbol for a conjunction, disjunction, and/or a conditional are at work in a formula, it is necessary that we always use parentheses, braces, and brackets to show what simpler statement is being joined to what. If the formula is already presented to us in good form, then it is usually a straightforward matter to determine which operator is doing what work. You will learn in Chapter 7 that the most important task is to identify the main operator. A simple rule to help you find it is that it is usually the operator enclosed by the *fewest* parentheses or brackets. Usually it is enclosed by none or one pair. When a denial stands outside parentheses or brackets that otherwise enclose a whole formula, it is important also to be able to determine what the next main operator is inside the main brackets or parentheses.

In English there are many ways special words and punctuation are used to show which operator is doing the main work. "Either-or" helps punctuate disjunctions; "neither-nor" punctuates denied disjunctions; "both-and" can help group components of a conjunction. Commas are often used to show what parts are most closely grouped together. For now we shall simply practice a few exercises. Chapter 9 will discuss this matter further.

△▼ EXERCISE 6-C

For the following formalized statements determine what the main operator is. If the main operator is a denial, –, then determine what the next main operator is as well.

▶ 1. $(A \lor B) \supset (C \,\&\, D)$

  2. $A \,\&\, (B \supset C)$

▶ 3. $A \lor [(B \,\&\, C) \supset D]$

▶ 4. $-(A \,\&\, B) \lor (C \,\&\, D)$

  5. $-A \supset (B \,\&\, C)$

▶ 6. $-[(A \supset -B) \lor C]$

  7. $-A \lor -(B \,\&\, C)$

▶ 8. $-[A \supset (B \lor C)]$

  9. $A \supset (-B \,\&\, C)$

  10. $-(A \,\&\, B) \supset C$

△▼ EXERCISE 6-D

Use letters and symbols to represent the following statements. Then identify the main operator of the complex statement. If the main operator is denial, go on to identify the next main operator in the representation. Sometimes there will be more than one possible interpretation of what the English means. You will have to make a choice in order to decide exactly what you think the main operator is. Use parentheses, brackets, and/or braces to show exactly how the operators are working.

  1. If Tom really wants to meet Sally, then he will do something crazy, and he really wants to meet Sally.

▶ 2. Paul and Don read the news and immediately decided to join either the Navy or the Marines.

  3. If there is life on other planets, then either it is too primitive to try to communicate with us or it is too advanced for us to understand what it is saying.

▶ 4. If neither Ruth nor Susan makes the team, then I will be surprised.

  5. If it rains this week, and it won't, the harvest will be saved. [Explain how the following sentence differs:] Only if it rains this week, and it won't, will the harvest be saved.

▶ 6. Either Smith or Jones and Paulsen will be the candidates for mayor.

  7. Your instructor may draw further assignments from Appendix A.

△▼ EXERCISE 6-E

Write out the denial of the following sentences.

▶ 1. John plays tennis.

  2. Mary is a physician.

▶ 3. It is easy to understand denials.

  4. The piano is a percussion instrument.

▸ 5. The stablemaster stole the horse.

6. The slave boy knew the Pythagorean Theorem.

6.5 Equivalences for Complex Denials

Denials can create many difficulties in complex statements. Students must be very careful not to think that statement-logic symbols will work the way mathematical symbols do. The denial symbol (–) is not at all like the symbol for subtraction and negative numbers in mathematics. For example, in math you can turn –(3 + 5) into –3 + –5. In statement logic, however, you can never turn a statement like –(A & B) into –A & –B. The logical relationships change when denial is applied to a conjunction.

Still, it is useful to be able to take a statement that has denial as its main operator and write in its place an equivalent statement in which denial is no longer the main operator. On the basis of your understanding of the truth value rules for our symbols, you will be able to see how the logical relationships change when a denial is applied to conjunctions, disjunctions, and conditionals.

The denial of a conjunction is equivalent to a disjunction which joins the denial of each component of the original conjunction. The basic idea is that a conjunction is true only when both components of the conjunction are true. If one or the other or both components are false, then the conjunction is also false. This gives us the following equivalence for denial of conjunctions.

_ ▲

Equivalence for Denial of a Conjunction: –(A & B) is equivalent to –A ∨ –B.

The denial of a disjunction is equivalent to a conjunction which joins the denial of each component of the original conjunction. The basic idea is that since disjunction uses the inclusive sense of "or," a disjunction is false only when both components of the disjunction are also false. So in order to deny a disjunction it is necessary that both of its components be denied. This gives us the following rule for denial of disjunctions.

_ ▲

Equivalence for Denial of Disjunctions: –(A ∨ B) is equivalent to –A & –B.

The preceding two equivalences are known as De Morgan's equivalences. De Morgan was a logician who lived 1806–1871. It is important that you thoroughly learn these equivalences and overcome the temptation to work with logical formulas as though they were mathematical formulas.

One other rule can be helpful. We have learned that a conditional statement will be false if and only if the antecedent ("if" component) is true while the consequent ("then" component) is false. This gives us the following equivalence for conditionals.

___ ▲ _____

Equivalence for Denial of Conditionals: $-(A \supset B)$ is equivalent to $A \,\&\, -B$.

_____

It is also worth remembering that we have seen a similarity between conditionals and disjunctions. We have already learned the following equivalence.

___ ▲ _____

Equivalence Between Conditionals and Disjunctions: $(A \supset B)$ is equivalent to $-A \lor B$.

_____

△▼ EXERCISE 6-F

For each of the following statements, indicate which of the given alternatives is equivalent to the original denied statement. It may help you to represent the statements in statement-logic symbols. Remember that a denial definitely changes the truth value of the statement it is denying. A denial always changes a true statement to false and a false statement to true. In some of the following choices there are not only exact equivalents to the original denied statement, there are also some statements which only partially capture what is happening in the original denied statement. Such statements are tempting but are not true equivalents to the originally denied statement. In the following, find *exact* equivalents of the denied statement. The statements are given mostly in English, but parentheses are sometimes used to make it clear that denial is the main operator in the first sentence. $-(A \text{ or } B)$

▶ 1. It is not the case that (Harold lives in Indiana or Elizabeth lives in Indiana).

   a. Harold does not live in Indiana but Elizabeth does.
   b. Both Harold and Elizabeth live in Indiana.
   c. Harold does not live in Indiana and neither does Elizabeth.
   d. Harold lives in Indiana and Elizabeth does not.

▶ 2. It is not the case that Harold and Elizabeth both live in Florida. $-(A \,\&\, B)$

   a. Either Harold does not live in Florida or Elizabeth does not.
   b. Harold lives in Florida and so does Elizabeth.
   c. Harold does not live in Florida and neither does Elizabeth.
   d. Harold lives in Florida and Elizabeth does not.

$\lnot (H \& F)$

3. It is not the case that Sue hunts and fishes.

    a. Sue does not hunt and does not fish.
    b. Either Sue does not hunt or she does not fish.
    c. If Sue does not hunt, then she fishes.
    d. Sue hunts and does not fish. $\lnot (H \supset I)$

4. It is not the case that if Harold lives in Florida, then Elizabeth lives in Indiana.

    a. Harold lives in Florida and Elizabeth lives in Indiana.
    b. Harold does not live in Florida but Elizabeth does.
    c. Harold does not live in Florida and Elizabeth lives in Indiana.
    d. Harold lives in Florida and Elizabeth does not live in Indiana.

▶ 5. It is not the case that if Tom pitches, then the team wins.

    a. Tom pitches and the team does not win. $\lnot (T \supset W)$
    b. Tom does not pitch and the team does not win.
    c. If Tom does not pitch, then the team does not win.
    d. If Tom pitches, then the team does not win.

▶ 6. It is not the case that all work and no play makes Jack a dull boy.

(This exercise cannot be handled with our rule for denial of an "and" sentence. Note carefully that there are not two separate statements here which could each be treated separately from the other. So we cannot use our statement-logic insights. Still, you can try to find an equivalent among the following alternatives. Ask yourself which of the following statements captures the meaning of the original.)

    a. All work and some play makes Jack a dull boy.
    b. Some work and some play makes Jack a dull boy.
    c. All work and no play does not make Jack a dull boy.
    d. Some work or some play makes Jack a dull boy.

$\lnot (W \& \lnot P) \supset D$

$.7$

Statement Logic and the Table Method

Our study of statement logic so far has enabled us to focus on some of the main ways in which simple statements are modified and joined by the logical operators into more complex statements. There are many things we can do with our statement logic, but in this brief study we shall now focus on testing given premises and conclusions for validity. Testing for validity involves an exhaustive search for counterexamples. A **counterexample** is a case in which you show all the initial premise statements can be imagined to be true while at the same time at least one ultimate conclusion statement can be imagined to be false. If we find a counterexample, the relationship between the initial premises and the ultimate conclusion is invalid. If, after a complete search, we fail to find one, the relationship is valid.

— ▲ _____

Valid Deductive Inference: An inference in which the relation between the premise(s) and the conclusion(s) is such that it is *impossible* to imagine any conclusion false while imagining at the same time all the premise(s) to be true.

117

Invalid Inference: An inference in which it remains possible to imagine a way for the conclusion to be false while imagining all the premise(s) to be true.

Counterexample: An imaginable situation in which the premise(s) all turn out to be true while the conclusion turns out to be false.

7.1 The Table Method

Part 1 of the book explained how most inquiries involve both interrogative steps and deductive logical inference steps. Deductive logic, however, is a special type of inquiry in which only initial premises and logical inference steps are used in the attempt to establish the ultimate conclusion. No interrogative steps are taken.

Nevertheless, because deductive logic is a special type of inquiry, the table method—introduced in Chapter 2 as the bookkeeping method for inquiry—can easily be applied to deductive logic. (Other approaches can be taken, but none of the others is as clearly related to inquiry in general as is the table method.)

As the table method for deductive statement logic is described, keep in mind that it is a special case of the interrogative table method explained in Chapter 2. Use of the table method will make it easy for us later to incorporate deductive "thought experiments" into interrogative inquiries generally. (Note that in this chapter we will usually speak of "premises" rather than "initial premises" and of "conclusions" instead of "ultimate conclusions.")

Consider first a simple example:

p1. $(A \lor B)$

p2. $-A$

c1. B

Here is how we study the relationship between the premises and the conclusion in a table: We put the premises (prem) on the left side of the table and the conclusion on the right side.

Premises and Deductive Inferences	Conclusion
1. $A \lor B$ (prem) 2. $-A$ (prem)	B

Then we try systematically to check all the ways the premises can be true, while looking for a way for the conclusion to be false. Because $(A \lor B)$ presents us with two possibilities as to which one is true, we split the premise side into two paths. As you learned in Chapter 2 (Section 2.4), whenever we find a path that contains both a statement and a denial of that same statement, it will not provide us with a counterexample in which all the lines in the path can together be imagined to be true. Also, whenever we run into the truth of the conclusion as we develop a path, we know that that means we cannot imagine the conclusion false while the premises are in this way imagined true, so we again end that path. It will not produce a counterexample. Here is how our argument looks:

Premises and Deductive Inferences	Conclusion
1. $A \lor B$ (prem)	B
2. $-A$ (prem)	
3. A | B (from 1)	
x | (Entire table closes; there is a bridge between the open paths.)	

The line of thought that leads to A in line 3 is closed because it conflicts with line 2, which told us that $-A$ is the case. (We put an x at the bottom of a closed path to show that it is closed.) The only open path on the left side leads to B in line 3, but this is exactly the same as the ultimate conclusion on the right side. Therefore, as you learned in Chapter 2 (Section 2.4), the table is entirely closed. The two paths on the left side showed the only two possibilities we can imagine under which both premises could be true. Because neither possibility enables us to imagine the conclusion false while the premises are all imagined true, we have shown that the relationship between premises and conclusion is valid.

Here is another example:

Premises and Deductive Inferences	Conclusion
1. $A \lor B$ (prem)	B
2. A (prem)	
3. A | B (from 1)	
(Entire table does not close; there is not a bridge between all the open paths.)	

In this case the path that leads to B in line 3 still produces a bridge to the ultimate conclusion, but the path that leads to A in line 3 is also open. This path does not produce a bridge to the ultimate conclusion, enabling us to imagine a counterexample. Let A be true and let B be false. The first premise ($A \lor B$) will be true, and the second premise A will be true, but the conclusion B will be false. This is the counterexample, which shows the relationship between premises and conclusion to be invalid.

These first two examples were simple, but they illustrate how the table method works. Now we shall learn rules enabling us to handle very complicated statement-logic problems. The basic idea is that in the development of the table we are going to take apart our premises into simpler units. (For now our conclusions are already taken apart. In the next chapter you will learn how to deal with complex conclusions.) Once a premise is taken apart, we will put a check mark by it. This is so we know we are on the way to trying every possible counterexample.

Before we learn the rules we need to agree on some terminology. By *table* we mean the whole construction consisting of the premise information and left-side logical inferences on the left side and the conclusion information and right-side logical inferences on the right side.

By *path* we mean a series of statements that always begins on the first line of the table and works down toward the bottom of the table. On the left (premise) side we always begin with a single path consisting of all the premise statements one after the other. Some rules will require you to split this left side into two paths. Each path always begins at the top with the first line and then follows down, with one path going to the left and the other to the right. The rules may require that these paths also be split, so often several paths can be running down the left side at the same time. The most important thing to remember is that *every path begins at the top*. Thus, the initial premises all belong to every path. Similar considerations apply to the right (conclusion) side of our tables, except that when we have more than one conclusion statement, we immediately begin on line 1 of our table with a separate path for each conclusion statement.

A *subtable* is made up of the pairing of open paths from the left (premise) side and right (conclusion) side of our tables. For a complete analysis each open path on the right side must be paired in a subtable with every open path on the left side. Our tests for validity and invalidity will require that we deal with each subtable in turn. This will be explained in detail when we come to those tests.

▲

Table: The whole construction consisting of the premise information and left-side logical inferences on the left side and the conclusion information and right-side logical inferences on the right side.

Path: A series of statements that *always begins on the first line of the table* and works down toward the bottom. There can be any number of paths on either side of the table.

Subtable: The pairing of open paths from the left (premise) side and right (conclusion) side of a table. For a complete analysis each open path on the right side must be paired in a subtable with every open path on the left.

The rules for table analysis of deductive logical inferences are as follows:

1. **Rule for Initial Premises:** Put each initial premise on a separate line on the left side of the table.

2. **Rule for Ultimate Conclusion:** Put each conclusion in a separate path on the first line on the right side of the table. (In this chapter we will always have only one simple conclusion.)

3. **Rule for Conjunctions:** Anytime a conjunction appears with & as the main operator on a full line on the left side of a table, put each of the components on a separate line in the open path (or paths) underneath the conjunction. Put a check mark by this conjunction.

Table illustration for conjunction rule:

Premises and Deductive Inferences			Conclusion
1. √ (A ∨ B) & C		(prem)	. . . . $A \vee (B \ \& \ C)$
2.		(prem)	
3. A ∨ B		(from 1 by 3)	
4. C		(from 1 by 3)	

The rationale for this rule is that & means that when the full conjunction line is taken to be true, the components on either side of the & must also be true. So lines 3 and 4 in the illustration will be true because we are imagining the premises to be true. Notice carefully that in line 1 & is the main operator. If ∨ had been the main operator, we would not be able to use this rule for &. Now that the premise line 1 has had its information spelled out, we put a check mark by it to show that we have no need to return to it and to prepare the way for testing for invalidity. Lines 3 and 4 are justified by noting in parentheses that they are based on line 1 using Rule 3.

For the most part, the statement-logic table rules we are currently studying are definitory rules. The check-mark procedure is a partial exception to this. Soon we will learn how to use our tables to test for invalidity. In that test the check-mark procedure plays an important definitory role.

But we also advise that a check mark on a line indicates we need not apply a rule to that line ever again. Strictly speaking, if one were to disregard that advice, there would be no violation of the rules of correct deductive reasoning. Table rules can be applied to the same line over and over without a definitory mistake being made. It is, however, terrible *strategy*, if, in statement logic, we work on a line more than once. The check-mark procedure is designed to assure that we work on a line only once. This is a good example of a strategic rule. In later chapters of the book we shall turn our entire focus toward strategic rules of reasoning.

4. **Rule for Disjunctions:** Anytime a disjunction appears with ∨ as the main operator on a full line on the left side of a table, put each of its components on the same line in the open path (or paths) underneath the disjunction. Separate these components into two paths. Put a check mark by the disjunction.

Table illustration for disjunction rule:

Premises and Deductive Inferences				Conclusion
1. √ (A & B) ∨ C (prem)				. . . .
2. . . . . (prem)				
3. (A & B) C (from 1 by 4)				
4.				

The rationale for this rule is that ∨ means that when the full disjunction line is imagined to be true, one or the other or both components on either side of the ∨ must be true. So line 3 in the illustration will be true in one path or the other, or possibly both, because we are taking the premises to be true. Our search for counterexamples will require that we follow both possible lines of thought in the two paths to see whether they close. Notice carefully that in line 1 ∨ is the main operator. If & had been the main operator, we would not be able to use this rule for ∨. Line 3 is justified by noting in parentheses that it is based on line 1 using Rule 4.

5. **Rule for Conditionals:** Anytime a conditional appears with ⊃ as the main operator on a full line on the left side of a table, put the denial of its left component on the same line with the right component in the open path (or paths) underneath the conditional. Separate these components into two paths. Put a check mark by the conditional.

Table illustration for conditional rule:

Premises and Deductive Inferences				Conclusion
1. √ (A & B) ⊃ C (prem)				. . . .
2. . . . . (prem)				
3. –(A & B) C (from 1 by 5)				
4.				

The rationale for this rule is that in statement logic we can treat ⊃ as a special kind of disjunction so that A ⊃ B is equivalent to –A ∨ B. Application of Rule 4 will then give the rule for conditionals. So line 3 in the table will be true in one path or the other, or possibly both, because we are taking the premises to be true. Our search for counterexamples will require that we follow both possible lines of thought in the two paths to see whether they close. Notice carefully that in line 1 ⊃ is the main operator. If & had been the main operator, we would not be able to use this rule for ⊃. Line 3 is justified by noting in parentheses that it is based on line 1 using Rule 5.

6. **Rule for Statements in Which Denial Is the Main Operator:** Anytime a denial appears with – as the main operator on a full line in a table, determine the next main operator. This will make it possible to determine the appropriate equivalent of the denial. Put the appropriate equivalent in the open path (or paths) underneath the denial. Put a check mark by the denial. The appropriate equivalents of denied statements are as follows:

Double Denial: Anytime a double-denied statement appears with – as the main and next main operators on a full line on the left side of a table, the appropriate equivalent will be the part that follows the --.

Table illustration for double denials:

Premises and Deductive Inferences			Conclusion
1. √	--(A & B)	(prem)	. . . .
2.	. . . .	(prem)	
3.	A & B	(from 1 by 6)	

The rationale for this equivalence is that -- reverses the truth value of the line twice. Thus, if the double-denied statement is taken to be true, then the statement that has been doubly denied must also be true. So line 3 in the illustration will be true because we are taking the premises to be true.

Denied Conjunctions: Anytime a denied conjunction appears with – as the main operator covering & as the next main operator on a full line in a table, the appropriate equivalent can be written by joining denials of each of the components of the original & with ∨.

Table illustration for denied conjunctions:

Premises and Deductive Inferences			Conclusion
1. √	-[(A ∨ B) & C]	(prem)	. . . .
2.	. . . .	(prem)	
3.	-(A ∨ B) ∨ -C	(from 1 by 6)	

The rationale for this rule is that -(&) means that when the full denied conjunction line is taken to be true, at least one of the components on either side of the & must be false. So line 3 in the illustration will be true because we are taking the premise to be true.

Denied Disjunctions: Anytime a denied disjunction appears with – as the main operator covering ∨ as the next main operator on a full line in a table, the appropriate equivalent can be written by joining denials of each of the components of the original ∨ with &.

Table illustration for denied disjunctions:

Premises and Deductive Inferences			Conclusion
1. √	–[(A ⊃ B) ∨ C]	(prem)	. . . .
2.	. . . .	(prem)	
3.	–(A ⊃ B) & –C	(from 1 by 6)	

The rationale for this rule is that –(∨) means that when the full denied disjunction line is taken to be true, the components on either side of the ∨ must both be false. So line 3 in the illustration will be true because we are taking the premises to be true.

Denied Conditionals: Anytime a denied conditional appears with – as the main operator covering ⊃ as the next main operator on a full line in a table, the appropriate equivalent can be written by joining the left component of the original ⊃ with the denial of its right component by means of &.

Table illustration for denied conditionals:

Premises and Deductive Inferences			Conclusion
1. √	–[(A ∨ B) ⊃ C]	(prem)	. . . .
2.	. . . .	(prem)	
3.	(A ∨ B) & –C	(from 1 by 6)	

The rationale for this rule is that in statement logic we treat ⊃ as a special kind of disjunction so that A ⊃ B is equivalent to –A ∨ B. (See the discussion of "if-then" in Chapter 6.) Application of the equivalence for denied disjunction and for double denial will then give this equivalence. So line 3 in the illustration will be true because we are taking the premises to be true.

(Important note about Table Rules 3, 4, and 5, and the equivalences in Table Rule 6: Rules 3, 4, and 5 can *only* be applied to full lines in paths on the left side of the table. The equivalences in Rule 6 are less restricted. We will learn in the next chapter that they can be used in exactly the same way on the right [conclusion] side of our tables. Furthermore, they can also be safely applied to portions of lines as well as to full lines. This latter application is, however, not necessary in our method, and we recommend that students apply the insights of Rule 6 *only* to full lines. In this way you will not be tempted to apply Rules 3, 4, and 5 to parts of lines.)

7. **Rule for Path Closure by Contradiction:** Anytime a statement and its denial both appear as separate full lines in a path in the table, close its path by writing "x" underneath it.

Table illustration for path closure by contradiction:

Premises and Deductive Inferences	Conclusion
1. . . . . (prem)	. . . .
2. . . . . (prem)	
3. $A \vee B$ (from . . .)	
4. . . . . (from . . .)	
5. $-(A \vee B)$ (from . . .)	
x (from 3 & 5 by 7)	

The rationale for this rule is that we are trying to make every line on the left side of the table be true, starting from the premises. If a line of thought (a path in a table) leads simultaneously to a statement and its denial, one or the other line must be false. This line of thought will not produce a counterexample, because not all the lines in the path can be imagined true at the same time. Note carefully that the relevant line and its denial must be full lines.

8. **Rule for Closure of Entire Table by Left-to-Right Bridges:** Each possible pairing of an open path on the left (premise) side of a table with an open path on the right (conclusion) side constitutes a **subtable.** Whenever every subtable in the table contains matching full statement lines in the two open paths constituting the subtable, the entire table is closed because there is a bridge from every open path on the left to every open path on the right. The relationship between premises and conclusion is valid.

Simple illustration of table closure by left-to-right bridge:

Premises and Deductive Inferences	Conclusion
1. . . . . (prem)	6. $A \vee B$
2. . . . . (prem)	
3. D (from . . .)	
4. . . . . (from . . .)	
5. $A \vee B$ (from . . .)	

Entire table is closed by bridge from line 5 to line 6.

The rationale for this rule is that we are trying to find a line of thought (a path through a table) on the left side that allows the premises to remain true while the conclusion on the right side could still be imagined to be false. If a path forces the conclusion to be true, then it will not produce a counterexample to show invalidity. Note carefully that the line on the left side must be a full line that is identical to the full conclusion line. If every open path on the left contains such a bridge to every open path on the right, then no counterexample can be found and the relationship between premises and conclusion is valid.

7.2   Using Tables to Test for Validity and Invalidity

To test a relation of premises and conclusions for validity, begin with Table Rules 1 and 2. Then apply the other rules to unchecked lines of open paths until the table is finished. A table is finished when all of its paths are closed, or when the entire table is closed, or when the only unchecked lines in subtables lacking bridges are statement letters and denials of statement letters. If all paths on the left side in the finished table are closed, i.e., have "x" at the bottom (Rule 7), or, if the entire table is closed (Rule 8), then the relationship of premises to conclusion is valid. Otherwise the finished table will produce a counterexample showing the relationship of premises to conclusion to be invalid.

Constructing a Counterexample

If the table is finished and not entirely closed, the inference is invalid. It will be possible to find a subtable that does not contain a bridge from its open path on the left to its open path on the right. The subtable consisting of two open paths which lack a bridge shows us how to construct the counterexample showing invalidity: go backwards through the open path on the left side, treating each full line in the path as true. This procedure will show in what way the premises can be made true without forcing the conclusion line in the open path on the right side to be true. The fact that the paths are open means that we will not be forced to try to make a line and its denial both true, and the lack of a bridge will mean that we will not run into the truth of the conclusion. This procedure shows us a way to imagine all the premises to be true at the same time that we are free to imagine the conclusion to be false. This produces the counterexample, which shows that the relation between the premises and the conclusion is invalid.

▲

Finished Tables: A table is finished when all of its paths are closed, or when the entire table is closed, or when the only unchecked lines in subtables lacking bridges are statement letters and denials of statement letters.

Testing for Validity and Invalidity: If all paths on the left side in a finished table are closed, i.e., have "x" at the bottom (Table Rule 7), or if the entire table is closed (Table Rule 8), then the relationship of premises to conclusion is valid. Otherwise the finished table will produce a *counterexample* showing the relationship of premises to conclusion to be invalid.

Inconsistent Premises

Notice that if all the paths on the left side can be closed by Table Rule 7, then there is no way whatsoever to imagine all of the premises true at the same time. No counterexample can be found, and the relationship between premises and conclusion is technically valid. In this case, however, the problem is that the premises are never able all to be imagined true at the same time. Logicians say that the premises are *inconsistent* with each other.

If we want to test whether a set of premises is inconsistent, the method is to use only the first seven table rules. If we can produce a finished table in which every left-side path has been closed by Rule 7, then we know there are inconsistent premises. We must omit use of Rule 8 during this test, because the presence of inconsistent premises might be masked by our finding bridges in open paths.

An argument beginning with inconsistent premises is of little use in rational inquiry. Such an argument can, however, deceive the unwary. In Part 3 we shall discuss strategic advice for dealing with inconsistent premises. Usually our goal will be to eliminate the inconsistency from the premises by changing the information on which we are relying.

Examples

Example One: A Valid Relationship

Premises and Deductive Inferences					Conclusion	
1. √	$P \supset Q$			(prem)	9.	Q
2. √	$S \vee P$			(prem)		
3. √	$-S \& T$			(prem)		
4.	$-S$			(from 3 by 3)		
5.	T			(from 3 by 3)		
6.	S		P	(from 2 by 4)		
7.	x				(from 4 & 6 by 7)	
8.		$-P$	Q		(from 1 by 5)	
		x			(from 6 & 8 by 7)	
				Bridge from line 8 to line 9.		

This table is finished and it shows a valid relation between premises and conclusion, because the entire table is closed. Rule 8 had to be used to close the entire table; Rule 7 by itself could not close all the paths. (You should check for yourself that the subtable containing the bridge cannot result in a Rule 7 closure.) No counterexample can be constructed, and the premises are not inconsistent.

Example Two: An Invalid Relationship

Premises and Deductive Inferences				Conclusion	
1. √	$P \supset Q$		(prem)	8.	Q
2. √	$S \vee P$		(prem)		
3. √	$S \& T$		(prem)		
4.	S		(from 3 by 3)		
5.	T		(from 3 by 3)		
6.	S	P	(from 2 by 4)		
7. −P	Q	−P	Q	(from 1 by 5)	
		x		(from 6 & 7 by 7)	
No Bridge	Bridge		Bridge from line 7 to line 8		

(handwritten left margin: Counter example; S; T; ¬P; ¬Q; √; not agreeing to a bridge)

In this example the left-most path is open and has no bridge in it, but the table is finished. It is finished because the only unchecked lines in the subtable which lacks a bridge are statement letters and denials of statement letters. This subtable will enable us to construct the counterexample we need to show that the relation between premises and conclusion is invalid. Let −P, S, and T all be true. Premise 3 will be true because (S & T) is true whenever both S and T are true. Premise 2 will be true because ($S \vee P$) will be true whenever at least one component is true. Premise 1 will be true because whenever the antecedent of a conditional (in this case P) is false, then the conditional is considered to be true. (Remember what we said about the truth of the example, "If your foot touches the line, you are out of bounds." If your foot does not touch the line, the rule about boundaries can still be considered true.) So, premises 1, 2, and 3 can all be imagined to be true simply by imagining −P, S, and T all to be true.

Does this prevent us from imagining the conclusion Q to be false? No, nothing in the premises prevents us from imagining Q to be false. Therefore, we have found a way to imagine the premises all together true and the conclusion false. We have a counterexample showing the relationship to be invalid.

Example Three: A Case of Inconsistent Premises

Premises and Deductive Inferences		Conclusion	
1. $P \supset (Q \supset R)$	(prem)	5.	$Q \supset R$
2. $S \vee P$	(prem)		
3. −($S \vee P$)	(prem)		
4. x	(from 2 & 3 by 7)		

(handwritten at bottom: Automatically valid)

The only path on the left side certainly closed quickly! The reason it did is that premises 2 and 3 cannot possibly both be imagined true at the same time. Premise 3 is simply the denial of premise 2. Because all paths are closed, there are no subtables in which we need to find a bridge. We can say that the relation between premises and conclusion is valid. We note, however, that we closed all the left-side paths (there was just one) using only Table Rule 7. Even in a very complicated table, this would be the clear indication that the premises are inconsistent. In an important inquiry it would be necessary to go back and try to figure out which of the premises should be changed or eliminated.

Example Four: Another Valid Relationship

Premises and Deductive Inferences				Conclusion
1. $\checkmark$	$(G \lor H) \supset (M \,\&\, K)$	(prem)		8. $\qquad$ M
2.	G	(prem)		
3. $\checkmark$	$-(G \lor H)$ $\mid$	$\checkmark$	$M \,\&\, K$	(from 1 by 5)
4a.	$-G \,\&\, -H$	4b. M	(4b from 3 by 3)	(4a from 3 by 6)
5a.	$-G$	5b. K	(5b from 3 by 3)	(5a from 4a by 3)
6a.	$-H$	Bridge from line 4b to line 8		(6a from 4a by 3)
7a.	x			(7a from 2 & 5a by 7)

The table above is finished and entirely closed. The relationship is valid. Notice that we could not have closed the path with M and K in it by using Table Rule 7. This indicates that we are not dealing with inconsistent premises. This path provides a way for us to show that all the premises can be true at the same time. Let K, M, and G be true. Premise 2 is clearly true. The antecedent of premise 1 is true because $(G \lor H)$ is true. The consequent $(M \,\&\, K)$ also is true, so premise 1 can be imagined to be true. It turns out, however, that in imagining all the premises to be true, we have been forced to imagine the conclusion, M, also to be true. We cannot find a counterexample to prove invalidity.

△▼ EXERCISE 7-A

1. For the following formalized statements determine what the main operator is. If the main operator is a denial, –, then determine what the next main operator is as well. (These are the same ones you studied in Chapter 6, Exercise 6-C in Section 6.4, so you may already have this part of the exercise finished.)

▸ a. $(A \lor B) \supset (C \,\&\, D)$

  b. $A \,\&\, (B \supset C)$

▸ c. $A \lor [(B \,\&\, C) \supset D]$

▸ d. $-(A \,\&\, B) \lor (C \,\&\, D)$

  e. $-A \supset (B \,\&\, C)$

▸ f. $-[(A \supset -B) \lor C]$

  g. $-A \lor -(B \,\&\, C)$

▸ h. $-[A \supset (B \lor C)]$

  i. $A \supset (-B \,\&\, C)$

  j. $-(A \,\&\, B) \supset C$

▶ 2. Review your work in section 1 of the exercise and decide which of the Table Rules 3 through 6 can be applied to each formalized statement. *One and only one rule will be appropriate, and this is determined entirely by the main operator.* It is essential that you learn this simple part of statement logic. There is no need to guess which of the Rules 3 through 6 to use on a complex statement; the main operator tells you which is the only rule possible.

▶ 3. Using what you discovered in sections 1 and 2 of the exercise, construct a table for each complex statement, showing what happens when the appropriate rule is applied to the statement.

▶ 4. Tell which of the tables you constructed in section 3 still contain unchecked lines to which one of the Table Rules 3 through 6 could be applied. Go on to apply the rules to lines in the tables until it is no longer possible to apply any of them.

△▼ EXERCISE 7-B

Use the techniques of table analysis to determine whether there is a valid connection between the premises and the conclusion given in the following tables. Check also for inconsistent premises.

▶ **Table 1.**

Premises and Deductive Inferences	Conclusion
1. $P \supset -Q$ (prem) 2. $-Q \supset -R$ (prem) 3. R (prem)	4. $-P$

▶ **Table 2.**

Premises and Deductive Inferences	Conclusion
1. $P \supset -Q$ (prem) 2. $-Q \supset -R$ (prem) 3. $-R$ (prem)	4. $-P$

Table 3.

Premises and Deductive Inferences	Conclusion
1. $P \supset R$ (prem) 2. $R \supset [-P \lor (S \supset T)]$ (prem) 3. $P \& S$ (prem)	4. $S \supset T$

▶ **Table 4.**

Premises and Deductive Inferences	Conclusion
1. $P \supset R$ (prem) 2. $P \supset (Q \& -R)$ (prem) 3. $P \& S$ (prem)	4. $S \supset T$

7.3   Strategic Rules in Statement Logic

The table rules that say we should put check marks on lines to which we have applied a rule have helped us formulate a procedure for recognizing invalidity. In this role, checking is part of the definitory rules of statement logic. Remember that a definitory rule tells us how to play the game correctly. You cannot correctly test for invalidity without observing the checking part of the procedure. This is because the checking of lines puts us in a position to know when a table has been finished.

But checking also enables us to formulate an important strategic rule. Remember that strategic rules tell us how to play a game well. Checking enables us to construct our tables in an efficient way. The strategic Checking Rule can be formulated as follows: *Never apply Table Rules 3 through 6 to a line that has already been checked.*

If you break this rule, you are not committing a sin against deductive logic. You are not breaking any definitory rules. But you do risk making a fool of yourself by working inefficiently and perhaps ineffectively. If you break this strategic rule, you are making unnecessary work for yourself and you are making your tables longer and more complicated than they need to be.

The reason for this will be clear to you if you look carefully at Table Rules 3 through 5. Each of these rules effectively breaks a complex line down into simpler parts. The rules of table construction work in such a way that the entire complex line is completely dealt with in terms of its simpler parts. To go back to the complex line later on and once again break it down would be simply to repeat what had already been accomplished. Similarly, Rule 6 provides equivalent lines to write in place of lines that have denial as the main operator. The equivalent line contains all the information available in the original line, so again there is no point in going back and once again working on the denied line.

To go back and work again on a checked line will not introduce errors into the reasoning, but it *will* mean that the inquirer is going back over ground that has already been covered. This is simply a waste of time. Thus, this strategic checking rule tells us not so much how to play the game of statement logic correctly, but how to play it efficiently.

This is a simple but important illustration of the difference between definitory and strategic rules for inquiry. We are currently concentrating on the definitory rules, but it is equally important that we allow time for studying strategic rules.

Following, along with our Checking Rule, are a few other strategic rules for statement logic. (The second rule is not strictly strategic, but it *is* useful.)

Checking Rule (strategic): Never apply Table Rules 3 through 6 to a line that has already been checked.

Recognize that there will be *only one rule* relevant to any given complex line anywhere in the table in any path. If you understand this, you will get in the habit of identifying the main operator in the line and then finding the only rule that can be applied to it.

Work with nonbranching lines first. In most cases, when you have a choice, it will be wiser first to apply the nonbranching Table Rules 3 and 6 first before applying Table Rules 4 and 5, which split the table into multiple paths. This will tend to keep the number of paths from multiplying more than need be.

Give priority to working on complex lines that contain part or all of the conclusion. This approach may more quickly put you in a position to find bridges in subtables.

As paths multiply look for complex lines containing elements which may permit application of Table Rule 7 to close some of the paths.

7.4   Some Simple Argument Patterns

Several patterns of inference appear regularly in everyday reasoning. Some are deductively valid and others tempt us to think they are valid, but they are not. We are now in a position to study these through use of the table method. Because they are so simple, they can be made part of another exercise to give you practice in using the method.

△▼ EXERCISE 7-C

Use the table method to determine which of the following argument patterns are valid. (You may find it useful to learn the traditional names for these patterns, given on the right.)

1. $P \supset Q$ ← $-P \vee Q$ Modus Ponens
   P
   Therefore, Q

2. $P \supset Q$ Affirming the Consequent
   Q
   Therefore, P

   Counter example $Q \, \& -P$

3. $P \supset Q$ Denying the Antecedent
   $-P$
  Therefore, $-Q$

4. $P \supset Q$ Modus Tollens
   $-Q$
  Therefore, $-P$

5. $P \lor Q$ Disjunctive Syllogism
   $-P$
  Therefore, Q

6. $P \lor Q$ (No name; the problem involves the
   P temptation to assume an exclusive "or.")
  Therefore, $-Q$

In the preceding exercise you should have found that items 1, 4, and 5 were valid. It is worth learning these patterns, and in Chapter 9 we will incorporate them into our interrogative tables. Items 2, 3, and 6 are patterns which people are often tempted to follow, but which are invalid. You will want to learn to avoid them.

△▼ EXERCISE 7-D

▶ The following premises and conclusion give you some more opportunities to practice the table method.

1. $[(A \lor -B) \& C] \supset D$
   $A \& C$
  Therefore, D

2. $-(A \& B)$
   B
  Therefore, $-A$

3. $-(A \lor B) \lor (C \& D)$
   $-C$
  Therefore, $-B$

4. $A \supset [B \lor (C \& D)]$
   $A \& -B$
  Therefore, C

5. $-A \supset [(-B \& -C) \lor -(-D \lor B)]$
   B
  Therefore, A

8

Complex Conclusions in Statement Logic

8.1 Rules for Multiple Conclusion Lines

We have made good progress in our study of statement logic, but we have not yet carefully studied what to do when there is more than one conclusion in a table. Table Rule 2 in Chapter 7 already tells us: If there is more than one conclusion, we put all the conclusion statements on the same first line on the right side, but each conclusion statement is put in a separate path. The idea here is that the inquirer is trying to show how there is no way to imagine the conclusion to be false. In order to show this when there is more than one conclusion line, we need to deal with each separate conclusion in a separate path on the right side of the table. If we set the table up in this way, then we will automatically use Table Rule 8 in a way that guarantees that we have checked all possibilities for imagining each separate conclusion to be false.

As paths multiply on the right side of a table as well as on the left side, it can become confusing to check all the subtables made up of pairings of open paths from left and right sides. In the case of multiple conclusion lines, one way to keep things from getting out of hand is to construct a table using only the first conclusion statement. If we find a counterexample, we have shown invalidity. If the table closes (Rule 8), then we go on to construct another table using the next conclusion statement. If we find a counterexample, we have shown invalidity. If the table closes (Rule 8), we go on to the next conclusion statement. Once we have constructed a table for each separate conclusion line and have shown that the tables always close, then we have shown validity.

If we construct separate tables in this way, what we are actually doing is examining what we have called subtables one at a time. Recall that we said a subtable is made up of the pairing of open paths from the left (premise) side and right (conclusion) side of our tables. For a complete analysis each open path on the right side must be paired in a subtable with every open path on the left side. When we construct a separate table for each conclusion line, we pair all open paths on the left with the first conclusion statement. Then, if we do not find invalidity or inconsistency, we pair all paths on the left with the next conclusion statement and so on. In this way we systematically examine all the possible subtables for a counterexample.

△▼ EXERCISE 8-A

1. Write a brief essay explaining how and why Table Rule 2 is different from Table Rule 1.
2. Write a brief essay explaining how Table Rules 2 and 8 are designed in such a way that they require us to check whether any of the conclusion lines may still be imagined false.

8.2 Rules for Complicated Conclusions

Times will occur when a single, complex conclusion statement needs to be taken apart. In such cases what we need are inference rules that allow us to write less complex conclusion statements that must also be able to be imagined false if the original line is to be imagined false. As we saw in Chapter 2 (Section 2.4), the rules we need in working on complicated conclusion statements on the right side of a table are reverse images of the rules we follow on the left. This is because on the left (premise) side of a table, we are trying to preserve truth from premises to later statements, but on the right (conclusion) side of a table, we are trying to preserve the possibility of imagining the conclusion false. We follow this procedure because we are looking for counterexamples that would show invalidity in the relation between the premises (left side) and the conclusions (right side).

Table Rules 1 and 2 on the Right Side

The right-side counterpart of Table Rule 1 has already been given as Table Rule 2. The only thing we note here is that, as already mentioned, when there is more than one conclusion statement, our procedure will be to study conclusion statements thoroughly one at a time. We will first build a table relating to only one of them. If we find a counterexample, we have shown invalidity. If the table completely closes, then we will go on to another of the conclusion statements, and so on. If the tables close in connection with each of all the conclusion statements, then we have shown validity. It does not matter what order we take up the conclusion statements, but it is necessary to deal with only one at a time.

Obviously, having more statements in a conclusion makes it harder to establish validity. This is what we might have expected, because the more we want to claim in our conclusions, the more we will have to expect to work at showing we have a valid argument.

Table Rules 3–5 on the Right Side

Table Rules 3 through 5 are more complicated in the ways in which they operate on the right side. Here you have to remember that they really are reverse images of their left-side counterparts. Because they operate so differently, we will give them slightly different numbers. The counterpart to Rule 3 will be numbered 3r, Rule 4's counterpart will be 4r, and Rule 5's counterpart will be 5r. Discussion of the differences may seem confusing at first, but if we pay careful attention, this part of the study should actually help us fix more clearly in our minds the relationships among our various rules.

Table Rule 3r   Like Table Rule 3, Rule 3r deals with conjunctions. You will recall that a conjunction is a complex statement making the claim that both of its components are true. This made things easy for us on the left (premise) side of a table because on the left side we are trying to preserve truth. If a conjunction is imagined to be true, then it is also necessary for us to imagine that its left component is true and that its right component is true. We could therefore put both components in the same path(s) the conjunction was in.

The fact that a conjunction is making such a claim, however, makes things complicated for us on the right (conclusion) side of a table. On the right side we are trying to imagine that the conjunction line could be false. Because a conjunction makes the claim that both of its components are true, we have a choice when we want to imagine that the conjunction is false: We can imagine that the left component is false, or we can imagine that the right component is false. But this means that, if we need to take apart the conjunction line, we now have to split the right side of our table into two paths. We have to test all the open paths on the left (premise) side not only in relation to one conclusion path, but also in relation to the other. In a moment we will discuss ways of keeping this splitting of the tables from getting out of hand. But first, here is Table Rule 3r:

3r. **Rule for Right-Side Conjunctions:** Anytime a conjunction appears with & as the main operator on a full line on the right side of a table, put each of its components on the same line in the open path (or paths) underneath the conjunction. Separate these components into two paths. Put a check mark by the conjunction.

Table Illustration for Right-Side Conjunctions

Premises and Deductive Inferences	Conclusion
1. . . . . (prem)	5. √ (A ∨ B) & C (conclusion)
2. . . . . (prem)	. . . .
3. . . . . (. . . .)	. . . .
4. . . . . (. . . .)	6. (A ∨ B) │ C (from 5 by 3r)

Table Rules 4r and 5r   The right-side reverse image of Table Rule 3 was the most difficult one we have to deal with. Rule 4 for disjunctions and Rule 5 for conditionals are, as we saw in Chapter 7, similar to each other. Disjunctions and conditionals make "weak" claims in the sense that they do not tell us which component is true but rather that there is a relationship between the truth and falsehood of the simple statements joined disjunctively or conditionally. Because they make rather weak claims, they require split tables on the left (premise) side. On the right (conclusion) side, however, they do not split the table.

Table Rule 4 dealt with disjunction. All a disjunction claims is that one or the other of its components is true. (Maybe both are, but there is no guarantee.) On the left (premise) side we had to split the table, because we did not know which one was true. Each component of the disjunction had to be pursued in its own path. On the right (conclusion) side we are trying to imagine that the disjunction is false. In order to do this we have no choice; we must imagine that both of its components are false. Therefore, we add each component to the same path as the disjunction. All of the elements in a path on the right side are elements that must together be imagined false if the conclusion is to be imagined false. Here, then, is Rule 4r:

4r. **Rule for Right-Side Disjunctions:** Anytime a disjunction appears with ∨ as the main operator on a full line on the right side of a table, put each of its components on a separate line in the open path (or paths) underneath the disjunction. Put a check mark by this disjunction.

Table Illustration for Right-Side Disjunctions

Premises and Deductive Inferences	Conclusion
1. . . . . (prem)	5. √ $(A \& B) \lor C$ (conclusion)
2. . . . . (prem)	. . . .
3. . . . . (. . . .)	6. $A \& B$ (from 5 by 4r)
4. . . . . (. . . .)	7. C (from 5 by 4r)

Rule 5 dealt with conditionals. But the conditional $A \supset B$ is treated in statement logic as equivalent to $-A \lor B$. So application of Rule 4r gives us Rule 5r:

5r. **Rule for Right-Side Conditionals:** Anytime a conditional appears with $\supset$ as the main operator on a full line on the right side of a table, put the denial of its left component and its right component each on a separate line in the open path (or paths) underneath the conditional. Put a check mark by this conditional.

Convert $\supset$ to $\lor$ and deal with it

Table Illustration for Right-Side Conditionals

Premises and Deductive Inferences	Conclusion
1. . . . . (prem)	5. √ $(A \& B) \supset C$ (conclusion)
2. . . . . (prem)	. . . .
3. . . . . (. . . .)	6. $-(A \& B)$ (from 5 by 5r)
4. . . . . (. . . .)	7. C (from 5 by 5r)

This finishes our discussion of the reverse-image versions of our Table Rules 3, 4, and 5 for use on the right (conclusion) side of a table. It remains for us to look a little more closely at how Rules 6, 7, and 8 work in the more complicated situations posed by the right side of a table.

Table Rule 6 on the Right Side

We mentioned in Chapter 7 that Table Rule 6, the rule for denials, operates the same way on both the right and left sides. Rule 6 simply provides equivalences that allow us to substitute statements which do not have denial as the main operator for statements which do. On both the left (premise) and the right (conclusion) sides of our tables we can write an equivalent of a denied statement in the open paths beneath it and check off the denied line. Imagining the equivalent statement false will accomplish the same task as imagining the original denied statement to be false. The equivalences made available in Rule 6 make it possible to transform denied statements into statements to which the other rules may be applied.

Table Illustration for Writing an Equivalent in Place of an Original Denial

Premises and Deductive Inferences	Conclusion
1. . . . . (prem)	4. √ $-(A \supset B)$ (conclusion)
2. . . . . (prem)	. . . .
3. . . . . (. . . .)	5. A & $-B$ (from 4 by 6)

Table Rule 7 on the Right Side

Table Rule 7 (Path Closure by Contradiction) operates the same way on both the right and left sides. Whenever we have a statement and its denial as two separate lines in the same path, we know that it is impossible for all the lines in the path to have the same truth value. On the left side we will not be able to have all the lines in the path be true at the same time; on the right side we will not be able to have all the lines in the path be false at the same time. Therefore, we can close such paths.

Table Rule 8 When the Right Side Has More Than One Path

Table Rule 8 (Closure of Entire Table by Left-to-Right Bridges) involves both the left (premise) side and the right (conclusion) side together. This is the rule that seeks bridges between open paths on the left and right sides. Whenever an open path on the left side has led to a truth that matches a statement we were trying to imagine false in a path on the right side, we know that this particular pair of right and left paths (a subtable) cannot work together to produce a counterexample. *The matching of one of the statements in both a left and right path (a subtable) shows that we cannot hope to keep the left (premise) path statements all together true while imagining the right (conclusion) path statements all together false.* If each subtable made up of the pairing of open paths from the left and right sides has a bridge, then there can be no counterexamples and the relationship between premises and conclusion(s) is valid.

It is very important to understand that we must always systematically check each open right-side path in connection with each open left-side path to have tested for all the possible combinations in which a counterexample might arise. (We can, however, omit any path on the left or the right that has been closed by Table Rule 7—Closure by Contradiction. This is because such a path can never help produce a counterexample.)

Testing for Validity When There Are Multiple Paths on the Right Side

Whenever the right side divides into more than one open path, our usual practice will be to do a complete study of only one of the right-side open paths in connection with all of the left-side open paths, until we either find in it a counterexample or find that every open left-side path has a bridge into the one open right-side path. (You might even think of this as a table containing only one right-side path.) Then, if no counterexamples were found, we can go on to another of the open right-side paths. (Again, you might think of this next step as doing a new table, now with the next right-side path as the only conclusion.) Once again, we will make a complete study of this one path in relation to all the left-side paths. Notice that a left-side path could easily happen to have a bridge to one of the right-side paths but not to another. Notice also that *any* matching of whole lines from the left and the right will suffice to produce a bridge. One line in a given path may help produce a bridge for one subtable but not for another.

If we manage to find bridges from all left-side open paths in connection with every one of the open right-side paths, then we know we have a valid relationship between the initial premise(s) and the ultimate conclusion(s).

One way of summarizing Table Rule 8 and the test for validity discussed in this section is as follows:

1. Remember that we have called any pair of a left-hand open path and a right-hand open path a subtable.

2. An entire table is closed if *every* subtable of this table contains a bridge.

Illustration: Table with a Complex Conclusion   We present the following illustration in a somewhat different form from that used previously. We encourage you to work with the details of your tables in whatever way enables you to present and discuss the material in an orderly fashion.

1. √	(A & B)	(prem)	‖	2. √	(A & –D)		(conclusion)
3. √	–(B ⊃ C)	(prem)					
4. √	D ⊃ C	(prem)					
5.	A	(from 1 by 3)					
6.	B	(from 1 by 3)					
7. √	B & –C	(from 3 by 6)					
8.	B	(from 7 by 3)					
9.	–C	(from 7 by 3)					
10. –D		C (from 4 by 5)	‖	11. A		–D	(from 2 by 3r)
		x (from 9 and 10 by 7)					

Discussion   Notice that we followed the strategy of postponing branching of the paths as long as possible. At line 10, the left side of the table branched as a result of applying Table Rule 5 to line 4. The right path was closed immediately by Rule 7, because both *C* and –*C* are contained in the same path. Meanwhile, the conclusion (line 2), which had been left alone up to this point, now has Rule 3r applied to it, producing line 11. This causes the table to branch into two paths on the right side. This results in two subtables being formed: The remaining open path on the left side must be paired with *each path* on the right. (Fortunately, the other path on the left side has closed, otherwise there would be a total of four subtables to consider.) In order to check for validity, we must find a bridge in both of these subtables. We examine first the subtable formed by pairing the only open path on the left side with the left path on the right side. Line 5 on the left side goes together with the left path in line 11 to produce the bridge we need in this subtable. That takes care of the first of the two subtables. We finish now by examining the subtable formed by pairing the only open path on the left side with the right path on the right side. In this case line 10 on the left side goes together with the right path in line 11 to produce the bridge we need for this subtable. That takes care of the other subtable. Both subtables have bridges, so by Table Rule 8 we have shown that there is a valid connection between the original premises and the conclusion.

8.3   Conclusions That Cannot Be Imagined False

Some complex statements have the interesting feature that they cannot in any way be imagined false. A simple example is the formula $A \lor -A$. Try to imagine it false. You will need to imagine both components of the disjunction false at the same time, which is not possible.

Our table rules give us a method for discovering whether a complex statement cannot after all be imagined false. We can put the complex statement on the right side of a table that has no premises on the left and then apply Rules 3 through 7 to it. If, by the time the table is finished every path on the right side has been closed by Rule 7, then we know we have a complex formula that cannot consistently be imagined to be false.

Just as Rule 7 enabled us to find inconsistent premises on the left side of our tables, so the same rule enables us to find these unfalsifiable statements on the right side. Such statements are sometimes called **tautologies.**

△▼ EXERCISE 8-B

▸ Use a table to show that $A \lor -A$ cannot be imagined false.

8.4   Strategic Rules for Complex Conclusions

Two rules govern efficient management of complex conclusions:

1. If the conclusion line you are working with can be seen to be part of a complex premise line, then refrain from breaking down the conclusion line with right-side rules. If, however, the conclusion line is complex and is not to be found all in one piece in a complex premise line, apply right-side rules to simplify the conclusion line.

2. *Analyze subtables in an orderly fashion.* Our strategic advice is to work with only one path on the right side until all the subtables of which it is a part have been analyzed. Then go on to the next right-side path.

△▼ EXERCISE 8-C

In Chapter 7 (Exercise 7-C in Section 7.4) we used the table method to examine some standard argument patterns. Now we have the tools to deal with a couple of others. Use the table method to determine which of the following are valid.

1. $P \supset Q$ Hypothetical Syllogism
$Q \supset R$
Therefore, $P \supset R$

2. $P \supset Q$ Conversion
Therefore, $Q \supset P$

3. $P \supset Q$ Transposition
Therefore, $-Q \supset -P$

You should discover that hypothetical syllogism and transposition can be shown to be valid, whereas conversion cannot. The valid patterns can come in handy in everyday reasoning, and in the next chapter we will discuss how they may be incorporated into the table method.

△▼ EXERCISE 8-D

More practice: Determine whether the following are valid or invalid.

▶ 1. $-[A \supset (B \vee -C)]$
Therefore, $(A \supset -B)$ & C

2. $B \supset (A \vee C)$
$D \vee B$
$-(-C \supset A)$
Therefore, $(D$ & $B)$

▶ 3. $A \vee (B \supset C)$
$C \supset D$
$D \supset (-A \vee -C)$
Therefore, $-[D \supset (A \vee D)]$

4. C & $(D \supset A)$
   $A \supset (B \vee C)$
   Therefore, $(B \vee -A)$ & $(-C$ & $-A)$

▶ 5. $[(A \vee -B)$ & $C] \supset D$
   A & C
   Therefore, $-(D \supset C)$

6. $-(A$ & $B)$
   B
   Therefore, $-(A \vee B)$

▶ 7. $-(A \vee B) \vee (C$ & $D)$
   $-C$
   Therefore, $-(B \vee D)$

8. $A \supset [B \vee (C$ & $D)]$
   A & $-B$
   Therefore, $-A \vee C$

▶ 9. $-A \supset [(-B$ & $-C) \vee -(-D \vee B)]$
   B
   Therefore, A

8.5 Indirect and Conditional Proofs

Many systems of statement logic teach students methods for indirect and conditional proof. The right-side rules you have learned in this chapter make it unnecessary for you to study these methods.

A common form of indirect proof involves the following technique: To show that a complex conclusion, for example $[A \supset (B$ & $C)]$ is a valid consequence of a set of premises, put the *denial* of the conclusion along with the premises all on the left side of the table. Then examine whether all the paths generated on the left side of the table can be closed by Table Rule 7. Assuming that the original premises were not inconsistent, then closure of all paths by Table Rule 7 would show that the denial of the conclusion is inconsistent with the premises. But this inconsistency means that the denial of the conclusion cannot be imagined true while the premises are imagined true, and thus the original conclusion cannot be imagined false while the premises are imagined true. The conclusion has been shown to be a valid consequence of the premises. No work is required on the right side of the table.

The method of indirect proof will yield the same results in tests for validity and invalidity in statement logic as the method you have learned in Chapter 8. We, however, prefer the method of Chapter 8 because it extends beyond deductive logic to interrogative inquiry in general.

▲.9 ▼

Statement Logic in Everyday English

At this point, we are facing important unfinished business. In Chapters 7 and 8 a number of rules of logical inference were presented and discussed (Table Rules 1–8), which were formulated so as to apply to statements in formal logical notation, that is, in terms of &, ∨, ⊃, and –. Obviously, this is not what you really need in everyday life. Many of the actual arguments you want to construct or to evaluate are expressed in more or less plain English rather than in logical notation. Hence, in order to bring Chapters 7 and 8 to bear on real-life arguments, we somehow have to bridge the gap between formal means of expression and natural languages like English.

9.1 The Translation Problem

Bridging the gap might not seem to be much of a problem. In Chapter 6 we explained the meanings of logical operators like & and ∨ by reference to the English words "and" and "or." If you were to try, however, to translate any of a number of the argument sketches in Appendix A into formal language, you would likely experience considerable frustration. Partly this is because there is more to logic than statement logic, but, more fundamentally, when you are frustrated by translation problems, you are in good company, and in a large company. The problem of translating between natural and formal languages is a much more difficult problem than first meets the eye (or, rather, first meets the mind).

One context in which these problems come up is when attempts are made to design computers which can use something like a natural language for programming rather than a formal one. To do this, the computer must in effect translate a given sentence in a natural language into its own logical language. A computer language is not unlike the formal language used in Chapters 7 and 8, and extended later in Chapter 14. In fact, some computer languages, for example PROLOG, are fairly closely related to our formalism. If a computer could translate from English (or Japanese or . . .) into our notation, it would be relatively easy for it to translate from it into an actual computer language.

In practice, alas, translation has turned out to be exceedingly difficult to implement. Devising translation methods is an integral part of Japan's plan to develop a "fifth generation" of computers. This project is so formidable that Japanese government and industry have committed to spending a cool billion dollars to carry it out.

9.2   Simpler Statements and the Main Operator

In view of the formidable difficulties posed by translation, is there any hope of applying our results in Chapters 7 and 8 to arguments in English? Fortunately, the answer is yes. The process is even simple in many cases.

To see what it is, let us look again at Table Rule 3. In the example used in Chapter 7, the conjunction rule is applied to the statement $(A \vee B)$ & C in the left side of a table so as to add a new line $(A \vee B)$ and another new line C in the left side. Why was a rule for conjunction used and not a rule for disjunction? After all, both & and $\vee$ occur in $(A \vee B)$ & C.

You will remember that & rather than $\vee$ is the main operator in the statement, and that the main operator is the only one to which a rule of inference may be applied in any given line. The conjunction symbol & is, as it were, the most important logical concept in the statement in question, and accordingly has to be dealt with first. In the logical notation we have been using, this is indicated by parentheses and brackets. As we learned in Chapter 6 (Section 6.4), the main operator is the one which is enclosed in the smallest number of pairs of brackets or parentheses, usually none or one.

Having recalled these fundamentals, we can now study how Table Rule 3 can be applied to an English statement. In order to do so, you do not have to translate the entire statement into a formal notation. (You do not have a billion dollars, anyway, to develop a set of explicit rules for doing so!) All that you need to do is to be able to recognize when the main operator in a statement means "and." How can you do this? *Not* by looking simply for the word "and" or one of its cousins.

You learned in Chapter 6 that the apparent form of a statement can be misleading. "And" is used for more tasks in English than simply to join statements in conjunctions. We noted also that there are many ways in English to express the relationship indicated by ⊃. Furthermore, when several operators are at work in an English statement, words and punctuation are used in a wide variety of ways to indicate which operator is the main one.

You have developed over the years a natural ability to understand what is happening in complex statements in natural language. When it comes to translation, you can rely on this ability to help you find the main operator. You can then apply the appropriate rule of logical inference directly to statements in English without first translating them into formal notation. You should ask yourself: What does the statement say? Are there simpler statements within the complex statement, and if so what are they? As you identify the simpler statements, you can then ask how they are being related to each other.

If the complex statement asserts two different statements at the same time, it is in a logician's eyes a conjunction, no matter how it is formulated. Once you know you have a conjunction and can see what the two different statements are that are being made, you can apply Table Rule 3. If you were working on the left side of a table, you would add one of the component statements on one new line and the other component statement on another.

For instance, suppose you have the statement:

We'll lose the house if the volcano erupts, and either it has already erupted or it soon will.

The comma and the word "and" seem to indicate a break between two simpler statements. One of these is

1. We'll lose the house if the volcano erupts.

and the other is

2. Either it has already erupted or it soon will.

Thinking about the complex statement in this way indicates it is asserting the two simpler statements in a conjunction. The application of Rule 3 would consist in adding statements 1 and 2 to the left side of your table on separate lines in the same path. No further translation is needed. Had we been working on the right (conclusion) side of the table, we would have split the side into two paths and put statement 1 in one path and statement 2 in the other.

But it is well to remember that you cannot always go by the form of a statement alone. For instance, the following statement contains "and" just as the previous statement did:

Tom and Dick lifted the stone.

Yet this statement normally means that Tom and Dick lifted the stone by their joint efforts. So we hesitate as we start to formulate the separate statements

1. Tom lifted the stone.

and

2. Dick lifted the stone.

In this example there is only one basic statement, so none of the table rules is appropriate. There is no way to break the statement down any further by the methods of statement logic.

You really do have to ask yourself questions and consult your own understanding of what is meant by a statement in English in applying logical rules to it. Once you do so, however, the task is usually less difficult than it might appear. For instance, if you understand the last example, you can immediately see that, on its intended reading, it does not make two separate statements.

Thus, an important way to ask yourself what a statement means is to ask what the simpler statements are (if any) that are being combined in a more complex statement. In the first example above, we readily grasped that at least two statements were involved. (There are more, of course, and we shall talk about these in a moment.) In the second, on the other hand, the attempt to phrase two separate statements showed that we would miss the meaning most likely intended.

Again, for an application of any of the Table Rules 3, 3r, 4, 4r, 5, and 5r, *you have to find out what the main operator is in the statement.* And you can do that by asking yourself: What simpler statements (if any) are being joined in this complex statement? Are two statements both being asserted together? If so, then we have a conjunction. Does the statement leave more than one possibility open, but not tell exactly which statement is true? If so, the statement involves a disjunction, and Rules 4 or 4r can be applied to it. Does the statement make a conditional claim, that is, does it somehow say that one statement becomes effective if (or only if) another statement is true? If so, the statement is a conditional and Rules 5 or 5r can be applied to it.

At this point, you should also remember that disjunctive ("or") statements and conditional ("if-then") statements are very similar to each other as far as statement logic is concerned. You may identify a given statement as a disjunction while another person might say it is a conditional. For example, we learned in Chapter 6 that "unless" can be treated like "or." Some people, however, prefer to think of *unless* as functioning like "if not." "Or else" is easily handled like "or," but again some people prefer to think of *or else* as being like "if not." Toward the end of this chapter, Exercise 9-C probes the meaning of these words a little further.

Whenever you have determined that a complex statement is offering alternative simpler statements, you will know that Table Rule 4 can be applied to it. If you are working on the left side of a table, you will split the table and add one of the component statements to one path and the other component statement to the other path.

For instance, if you have the statement

Either the volcano has already erupted or it soon will.

the two separate claims made in 1 are clearly expressed by

1. The volcano has already erupted.

and

2. The volcano soon will erupt.

An application of Rule 4 (Disjunction on the Left Side) would consist in adding statements 1 and 2 to separate paths on the left side. No further translation is needed. Had you been working on the right (conclusion) side of the table, you would add statements 1 and 2 to the same path.

In everyday reasoning you will often encounter complex premise statements or interrogative-move statements that offer alternatives and are thus disjunctions. The way to handle these complex statements is quite straightforward. Simply develop a separate line of thought (a separate path) for each of the alternatives if you are working on the left side of a table.

Whenever you determine that a complex statement is offering a simpler statement that is a condition for the truth of another, you will know that Table Rule 5 can be applied to it. In working with conditionals you have to be very careful to identify which of the simpler statements is the sufficient ("if") condition and which is the necessary ("then" or "only if") condition. Then you will know which statement belongs on the left (antecedent) side of the conditional and which on the right (consequent) side. If you were working on the left side of a table, you would split it and add the denial of the antecedent to one path and the consequent to the other.

For instance, if you have the statement

Nathan will win only if Katie helps him.

the two separate claims made in 1 are clearly expressed by

1. Nathan will win.

and

2. Katie helps him.

Remember that the phrase "only if" precedes the consequent (necessary condition) of a conditional. So an application of Table Rule 5 would consist in splitting the table on the left side and adding the denial of statement 1 to one path and statement 2 to the other. No further translation is needed. Had you been working on the right (conclusion) side of the table, you would add the denial of statement 1 to one line and statement 2 to the next line in the same path.

Here is another conditional:

We'll lose the house if the volcano erupts.

The two separate claims made in the statement are clearly expressed by

1. We'll lose the house.

and

2. The volcano erupts.

Remember that the word "if" precedes the antecedent (sufficient condition) of a conditional. So an application of Table Rule 5 would consist in splitting the table on the left side and adding the denial of statement 2 to one path and statement 1 to the other. No further translation is needed. Had you been working on the right (conclusion) side of the table, you would add the denial of statement 2 to one line and statement 1 to the next line in the same path.

Often complex premise statements or interrogative-move statements express conditional relationships. In analyzing these on the left side of a table, simply develop a separate line of thought (a separate path) for the denial of the antecedent statement and for the consequent statement.

Table Rule 6 can be applied to English statements in the same way we have been describing, except for one thing. Often your own natural understanding will enable you to think your way through to an expression in which denial is no longer the main operator in the complex statement. For example, how would you understand the following:

Neither Sam nor Sue will get the job.

The two statements involved are simple and clear enough:

1. Sam will get the job.

and

2. Sue will get the job.

Once you are clear about what the simpler statements are, you can ask what the denial in "neither-nor" is doing. You are likely to see fairly directly that both statements 1 and 2 are together being denied. Thus you have a conjunction as the main operator joining two denied statements. Table Rule 3 (or 3r) would apply. You might, however, have thought that the complex statement is saying "It is not the case that either Sam or Sue will get the job." This looks like a denied disjunction, and it is. The equivalence for denied disjunction produces the conjunction of two denials, so in this way too we would get in position for using Rule 3 (or 3r).

Summary

In applying Table Rules 3, 3r, 4, 4r, 5, 5r, and 6 to English statements, the basic question concerns *what the main operator is in the statement*. The procedure we are recommending goes back to where we started in Chapter 6. Two different approaches were used.

1. Try to isolate the simpler statements that can be taken to be parts of a more complex statement.
2. Keep an eye on how *not, and, or, if-then,* and their cousins are complicating a statement.

The first approach continues to be the more fundamental. As we identify simpler statements, we ask ourselves how they are being related to each other: whether by conjunction, disjunction, conditional, or denial. The process of identifying the simpler statements usually helps determine what the main operator is in the complex statement. Then we are able to apply the appropriate rule. We get additional help by inspecting words such as "not," "and," "but," "or," "if-then," "only if," and "unless" and by keeping in mind the insights we have learned about how they operate on statements. But above all we try to identify simpler statements and their relationships. Notice that in this chapter we have followed our own strategic advice about reasoning. We have tried to develop your ability to question your own store of tacit linguistic knowledge in analyzing the logical form of various English sentences.

△▼ EXERCISE 9-A

1. Identify the simpler statements (if any) in the following English sentences:
   a. John forgot to turn off the faucet and the oven.
   ▶ b. John did not win the race but he did manage to finish it.
   ▶ c. If Mary comes to Sue's party, she will be surprised.
   ▶ d. A visitor is not allowed to step on the grass unless they are accompanied by a member of the college.
   e. Sue is surprised if Tom, Dick, or Harry comes to her party.
   ▶ f. Sue is surprised if Tom, Dick, and Harry come to her party.
   ▶ g. James and Susan are lovers.
   h. Kevin and Tom help each other.
   i. Clara or Norma helps herself.

▶ 2. What is the main logical operator (if any) in the above English statements?

▶ 3. Apply appropriate left-side table rules to the above English statements if possible. Your task is *not* to translate but to identify the appropriate rule of logical inference that should be applied and to show what application of that rule would do on the left side of a table.

▶ 4. Apply appropriate right-side table rules to the above English sentences if possible. Your task is *not* to translate but to identify the appropriate rule of logical inference that should be applied and to show what application of that rule would do on the right side of a table.

9.3 Denial (Negation) in English

One more remark is needed concerning Table Rules 5 and 5r for conditionals. In applying the conditional rules to a complex statement, you are instructed to insert the denial of the antecedent in the left path of the branching caused by Rule 5, or as the first of two new lines when using Rule 5r on the right side. To do so, you must be able to form the denial (negation) of an English statement.

Thus a little bit more is required of you when you are to apply our logical inference rules to English statements than merely the ability to recognize the main operator. You must also be able to form the negation (the denial) of a given statement.

Now how is this neat trick performed? This is one of many linguistic operations that are (to invert the old phrase) more easily done than said. Often it is not easy to say just exactly how it is accomplished. Most of the time we can simply think about what a statement says and then formulate its denial. But do not ask yourself *how* you do it! Simply put the question to your store of tacit information. Do not proceed step by step, word by word! If you try to use the wording of a statement as a guide to forming its denial, you are likely to go wrong. This is illustrated by the old story of a senator who was taken to task for insulting his colleagues. He had said: "Half of the senators are idiots!" He was reprimanded and told to retract his statement, whereupon he quickly declared solemnly and in a contrite voice: "I was wrong—half of the senators are not idiots!"

— ▲ ——————————————————————

Denial (Negation): Denial (negation) of a true statement makes it false. Denial (negation) of a false statement makes the statement true.

△▼ EXERCISE 9-B

Form the negation of the following statements:

▶ 1. Jimmy can beat anyone.
2. Jimmy can beat everyone.
▶ 3. Jimmy cannot beat anyone.
4. Jimmy cannot beat everyone.
▶ 5. Many senators are wise.
6. Few senators are wise.
▶ 7. Not many senators are wise.

△▼ EXERCISE 9-C

Discuss how both Table Rules 4 and 5 can be applied to the following cases.

1. Mary will go out with John unless Harold calls.

2. Jack had better come up with the money or else he will be in big trouble with Harry.

It is instructive to think about the preceding exercise. Many people are tempted to think that the statement in case 1 means "If Harold calls, Mary will not go out with John." Strictly, however, it only says for sure that "If Harold does not call, Mary will go out with John." If Harold does call, she may or may not go out. What is involved here is the difference between inclusive and exclusive "or." This case can also be treated as "Mary will go out with John or Harold calls." With the weaker, inclusive sense of "or," it is possible both that Harold would call and that Mary would go out with John. If, however, we take the stronger, exclusive sense of "or," then the truth of John calling will eliminate the possibility that Mary would go out with John. "Unless" is a source of confusion for people precisely because there is often no clear indication whether it should be taken in the weaker, inclusive sense of "or" or the stronger, exclusive sense. You should remember that the logician's strategy is, in the absence of any clear indication, to assume the weaker sense.

Similar problems arise with case 2. Many people would be tempted to think that the statement tells us that "If Jack comes up with the money, he will not be in big trouble with Harry." Strictly, however, the statement only says for sure that "If Jack doesn't come up with the money, he will be in big trouble with Harry." The problem can be understood again in terms of inclusive and exclusive "or." Another way, however, to think about these problems is to say that "Coming up with the money" is definitely a necessary condition for staying out of trouble with Harry, but it may or may not be a sufficient condition. People can become confused because it is often not made clear in English whether a necessary condition is being indicated only or a sufficient condition also.

— ▲ ——————————————————————————————————

Applying Formal Logic to English Statements: Our study of formal logic has revealed many details of logical inference. From a practical standpoint it is not wise to spend a lot of time translating everyday English into formal representations. This is both extremely difficult and unnecessary. Instead, when you are working with a logical inference involving a complex English statement, ask yourself what the simpler statements are and how they are being joined by the main logical operator in the statement. You do not need to do any other translating, because once you have identified the simpler statements and the main logical operator in the statement, you will know which rule of logical inference to apply and how to apply it.

Main Logical Operator: The primary logical concept in the statement; the one that must be dealt with first in logical inferences as we have formulated them; the one which, in a formal notation, would be enclosed in the smallest number of pairs of brackets or parentheses. No automatic, mechanical rules exist for determining the main operator of an English statement. The most important thing is to ask oneself what precisely is the meaning of the statement, how is it to be understood? What are the simpler statements and how are they being related to each other? Answers to these questions, combined with an understanding of formal logical operators, will usually produce correct logical inferences.

9.4   Basic Argument Patterns in Table Analysis

In Chapters 7 and 8 (Exercises 7-C and 8-C) you were introduced to some common patterns of inference and you used the table method to find which were valid and which invalid. You are perhaps already aware or have noticed that both the valid and the invalid patterns are often found in everyday reasoning.

To reason well you will of course want to avoid the invalid patterns. These were:

1. $P \supset Q$
Q
Therefore, P

Affirming the Consequent

2. $P \supset Q$
$-P$
Therefore, $-Q$

Denying the Antecedent

3. $P \supset Q$
Therefore, $Q \supset P$

Conversion

4. $P \vee Q$
P
Therefore, $-Q$

(No name; the problem involves the temptation to assume an exclusive "or.")

As you analyze and construct interrogative tables, you will come across (or be tempted to use) invalid patterns of reasoning such as the above. You should try not to let them slip into your tables. As you review your tables, eliminate any that you find.

On the other hand, the following patterns are valid:

1. $P \vee Q$
$-P$
Therefore, Q

Disjunctive Syllogism

2. $P \supset Q$
P
Therefore, Q

Modus Ponens

3. $P \supset Q$ Modus Tollens
   $-Q$
   Therefore, $-P$

4. $P \supset Q$ Hypothetical Syllogism
   $Q \supset R$
   Therefore, $P \supset R$

5. $P \supset Q$ Transposition
   Therefore, $-Q \supset -P$

These five valid patterns are regularly useful in everyday reasoning. They can help you quickly check whether a particular inference is a truth-preserving logical inference. You may also find it convenient to use the five valid patterns in the tables you create for argument analysis and argument construction. They can work like the logical inference table rules we have studied in Part 2.

Anytime you already have two full lines in your table that conform precisely to one or another of the patterns, then you can readily justify writing the concluding part of the pattern as a new line in your table. For instance, suppose you have constructed a table containing (in English or in formal language) the two-line pattern $(A \supset B)$ and $-B$ in a path (or paths) on its left side. These are the premises of the pattern traditionally called modus tollens. You would be justified in going on to introduce $-A$ into the same path (or paths). Modus tollens is a valid inference pattern.

Note carefully that, as always, to use one or another of these patterns, you must be working with a line that has precisely the right main operator. In the case of disjunctive syllogism, the main operator must be "or." In the case of the other patterns, the main operator must be "if-then."

These patterns are designed only for work on the left side of tables, and it is here that they offer a special virtue. All of them involve main operators that would split the left side if we used our Table Rules 4 and 5. But these patterns do not require any splitting. What they do is sum up the results of splitting the table and then finding that certain paths close or are structured equivalently to the concluding line of the pattern. In other words, they can keep tables less complicated and speed up analysis and construction.

Many logic books develop their whole system of logical inference rules in terms of such patterns. The five valid inference patterns listed above are among the most useful, and it is well worth learning them and using them in your tables.

△▼ EXERCISE 9-D

Review (or now complete) standard table rule analyses of the validity and invalidity of the above argument patterns.

△▼ EXERCISE 9-E

Your instructor will assign some simple English arguments from Appendix A. Use the skills you have learned in Chapter 9 to check the arguments for validity.

Use the table rules from Chapters 7 and 8, and, if they are helpful, the valid argument patterns we have studied in Section 9.4.

9.5   Argument Analysis and Construction

At the end of Part 1 we studied argument analysis and construction in detail. You worked at constructing some simple arguments and perhaps at writing a simple argumentative essay. Now you are in a position to return to Chapters 3 and 4 with deeper insight into the nature of logical inference. You also have a better grasp of basic rules and patterns for valid logical inference. You can now incorporate the insights from Part 2 into your understanding of analysis and construction.

You are now also ready to tackle larger projects of analysis, construction, and essay writing. After administering an examination on Part 2, your instructor may assign a major argument construction and essay project to be worked on as you study Part 3.

Throughout Part 3 you will be given advice and strategies for analyzing and evaluating interrogative moves. As you work on your major project, you should also use the insights summed up in Chapter 9 to make your logical inferences genuinely truth-preserving.

As you proceed, however, you will discover that a number of inferences you think are valid are nevertheless not able to be understood according to the rules and patterns we have studied. This is because there is much more to inference than what we have thus far explored. Still, now that you have much experience with what logical inferences are supposed to do, you will be able to be more careful even with inferences for which you have no explicit rule.

One other problem with logical inferences should be noted as you embark on your project. Sometimes an everyday inference depends on more or less obvious background knowledge to be a valid inference. If the background knowledge is not mentioned, the inference will not actually be a valid logical inference as it is written. Yet, bringing in all the background information can quickly become tedious. What should you do?

It depends on your situation and your purposes. Even in an important argument it can be justifiable not to burden yourself and others with tedious details. The important thing is both to recognize that the goal is to have only valid logical inferences and to be reasonably confident that you could defend the validity of your inferences in detail if doing so became important.

Being "reasonably confident" and assessing when defending an inference might become "important" are once again strategic matters. There are no mechanical rules of right and wrong about how thoroughly you must prepare the logical inference work in your tables. Practice and experience are needed. You already have engaged in much unreflective practice in everyday life. You are now equipped to examine more critically the standards you use for accepting and rejecting your own and others' inferences.

9.6 Argument Evaluation

It should be clear, or becoming clear, by now that skills in argument analysis and construction also enable us to evaluate arguments. The ability to take arguments apart and the knowledge of how they are built give us a good perspective for evaluating whether an argument or inquiry is effective. We have more to learn about evaluation, but at this point we are able to perform well two main tasks.

First, we have learned some of the most important rules of correct logical inference and have also learned about the basics of interrogative moves. Thus, we are able to determine what the basic steps of an argument are and to ask in some important ways whether they have been made correctly. If they have not, then we are in a position to evaluate where some important weaknesses are.

Second, we understand what it means that an argument is valid, that is, that its table closes. Thus, we are able to evaluate whether an argument or inquiry has reached (or has claimed to reach) a successful conclusion. We are able to test whether it is indeed valid—whether its table does, in fact, close. If the argument is not valid, then again we know where some important weaknesses are in it.

— ▲ _____

Argument Evaluation: The process of checking the steps of an argument for definitory correctness, for strategic excellence, and for whether the argument is valid, i.e., whether its table closes. Skills in argument evaluation are closely related to skills in argument analysis. The ability to analyze an argument provides a foundation for the evaluative tasks. Other evaluative tasks will be learned in the remaining parts of the book.

A crucial remaining skill is that of knowing how to highlight and cope with places in an argument where uncertain information is in use because the oracle has provided information about which we are doubtful. This is a central topic in Part 3 and will be addressed in Chapters 12 and 13.

△▼ EXERCISE 9-F

Analyze the following argument. On the basis of your analysis evaluate whether the moves have been made correctly and whether the argument is valid. As you are aware, you must often supply a number of the steps. Be sure to discuss whether this argument is asking you to supply too much in the way of intermediate steps.

con — Nuclear energy should remain an important energy source for this country. Our energy needs are growing, and there is every reason to expect this trend to continue. We cannot rely upon oil to meet these needs, as this resource is becoming scarcer. The only sources of energy plentiful enough to solve the impending energy crunch are nuclear energy and coal. But, compared to coal, nuclear energy is both less expensive and less hazardous.

It is less expensive because fuel costs are only a fraction of the cost of coal, while the costs of building nuclear power plants are comparable to those of traditional fossil-fuel burning plants. And although nuclear power does pose a minor safety hazard, the threat posed by coal-burning power plants is far greater. Coal-burning plants currently release ten times as much radiation into the atmosphere as nuclear plants do, and they pose additional health risks stemming from the release of other contaminants as well. So when you compare the options, nuclear is clearly the way to go.

You may find yourself sufficiently interested in this topic to go beyond *analysis* of the given text to *construction* of your own argument. Constructing your own argument would require that you gather and analyze more information and arguments on both sides of the issue and then assemble the materials into your own sequence of interrogative and logical inference moves.

For example, you are likely to need to consider the implications of the severe nuclear accident at Chernobyl in the Soviet Union in 1986. Some argue that this accident shows nuclear energy to be far more hazardous than the above argument suggests. Here is how the author of the above argument responded to that challenge:

The nuclear accident in Chernobyl in 1986 does not show that nuclear power plants are inevitably dangerous. What it proves is the incompetence of the planning and managing of nuclear power plants in the Soviet Union. The reactor in which the explosions occurred was a graphite-modulated type built without any airtight containment structure, unlike American water-modulated reactors. It was not tested for safety when it was installed in 1983. When the operators attempted a safety test in 1986, the core of the reactor was heavily contaminated with radioactive fission products. The operator in charge of the test was inexperienced and tired. When the disaster occurred, the initial attempts to deal with it were ill-advised and merely accentuated the problem.

With proper reactor planning and management, several of these errors could have been avoided. The accident would not have happened or would have been quickly contained. Hence the accident shows not the intrinsic dangers of nuclear energy but the weakness of Soviet planning and management.

Analysis and evaluation of this additional material will take you further into the issues and might serve as a beginning point for your own attempts to construct arguments for or against the use of nuclear energy.

PART △ THREE

Interrogative Moves in Detail

10

Fundamental Aspects
of Questioning

As we study how reasoning in general can be understood through the interrogative game model, we consider both its definitory and strategic aspects. In Part 2 we examined many of the definitory aspects of logical inference moves and some of the strategic aspects. In this chapter we discuss some of the basic *definitory aspects of interrogative moves*.

In the preceding chapters we have said that interrogative moves introduce new information into an inquiry, whereas logical inference moves spell out the information already available. After first discussing what is meant by "information," we examine what is meant by saying that interrogative moves provide new information. The remainder of the chapter will be devoted to studying closely the two different roles questions play in reasoning.

10.1 New Information and Interrogative Moves

In an interrogative move the inquirer asks a question. A question can be understood as a request for information. In Chapter 1 (Section 1.8) we said that, according to the interrogative model, having information involves being able to eliminate from our inquiry certain alternative situations that we otherwise might have thought possible. For example, consider the question

Is Mary in class today?

Here the alternatives are that Mary is in class or that she is not in class. By asking the question, I am trying to eliminate one or the other alternative from what I think is possible. Another question might be

Is Mary staying on campus over the holiday or is she going home or will she be visiting her boyfriend?

Here the alternatives are more complicated, and by asking the question, we are trying to get more information by eliminating one or another of them from what we currently think is possible.

Turning to a different type of question, I may be wondering

Who finished as the National College Football Champion in the 1988 season?

If I am given the information that it was one of the three major Florida teams, that enables me to eliminate a lot of teams I might otherwise have considered. If someone goes on to tell me that it was either Florida State or the University of Miami, that helps me eliminate the University of Florida. If I remember that Miami beat Florida State in 1988, I might conclude that Miami was the National Champion.

Notice how each additional piece of information enables me more and more to eliminate alternatives. This gives us a way to explain what it means to know something: *To know something is to be able to eliminate alternatives.* By the same token, receiving new information means becoming able to eliminate more possibilities than before.

___ ▲ _____

Information: That which enables us to eliminate from our inquiry certain alternative scenarios that we otherwise could have thought possible. Information enables an inquirer to rule out possibilities that could otherwise be imagined to be realized. This idea is sometimes expressed in the form of the slogan "Information means the reduction of uncertainty."

_____

It is important to notice that there is always a lot we do not know. This means that we always have a number of different alternative ways of thinking about the world. For example, you may not know who won the singles' championships at Wimbledon in 1988. We shall tell you that Steffi Graf and Martina Navratilova competed in the women's final, and Boris Becker and Stefan Edberg competed in the men's. That eliminates a lot of other possibilities, but, assuming you do not know who won the finals, you are left with several different alternative ways of thinking about the world. You could think ours is a world in which Graf and Becker were the champions, or Graf and Edberg, or Navratilova and Becker, or Navratilova and Edberg.

Because it is not too painful to be in this fix, we are not going to tell you who the champions were. However, it is a fact that the Miami Hurricanes were the National College Football Champions at the end of the 1988 season and that Florida State ranked third. This will help us get at one more important idea. That you have complete information about who won the National College Football Championship means that Miami will be the winner in all the different alternative worlds left open by your not knowing who won Wimbledon. You may not know which alternative is correct about Wimbledon, but you do know that whichever alternative is correct, Miami will always be the right answer for the National College Football Championship in the 1988 season.

△ ▼ EXERCISE 10-A

Use your understanding of the nature of information to determine which statement of the following pairs contains the most information:

1. a. Today is Sunday.
   b. Today is a weekend day.
► 2. a. Someone is at the door.
   b. Tom is at the door.
3. a. Sue or Pam will drive.
   b. Pam will drive.
► 4. a. Someone trusts everybody.
   b. Everybody is trusted by someone.

[handwritten annotation: – why the someone in "a" must be one person / know / FINAL EXAM QUESTION]

10.2 Conclusive and Partial Answers

The question of alternatives in the last section will help us understand what a *conclusive* answer to a question must look like: A conclusive answer gives me information that picks out the same item in every alternative situation left open by what I do not know. We shall illustrate this further by looking at answers which are not conclusive: A *partial* answer gives information that does not necessarily pick out the same item in every alternative situation left open by what I do not know.

For example, the story is told of an ancient king who asked the oracle at Delphi in Greece, "If I go to war tomorrow, who will win the battle?" The oracle answered, "If you go to war tomorrow, you will destroy a mighty army." Let us assume that the oracle was giving a truthful answer. The king did not pause to wonder whether it was a partial or a conclusive one. He assumed that the answer picked him as the winner in every alternative situation before him.

If you think about it, however, the answer only tells us that some army will be destroyed by the king's going to war. It does not give enough information for us to be sure whether it is picking out the enemy army or the king's. The answer leaves open two different alternative views of the likely outcome. As it happened, the king suffered a disastrous defeat. By giving a not-very-informative, partial answer, the oracle was able to give an accurate prediction. This was probably not much consolation to the king.

△▼ THINK ABOUT IT

Analyze one of the horoscopes in a current newspaper. Determine what sorts of questions the horoscope seems to be answering and then consider whether the answers offered are conclusive or partial. Give your appraisal of just how much useful information is being offered in the horoscope.

The illustration given of a partial answer may give you the mistaken impression that such answers are not useful. This is not the case at all. Partial answers can be both helpful and necessary. All we are demonstrating at this point is that partial and conclusive answers must be carefully distinguished. We shall learn more about this as we go along.

— ▲ ――――――――――――――――――――――――――――――――――――

Conclusive Answer: An answer providing information that picks out the same item in every alternative situation left open by what I do not know.

Partial Answer: An answer providing information that does not necessarily pick out the same item in every alternative situation left open by what I do not know.

△▼ EXERCISE 10-B

Which of the following alternatives are conclusive answers to the corresponding question? Explain your choices. If an answer is partial, discuss what other information might be available to make it conclusive.

▶ 1. Who won the last presidential election?
   a. The best man for the job won the election.
   b. The republican candidate won the election.

   c. The vice president won the election.
   d. George Bush won the election.
2. When did you change the oil in the car?
   a. I changed the oil before our last vacation.
   b. I changed the oil when we had the car tuned up.
   c. I changed the oil last Friday.
   d. I changed the oil on Mother's Day.

10.3 Interrogative Moves Introduce New Information

We have seen, then, that information enables us to eliminate from our inquiry alternatives that we otherwise might have had to consider. Because a question can be understood as a request for information, an interrogative move (a question/ answer step) in our interrogative games is an attempt to gain new information. If the move is successful, that is, if we get an answer, then we have more information than we had before. We have new insight into which alternatives can be discarded and which need further attention in our inquiry. The interrogative move has introduced new information into the inquiry.

> **New Information:** Information that was not previously available for use in a given inquiry. New information will always be analyzed as coming into the inquiry by way of an interrogative step.

Illustrations   Consider this brief argument:

> The best person for the job is the one with the most experience, and the best person for the job should get the job. Jill has the most experience, so Jill should get the job.

The first two premises in this argument set the stage for an inquiry into who should get the job, but they alone do not provide enough information. The extra information is provided as a response to the question, "Who has the most experience?" Notice how a less informative, partial answer would have been less effective. Suppose, for instance, that the response provided was, "Someone from the downtown office has the most experience." The process of inquiry would have been only partially completed.

Here is another illustration:

> If an American is to win the Tour de France, either Hampsten or LeMond will have to win. But all winners must be good climbers, and Hampsten is not a good climber. So if an American is to win, it will be LeMond.

Again, in this argument the first two premises are insufficient to complete the process of inquiry. But the third statement, seen as a response to the question "Is Hampsten a good climber?" makes more information available.

10.4   The Socratic Questioning Method

Historically, the most famous type of questioning procedure is the one illustrated by the example of Meno's slaveboy given at the end of Chapter 1. As was mentioned there, Socrates's questions have to be looked upon in a special way to make them comparable with the other questioning processes we are studying. Socrates is not so much constructing a line of argument himself. He is helping the slaveboy to construct one. His questions are, as it were, asked on behalf of the slaveboy. The slaveboy example is in fact an instance of the famous Socratic method of questioning, sometimes called Socratic *elenchus*.

The following is a scholar's description of the Socratic method:

> The outstanding method in Plato's earlier dialogues is the Socratic elenchus. "Elenchus" in the wider sense means examining a person with regard to a statement he has made, by putting to him questions calling for further statements, in the hope that they will determine the meaning and the truth-value of his first statement. Most often the truth-value expected is falsehood; and so "elenchus" in the narrower sense is a form of cross-examination or refutation. In this sense it is the most striking aspect of the behavior of Socrates in Plato's early dialogues. He is always putting to somebody some general question, usually in the field of ethics. Having received an answer (let us call it the primary answer), he asks many more questions. These secondary questions differ from the primary one in that, whereas that was a matter of real doubt and difficulty, the answers to all these seem obvious and inescapable. Socrates usually phrases them so that the natural answer is yes; and if you say anything else you are likely to seem irrational or at least queer. In other words, they are not so much requests for information as demands for an assent that cannot very well be repelled. They often seem at first irrelevant to the primary question, and sometimes they seem to fall into two disconnected groups among themselves. But at last Socrates says: "Come now, let us add our admissions together" (*Prt.* 332D); and the result of doing so turns out to be the contradictory of the primary answer. Propositions to which the answerer feels he must agree have entailed the falsehood of his original assertion.

> Such is the Socratic elenchus, often referred to also as *exetasis* or scrutiny and as *basanismus* or assay. It is so common in the early dialogues that we may almost say that Socrates never talks to anyone without refuting him. An exception is his conversation with Cephalus in the first book of the *Republic* (the first book of the *Republic* may be regarded as an early dialogue); but there the subject is personal experience and not abstract ethics.

> The sureness of the refutation gives the impression that Socrates possesses knowledge about the subject on which he refutes others. This, however, he invariably

denies. "You treat me", he says in the *Charmides* (165B), "as if I professed
to know the matters I ask about, and if I might agree with you if I wish to.
But that is not so. On the contrary, I am inquiring into the proposition along
with you because I do not know. I will tell you whether I agree or not when
I have examined it." (Cf. *Ap.* 23A) That is always his attitude; and in harmony
therewith he always puts the primary question as a request for information
and not as if he were examining a candidate. Throughout the early dialogues,
whether engaged in elenchus or not, he usually declares himself ignorant of
the answers to all the general ethical questions that he raises. There are some
extreme confident statements in the *Apology* and the *Crito,* and in the *Euthydemus*
(293B). He admits knowing many small matters; but *Meno* 98B seems to be the
only place where he actually professes to know something important. (Excerpted
from Richard Robinson, *Plato's Earlier Dialectic* [Oxford: Clarendon Press, 1953],
pp. 7–8.)

Some comments on this description are in order. We can distinguish in the
Socratic procedure features peculiar to it and features it shares with other types
of reasoning which combine questions and logical inferences.

The most important shared feature is that all new information brought to
bear on the reasoning is elicited by means of questions. This is to say, the new
information comes in the form of answers to suitable questions. Peculiarities of
the Socratic questioning procedure include the following:

1. The ultimate conclusion at which Socrates is tacitly aiming is usually the denial
   of an assertion his discussion partner had made in the beginning of the
   dialogue. The only essential thing here is that the questioning procedure has
   a definite end or aim. From the point of view of our general theory of reasoning, it does not matter how this predetermined ultimate conclusion comes
   about, for example, whether it is put forward by one of the dialogue partners,
   whether it is the denial of such an assertion, whether it is agreed by all parties,
   or whether it is chosen by a lone investigator. We shall return to the nature
   of the ultimate conclusion later. In particular, we shall return to the curious-
   looking fact that the thesis (assertion) which Socrates and his friend usually
   end up disproving by means of answers to questions is itself obtained originally
   as an answer to one of Socrates's questions.

2. In a Socratic dialogue, the source of answers is normally the dialogue partner's
   tacit knowledge. Hence the questions might as well have been asked by
   Socrates's dialogue partner himself. Socrates's role is to guide the choice of the
   questions. These features do not characterize interrogative reasoning in general.
   Usually we are dealing with only one inquirer who chooses his or her questions
   without the help of a mentor like Socrates.

This peculiarity of the Socratic questioning method is what lends it its special
flavor. For Socrates's role in his partner's reasoning is like the role of the partner's
own intellectual conscience, as it were. Socrates tells him what he ought to
ask even though the other person may be perfectly capable of choosing questions on his own.

3. An especially poignant aspect of Socrates's method is his claim to ignorance. This claim is what was originally meant by an expression which you may have heard, namely, "Socratic irony." In our days, speaking ironically means saying something but meaning something else, usually the opposite to what one appears to say. (Suppose a running back fumbles the ball and I say in disgust, "Well, there's a sure-handed player." That is an example of irony.)

However, originally Socrates's "irony" meant only his pretended ignorance. It is easy to see how the present-day meaning of the term developed, for in a sense Socrates merely pretended ignorance. He could not have chosen his questions in the masterful way he did without a firm grasp of where he was going and by what route. Otherwise he could not have asked the right questions in the right order.

Socrates was insisting on his ignorance to make a point. He wanted to highlight the fact that he was not imparting any new information to his dialogue partner. Most of his questions merely prompted his partner to realize something he had always known without realizing it. In other words, Socrates pretended to be ignorant to highlight the fact that his questions were supposed to be answered on the basis of the tacit knowledge of the person to whom they were addressed.

We note also, however, that in another sense Socrates was often quite serious about his "not knowing." He often knew very well how to defeat a partner's assertion, but he also often meant it when he said that he did not know the true assertion that could be put in place of the one that was defeated.

So what is, after all, the famous "Socratic method" that much of actual education and instruction is supposed to be based on? The following is the best brief answer:

What Socrates is trying to teach his interlocutor is to ask the right questions. He is confident that the student will find (or will learn to find) the answers himself or herself. Socrates teaches by putting himself in the position of his students and asking them the questions they ought to ask themselves. This is what distinguishes Socratic questions from the usual teacher's questions, which are typically attempts to find out whether the student has learned something the teacher knows and is trying to impart. Socrates is not giving his interlocutor new information; he is trying to teach his dialogue partner the art of asking questions.

Here you can perhaps see that what we are attempting in this book is not so different from what Socrates was doing. One difference is that Socrates was teaching the art of questioning by example only. We are trying to give you explicit guidelines for this purpose.

10.5   Answering Questions by Means of Questions

In this chapter we are studying the definitory aspects of interrogative moves in the interrogative model of inquiry. Up to this point we have examined what it means to say that interrogative moves introduce new information into an inquiry, and we have taken a detailed look at Socratic questioning. Our next task is to learn how questions and answers can have different roles in inquiry.

You may have noticed a feature of Socratic question-answer dialogues which does not fit into the interrogative games described in Part 1 of the book. On the one hand, in harmony with our analysis in Part 1, Socrates reached the ultimate conclusion by means of eliciting answers to simple questions and then "adding the admissions [answers] together." But, on the other hand, even the ultimate conclusion itself was set up by Socrates as an answer to a question he had initially put to his dialogue partner.

You will note that the initial question of a Socratic dialogue differs essentially from the subsequent ones. "These secondary questions differ from the primary one in that, whereas that was a matter of real doubt and difficulty, the answers to all these seem obvious and inescapable. . . . In other words, they are not so much requests for information as demands for an assent [agreement] that cannot very well be repelled" (Robinson, p. 7).

This feature of the Socratic dialogues illustrates an important fact about the roles of questions in knowledge seeking: Questions can play more than one role. We now have to do justice to this important fact.

10.6   Principal and Operational Questions

We are discovering that questions and answers have two different functions in inquiry. The overall purpose of an interrogative "game" may be to answer a question. Such a question will be called the **principal question**. What happens in interrogative reasoning is that the inquirer tries to answer this "big," principal question by putting a number of "small" questions to the oracle (to her or his source of information) and by using the answers as additional information to be used in logical inferences. By means of these "small" answers the inquirer hopes to arrive at an answer to the principal question. The inquirer is thus trying to answer a principal question by means of other, "small" questions.

Having called the "big" question the principal question, we shall call the "small" questions the **operational questions**. (We will also often continue to speak of "big" and "small" questions in this sense.)

▲

Principal Question: The question which sets up the goal or purpose of an inquiry. A conclusive answer to the principal question comes not in a single move, but through the whole inquiry, made up of a number of interrogative steps and logical-inference steps.

Operational Question: A question which forms the basis of one particular interrogative move in an inquiry. Such a move seeks part of the information needed to answer the principal question.

In the example found in Section 4.2 of Chapter 4 the *principal* question is, "Shall I take a course in reasoning and critical thinking?" The conclusion, "I will take a course in reasoning and critical thinking," is the answer to this principal question and is arrived at by means of an interrogative inquiry. The *operational* questions in the inquiry are those found in lines 2.1, 3, 4, 6.1, 7.2, 8.1, and 10. (Line 1 is the initial premise and can also be treated as an answer to an operational question.) Operational questions have, for the purposes of this inquiry, immediate answers; these are not taken to be the result of a process of inquiry but rather as being provided directly by an oracle.

10.7 The Double Role of Questions in a Court of Law

It is easy to find other kinds of large-scale examples of situations in which an inquirer is trying to answer a big question by means of small ones. A case in point is criminal prosecution in a court of law. There the principal question is, for each particular charge, "Is the defendant guilty as charged or not?" And as a part of the attempt to answer this big question, other operational questions are put to witnesses and also to the evidence, questions whose "answers" might even be present there in the courtroom in the form of exhibits.

What is peculiar to the judicial system in most of the English-speaking parts of the world is that the task of answering the principal question—"Guilty or not?"—is divided into two parts. In other words, the role of the inquirer is now played by two different lawyers (or teams of lawyers together with their aides). On the one hand, the prosecutor is trying to construct an argument that would show that the defendant is guilty. On the other hand, the defense attorney is endeavoring to put together a line of reasoning to establish that the person in the dock cannot be proved guilty. It is interesting to see that both sides are not only seeking to draw suitable logical inferences. In fact, their main task is to find the right information, that is, the right answers to questions put to the witnesses and/or the material evidence.

This division of labor in our courts is called the *adversary system*. We shall have more to say about it in Chapter 11. It is mentioned here as an example of a process of answering principal questions by means of small, operational questions.

10.8 Operational and Principal Questions in Science

The double role of questions and answers in inquiry can also be seen in science. For instance, the famous German philosopher Immanuel Kant (1724–1804) treated scientific experiments as operational questions put to nature. In his classic work *Critique of Pure Reason* Kant compared the method of experimental science to "constraining nature to give answers to questions of reason's own determining" (*Critique of Pure Reason*, original 2d German edition, translated by N. Kemp Smith [London: Macmillan, 1933], p. xiii).

What makes it possible to consider experiments as questions put to nature is that they serve the same role in inquiry as questions put to a witness. They serve to bring new information into one's line of reasoning, just as a witness's answers provide in a court of law more material on which the jury can base their deliberations. Moreover, Kant's brief statement calls our attention to another aspect of the same similarity between questioning and empirical inquiry. Just as a good lawyer can guide the course of a cross-examination through a skillful choice of the questions she or he puts to a witness, in the same way an empirical scientist can guide the course of her or his inquiry by a careful choice of experiments. In Chapter 19 we shall return to the special character of experimental "questions put to nature."

▲

Kant: The German philosopher Immanuel Kant (1724–1804) is one of the most famous of relatively modern philosophers, who worked at about the time of the American revolution. He rarely traveled from his home, and he was so regular in his habits that people were said to set their clocks on the basis of his afternoon walks. Nevertheless, his mind ranged widely and powerfully over the most difficult problems in philosophy.

Kant produced one of the most challenging accounts of how human beings know what they think they know. Both those who accept and those who reject Kant's account agree that it is very important to work through the insights Kant offers.

The contemporary American philosopher of science Larry Laudan also stresses the importance of questions in science. Whereas we have just seen Kant speaking of the importance of operational questions, Laudan emphasizes the importance of principal questions. He in effect argues that the value of a scientific theory depends crucially on the number and importance of the principal questions it enables scientists to answer. Laudan identifies such questions with problems and speaks of the problem-solving power of a theory as a crucial measure of its value. In fact, he argues that a new scientific theory is typically accepted on the strength of its capacity for solving one or two especially important problems.

10.9 Suppressed (Unstated) Operational Questions

The distinction between principal and operational questions helps us extend and refine our discussion of interrogative games in a number of ways. First, we will consider the important problem of *suppressed* operational questions.

In Part 1 we saw that many real-life sketches of inquiries make use of background or tacit (unmentioned) knowledge without explicitly indicating where and how. We saw then that it is instructive and difficult to take a description of one of these inquiries literally and to try to construct an interrogative game table. If you apply any half-way stringent standards of reasoning simply to the sketch of the inquiry, you will find that the inquiry does not meet the standards of good reasoning unless and until many new steps have been supplied. We have already noticed the need to supply new steps in many examples in Part 1. To make everyday arguments conform to the standards of interrogative inquiry, several steps had to be added to the argument that were not explicitly contained in its original sketch. Without such added steps, many real-life reports of inquiries and arguments appear to have more holes in them than a Swiss cheese.

Often, however, there is nothing deeply wrong with everyday arguments that contain gaps. Normally, the hearer or reader of such an argument will tend rather automatically to assume that what is missing can be supplied. But in order to analyze and to evaluate such incomplete inquiries, we have to be able to supply the missing links in detail.

How is this to be done? A tempting way of turning an incomplete inquiry into a better one—the method you would find in most textbooks on argumentation—is to consider the inquiry as an argument with unstated initial premises. To study an incomplete argument, according to this view, we must do two different things: first, find somehow the missing initial premises and, second, amplify the argument table to which these new premises have been added, trying to turn it into a purely deductive argument.

There is nothing wrong with doing this, if it can be done. Unfortunately, the missing premises cannot always be found in the beginning of the inquiry. Here the interrogative model shows what is possible and what is impossible. First, there are no general principles which would enable us to study where and how the suppressed initial premises might be found. The interrogative model suggests that **the missing premises can most naturally be thought of as answers to suitable operational questions.** The missing questions usually have to do with tacit knowledge the inquirer seems to be using.

But questions cannot always be asked whenever the inquirer so wishes. We shall see in Chapter 11 that a question, even a question addressed to one's own tacit knowledge, cannot be asked before its presupposition is established. But logical inferences may be needed to establish a required presupposition. Therefore, it is often impossible to ask all the questions first, as though logical inferences will be needed only after the missing information has been supplied. Furthermore, we may not even know which questions to ask until we have worked our way some distance into the inquiry.

The interrogative model is helpful with the problem of suppressed information for the following reason. The choice of operational questions to cover missing steps in an inquiry is subject to the same principles as the choice of knowledge-seeking questions in general. As we will see in Part 4 of the book, the presuppositions of unstated questions are the same as the presuppositions of explicit questions. In general, the unstated (suppressed) questions can be studied in the same way as stated ones, which makes the study of incomplete arguments much easier. In contrast, there are no general methods for evaluating the reasoning performance of an inquiry which is considered to be missing some suppressed premise(s).

Thus, in studying real-life examples of reasoning, one has to be constantly alert to the following questions: What unspoken operational (small) questions is the inquirer raising? and What answers is he or she assuming are available?

△ ▼ EXERCISE 10-C

Return to the illustration about losing the drug war, found in Section 3.4 of Chapter 3. Briefly describe how this example required the supplying of suppressed information at various steps along the way. Indicate how steps 2, 6a, and/or 8 might be further developed by posing additional operational questions.

△ ▼ EXERCISE 10-D

If you are working on a major argument construction and essay project, devote some time to examining your work for suppressed operational questions. Consider whether these can safely be left in the background or whether some of them need to be given more explicit attention in your table and/or in your essay.

△ ▼ EXERCISE 10-E

Your instructor may assign argument sketches from Appendix A. Identify the suppressed (unspoken or tacit) operational questions in the assigned sketches, and discuss what the answers are the inquirer seems to have been expecting. Indicate also what source of information may be functioning as an oracle for these questions. Discuss whether the unspoken questions were easy to supply and answer. Was the inquirer justified in expecting the reader to supply the missing information?

△ ▼ **EXERCISE 10-F**

Find a report of an inquiry or an editorial or commentary that presents an argument. Alternatively, your instructor may assign one. Indicate what suppressed operational questions (if any) are involved in the inquiry and discuss whether the unspoken questions would be easy to supply and answer. Was the inquirer justified in expecting the reader to supply the missing information?

10.10   Sequential Reasoning

The difference between principal questions and operational questions can also help us understand complex sequences of reasoning. Suppose that an inquirer has successfully completed a particular process of reasoning. In terms of an interrogative game this would mean that the ultimate conclusion has been established. Often, however, this success does not finish the inquirer's life work, nor usually even his or her day's work.

What does the inquirer usually do? The answer is clear. After a particular ultimate conclusion has been established, this conclusion may, in the next act of the drama of questioning, be treated as one of the initial premises of a new inquiry.

It is important to note, by the way, that *this is the only situation in which propositions may be transported from the right side of an interrogative table to the left side.* Furthermore, such transportation may take place only after a logical table has been successfully completed, *never before*.

Illustration   Return to the example concerning salaries paid to teachers and to professional athletes in the middle of Section 3.1 of Chapter 3. Notice that each of the first three lines of the table could be considered to be the result of a separate process of inquiry whose goal is to establish that particular bit of information, which in turn serves as a premise in this particular inquiry.

Likewise, in the first table of Exercise 3-B from the same section of Chapter 3, the first two lines could be considered as the goals of separate processes of inquiry. For instance, the second line, that children infected with the AIDS virus cannot transmit it to other students, involves both information on the way the virus may be transmitted and the types of interaction between children at school. A sequence of processes of inquiry might begin by first establishing this result and then continue by using the information it provides to reach a conclusion about correct policies involving these children, as in the exercise.

10.11   Questioning as a Multilevel Process

A related insight which the distinction between principal and operational questions helps us to reach is that interrogative reasoning can be a *multilevel* process.

What, from the perspective of a higher-level questioning game, is a "small," operational question can, on the basis of a finer analysis, turn out to be itself answerable on the basis of a series of even smaller questions, that is, answerable as the principal question of a lower-level interrogative game. On these occasions it becomes important to distinguish from each other the different levels of questions and the different levels of interrogative games.

Please note that no value judgment is intended when we speak of different *levels* of questions and questioning. An example might be offered by the scientific "game" of "exploring the world." A controlled experiment may serve as an operational ("small") question for a theoretical scientist who uses the results of experiments as stepping stones in quest of a theory. The result of an experiment—for instance, a mathematical function expressing the dependence of one variable on another—enters into the reasoning of a theorist as a ready-made answer to an operational question. Yet, for an experimental scientist the very same result may play the role of an answer to a principal question. Answering this principal question itself involves a complex process of reasoning, which can also be interpreted as a questioning game.

Advisers and Levels of Inquiry

A different kind of example might be offered by considering a scientific adviser to a governmental agency or administrator. Questions put to the adviser are dealt with by the administrative or political decision makers as operational ("small") questions. The administrator or politician is usually not interested in the foundation of such answers. Yet answering such questions may require a careful and lengthy process of reasoning on the part of the adviser. What for the administrator was an operational question may therefore play the role of a principal question for the adviser.

The multilevel character of questions and questioning is important to keep in mind when analyzing actual arguments from real-life sources. For one thing, the analyst has to know on what level the analysis is supposed to come to an end. Otherwise, the task of analyzing an argument may never do so.

On the other hand, before the agreed-on, rock-bottom analysis has been reached, we always have to keep in mind *the possibility that what looks like a "small" (operational) question really should be considered as the principal question of a lower-level questioning process.*

We may here recall also what was said above about incomplete arguments. Sometimes an argument may look incomplete because it moves on a level in which certain answers are taken for granted, that is, are considered as answers to operational questions. The argument will then be incomplete only from the viewpoint of another, deeper level of inquiry. On that lower level, the same answers are considered as responding to principal questions, to be reached through lower-level interrogative reasoning.

Illustration   In the Smith-Jones-Robinson puzzle (at the end of Chapter 5) most of the work is done by logical inference steps. An example in which most of the weight falls on interrogative steps is offered by the main character's reasoning in a novel by Dick Francis, *Hot Money* (London: Pan Books, 1987). It also illustrates how a final argument can consist of assembling the results of a number of lower-level inquiries.

The outline of the plot is as follows: An oft-married multimillionaire Malcolm Pembroke finds his latest estranged wife murdered and himself the target of murder attempts. He contacts his son from an earlier marriage, Ian Pembroke, and asks him to act as his bodyguard. The result is an attempt to kill both of them with a bomb that destroys much of Malcolm's mansion, where all his children had spent some of their childhood. It quickly turns out that only an immediate family member could have made all the murder attempts. But with six sons and two daughters from five marriages, four current daughters-in-laws, one son-in-law, and three surviving ex-wives, that still leaves the field pretty open. Malcolm Pembroke hires a private investigator named Norman West to check on all of them.

Ian Pembroke also checks on his half-brothers and half-sisters and their spouses. He decides he knows who the culprit is, but in order to convince the police and his father, he has to set a trap that would force the murderer to reveal his or her identity by trying to destroy incriminating evidence. To Malcolm's surprise, his favorite daughter Serena shows up and is killed by the self-made bomb she was carrying.

How did Ian know it was Serena? Here is part of his reasoning.

"How did you know?"

"I saw everyone, as you know. I saw what's wrong with their lives. Saw their desperations. Donald and Helen are desperate for money, but they were coping the best way they could. Bravely, really, pawning her jewellery. They thought you might help them with guaranteeing a loan, if they could find you. That's a long way from wanting to kill you."

Malcolm nodded and drank, and watched life proceeding outside.

"Lucy," I said, "may have lost her inspiration but not her marbles. Edwin is petulant but not a planner, not dynamic. Thomas . . . " I paused. "Thomas was absolutely desperate, but for peace in his house, not for the money itself. Berenice has made him deeply ineffective. He's got a long way to go, to climb back. He seemed to me incapable almost of tying his shoelaces, let alone making a time-bomb, even if he did invent the wired-up clocks."

"Go on," Malcolm said.

"Berenice is obsessed with herself and her desires, but her grudge is against Thomas. Money would make her quieter, but it's not money she really wants, it's a son. Killing Moira and you wouldn't achieve that."

"And Gervase?"

"He's destroying himself. It takes all his energies. He hasn't enough left to go around killing people for money. He's lost his nerve. He drinks. You have to be courageous and sober to mess with explosives. Ursula's desperation takes her to churches and to lunches with Joyce."

He grunted in his throat, not quite a chuckle.

"Joyce had been thanked by us on the telephone on the Saturday night when we'd come back exhausted. She'd been devastated to the point of silence about what had happened and had put the phone down in tears. We phoned her again in the morning. "I got Serena first," she said sorrowfully. "She must have gone out and bought all the stuff . . . I can't bear it. That dear little girl, so sweet when she was little, even though I hated her mother. So *awful.*"

"Go on, then," Malcolm said. "You keep stopping."

"It couldn't have been Alicia or Vivien, they're not strong enough to carry you. Alicia's new boyfriend would be, but why should he think Alicia would be better off with you dead? And I couldn't imagine any of them constructing a bomb."

"And Ferdinand?"

"I really couldn't see it, could you? He has no particular worries. He's good at his job. He's easy-going most of the time. Not him. Not Debs. That's the lot."

"So did you come to Serena just by elimination?" He turned from the window, searching my face.

"No," I said slowly. "I thought of them all together, all their troubles and heart-aches. To begin with, when Moira died, I thought, like everyone else did, that she was killed to stop her taking half your money. I thought the attacks on you were for money, too. It was the obvious thing. And then, when I'd seen them all, when I understood all the turmoils going on under apparently normal exte-riors, I began to wonder whether the money really mattered at all . . . And when I was in New York, I was thinking of them all again but taking the money out . . . and with Serena . . . everything fitted." (pp. 264–265)

From this example, you can see how different types of inquiry differ from each other. In the Smith-Jones-Robinson exercise, the main problem was to find the right logical inference moves. Here it is to find answers to the relevant ques-tions. The questions, mostly obvious, are mostly of the form: Could X have done it? Each such question must actually be answered by a separate smaller (lower-level) inquiry of its own. In fact, in the novel itself, much of the story centers on Norman West's and Ian Pembroke's investigation of the different family members, in the course of which the character, lifestyle, financial condition, and emotional state of each of them slowly emerges. Here, we are nevertheless interested primarily in the overall line of reasoning of Ian Pembroke.

Notice that other types of inquiry differ from Ian Pembroke's in that in many of them the crucial problem is to find the right questions, which here are relatively obvious.

One possible reconstruction of Ian Pembroke's line of inquiry (left side of the interrogative table) might run as follows:

1. Question-answer step: Was the murderer a family member? Yes, for he or she knew Malcolm Pembroke's habits (p. 104) and did not make his dogs suspi-cious. All and only family members filled this bill (p. 104). Moreover, the

murderer was likely to have had keys to Malcolm Pembroke's house in his or her possession (p. 127).

2. Question-answer step: Was the murderer an adult? Yes, for he or she carried Malcolm Pembroke to the garage.

3. Question: Who are the adult family members? Answer:

   Mrs. Vivian Pembroke (first wife). Children: Donald Pembroke, Lucy Pembroke, Thomas Pembroke. Their spouses: Helen Pembroke, Edwin Bugg, Berenice Pembroke.

   Joyce Pembroke (second wife); Ian Pembroke (her son).

   Alicia Pembroke (third wife). Children: Gervase Pembroke, Ferdinand Pembroke, Serena Pembroke (unmarried). Their spouses: Ursula Pembroke, Debs Pembroke.

4. Question-answer step: Is Ian Pembroke the murderer? No, he was at the racing stable with about thirty people as witnesses when the first attempt was made on his father's life, and he was himself nearly killed together with his father when someone tried to run over them with a car.

5. Question-answer step: Is Donald or Helen Pembroke the murderer? No, even though they are desperate for money, they are dealing with their problems rationally.

   [In the same way the inquirer (Ian Pembroke) eliminates all the family members except Serena Pembroke.]

18. Logical-inference step: The murderer is Serena Pembroke. (Inference from all the earlier steps.)

This example also illustrates the multilevel character of inquiry. As was indicated, each of the questions 1–2, 5–17 is answered by means of a separate "mini-inquiry" or line of thought of its own. They must be thought of as lower-level inquiries, for the questions 1–2, 5–17 (which in Ian Pembroke's overall line of reasoning are operational questions) serve in these separate lower-level inquiries as their respective principal questions. Some of the steps of these subordinate inquiries are in fact indicated in the reconstruction above as parts of the answers to the questions 1–2, 5–17.

△ ▼ THINK ABOUT IT

Persons who have access to the book *Hot Money* might reconstruct Ian Pembroke's lower-level line of inquiry in answering one of the questions 5–17. Note that in these lower-level inquiries the choice of the right (psychologically revealing) questions is the crucial strategic consideration.

In Chapter 12 we shall discuss how a line of argument can be strengthened by constructing alternative lines of reasoning. Here Ian Pembroke clearly is backing up his own conclusion by also explaining Serena's motives.

10.12   Fallacies and Begging the Question

The distinction between principal and operational questions and our understanding of the multilevel nature of reasoning gives us an occasion to discuss the famous fallacy called **begging the question.** As we make progress in our study of reasoning, we have from time to time been pointing out specific mistakes that need to be avoided. Certain mistakes in reasoning are made so regularly that it has seemed wise to identify them and give them a name. Traditionally, these have been called **fallacies.** Interestingly, although it seems easy enough to notice that something has gone wrong in a line of reasoning, there has frequently been much confusion and difficulty in pinning down exactly what is going wrong.

▲

Fallacy: A mistake in reasoning. As reasoning involves both logical inference steps and interrogative steps, there can be *logical fallacies* and *interrogative fallacies*. Alongside definitory and strategic rules of reasoning exist *definitory fallacies* and *strategic fallacies*.

Many more errors occur in deductive reasoning than could possibly be given specific names. For example, invalid attempts at deductive inferences are examples of definitory logical fallacies. Some, such as "affirming the consequent" and "denying the antecedent," which we studied in Part 2, have labels but most do not. One can also make strategic errors in deductive reasoning. An example would be to apply a statement-logic rule to a line which has already been checked off. An example of an interrogative fallacy is given in the following discussion of "begging the question."

Our interrogative model of inquiry can help us avoid many of the more dangerous errors in reasoning. You will find that if you learn how to use the interrogative model effectively, you will avoid many errors without ever having had to study them by name. In Appendix C, however, we collect together our insights into the so-called fallacies. For the moment we will take a look at the famous fallacy called **begging the question.** Its Latin name is *petitio principii.*

Probably neither the Latin nor the English name tells you very much about the mistake. And, in fact, in many traditional explanations of the mistake the name still remains rather puzzling. For example, one of the better traditional explanations says that begging the question involves making an assumption in the premises of an argument that is equally or more contentious than the conclusion a person is trying to establish.

Now why should we call that "begging the question"? We could twist it around a bit to help you tie the name to the described error, but our interrogative model will show us a better way.

The problem in explaining the fallacy is partly due to an understandable historical mistake. Aristotle is the grandfather of most discussions of the so-called fallacies. As was indicated in Chapter 3, he is also famous for having given one of the first detailed discussions of logical inference. This has led many commentators to assume that when Aristotle warned us against fallacies like begging the question, he was trying to help us avoid a mistake in logical inference, a logical fallacy. This then leads to an explanation like the one given above. Notice how that explanation talks about premises and conclusions in a way that assumes we are trying to make a logical inference.

As it happens, however, Aristotle also had a lively interest in interrogative procedures. And it turns out that when he warned us against "begging the question," he was actually discussing an important mistake in questioning rather than in logical inference.

Like his predecessors, Socrates and Plato, Aristotle was deeply interested in how questioning games help us in rational inquiry. One of the things they early discovered is something you have been learning. This is that significant inquiry usually requires a series of question-answer steps. Important problems are rarely solved in one big jump. For various reasons, the big questions we ask, which get us started on an inquiry, are not questions that can be immediately answered. Instead, we must proceed by careful, smaller steps toward the conclusive answer. In this light, begging the question is easily understood: Begging the question occurs whenever we try to answer the big (principal) question too soon. Begging the question is a matter of taking questioning shortcuts that are not appropriate to our purposes.

In an extreme case the fallacy of begging the question occurs when the questioner entirely overlooks the difference between operational and principal questions. Instead of trying to answer the principal question by means of operational questions, the inquirer mistakenly asks ("petitions") the principal question directly. This is, incidentally, where the name *petitio principii* comes from.

Some Examples   There are various reasons for which such shortcuts are closed and not available. Consider an artificial, but quite ordinary example. When you study math in college, you can be sure to get examinations in which you will be asked to answer some tough principal questions. If all we were ever interested in were the conclusive answer to the questions, a good method for getting it would be simply to ask the teacher! The teacher presumably already knows the answer. This, however, would be an inappropriate begging for the question's answer. (Perhaps you know some students who in desperation have been driven to do this.)

The teacher, however, is usually not interested in how creatively you are able to beg for mercy. In math the goal is not to find out whether your hearing is good and whether you can copy down an answer. The teacher is interested in whether you can work out a line of inquiry on your own that will lead to the answer. This line of inquiry will include appropriate operational questions addressed to the available information, combined with mathematical logical inferences. Therefore, the shortcut of begging for the question's answer is not usually available to you.

In Appendix B you can read about some recreational questioning games like "twenty questions" and "Botticelli." The whole point of games like these is that the shortcut of begging for the main question's answer is not available.

Human beings set up artificial situations like the math exam and the recreational questioning games partly because life itself presents us with so many similar situations. For example, for many centuries people wanted to know the answer to why things stay in motion the way they do and why things fall to the ground. Powerful theories in physics now help us understand these matters. But we did not get these theories simply by asking Nature one big question and getting a prompt reply. Nature does not usually permit such shortcuts. It has instead required centuries of patient inquiry, including the asking of many smaller questions, for us to get where we have.

Or again, if an engineer is involved in a complex building project, questions about strength of building materials are not answered simply by looking at a piece of steel or wood or plastic. Instead, a complex series of operational questions must be developed in order to match what is known about the materials to what is needed in the project.

Politicians regularly run the risk of begging the question. The people who elect them often want some very big problems solved. They want the national deficit eliminated. They want to avoid inflation or a recession. They want the homeless to be helped. How tempting it is for everybody involved to look for quick answers. Being alert to the problem of begging the question, however, should cause us to be wary of the quick solutions that are so often suggested.

Purposes, Strategies, and Begging the Question

Notice, however, that begging the question is in part a strategic matter. Our definition says that the error involves taking questioning shortcuts that are "inappropriate to our purposes." Determining what questions are "big" for us and what are "small" is often dependent upon our situation and the purposes we have in mind with our questions.

For example, an engineer may need a quite complex series of questions to determine what materials to specify in a building project. But the construction foreman can simply consult the blueprints and get an answer about required materials directly. What was a principal question for the engineer's purposes is operational for the construction foreman.

An accountant may require pages of analysis to produce a company's annual financial statement, but the chairman of the board may be interested only in the "bottom line." Determining the "bottom line" was the principal question guiding the accountant's reasoning, but it is likely to be an operational question in the chairman's decision-making inquiries. If you are in a physics class, you will be expected to develop a deep grasp of the nature of electricity. But someone else may need only know that when the switch is turned, the radio plays.

Our discussions of sequential reasoning and of the many levels of inquiry in preceding sections of this chapter have helped us understand how questions play different roles in different situations. Aristotle's warnings about begging the question thus involve something much more complicated and significant than pointing out a mistake in logical inference. Warnings against begging the question remind us what rational inquiry is really like. And begging the question is not so much about logical inference as about the different roles questions may play in rational inquiry.

___ ▲ _____

> **Begging the Question:** An interrogative fallacy involving an attempt to answer a big, principal question in an inquiry too soon. In so far as "too soon" is determined by our situation and purposes, this fallacy involves strategic considerations. In other cases, "begging the question" is forbidden by rules restricting questions and answers in specific types of interrogative games.

△ ▼ EXERCISE 10-G

Describe and discuss how "begging the question" might arise for different people in different ways in the following cases.

▸ 1. What will the weather be tomorrow? A meteorologist; a skier.

2. Is this used car in good shape? A potential buyer; a mechanic.

3. How does this compact disc player work? The owner; a consumer magazine; a digital electronics engineer.

▸ 4. Should Sally marry Sherman? Sally; Sherman; Sally's father; Sherman's roommate.

5. Should you major in philosophy? You; your philosophy instructor.

△ ▼ EXERCISE 10-H

Continue (or your instructor may now have you begin) work on your major assignment in constructing an argument and writing an essay based on it.

▲11
▼

Three Further Aspects of Interrogative Moves

In Chapter 10 we studied fundamental aspects of the questioning process, noting various implications of the difference between principal and operational questions. In this chapter we turn our attention to three further aspects of interrogative moves: (1) the influence of complex principal questions on the structure of rational inquiry, (2) operational questions and the importance of their presuppositions, and (3) the many different sources of information that are typically found in rational inquiry.

11.1 Complex Principal Questions

The distinction between principal questions and operational questions leads us to extend the characterization of interrogative games given in Part 1. We can now see that we have to allow for situations in which the aim of the game is not to prove a given ultimate conclusion but to answer a principal question.

The simplest new case is the one in which the principal question is a yes-or-no question. Then the only difference as compared with the original games is that the inquirer is now trying to construct two lines of reasoning, one with an affirmative answer to the principal question as its ultimate conclusion and one with a negative answer as its ultimate conclusion. This will require the construction of two different game tables.

Thus we can distinguish two different types of interrogative games (among others). In the first type of game, the inquirer is simply trying to establish a given conclusion. We might call such a game a *simple interrogative game.*

In the other type of game, the inquirer is trying to answer a question of the form "B or not-B?" We might call this more complex type the *Shakespearean type of interrogative game* in honor of Hamlet's famous question, "To be or not to be?"

In this second type of game, the inquirer will need two different logical tables as his or her bookkeeping method. Both tables have in the beginning the same initial premise(s) on their left sides, but different ultimate conclusions (indeed, contradictory ones) on their right sides. The two lines of reasoning (the two logical tables) have to be constructed separately.

This helps us notice a common mistake committed in many different walks of life. It is often assumed that we can examine a principal yes-or-no question through a single line of reasoning. It is thought that one and the same process of inquiry can determine whether an affirmative or negative answer to a principal yes-or-no question is the correct answer. This is usually not possible, however. The reason is that the construction of a logical table also depends on what there is in its right column, not just on what there is in its left column.

This can be illustrated by a variety of examples. The most obvious ones are perhaps the rules of questioning for successful reasoning in a court of law. If you are a defense attorney, you do not usually ask questions about the defendant's criminal past. If you are the prosecuting attorney, that might be just the kind of question to raise.

But the difference is not just a matter of tactics. It also concerns the logic of the case. Suppose, for instance, that you are trying to answer the question of whether all the individuals in some group are of a certain kind or whether there are exceptions. Then the top right-hand entries (possible ultimate conclusions) in the two logical tables might be, respectively,

1. Everything is A.
2. Something is not-A.

Now in the table with statement 1 as the proposed ultimate conclusion, the argument takes the form of postulating, as a thought-experiment, an exception. Let us name the exceptional individual α. Now part of this inquiry will typically take the form of an examination of what one can and must say of this proposed imaginary counterexample. Questions about α will therefore play a major role in the inquiry.

In contrast, in the other logical table α cannot play any role, because it does not even enter the argument. When the ultimate conclusion is "Something is not-A," the corresponding counterassumption is that "Everything is A." On this assumption α does not even exist. Therefore, questions about α will not play the role they played in the other table. Hence it will often make a major difference to the structure of the argument which of the two contradictory propositions is inserted in the top of the right column.

Understanding the Adversary System in Law

The need to split up the line of reasoning into two when the inquirer is trying to answer a yes-or-no question is also an unspoken presupposition of the adversary system in our courts. If the two lines of thought that are involved in answering a yes-or-no question depended on each other in order for the questioning process to lead to the truth, then the prosecutor and the defense attorney would have to cooperate if the criminal process were to lead to a decision. We have already seen, however, that attorneys on opposite sides of a case routinely follow very different lines of questioning.

"Wh-" Questions

When the question the entire reasoning process is to answer is a "who-" or a "what-" question (see Section 11.2), then the desired ultimate conclusion becomes even more complicated. To come to know "who did it," the inquirer must come to know of some one person that he or she did it. But, sight unseen, the inquirer does not usually know who that person is. How this idea can be incorporated into the rules of interrogative games will be studied in Part 4.

△ ▼ EXERCISE 11-A

▶ 1. Give an example of an inquiry in a field other than law in which the inquiry generally proceeds by trying to establish one member of a statement-denial pair. Discuss how this affects the construction of interrogative tables for such an inquiry.

2. Return to the illustration about taking a course in reasoning and critical thinking discussed in Section 4.2 of Chapter 4 and Section 10.6 of Chapter 10. Under what conditions might we consider the resulting interrogative game to be a simple one? Under what conditions might it be considered to be one-half of a Shakespearean interrogative game?

△ ▼ EXERCISE 11-B

Continue to work on your argument construction and essay assignment. Examine how the principal question involved in your project may suggest more than one line of reasoning leading to alternative conclusions. Ask yourself whether you have sufficiently considered alternative ultimate conclusions that would correspond to alternative answers to the principal question.

11.2 Presuppositions of Questions

In this section you will first learn how to identify two fundamentally different types of questions, after which we shall examine the importance of establishing presuppositions for the questions we wish to ask in our interrogative inquiries.

Statement Questions

Some questions are statement (propositional) questions; others are "wh-" questions. Examples of the latter are questions that use words like *who* and *what*. The simplest statement questions can be answered with a "yes" or "no." For example:

Is Mary in class today?

In the usual use of such a question a simple "yes" or "no" will provide an answer. Reaching back to the statement logic we learned in Part 2, we can represent "Mary is in class today" by A and "Mary is not in class today" by $-A$. Our simple question will now expect either the answer A or the answer $-A$.

In a moment we will be looking at "wh-" questions, but first we have to talk about *whether*. *Whether* looks like a "wh-" word but it actually produces statement questions rather than "wh-" questions. For example, the question

Let me ask you whether you plan to come to class or to go skiing?

is a statement question. It cannot be answered by a simple "yes" or "no," but it can be analyzed in a way similar to yes/no questions. Let C represent "You plan to come to class" and D represent "You plan to go skiing." The questioner obviously wants to find out if C is true or D is true. The two alternative answers to the question are therefore C, on the one hand, and D on the other.

In this particular question the two available answers are mutually exclusive. C and D cannot be true together. We do not, however, want to build this requirement of mutual exclusiveness into our concept of a statement question. For example, if the question had been

Did Mats Wilander win the U.S. Open or the Australian Open in 1988?

then the two possible answers are

1. Mats Wilander won the U.S. Open in 1988.

and

2. Mats Wilander won the Australian Open in 1988.

As it happens, both statements 1 and 2 are true. In this book we shall consider both of these to be acceptable answers. In other words, we are not assuming that in the two previous example questions only one of the options is true. This relates to the strategy of logicians in focusing on "inclusive" *or* rather than "exclusive" *or.*

It is nevertheless a good strategy to ask questions whose possible answers exclude each other. For this reason in the second statement question we are right to assume that the different answers *C* and *D* cannot both be true together. Furthermore, at least one of them ought to be true, for otherwise it would not make much sense to raise the question.

Here is another statement question:

Is Mary staying on campus over the holiday or is she going home or will she be visiting her boyfriend?

This example involves three statements. Let *E*, *F,* and *G* represent the first, second, and third, respectively. We are asking which of the statements is true without assuming that the other two will be false.

There is more to be said about statement questions, but first we must contrast them with "wh-" questions.

"Wh-" Questions

"Wh-" questions are questions that use words like *who* and *what*. There are many different kinds of "wh-" questions; they make use of all the famous newspaper reporter words such as *who, what, where, when, why,* and *how.* (*How* can be used to ask a "wh-" question even though it is not literally a "wh-" word. Remember also that *whether* looks as though it should introduce a "wh-" question, but it actually introduces statement questions.) For the moment we will concentrate on "wh-" questions using the words *who* and *what.*

Consider the following example:

Who stole my pickup truck?

This cannot easily be represented as a statement because the word *who* indicates that there are an indefinite number of specific statements which need to be considered: "Did Mary steal it?" "Did Harry steal it?" "Did someone I don't know steal it?" The list could go on and on. "Wh-" questions require use of a more powerful formal logic than the statement logic we learned in Part 2. In Part 4, Chapter 16, you will learn about their formal representation.

For now we simply observe that in ordinary use the alternatives involved in a statement question are specified by statements or words like "yes" and "no." In a "wh-" question, the alternatives are usually specified by names designating, for example, persons or objects.

△ ▼ EXERCISE 11-C

Which of the following are statement questions and which are "wh-" questions?

1. Did you go to the play?
2. What is your favorite play?
▸ 3. Is your favorite play *Hamlet* or *Happy Birthday, Wanda June*?
▸ 4. Who is your favorite author?
▸ 5. Do you have a favorite author?
▸ 6. How did you like the play?
7. How did the theater burn down?

Structure of Statement Questions

We can get a more detailed understanding of the reasoning process by examining the structure of questions. The first thing to notice is that we are studying how questions are used to increase our information, to expand our knowledge. (You may wish to review the explanation in Chapter 10 of how interrogative moves introduce new information into an inquiry.) This suggests that the questions we are studying can all be put into the form of a request:

Bring it about that . . . I know that . . .

This request might be addressed to another person or to our own memory or to Nature or to a computer database or to any of a number of different sources. The point is that the questioner desires further information. It is this feature of questions which leads us to use the technical term **desideratum** to refer to whatever it is we are searching to know.

For example, we are already well on the way to understanding the structure of statement questions. Consider again the example question from the beginning of this chapter:

Is Mary in class today?

If *A* represents "Mary is in class today" and –*A* represents "Mary is not in class today" then our question can be analyzed as:

Bring it about that (I know that *A* or I know that –*A*).

What is desired in this question is what is in parentheses:

I know that *A* or I know that –*A*.

So this sentence is the desideratum of the question.

The subsequent example question was

Let me ask you whether you plan to come to class or to go skiing?

Using statement letters *C* and *D* again, the form of this question is

Bring it about that (I know that C or I know that D).

The desideratum will then be

I know that C or I know that D.

Statement questions are thus not too difficult to analyze. The general form of a statement question will be

Bring it about that (I know that $A \lor$ I know that $B \lor$ I know that $C \lor \ldots$).

Yes/No questions have the general form

Bring it about that (I know that $A \lor$ I know that $-A$).

The desideratum of the question is the part that follows the phrase "Bring it about that . . . " This means that the desideratum of a statement question can be formed simply by putting "I know that" in front of each of the alternative statements suggested by the statement question and joining the resulting sentences with the word *or*. (The word *whether* introduces such alternatives joined by *or*, and this is why *whether* indicates a statement question rather than a "wh-" question.) So, the desideratum of a statement question will in general look like this:

I know that $A \lor$ I know that $B \lor$ I know that $C \lor \ldots$

The general form of the desideratum of a yes/no question will simply be

I know that $A \lor$ I know that $-A$.

Structure of "Wh-" Questions

"Wh-" questions are a little more tricky to analyze, but the ideas will be the same. As with statement questions the general form of a "wh-" question also begins with the request

Bring it about that . . . I know that . . .

In "wh-" questions the part that begins "I know that" will, as before, be called the desideratum. The problem is how to represent what replaces the dots in our schematic analysis. We are not in a position to give a formal analysis, but the basic idea can be illustrated as follows. Let us return to the preceding example:

Who stole my pickup truck?

Putting this question in more general form, we get

Bring it about that I know who stole my pickup truck.

The troublesome word *who* is still in the picture, but we can at least see that the desideratum here is

I know who stole my pickup truck.

Notice how the "wh-" question "Who stole my pickup truck?" is similar to, but very different from the statement question, "Did someone steal my pickup truck?" Examine these two questions carefully to make sure you understand the difference. Here is another example:

What is the capital of Nebraska?

We shall rewrite this as

Bring it about that I know what the capital of Nebraska is.

The desideratum of this question is thus

I know what the capital of Nebraska is.

△▼ EXERCISE 11-D

1. Analyze the question "Is there a capital of Scotland?" and discuss how it is different from the question "What is the capital of Scotland?"

▶ 2. Return to Exercise 11-C. Identify and give the form of each of the questions found there.

Presuppositions of Questions

The analysis of statement and "wh-" questions has now put us in a position to get at one of the most important principles of the questioning process: that we cannot make much progress in questioning unless what logicians call the **presuppositions of the questions** have been established. But we cannot check up on the presuppositions of our questions unless we know what they are.

Fortunately, if you are able to identify the desideratum of your question, you can easily get at its presupposition, for the presupposition of a question can be found simply by omitting all occurrences of the phrase "I know" or "I know that" from the desideratum. In the case of "wh-" questions it is also necessary to substitute words like "someone," "something," or "there is" for "who," "what," or "what is."

Presuppositions of Statement Questions

Look again at the general form of a statement question.

Bring it about that (I know that A ∨ I know that B ∨ I know that C ∨ . . .)

The desideratum is

I know that A ∨ I know that B ∨ I know that C ∨ . . .

So the general form of the presupposition of a statement question is

A ∨ B ∨ C ∨ . . .

Recall that the general form of the desideratum of a yes/no question is

I know that A ∨ I know that $-A$.

So the general form of the presupposition of a yes/no question is simply

A ∨ $-A$

In general, then, the presupposition of a statement question is simply the statement letters joined by ∨. Whenever we want to ask a statement question, we can check rather easily to see what our presupposition is and whether we are in a position to make the assumption the question requires.

Presuppositions of "Wh-" Questions

Now look again at the form of a "wh-" question:

Bring it about that I know who stole my pickup truck.

The desideratum here is

I know who stole my pickup truck.

For our informal analysis of "wh-" questions, we drop the phrase "I know" and substitute a word like "someone" or "something" for the occurrence of "who" or "what" in the desideratum. So the presupposition of this "wh-" question is

Someone stole my pickup truck.

As we shall see, it is always well worth checking whether a presupposition like this can be established when we want to inquire into a question like "Who stole my pickup truck?"

Here is one more "wh-" example, taken from a previous question put into the general form

Bring it about that I know what the capital of Nebraska is.

The desideratum of this question is thus

I know what the capital of Nebraska is.

Substituting "there is" for "what . . . is," the presupposition of this "wh-" question is consequently

There is a capital of Nebraska.

The state of Nebraska ought to have a capital, so this presupposition seems like a pretty safe assumption. Our question is not likely to lead to any trouble. How would things turn out in the exercise if we asked about the capital of Scotland?

△ ▼ EXERCISE 11-E

Write out the presuppositions of the following questions.

▸ 1. Will you watch the game on TV?

2. Is Mexico City larger than Tokyo?

▸ 3. Which is larger, Mexico City or Tokyo?

4. Where is Tegucigalpa?

▸ 5. Who is the president of France?

11.3   Putting the Analysis to Work

We now proceed to put our knowledge about partial and conclusive answers (cf. Chapter 10) and about the structure of questions to work.

The Fallacy of Many Questions

One has to be very careful in dealing with yes/no questions in ordinary language. Sometimes what looks like a yes/no question and is even formulated as one, in reality is not of the form "Bring it about that I know that A ∨ or that I know that $-A$." Consider, as an example, the question

Have you stopped cheating on your homework?

This looks like a yes/no question, but in reality it is not. In other words, it looks as if it needed only an obvious presupposition of the form $(A ∨ -A)$, but actually it needs a much stronger presupposition. What the two alternative answers really say is, respectively,

1. I used to cheat on my homework, but I am not cheating on my homework now (any longer) and

2. I used to cheat on my homework, and I am (still) cheating now.

Neither statement 1 nor statement 2 can be true unless it is true that

3. I used to cheat on my homework.

Hence, for a logician, the real form of the original question is

Bring it about that I know that $(B \& A)$ or I know that $(B \& -A)$.

where B stands for "I used to cheat on my homework" and A stands for "I am now cheating on my homework."

The presupposition of the question is not a tautological (always true) one but rather includes the statement B, that is, "I used to cheat on my homework." It is the presence of this hidden part of the presupposition that results in a trick question (a fallacious one), which the questioner is not entitled to ask before the presupposition B has been established. Of course, this is precisely the presupposition the questioner is trying to trick the answerer into admitting.

Because this move in questioning in a sense involves asking more than one question under the guise of asking only one, it has been called the **fallacy (or error) of many questions.** The hidden presupposition ought to have been established by a different preparatory question or questions. What is happening is that these preparatory questions are assimilated into the stated question, which therefore is really "many questions" even though it should be only one. Because this move loads more than one question into what looks like a single question, another name that is often used is the "fallacy (or error) of asking loaded questions." (Strictly speaking, these explanations are themselves a little fallacious, however, for the hidden presupposition could perhaps be established by making logical inferences rather than by asking other, earlier questions.)

Drawing an unauthorized logical inference is sometimes called "jumping to a conclusion." Committing the "fallacy of many questions" might then as well be called "jumping to a presupposition"! More generally, the inquirer commits the fallacy of many questions whenever she or he asks a question whose presupposition has not yet been established.

The classic example of this fallacy is the query, put to a kind and considerate husband, "When did you stop beating your wife?" A less sexist illustration might be, "When did you stop taking steroids?" addressed to an athlete, or "When did you stop your heavy drinking?" put to a nominee for the position of Secretary of Defense. Any attempt to answer such questions will lead the answerer into trouble.

Now we can see that the proper response to such a question is not to attempt to answer it, but to point out that it depends on a presupposition that has not been established and maybe cannot be established. In other words, the appropriate response is to accuse the questioner of committing the fallacy of many questions or "jumping to a presupposition."

As we have often seen with the complexities of reasoning, however, there are sometimes contexts in which a reasoning move usually called a fallacy is not after all a mistake but rather a strategy serving a useful purpose. Some child psychologists suggest that combining questions in the way we have been studying can sometimes help children through certain difficult stages.

For instance, consider a small child who is just beginning to assert his or her independence. If the mother says, "Gail, put your shirt on" or "Gail, don't you want to put your shirt on," the child is likely almost automatically to refuse. Child psychologists recommend that, in such a situation, parents should say something like, "Gail, do you want to put your pants or your shirt on first?" This gives the child some scope to exercise his or her own will while at the same time accomplishing the parent's goal of getting both items of clothing on.

△ ▼ EXERCISE 11-F

1. Indicate and represent the presuppositions of the following questions a–i. Note carefully which have a presupposition of the logical form ($A \lor -A$) and which have a stronger presupposition.

▶ a. Is the present king of France bald? $(A \& B) \lor (A \& -B)$

▶ b. Does Nelson live in an apartment? $A \lor -A$

▶   c. Does Nelson live in a luxury apartment? $(A \& L) \vee (A \& \sim L)$
    d. Did Tom arrive before Dick and Harry?
    e. Is Mexico City larger than Tokyo? $A \vee \sim A$
▶   f. Which is larger, Mexico City or Tokyo? $A \vee B$
    g. Did you go to the play? $(P \& A) \vee (P \& \sim A)$ $A \vee \sim A$
▶   h. Do you have a favorite author? $A \vee \sim A$
▶   i. Do you have a favorite Jabberwock? $(E \& F) \vee (E \& \sim F)$

2. Give some thought to how questions and hidden presuppositions are used to create friction in interpersonal communication. For example, I may know that you have not yet done your math homework, but I might ask "Were the problems very difficult?" What is the irritating hidden presupposition of my question? Give and analyze your own example of this sort of problem.

On the other hand, people often read extra presuppositions into questions that in themselves do not make the offending assumption. For example, a wife might ask, "What time should the kids go to bed tonight?" and the husband might irritably infer that she is presuming that it is his turn to take care of that problem. Give and analyze your own example of this sort of problem.

Illustration of a Failure to Check Presuppositions

The example question above, "Who stole my pickup truck?" might be somebody's very serious request for information. We shall now examine how an inquiry started by this question might proceed.

    Our first hope might be that someone would directly answer the question by saying something like

> The notorious pickup thief Jack Rothals has just been captured in your unharmed truck.

If true, this answer would bring the inquiry to a very satisfactory conclusion. Life, however, is not often like that, and as we learned in Chapter 10, we would likely be "begging the question" to hope that the problem could be solved so directly. Our interrogative model will help us understand how an everyday inquiry into the pickup problem might proceed.

    Our question is asking for some information. The desideratum, the information desired, in this question is, as we have seen,

> I know who stole my pickup truck.

The presupposition of the question is

> Someone stole my pickup truck.

Not every answer to my original question will put me in a position to say I know who stole my pickup truck. For example, you might say (truthfully) to me, "A red-haired person took it." I can now say, "I know that a red-haired person took my pickup." But that does not necessarily mean that I know who stole my truck. I may know several red-haired persons, and I may not yet know enough about them to eliminate all but one from suspicion. In fact, I may not be in any way acquainted with the red-haired person in question. I am likely to need much more information before I can catch up with the culprit. Your answer will be *conclusive* only if it enables me to zero in on the one red-haired person who stole the truck. (You may wish to review the discussion of partial and conclusive answers in Chapter 10.)

Your answer then was a *partial* answer, but that does not mean it is useless. If accurate, it does allow me to rule out a lot of other possible suspects. Your answer may also suggest some fruitful lines of inquiry for me. It will be at least worthwhile now to search my memory for a list of redheads I know. It will also be worthwhile to check with the police about suspicious redheads known to them. A number of new intermediate questions are suggested by your partial answer.

We need, however, to pause and notice that we might be getting ahead of ourselves with all this talk about answers. In asking the question I have been making an important assumption, and any assumption made in asking a question needs to be examined. In other words, we passed over the presupposition of the principal question too quickly. The presupposition was

Someone stole my pickup truck.

In asking my question I have been presupposing that somebody stole my pickup. Perhaps, however, I do not really know that. Maybe I parked in a tow-away zone. Maybe my sister, who has a key, borrowed it in an emergency. I would be really embarrassed if I did not check into these other possibilities, especially now that I remember that my sister is a redhead! This puts your partial answer in a whole new light! Perhaps nobody stole my pickup truck!

△▼ EXERCISE 11-G

▸ Can a yes/no question ever have a false presupposition? Explain your answer.

11.4 Definitory Rules for Interrogative Moves

Now we can state some definitory rules for asking questions in inquiry. The idea is very simple: Basically, the inquirer can address to any available oracle any question whatsoever whose presupposition has been established. The content of this principle becomes clearer when it is split up into two different rules, one for statement questions and the other for "wh-" questions. They can be stated as follows:

Q1. **Rule for Statement Questions:** If a statement of the form $(A \lor B \lor \ldots \lor D)$ occurs on the left side of the table, the inquirer may ask one of the oracles whether $A, B, \ldots,$ or D is true. The answer, if the oracle gives one, is added to the left side of the table. [Whether the oracle will actually yield an answer depends on the particular kind of inquiry in question. Nothing can be said about the availability of answers in general.]

Normally, the oracle's answer is a conclusive one, represented by A, B, . . . , or D. When it is conclusive, the questioning move will look "on paper" somewhat like certain logical inference moves. The situation before the question looks like this:

Premises, Interrogative Moves, and Logical Inferences	Conclusion and Logical Inferences
1. T (initial premise[s]) 2. . . . . (from . . .) 3. $A \lor (B \lor D)$ (from . . .) 4. . . . . (from . . .)	C (ultimate conclusion) . . . . (from . . .)

What happens when a statement question is asked and a conclusive answer is received is that A, B, . . . , or D is added to the left side of the table.

Table Illustration for Statement Questions

Premises, Interrogative Moves, and Logical Inferences	Conclusion and Logical Inferences
1. T (initial premise[s]) 2. . . . . (from . . .) 3. $A \lor (B \lor D)$ (from . . .) 4. . . . . (from . . .) 5. A (from 3 by Q1) 6. . . . . (from . . .)	C (ultimate conclusion) . . . . (from . . .) [Assuming the oracle answered A]

Notice now, however, an important difference as compared with the logical inference moves. In the logical inference move for a disjunction, the inquirer has to split the table into several paths, with A, B, . . . , D at the top of the branching paths. (See Table Rule 4 in Chapter 7.) In the case of Rule Q1 the inquirer has to deal with only one path (*if* the oracle responds with an answer).

Q2. **Rule for "Wh-" Questions:** If a statement of the form "Someone . . . " or "Something. . . . " or "There is a . . . " occurs on the left side of a table, the inquirer may ask one of the oracles who or what is the person or object about which the statement speaks. If the oracle gives an answer, it is added to the left side of the table. Normally, the oracle's answer is a name or a description that narrows our focus onto one or a few persons or objects. Because we have not studied the formal logic needed to represent "wh-" questions, we will not give a formal account of Rule Q2.

As you can see from Rules Q1 and Q2, it is a mistake (breach of definitory rules) to ask a question whose presupposition has not been established. A key reason for this is that if the presupposition is false, any answer the oracle would likely give will likewise be false, but we are looking for truths in our inquiries. Above we studied this kind of mistake under the traditional name "the fallacy of many questions" or our own suggestion of "leaping to a presupposition."

Notice that in both question rules *all the action takes place on the left side of the table.* There are no rules for asking questions for the right side of the table. In this respect interrogative rules and logical inference rules sharply differ from each other.

In Part 2, counting both left-side and right-side rules, we formulated no fewer than eleven for logical inference moves. We have also noted that these do not exhaust all possible rules for logical inferences. In contrast, here in Part 3 we shall formulate very few definitory rules for interrogative moves. This may seem surprising in view of the importance of questions for inquiry in general.

What the small number of definitory rules for questions illustrates is not the unimportance of questions, but the relative unimportance of definitory rules when it comes to interrogative moves and questioning. Anyone can ask questions, and the ways of going wrong in the sense of doing something incorrect are few. Almost all the interest lies in the choice of the best questions, that is to say, in the *strategic rules of questioning.*

In contrast, there are many ways of going wrong in making logical inference moves, as you undoubtedly have discovered yourself. As a consequence, we need a large number of detailed definitory rules for logical inferences.

△▼ EXERCISE 11-H

1. Construct tables for the following arguments. You do not need to put them in formal notation, but do create complete tables. By asking the right questions in the right way, you will be able to close the tables entirely. Assume that the oracle will answer any statement question and any "wh-" question with any acceptable answer you think you need, so long as the appropriate presupposition is in place.

   ▶ a. The last one to leave last night let the cat get out. Whoever let the cat get out should climb the tree to get him down. Conclusion: Leonard should climb the tree to get the cat down.

   b. The following is a more complex argument. Place the argument in table form, indicating any implicit statements and interrogative steps. Then try to name possible sources of information which might serve as an oracle. How does the presence of a presupposition in the table guide the course of the inquiry?

   > The murderer had to know the victim, because there is no sign of a struggle. Moreover, it took someone of great strength to inflict such a powerful blow. The murderer, then, was a member of the coach's own team. But Smith and Jones were the only teammates in town that evening, so the murderer is Jones.

2. Find examples of important interrogative moves in a report of a successful inquiry or in lines of reasoning set forth in newspaper editorials or commentaries. Alternatively, your instructor may suggest examples from Appendix A. Demonstrate your ability to isolate the presuppositions of the interrogative moves.

Combining Questions

When you are trying to locate presuppositions of real-life questions, you will find that very often two or more questions are in fact combined into one. For instance, in actual questioning processes, two questions are routinely assimilated to each other in the following way: The questioner first asks the question which is supposed to establish the presupposition of a "wh-" question. The answerer is prepared to give the response establishing the presupposition but skips it and, anticipating the questioner's impending next move, instead answers the "wh-" question itself.

Illustration

There was a stir in the courtroom when MacDonnell lifted his regular glasses over his brow and held the slug within two inches of his eyes. He had been myopic since childhood and rather than bother to change to other glasses, he always held small objects at the distance from which he could comfortably see them without help.

"I examined and weighed this slug in the office of Sheriff Dean, on the afternoon of April twenty-eighth."

"*Do you notice anything peculiar about it?*"

"The first thing is that the wadding is still attached to it. This is only possible if Roxbury was hit within thirty-six inches of the gun that fired it."

Tillman turned to the jury. "And we know that Ferry was standing one hundred fifty-five feet from Roxbury when he fired." He turned back to his witness. "*Is there any explanation that you can think of for this extraordinary bonding of slug and wadding?*"

"It could happen if there was some sort of obstruction in the barrel or muzzle of Ferry's gun." (From A. Lewis and H. MacDonell, *The Evidence Never Lies* [New York: Holt, Rinehart and Winston, 1984], p. 23)

Consider the two questions italicized for emphasis. In each, the questioner is asking a yes/no question but is not receiving an answer that would be appropriate in the case of such a question. Why? In the first question, the affirmative answer would have been something like

1. "Yes, there was something peculiar about it."

This is the presupposition of the obvious next question:

2. "What was peculiar about it?"

What MacDonnell does is to give tacitly the affirmative answer (1). However, instead of expressing it explicitly, he answers the anticipated question (2).

Similar things can be said of the second emphasized question and its answer. In both cases an answer and a question are tacitly skipped in an argument (line of questioning). There is nothing necessarily wrong about such a procedure, but it may need to be noted in argument analysis.

Summary

When we are engaged in significant pursuit of knowledge, it is important that we keep in mind the insights we have learned about presuppositions of questions and about partial and conclusive answers. In Parts 1 and 2 we learned how to rewrite a line of inquiry in an interrogative table and how to handle logical inference steps in a table.

In a position to analyze interrogative sequences even more closely, we can now examine whether the presuppositions of our questions are in order. If they are, well and good. If they are not, we need to back up and ask questions relating to the presuppositions. We are also in a position to consider more carefully whether the answers to our questions are partial or conclusive. If they are conclusive, well and good. If they are partial, our work is not finished, but we may have been given some new lines of questioning to pursue.

It is useful to notice that paying heed to the presuppositions of questions not only helps us avoid mistakes but also serves to open up our range of attention so that we are able to ask the probing questions that may make our inquiry more successful. In the Sherlock Holmes example of the "Curious Incident of the Dog in the Nighttime," the presupposition of Holmes's key question was that "there was a dog in the stable." If we discipline ourselves to examine our inquiries for presuppositions, we can learn not only to examine the questions we have already asked, but also to look for information that might give rise to presuppositions for new questions.

△▼ EXERCISE 11-I

Continue to work on your argument construction and essay assignment. Examine whether the interrogative moves involved in your project have problematic presuppositions. Ask yourself whether any of the questions in your argument presuppose something with which you cannot reasonably expect people to agree. Consider also whether there is information in your argument that could serve as the presupposition for an interesting and possibly significant question you have not yet asked.

11.5 Various Sources of Answers to Questions

Up to this point we have often spoken simply of the oracle as the source of answers. This enabled us to pass over questions about actual sources of information and about their reliability. As we turn to consider different sources of answers, it is well to remember that in everyday inquiry, interrogative moves often are not expressed as explicit questions. Still, we have seen that it is useful to analyze them as questions, and it is important to understand that questions can be addressed to many different sources of answers. In the following we shall illustrate this point by examining some of the more important sources of answers (oracles) involved in various types of inquiry.

Witness in a Court of Law

Sometimes we are dealing with explicitly formulated questions and answers. A familiar example is a cross-examination of a witness in a court of law. It is a well-established part of American folklore that a skillful lawyer like Perry Mason can uncover surprising truths by putting the right questions to a witness and by drawing the right conclusions from them.

Patient at a Diagnostic Interview

Often a doctor will put questions to his or her patient in order to reach a diagnosis. In such a situation, the physician is using questions to gather information which will help him or her reach a conclusion as to what is wrong with the patient. Laboratory tests and medical handbooks will also be a source of answers for the physician. It is interesting to note that Sir Arthur Conan Doyle modeled Sherlock Holmes after a teacher of medicine he had known as a student.

Experiments as Questions Put to Nature

In certain cases, the relevant steps of reasoning are not usually expressed in the form of a question. Yet it is valuable to understand what is going on as a questioning process. For instance, it is an old philosophical idea that scientific experiments can be thought of as questions put to nature. The best-known expression of this idea occurs in Kant's comment that experimental science involves "constraining nature to give answers to questions of reason's own determining" (*Critique of Pure Reason*, original 2d German edition, translated by N. Kemp Smith [London: Macmillan, 1933], p. xiii). In Chapter 10 (Section 10.8) we have already noted that nature can be viewed as a source of information. But nature does not always freely and easily yield the information we seek. Carefully chosen scientific experiments function as questions addressed to this very important source of answers. Experiments, as it were, force nature to answer a scientist's questions.

Observations as Questions Put to One's Environment

Experiments are a special case of what is more generally known as *observation*. Observations can be thought of as answers to questions put to one's environment.

Again, the justification for taking observations to be questions is that their role in a line of inquiry is the same as that of answers by a human witness: to provide more information for one's reasoning. This is in fact what several psychologists say about perception in general. For instance, the American psychologist J. J. Gibson has asserted that perception should not be thought of as a reception of sense impressions, but as a pickup of information about the perceiver's environment. Gibson writes, "In short, there can be sensationless perception, but no informationless perception" (*The Senses Considered as Perceptual Systems* [Boston: Greenwood Press, 1966], p. 2).

[handwritten margin note: perception is the integration of sensations. No perception is possible apart from sensation]

Illustrations of this point are not hard to find. Recall, for instance, the description of Sherlock Holmes's "Science of Deduction and Analysis" quoted above in Chapter 1 (Section 1.10). The science—or is it an art?—described there obviously includes observational skills. In fact, a little earlier it is stated that, according to Sherlock Holmes, "deceit . . . was an impossibility in the case of one trained to *observation* and analysis" (emphasis added). We interpret Sherlock Holmes's feats of reasoning as depending upon skillful questioning, which often involves keen observation of small details in our environment. Observations function as a very important source of answers to questions in our reasoning.

[handwritten margin note: initial source of all info – observation]

Contemporary Illustrations of the Role of Observation   You may find our examples from Conan Doyle a bit unrealistic. They admittedly depend on Sherlock Holmes's knowledge of the manners and customs of his time. However, even in the present one can sometimes "at a glance . . . distinguish the history of the man, and the trade or profession to which he belongs," as Sherlock Holmes put it in the passage we studied in Chapter 3 (Section 3.3). Following are two actual, real-life examples:

> 1. I am at Dulles International Airport near Washington, D.C., waiting for a friend to return from Europe. Two men walk back and forth, obviously also waiting for the same plane. I say, idly, to a knowledgeable friend who is accompanying me: "I wonder who those two guys are." He replies without hesitation: "Soviet or East European security personnel, probably from the KGB." I look surprised, and my companion smiles and says, "Elementary, my dear Watson." He explains: "This is a flight frequently taken by important government officials and diplomats coming from Europe. Those two men were waiting for someone, for they looked frequently at their watches and never strayed far from the gate. Since there are two of them, they are waiting for someone important. They are not Americans, for even though they are dressed rather inconspicuously, like businessmen, their style of clothing has a European touch rather than American or British. That is precisely how privileged Soviet officials tend to dress abroad. But the real give-away is their shoes. They are out of step with the rest of their clothing. They are so ugly that they could only have been made in Eastern Europe. They are even squeaking! Why should they wear such shoes? Obviously, because in their profession they have to walk a lot and therefore need to wear their comfortable old shoes. Now which kind of foreign embassy personnel have to walk a lot? The security personnel, of course."

This next, simpler example turns on recognizing particular people rather than kinds of people:

2. I am having an early dinner with a companion at a restaurant in Sausalito, California, in the early summer of 1976. Suddenly my companion says to me, "I see that the Oakland Raiders are trying to hire a new quarterback." I am nonplussed. She says: "Turn carefully around and have a look at the corner table on your right. Who are the two men engaged in a serious conversation there? They are Al Davis, the owner of the Raiders, and Terry Bradshaw, the quarterback of the Pittsburgh Steelers, this year's Superbowl winners. Do I have to say more?" (An historical footnote: The media never found out about Al Davis's meeting with Bradshaw. Bradshaw ended up staying with the Steelers. Eventually, the Raiders acquired another quarterback, Dan Pastorini, who was not very successful.)

△ ▼ EXERCISE 11-J

Represent the line of reasoning in one or the other of these two examples in an interrogative table.

△ ▼ EXERCISE 11-K

Continue to work on your argument construction and essay assignment. Identify the sources of information upon which you are relying.

Tacit Knowledge as a Source of Answers

Still further sources of answers exist. One of the most intriguing oracles is the inquirer's own tacit (unspoken) knowledge, including his or her memory.

It might seem that appeals to tacit knowledge, which do not seem to introduce new information, cannot be compared with answers to questions. The point, however, is that even though the information in question is perhaps not new to the inquirer, *it is new to the argument.* The activation of an item of tacit information means bringing previously unused information to bear on the argument. Indeed, tacit knowledge can be thought of as being brought into the reasoning by means of suitable questions.

This is illustrated by the example about Meno's slaveboy in Chapter 1, for the whole point of Socrates's questioning was to show that the slaveboy could be brought to recognize new truths apparently without giving him any new information. All the right answers the slaveboy gave were based on what he tacitly knew before the dialogue started. He already "knew" much of what Socrates brought to his attention, but the information did not become available for the inquiry until the right questions were asked. In this sense the information was new to the inquiry.

A more contemporary illustration might be to compare one's tacit knowledge with the database stored in a computer. The computer may be programmed to carry out certain reasoning processes. But the mere fact that some information is stored in the computer does not mean that it automatically uses this information as soon as it becomes relevant. No, the computer must be programmed to question the database at appropriate stages of the process, just as the slaveboy's tacit knowledge needed to be addressed by Socrates's questions before it was activated.

You may also recall our sample argument in Chapter 3 (Section 3.4) about ending the drug war. This relatively simple-looking argument turned out to depend on several tacit questions which were presumed to be answerable by reference to general background knowledge.

An Example   The following is an example of how the activation of information in a person's memory depends on the questions raised. It is from Rex Stout's detective novel *Fer-de-Lance* (New York: Bantam, 1983). Dr. Barstow was murdered by a device built into the golf club (a driver) that he had used while playing with his friend Mr. Kimball. The great private detective Nero Wolfe is questioning the caddies.

> "Then you must have had the bag with you while you were hunting the ball. In that case, you could not have handed Barstow his driver when he teed off, because you weren't there. He could not have removed it from the bag himself, because the bag wasn't there. Had you perhaps handed him the driver previously?"
>
> "Sure. I must have."
>
> "Michael! We need something much better than must have. You did or you didn't. Remember that you are supposed to have told us—"
>
> William Riley [another caddie] butted in: "Hey! Mike, that's why he borrowed old Kimball's driver, because you were off looking for the ball."
>
> "Ah." Wolfe shut his eyes for a tenth of a second and then opened them again. "William, it is unnecessary to shout. Who borrowed Mr. Kimball's driver?"
>
> "Barstow did."
>
> "What makes you think so?"
>
> "I don't think so, I know. I had it out ready to hand to old Kimball, and Barstow's ball rolled off his tee and I fixed it for him, and when I stood up old Kimball was saying to Barstow, 'Use mine,' and Barstow reached out and I handed old Kimball's driver to him."
>
> "And he used it?"
>
> "Sure. He drove right away. Mike didn't come back with the bag until after old Kimball had drove too." . . . [Wolfe next questions the other caddies.]
>
> . . . During all this William Riley was straining his politeness to keep still. Finally Wolfe got back to him:
>
> "Excuse me, William. Do not think I doubt your memory or your fidelity to truth. Corroboration is always helpful. And it might be thought a little curious that you had forgotten so informing a detail."
>
> The boy protested, "I hadn't forgotten it, I just didn't happen to think of it."

"You mean that you have not included that incident in any of your recitals to your friends?"

"Yes, sir."

"Good, William. I put my question badly, but I see that you have the intelligence to stick to the main clause. Possibly you mentioned the incident to Mr. Anderson?"

The boy shook his head. "I haven't seen Mr. Anderson. The detective came and asked me a few questions, not much."

"I see." Wolfe sighed, deep and long, and pushed the button. "It is tea time, messieurs." (pp. 120–121)

Thus the detective Nero Wolfe elicits *by means of suitable questions* the first breakthrough discovery in solving the murder mystery. He discovers the crucial information that the intended murder victim was not Dr. Barstow but Mr. Kimball, for it was in Mr. Kimball's driver that the infernal poison was hidden. The innocent bystander, Dr. Barstow, merely happened to borrow the club while his own caddie was away with Dr. Barstow's own golf bag. It is especially interesting to see that the caddie insists he had not forgotten the incident. Yet it takes the clever questions of Nero Wolfe to activate his tacit knowledge.

Interpretive Observations

Often, appeals to tacit knowledge are involved in what might at first look like observational question-answer steps. For instance, suppose I am interested in the identity of a certain man. I look at him and conclude that he is a police officer. But of course I do not literally see that. What my observational question yields as an answer is some observable fact about him, for example, that he is dressed in such-and-such a way. From this I can move to the conclusion about his profession only by activating (by means of a question) an item of tacit knowledge which says that anyone dressed in such a way is a police officer. From this answer and from the first observational answer I can then conclude by means of a logical inference step that the person I am observing is a police officer.

Thus, what looks like a simple observational question-answer move is often in reality a combination of three steps: (1) a question addressed to the inquirer's environment, (2) a question addressed to the inquirer's tacit knowledge concerning what the observational information obtained in step 1 tells the inquirer in general, and (3) a logical inference from the answers of the preceding two steps, applying the result of the second to the special case observed in the first.

Observational steps of this kind can be called *interpretive observations*. One reason why it is useful to divide them into three separate steps (two question-answer steps and one logical inference) is that the evaluation of the reliability of such interpretive observations, which we shall discuss later, depends on the reliability of the general answer obtained by the inquirer from her or his store of tacit knowledge.

An even more important reason to analyze steps of interpretive observation in this way is to call your attention to the fact that skill in making useful observations very much depends on the background knowledge, that is, the store of tacit knowledge, of the inquirer. Observation is not only a matter of having good eyes or ears but also a matter of having a good grasp of relevant background information.

△▼ EXERCISE 11-L

Continue to work on your argument construction and essay assignment. Reflect on the role of tacit information in your inquiry.

△▼ EXERCISE 11-M

1. Suppose that you have misplaced an item, for instance, your car keys. What questions might you put to yourself in order to activate tacit knowledge in the course of trying to locate the keys? The humor in the following passage from Dave Barry's *Dave Barry Slept Here* arises from his treating the story of the Lost Colony of Roanoke as though it were similar to a case of lost keys:

   > [Sir Walter Raleigh] went to an area that he called Virginia, in honor of the fact that it was located next to West Virginia, and he established a colony there, and then—this was the darnedest thing—he lost it. "Think!" his friends would say. "Where did you see it last?" But it was no use, and this particular colony is still missing today. Sometimes you see its picture on milk cartons. (*Dave Barry Slept Here: A Sort of History of the United States* [New York: Random House, 1989], p. 18)

▶ 2. Indicate which of the statements in the following passage might be taken to be the result of questions designed to elicit tacit knowledge:

   > Something must be wrong. It is now half past the hour, and Ellen said that she would be here by seven. It was important to her that we see this film, so I don't think she forgot about our plans. She is a very reliable person; whenever something has come up in the past which kept her from meeting a commitment she has let me know. I don't recall hearing anything about the traffic, no bad accident or traffic jam, which could explain her being late. Perhaps she had car trouble.

3. Your instructor may assign one or another of the argument sketches from Appendix A. Discuss how the activation of tacit knowledge is or is not involved in the assigned sketches.

4. Produce an example of your own that illustrates tacit knowledge being brought into an inquiry. Look for examples in reports of successful inquiries or in lines of reasoning set forth in newspaper editorials or commentaries. Alternatively, your instructor may suggest a source for you to look into.

Computer Memory

Another source of answers was mentioned earlier. One resource a reasoner frequently has these days is a computer memory in which pertinent information is stored. This information has to be brought to bear on one's argument by means of suitable question procedures, as suggested previously.

The searching of large computer databases requires some careful planning so that they are interrogated in an effective way. The goal is to find all and only the relevant information needed for the task at hand.

△ ▼ EXERCISE 11-N

Go to your library or learning resource center and learn about access to computerized research databases on your campus. Ask about techniques for effective querying of such databases and write a brief report about what you have learned.

Imagination as a Guide to New Information

It may at first sight seem strange to suggest that our imagination is a guide to finding useful, new information. Imagination, however, can prompt us to ask unexpected questions. In "The Curious Incident of the Dog in the Nighttime" Holmes may have imaginatively pictured what would happen to a thief at the stables, expecting his vision to include a barking watchdog. But the dog did not bark, so Holmes had a whole new line of inquiry open up.

We have seen how "asking the right question" is a key to effective reasoning. A strong and lively imagination can help us ask just such questions.

12

▼

Strategies for Reasoning
with Uncertain Answers

In Chapters 10 and 11 we studied fundamental aspects of the questioning process. In Chapter 10 we noted various implications of the difference between principal and operational questions. In Chapter 11 we surveyed the many different sources of information typically found in rational inquiry.

This survey leads us naturally to the problem of the reliability of the answers the inquirer receives to operational questions. Back in Part 1 we agreed mainly to accept information received from the oracle in interrogative moves and to imagine it is true. Now we will learn techniques for coping with the possibility that the information we receive is unreliable.

12.1 Argument Analysis, Construction, and Evaluation

Until now we have been working on a restrictive assumption: We have been assuming that all the answers the inquirer receives from the oracle are true or at least can be treated as if they were. Likewise, we have been assuming that the initial premises are all true or at least can be dealt with as if they were. These assumptions are obviously oversimplified and frequently limit the applicability of our results to real-life arguments. It is time to give up the restrictive assumptions.

Before doing so, however, it is useful to look back on what we have done and to see what difference the admission of uncertain answers and premises will make for our enterprise of learning effective reasoning and efficient argumentation. We have made a distinction between that of argument construction and that of argument evaluation. Essential to both tasks is the ability to analyze arguments. Thus far we have concentrated on argument analysis and construction. Argument analysis can tell us what steps are being taken in what ways. Then, if we are evaluating an argument (either our own or someone else's) that is already completed, our knowledge and skills in deductive logical inference help us determine whether the reasoning steps have been taken correctly. Our knowledge of strategic principles helps us judge how well the inquiry is proceeding. If we are constructing an inquiry of our own, the same knowledge can help us avoid mistakes and, more importantly, make effective steps toward our ultimate conclusion.

All this nevertheless does not yet by itself help you to evaluate the strength of many different sorts of reasoning. In real life, even though you have managed to construct a valid argument for the conclusion you want, someone might still try to cast doubts on it. This critic might claim that your argument as a whole was still not strong enough to persuade him or her.

For instance, let us go back once again to the "Curious Incident of the Dog in the Nighttime." You were undoubtedly impressed by Sherlock Holmes's skill in constructing his ingenious line of reasoning. But you might very well have had second thoughts. How can Holmes be sure that the watchdog did not bark when the horse was stolen? Maybe the stableboys were drugged or just were heavy sleepers. Or maybe the dog did not bark, not because the thief was its own master, but because it was drugged or had been secretly trained not to bark at someone else. Hence, there is plenty of room for doubt here. Holmes himself felt the need to test his own results by questioning the friendly neighborhood shepherd about whether the sheep had been hobbling. In other words, Sherlock was himself not relying blindly on his own reasoning. In particular, he was not one hundred percent sure that the answers to his tacit questions were true.

What this means is that *we need to study reasoning from uncertain answers and uncertain premises to round out our ability to analyze, construct, and evaluate arguments.* What we have done so far in this course fortunately helps us to break our tasks up into different parts. Given that logical (deductive) inferences are necessarily truth-preserving, we do not have to worry about our logical inference steps if they all follow valid rules of inference. We may still have a problem of finding the rule which justifies our attempted logical inferences in all cases. But because we understand the fundamental definition of valid logical inference, we can usually satisfy ourselves as to whether our inferences are valid.

Hence, if there is a false conclusion somewhere, it must have been initially introduced by a false answer or by a false initial premise. Thus, especially when we are evaluating arguments, our work falls into two parts. First, we have to ascertain whether the logical inference steps and interrogative steps are made correctly. Second, and of equal importance for evaluation of arguments, we must try to find out whether the answers in the interrogative steps are true or false as well as examine the initial premises for truth or falsity. Examining arguments for correctness of steps was discussed, although by no means exhausted, in Chapters 5 through 11. Now we must turn our attention to strategies for evaluating the reliability of answers and premises.

If an inquirer exercises sufficient care with the definitory rules of logical inference, logical inference steps can very often be handled satisfactorily so that no errors are made and each step validly connects with the preceding information. It is much more difficult, however, to handle interrogative moves in such a way that the inquirer can always be confident that answers to questions provide reliable information. The few definitory rules for questioning moves do not for the most part guarantee that answers given to appropriate questions are reliable. Therefore, uncertainty in an inquiry will usually arise as a result of uncertainty about the reliability of information that has been introduced into the inquiry through initial premises and answers to questions, that is, through interrogative moves.

△▼ THINK ABOUT IT: HOLMES VS. EUCLID

Dr. Watson reports that Sherlock Holmes claimed that "his conclusions were as infallible as so many propositions of Euclid." (Euclid was the famous ancient Greek mathematician who systematized geometry and tried to carry out his proofs in a strictly logical manner.) Is this comparison with geometry compatible with Holmes's practice of testing his conclusions by means of suitable questions which give rise to other lines of argument for the same conclusion?

Once you think for a moment about this question, one answer will be fairly obvious. If, by "conclusions," Dr. Watson means logical inferences, then Holmes's conclusions are indeed as truth-preserving ("infallible") as Euclid's. This is perfectly compatible with the fact that the premises Holmes uses, including the answers he receives from the different oracles he consults, are not by any means absolutely certain. The point of difference between Holmes and Euclid has to do with the relative certainty about truth that seems to attach to Euclid's premises and answers as opposed to Holmes's.

12.2   Definitory Rules for Games with Uncertain Answers

What happens when the reliability of information in premises and answers seems uncertain? How are we to change the rules of our questioning games for the purpose of doing justice to reasoning which may involve uncertain information?

To answer these questions, it is useful to recall the distinction between the definitory rules of a game and the strategic rules. When uncertain answers and uncertain initial premises are introduced, the definitory rules of our interrogative games do not have to be changed very much. All the inquirer needs is the permission to reject any earlier answer (or any initial premise) together with everything that depends on it.

In Chapter 11 we introduced two definitory rules for interrogative moves, Rules Q1 and Q2 concerning presuppositions of questions. The definitory rules for coping with uncertain premises and answers can be formulated as follows:

Q3. **Rule for Bracketing Lines:** At any stage of an interrogative game the inquirer may bracket any earlier answer or initial premise. Square brackets will normally signal that the inquirer thinks the answer or premise is uncertain.

Q4. **Rule for Bracketing Lines Derived from Bracketed Lines:** If a line in the table of an interrogative game is bracketed, all later lines dependent on it must also be bracketed.

To be able to apply Rule Q4, the game table must include, for each new line, an indication of where (which earlier line or lines) it comes from. Whenever we bracket a line, it is useful to label the brackets to indicate the line whose rejection necessitated (in virtue of Rule Q4) the bracketing of the line in question.

Q5. **Rule for Not Using Bracketed Lines in the Table:** When a line is bracketed, it may not be used in any application of the game rules, including the closure rules.

It should be noted that this rule may turn a closed subtable or path into an open one, thus forcing the inquirer to return to it and to try to close it in some other way.

Q6. **Rule for Unbracketing Lines:** At any stage of the game, the inquirer may unbracket any answer or premise bracketed at the time. Then all the later brackets caused by this line having been bracketed can also be removed.

You can indicate "unbracketing" in any of a number of ways. We recommend that you simply draw a line through the original brackets as a way of indicating they have been canceled.

In light of the possibility of unreliable information entering our tables, a little bit more must be said of the outcome of an interrogative game. Earlier in the book, we spoke as if any conclusion the inquirer is able to establish was true. Now a conclusion can be false. Obviously, a false conclusion is worthless. Hence a stipulation must be added to cover this possibility.

Q7. **Rule for Accepting or Rejecting the Ultimate Conclusion:** When an interrogative game table is closed, the inquirer may either accept the ultimate conclusion or refuse to. If the inquirer refuses to accept the conclusion, he or she must indicate why by explaining that at least one closing line on the left side should be bracketed.

One last rule spells out the idea that the inquirer is searching for truth and that success and failure have their attendant costs:

Q8. **Rule for Payoffs in an Inquiry:** If the ultimate conclusion the inquirer accepts is true, the inquirer receives a positive "payoff." If an accepted conclusion is false, the inquirer who accepts it receives a negative "payoff." If the inquirer rejects a true conclusion, this may also occasion a negative "payoff."

Rule Q8 profoundly affects the inquirer's strategies but does not, however, characterize all the different interrogative games we are interested in and want to study. For instance, in some situations you may merely want to refute an opponent's views, regardless of whether they are true or false. This you may try to do by putting questions to your opponent and by trying to derive a contradiction from them. Rule Q8 does not cover this kind of situation; instead, it characterizes only those games in which the inquirer aims at finding truths. Alternative rules for payoffs are required for games which do not aim at finding truth.

Even Initial Premises Can Be Given Up

Let us go back to Rule Q3, focusing our attention on an important feature: This rule allows the inquirer to bracket not only the oracle's answers but also any of the initial premises. In other words, initial premises can also be called into question through use of Rule Q3. There is no reason to think that initial premises are infallible and indubitable in interrogative arguments. Because they are not immune to error, they too can be rejected if need be. This opens up important opportunities for the critical evaluation of real-life arguments.

The possibility of revising one's initial premises is, among other things, relevant to the way you should think about science and scientific reasoning. A science is not merely a body of results. It is also characterized by a way of reasoning, many aspects of which are captured by the interrogative model, including the feature just noted. A science is not a closed system of results or tentative results, because any one of the premises on the basis of which a scientist is working can in principle be given up if necessary. This possibility is not a flaw in the scientific method, and it should not prompt you to distrust a scientist's conclusion. It is merely a feature of the reasoning process.

△ ▼ EXERCISE 12-A

▶ Go back to the "Nobody Leave the Room!" exercise at the end of Chapter 5. Carry out the line of reasoning that solves the problem, giving the full match between names, professions, and seats. Notice that there are two statements in the second set of clues. Bracket the first statement concerning the mechanic and the mirror. Which other lines must also be bracketed? Which conclusions will remain and which must be rejected because of the bracketing? What happens if you bracket the other statement in Clue 2?

△ ▼ EXERCISE 12-B

Your instructor may assign some statement-logic examples or problems from Part 2 or from Appendix A. You will be instructed to treat certain premise lines as unreliable using our new bracketing rules. Is the success of the argument (closure) affected by the bracketing? Why or why not?

12.3   Inconsistent Information

You are already familiar with a class of arguments which are put into a new light by Rule Q8. They are the interrogative arguments in which the table is completely closed by Table Rule 7 on the left side without any use of Table Rule 8. This means that the table closes because there is a statement (S) and its negation ($-S$) in the left side of each path. Consider first a logical table with only one left-side path.

What the presence of S and $-S$ in the left column means is that the information used is inconsistent, that is, cannot all be true at once. If so, we do not have any guarantee that the ultimate conclusion is true, even if the argument is valid. For what the validity of the argument means is only that *if* the information used (initial premises and the oracle's answers) is all true, then the ultimate conclusion is also true. This is vacuously the case if the information is inconsistent because Rule 7 path closure means there is *no* way to imagine all the information in the path true at the same time. The same can be said of a table with several paths if they are all closed by the Rule 7 applied on the left side.

You may very well have wondered about this strange situation when you encountered it above in Part 2. Now we can see what is wrong with arguments involving inconsistent information. They can be considered as logically valid, but they are useless for the purpose of reaching true conclusions. If Rule Q8 is in effect, the inquirer will want to take steps to avoid accepting what may be a false conclusion.

Can you think of how to react to a closure of a game table which shows that the premises together with available answers are inconsistent? Obviously the inquirer must, in such a situation, use Rule Q3 and reject (at least for the time being) one of the initial premises or one of the oracle's answers. In doing so, the inquirer hopes to construct an argument for the same intended conclusion which is valid but which does not depend on the inconsistency of the premises and answers, in other words, an argument with a table that cannot be closed by Rule 7 in every path on the left side.

Notice that this advice is not a definitory rule of the modified interrogative game. The inquirer does not break any (definitory) rules if he or she rests on his or her laurels after having closed the table. What is wrong with such a procedure is that the inquirer, by so doing, exposes himself or herself to a false conclusion and hence to a penalty (negative payoff). This leads us to formulate an important strategic rule:

Whenever all paths on the left side have been closed by Table Rule 7, the inquirer seeking a true conclusion ought to bracket at least one of the initial premises and/or at least one of the answers.

This strategic rule is applicable only if Rule Q8 has been adopted, that is, if it is important to find a true conclusion. Whenever this is not the case, as happens often in purely deductive inquiry, this strategic rule does not apply.

The situation with which we are dealing here is sometimes expressed by saying that *anything follows from inconsistent information.* For our purposes we can take this saying to mean the following: If all the paths of a table which starts from the initial premises *T* are closed by Table Rule 7 applied to the left side, then *T* is inconsistent either with itself or with ascertainable facts about the world. Therefore, any old ultimate conclusion follows from *T,* and *T* cannot help us in reaching true conclusions about the world rather than false ones.

The great British philosopher Bertrand Russell (1872–1970) was once challenged to show that this paradoxical situation really is the case. Does it really follow from 2 + 2 = 3, for instance, that you are the Pope? "But of course!" said Russell. "First subtract 2 from both sides and you get 2 = 1. Now Russell and the Pope are known to be two people. But if two is one, they must be the same person, and that is to say that Bertrand Russell is the Pope!" Needless to say, Russell was joking, but his joke illustrates the serious moral that any old ultimate conclusion follows from inconsistent information.

△▼ EXERCISE 12-C

Check the work you are doing on your argument construction and essay project to see whether there are inconsistencies in the information on which you are relying.

12.4   Which Answer to Bracket?

Rule Q3, which entitles you to bracket an answer (or an initial premise), may have disappointed you, because it does not tell you which earlier answer (or premise) to bracket. This disappointment is unjustified, however, for two reasons. First, the choice of an answer to bracket is obviously a strategic matter, whereas Q3 is merely a definitory rule.

Second, it is very hard to formulate foolproof strategic rules for the choice of an answer (or initial premise) to bracket. For let us think of what such a rule would need to do. Typically, the inquirer needs such a rule if he or she has discovered, or begun to suspect, that not all the information is true, discovering, for instance, that the available premises and answers are inconsistent with each other.

It is unrealistic to expect that the inquirer can always know which earlier answer or premise is the culprit. Hence, it is unlikely that one can ever formulate a strict strategic rule as to which answer the inquirer should bracket. Usually the inquirer has to experiment and to bracket tentatively this or that answer (or initial premise) and to see what happens. This means we must now turn our attention to strategic rules.

Bracketing Strategies

The technique of bracketing is used to indicate and keep track of lines containing information about which the inquirer is uncertain. Various strategic considerations can lead the inquirer to be suspicious about information in the inquiry:

1. Conflicting answers from different oracles or from the same oracle can raise doubts.

2. General background knowledge may make a reasoner question whether an answer to a given question is reliable.

3. Knowledge of the past reliability of an oracle may call current answers into question.

4. One may also choose simply to experiment with bracketing information in an inquiry to see what role a particular piece of information plays.

△▼ EXERCISE 12-D

Apply the bracketing rules to the work you are doing on your argument construction and essay assignment. Where in your work is there information that may be unreliable? Does this call your ultimate conclusion into question? As we proceed in this chapter we will learn some strategies for coping with unreliable information.

12.5 Strategies for Coping with Uncertain Answers

Sequential and Multilevel Inquiry

Once we have decided that one or another answer or initial premise should be bracketed, there are a number of different strategies we can adopt to address the problem of uncertainty. One of the most straightforward ways in which we may cope with uncertainty of answers is by reflecting on what we learned in Chapter 10 (Sections 10.10 and 10.11) about sequential reasoning and reasoning as a multilevel process.

The inquirer may be able to make the questionable piece of information the subject of a separate inquiry. In this case what was an operational question in the original inquiry becomes the principal question for a new one. If the new inquiry successfully establishes the reliability of the answer to this question, the inquirer can then return to the original inquiry with more confidence that the answer which was called into question by bracketing can now be unbracketed.

If there are several bracketed answers in the original inquiry, each of the affected operational questions can become the principal question of separate, lower-level lines of inquiry. The extended example in Section 10.11 of Chapter 10 from the novel *Hot Money* illustrates how ultimate conclusions (answers to principal questions) of lower-level inquiries can provide answers to operational questions in a higher-level inquiry that draws the separate lower-level inquiries together into a final solution to a problem.

△ ▼ **EXERCISE 12-E**

Your instructor may assign an example from Appendix A or from another source. Locate some potentially unreliable information in the example, and discuss whether the methods of sequential or multilevel reasoning would be appropriate for dealing with the bracketed answers.

△ ▼ **EXERCISE 12-F**

Apply the new bracketing rules to the work you are doing on your argument construction and essay assignment. Where in your work is there information that may be unreliable? Does this call your ultimate conclusion into question? Discuss whether the methods of sequential or multilevel reasoning would be appropriate for dealing with the bracketed answers. If it will help strengthen your project, you may wish to support one of your unreliable answers by developing a new lower-level inquiry. As we proceed in this chapter, we will learn further strategies for coping with unreliable information.

Random and Systematic Errors

It may happen in a given inquiry that only some types of answers can be uncertain. For example, it may be suggested that in empirical sciences the answers nature gives to questions concerning particular matters of fact are infallible (i.e., they can be relied on to be true), whereas general answers (e.g., answers specifying dependencies between different variables) can sometimes be false.

Usually, the inquirer has also some prior information as to how likely the oracle's answers are to be true. It is important to note that the probability of obtaining a true answer to a given question need not be a constant but may depend on the other answers the inquirer has received. Obviously, a great many different kinds of interrogative games can come about through different combinations of such probabilities and probability dependencies. As a result, the strategic rules for interrogative reasoning with uncertain answers vary from one kind of game to another and include at first sight a bewildering variety of considerations the inquirer has to keep in mind.

Nevertheless, many relatively simple strategic principles are relatively easy to understand and learn. For instance, consider a case in which the inquirer is a scientist or lawyer who wants to prove a certain conclusion C. Suppose he or she has constructed an argument which starts from known initial premise T and leads through a line of reasoning involving but one answer A to a yes/no question put to the oracle before reaching the ultimate conclusion C. Can the inquirer trust this conclusion? Perhaps not, for the answer A may be false. And if it is, the inquirer's line of reasoning, however correct it might be in all other respects, might very well lead to a false conclusion.

What can the inquirer do to increase the reliability of the conclusion C? We have seen that the inquirer could make the uncertain answer the subject of another inquiry, but other avenues are open as well. Here are two of them:

1. The inquirer could repeat the same question, hoping to receive the same answer A.

or

2. The inquirer could try to construct a new line of reasoning, not using the answer A, which would establish the same ultimate conclusion C.

Consider the first strategy. Why should the inquirer deem this a good idea? Most likely he or she is thinking: "Maybe the answer was a fluke. The oracle is perhaps known to give true answers with a relatively high probability. If the answer A is a false one, it is likely to be corrected by asking the same question again. For it is unlikely that the oracle should give the same wrong answer twice."

This line of thought relies on an important assumption—that the first wrong answer does not make a second wrong answer very likely, the probability of obtaining a true answer is not being affected by earlier answers. In other words, the second answer is probabilistically independent of the first one. When such independence is present, it may be reasonable to test a dubious answer simply by repeating the question.

In a scientific context, when the "question" is an experiment and probabilistic independence is present, a false "answer" is sometimes called a *random error*. Such errors are often a fact of an experimental scientist's life. Thus, we have arrived at a strategic principle for reasoning in situations in which random errors may provide unreliable answers: *In the presence of random errors, test a dubious answer by repeating the question*.

But often an error is not a random one. Many times a false answer makes a second false answer more likely. For instance, if a witness gives a mistaken answer under cross-examination, he or she is not very likely to change his or her testimony if the same question is repeated. Instead, the opposing attorney might perhaps object that the questioner is harassing the witness. When a false answer is likely to be repeated, we can speak of a *systematic error*. In science, such systematic mistakes might, for instance, be due to a systematic bias of an experimental setup.

When a systematic error is likely, a better idea might very well be strategy 2. In other words, the way to increase the credibility of a conclusion C that depends on the answer A is not to repeat the question but to try to prove the same conclusion in another way which does not depend on A. This is what both scientists and lawyers frequently do.

But what kind of new argument will best serve this purpose? We can give an answer to this question, even though we do not quite have the means yet to explain it. Time-honored advice that you will hear from scientists and philosophers of science, but which rightly understood is also likely to be familiar to criminal lawyers, is to try to prove your ultimate conclusion in two ways as unlike each other as possible.

When two unlike arguments both support the same conclusion, their joint effect is far greater than the support of the two lines of argument taken separately. This phenomenon is known as the *consilience* of evidence. In the presence of systematic errors, it is indeed a reasonable strategy to rely on consilience and to try to prove one's conclusion in different and indeed dissimilar ways.

But what is meant by dissimilarity here? A partial answer can be given to this question as follows: Let us assume, for simplicity, that the same conclusion C has been proved by two different interrogative arguments, each of which uses only one answer, A_1 or A_2, respectively. Let us assume that A_1 and A_2 are answers to yes/no questions. Now suppose that the answers A_1 and A_2 are initially very unlikely both to be true. Then it can easily be shown that the two independent arguments taken together greatly strengthen the probability of the conclusion C over and above what either one does singly. What this means is that in trying to strengthen the argument for your conclusion C, you should endeavor to prove it through different arguments based on answers which are unlikely to be true together. Such arguments are what we called earlier dissimilar arguments.

In sum, we have thus formulated another strategic rule for interrogative arguments with uncertain answers: *When systematic errors are likely, the inquirer should try to construct dissimilar arguments for the hoped-for ultimate conclusion.* The ability to find relevant and effective dissimilar arguments is an important skill in reasoning well. It is a significant tool for dealing with uncertain premises and answers.

△▼ THINK ABOUT IT

Look up the entire story "Silver Blaze" by Sir Arthur Conan Doyle. Find three dissimilar arguments used by Sherlock Holmes in solving the mystery. Discuss whether and how the cumulative effect of these arguments strengthens the probability of his conclusion.

△▼ EXERCISE 12-G

Your instructor may assign examples from Appendix A or elsewhere. Answers which are to be treated as uncertain will be indicated. Discuss why you think the strategy for coping with random errors and/or the strategy for coping with systematic errors would or would not be appropriate in the indicated cases. Would the strategy of making the uncertain answer the subject of a separate inquiry be better?

Strategy Choice, Resources, and Purposes

It is perhaps beginning to occur to you that choice of a strategy for coping with uncertain answers will not usually be made under ideal circumstances. For example, in the abstract, it may seem best always to construct a new inquiry to establish the reliability of an answer that has been called into question. But in real life there may not be time for that approach, or the information needed to construct the new inquiry may not be available or may be too costly to make available. Even if time and money are to be had, it may seem wasteful to employ this strategy when that for dealing with random errors is likely to be as effective. The importance of the inquiry to us will also affect our willingness to employ more or less expensive strategies.

Once again we are seeing that some of the most interesting and important parts of rational inquiry cannot be boiled down to definitory rules which once and for all tell us what is right to do and what is wrong. Instead, we must make our strategic choices in the light of our purposes and resources. In this book we can help you avoid definitory errors and we can help you broaden your appreciation of the strategies available to you, but many of the most important decisions involved in good reasoning can only be made as you assess the particular situation in which you find yourself working.

△ ▼ EXERCISE 12-H

Consider the strategies for random and systematic errors in connection with the work you are doing on your argument construction and essay assignment. Discuss whether these strategies would be appropriate for dealing with any of your bracketed answers. Do your purposes and resources affect the decisions you are making about strategy choice?

Statistical Reasoning

Earlier in this chapter we saw that relatively small additions to the definitory rules are needed in order to cope with uncertain answers and premises in interrogative games. In contrast, the strategic rules (in so far they can be formulated) for the same games are often quite complicated. In fact, many sophisticated rules for statistical reasoning can be considered to be special forms of such strategic rules for our interrogative games.

Because statistical reasoning involves strategic matters, it usually involves more than the mechanical application of definitory rules. This is why we are well advised not to exaggerate the mechanical effectiveness of statistical reasoning. The rules of statistical reasoning make good servants, but they should not be allowed to become our masters.

Illustration   A simple but typical example of statistical inference is the following:

A genetic theory tells us that the probability of a certain kind of offspring (say, white-colored offspring) of laboratory animals is either ½ or ¾. A sample of ten offspring is observed, of which six turn out to be white. What can we conclude?

It is natural and useful to think of the sample as a question put to nature. The question would be: Is the probability of a white offspring ½ or ¾? If the ratio of white offspring is closer to ½ than to ¾, the answer is ½, otherwise ¾.

But is the answer reliable enough to be accepted by an inquirer? This is precisely the kind of question statisticians are trying to answer. What their answers actually are is not our concern at this point. The answers depend both on the observed frequency (ratio) of white offspring and also on the size of the sample. For instance, if the observed ratio of white offspring had been five out of ten, nature's answer is firmer than if the frequency is six out of ten. Also, the answer would have been even more certain if the ratio had been fifty out of a hundred.

This example shows how principles of statistical inference can be understood as strategic rules for evaluating nature's (or others') answers to the inquirer's questions.

△▼ EXERCISE 12-I

Your instructor may assign an example from Appendix A or from other sources. Examine the role of statistical reasoning in the assigned example.

△▼ EXERCISE 12-J

What role does statistical reasoning play (if any) in the argument construction and essay project you are developing?

13

Strategies for Evaluating Oracles

In Chapter 12 we studied strategies for coping with uncertain answers. These strategies focused on ways of examining the content of the answers. In this chapter we study strategies for evaluating the oracles that provide the answers in the course of an inquiry.

13.1 Evaluating Answers by Evaluating Different Answerers (Oracles)

One of the most important strategic opportunities open to an inquirer in games with uncertain answers is to evaluate different sources of answers, or "oracles," as we have been calling them. In brief, we can assess the reliability of an answer by evaluating the answerer. Obviously a wide variety of different considerations can enter into such evaluations, and many different types of answerers must be evaluated.

For instance, a scientist can estimate the reliability of the result of an experiment by studying the experimental setup. The way the experiment was designed and executed may make it more or less dependable as a source of scientific information. This is why a description of the experimental apparatus and the way it was used is usually included in a scientist's report of his or her experimental results.

Similarly, a historian may try to evaluate the reliability of a document he or she is using in a historical inquiry. Both the internal characteristics of the document and information about its general historical situation can assist in the effort.

Likewise, when a witness is cross-examined in a court of law, much of the questioning is often aimed not at getting new information but at determining how reliable or unreliable the witness is. For instance, was the witness in a position accurately to perceive what happened in the particular situation in question? Was there enough light for the witness to see what happened? Was the witness situated in such a way that he or she could survey the scene of the crime? Is it in the self-interest of the witness to tell the truth? Could the witness be misled by his or her strong emotions concerning the incident under examination? Questions like this could easily be multiplied.

The credibility of a witness might also depend on what the cross-examiner can establish about the permanent characteristics of the witness. Is his or her eyesight good enough? Does he or she have a tendency to exaggerate or lie? An experienced attorney can think of many more lines of questioning that can shed light on the worth of a witness's testimony.

The importance of oracle evaluation is the reason for one of the most important rules of scientific and scholarly writing. You may have been told about this rule when you wrote your first term paper. It says: **Always indicate your sources.** If you got some of the information you are using from a book, you should tell your reader what the book is and who its author and publisher are. If you are using unpublished source material, you should state what the source is and where it can be located. If you performed an experiment that gave you the information, you should describe the experimental setup. You should also be prepared to make available the primary data from your experiment.

These rules for scientific and scholarly writing are not cosmetic ones. What they do is make it possible for your reader to ascertain which oracles you are consulting. This will in turn enable your reader to evaluate the answers you obtained from your different oracles. You will recall that in Chapter 4 (Section 4.3) we discussed the difference between simply reporting what someone else has said and creatively using information from various sources to construct your own arguments.

Inquiring into an Adviser's Interrogative Abilities

The need to evaluate the reliability of an oracle is especially important in situations involving advisers. Earlier, we envisaged a scientific adviser answering questions that a political decision maker puts to him or her. In such a situation, it is important for the administrator or politician to be aware of the fact that the adviser's answers are not automatic but rather are the results of reasoning processes which may be of a better or worse quality. It will help the person being advised to assess the advice if she or he has some sense of what those deeper-level reasoning processes are like. Of course, the politician cannot carry out the reasoning that is needed to answer all of her or his questions. But, she or he may, for instance, have to choose between different advisers and perhaps even between numerous answers different advisers are proposing to the same questions. In such decisions, some sense of the reasoning involved and of the reliability of the adviser is indispensable.

History shows that even some of the greatest world leaders lacked this quality. It is, for instance, by this time quite well established (though not generally known) that Winston Churchill made a serious error during World War II in trusting the scientific advice of Professor F. A. Lindemann and distrusting the advice of Sir Henry Tizard. Before the war, when Churchill was not in power, Tizard had been the key figure in putting the British ahead in their development of radar and, after the war began, in bringing the United States up to date on British developments. But Lindemann succeeded in removing Tizard from positions of influence. In 1942 Lindemann argued strongly that Britain should commit major resources to the strategic bombing of Germany. In a cabinet paper he argued that it was possible to destroy 50 percent of the homes of working-class Germans. Lindemann's calculations were challenged by several other leading British scientists, including Tizard; they calculated that his estimates were five to six times too high. But Lindemann had long prevailed with Churchill on scientific matters. "The bombing survey after the war revealed that [his estimates] had been ten times too high. . . . The actual effort in manpower and resources that was expended on bombing Germany was greater than the value in manpower of the damage caused." This story is told in a brief but fascinating way in C. P. Snow's *Science and Government*, published in 1961 (Cambridge: Harvard University Press, quote from p. 51).

Such experiences moved Snow, a British novelist and administrator (and, significantly, a former scientist) to plead for a higher degree of awareness of science and scientific thinking among politicians and administrators in his famous lecture "The Two Cultures and the Scientific Revolution" (1959). He also advised in *Science and Government* that "we ought not to give any single scientist the [governmental] powers of choice that Lindemann had" (p. 68). Still, he also thought that scientists are especially gifted in helping a society keep its sense of the future (pp. 81*ff*).

Some of the same truths about careful choice of advisers are applicable closer to home. We all need every so often the advice of various professionals, be they physicians, lawyers, accountants, stockbrokers, coaches, automobile technicians, or what not. There is admittedly a great deal of truth in the old saying that the man who thinks he is his own best lawyer has a fool for a client. Yet, even though the advice of professionals is indispensable, such advice is most useful when one can oneself judge something of the quality of one's advisers' reasoning.

As the principles of reasoning are basically the same in all fields, one of the purposes of the kind of training in reasoning we are attempting to impart here is to enable you to judge your advisers' arguments. Strategies for oracle evaluation can be of great help.

The choice of an oracle or oracles is often an important strategic consideration for an inquirer. But how can an inquirer evaluate the oracles that are available? The answer depends on the kind of inquiry engaged in. Sometimes right from the beginning of an inquiry one has some knowledge of the relative reliability of different oracles. Sometimes oracles can serve, so to speak, as "character witnesses" for other oracles.

An interesting and effective strategy is to use an oracle's own answers as a clue to its reliability. Sometimes an inquirer can compare an oracle's several answers with each other. A particularly effective way of discrediting an answerer's credibility is to show that the answers are inconsistent. Such an inconsistency can be established by means of interrogative reasoning, by deriving a contradiction from an oracle's answers, which shows that the answers cannot all be true (assuming of course the truth of all the other answers and other premises used in deriving the contradiction). Over and above that, such inconsistency may also throw doubt over the credibility of the oracle in general, including the oracle's other answers.

Sometimes an oracle's answers can be tested against answers from other sources which are independently known to be reliable. By following up such clues, the likelihood of the truth of an oracle's answers can be tested and perhaps even ascertained by means of the process of interrogative inquiry we have described in this book. Evaluation of the reliability of an oracle's answers need not be based on prior knowledge but can also depend on what is revealed in the course of the interrogative inquiry.

In yet another situation a subclass of a certain oracle's answers may be known to be true. Then the inquirer can test the same oracle's answers to other questions or another oracle's answers to questions, by comparing their consequences with the first oracle's indubitable answers. For example, assume that the inquirer has received a number of uncertain answers. Assume also that their consequences disagree with one of the indubitable answers. Then the inquirer knows that at least one of the uncertain answers was false and can attempt to find out which one must be rejected.

It is not necessary for the evaluation process, however, that some one subclass of answers be indubitable. It suffices that answers to a certain class of questions are known to be very likely true. In fact, successful scientific reasoning does not require that absolutely infallible answers be available to any particular questions.

Illustration   In the following, a famous example is given to show how an answerer's false responses can be exposed. On the surface, the passage demonstrates a simple conflict between an uncertain answer (that by a witness to a lawyer's question) and an indubitable answer (entry in an almanac). It is nevertheless interesting to see how the unfortunate witness was led to his crucial false answer by the lawyer's pursuing the consequences of his earlier testimony.

Grayson was charged with shooting Lockwood at a camp-meeting, on the evening of August 9, 18—, and with running away from the scene of the killing, which was witnessed by Sovine. The proof was so strong that, even with an excellent previous character, Grayson came very near being lynched on two occasions soon after his indictment for murder.

The mother of the accused, after failing to secure older counsel, finally engaged young Abraham Lincoln, as he was then called, and the trial came on to an early hearing. No objection was made to the jury, and no cross-examination of witnesses, save the last and only important one, who swore that he knew the parties, saw the shot fired by Grayson, saw him run away, and picked up the deceased, who died instantly.

The evidence of guilt and identity was morally certain. The attendance was large, the interest intense. Grayson's mother began to wonder why "Abraham remained silent so long and why he didn't do something!" The people finally rested. The tall lawyer (Lincoln) stood up and eyed the strong witness in silence, without books or notes, and slowly began his defence by these questions:

LINCOLN: And you were with Lockwood just before and saw the shooting?
WITNESS: Yes.
LINCOLN: And you stood very near to them?
WITNESS: No, about twenty feet away.
LINCOLN: May it not have been ten feet?
WITNESS: No, it was twenty feet or more.
LINCOLN: In the open field?
WITNESS: No, in the timber.
LINCOLN: What kind of timber?
WITNESS: Beech timber.
LINCOLN: Leaves on it are rather thick in August?
WITNESS: Rather.
LINCOLN: And you think this pistol was the one used?
WITNESS: It looks like it.
LINCOLN: You could see the defendant shoot—see how the barrel hung, and all about it?
WITNESS: Yes.
LINCOLN: How near was this to the meeting place?
WITNESS: Three-quarters of a mile away.
LINCOLN: Where were the lights?
WITNESS: Up by the minister's stand.
LINCOLN: Three-quarters of a mile away?
WITNESS: Yes,—I answered ye twiste.
LINCOLN: Did you not see a candle there, with Lockwood or Grayson?
WITNESS: No! What would we want a candle for?
LINCOLN: How, then, did you see the shooting?
WITNESS: By moonlight! (defiantly).
LINCOLN: You saw this shooting at ten at night—in beech timber, three-quarters of a mile from the light—saw the pistol barrel—saw the man fire— saw it twenty feet away—saw it all by moonlight? Saw it nearly a mile from the camp lights?
WITNESS: Yes, I told you so before.

The interest was now so intense that men leaned forward to catch the smallest syllable. The lawyer drew out a blue covered almanac from his side coat pocket —opened it slowly—offered it in evidence—showed it to the jury and the court— read from a page with careful deliberation that the moon on that night was unseen and only arose at one the next morning. (From Francis L. Wellman, *The Art of Cross-Examination* [New York: Collier Books, 1962], pp. 73-78)

We include this illustration not only for its intrinsic interest but also because there is a very interesting footnote to it that further illustrates problems with reliability of information. Wellman reports that this account of Abraham Lincoln's skillful cross-examination would itself not stand up in a court of law. The case probably did not happen in the way you just read. Many of the details do not fit with other known facts. For example, Lincoln was not, at the time of the case, a new young lawyer but rather a well-established, experienced attorney.

Wellman in fact analyzes the account you just read as an example of "the unreliability of honest testimony." The point comes through clearly, however, that a skillful examination of an oracle can help the inquirer assess the reliability of the answers.

Wellman offers other comments as well on the strategy of cross-examination. One of them is the following: "A difficult but extremely effective method of exposing a certain kind of perjurer is to lead him gradually to a point in his story, where—in his answer to the final question, "Which?"—he will have to choose either one or the other of the only two explanations left to him, either of which would degrade if not entirely discredit him in the eyes of the jury" (op. cit.).

△ ▼ EXERCISE 13-A

Assume you have moved into a new town and are faced with the problem of finding a new doctor, dentist, pastor, insurance adviser, automobile repairman, and so forth. Write a brief essay outlining the strategies you would pursue in trying to choose them.

13.2 Different Types of Arguments

It is important to realize that questions of reliability play a different role in different kinds of arguments. Sometimes the purpose of the interrogative game is simply to refute another person's claim. Even in Socrates's own practice of his Socratic method of questioning, the concrete outcome of his argument was to show that his interlocutor's proposal did not work. Our interrogative framework enables us to distinguish such arguments from the kinds of reasoning which seek truths about the world (or about ourselves).

In other cases, it is not sufficient merely to find the truth; you also have to prove that your conclusion is true or is likely to be true. Scientific inquiry is usually a case in point. Aristotle, the father of logic and the philosophical and scientific authority of the Middle Ages, also considered scientific truths as being established by an interrogative process. But in searching for answers, one quickly discovers that there is no single reliable and informative source but that scientific truth must be sought for by means of a variety of different methods, techniques, experiments, and observations.

In contrast, the purpose of a legal argument might be simply to show what follows from statutes and precedents. The answers the statutes themselves yield are not and cannot be challenged, except perhaps by reference to some higher legal authority, for instance, the Constitution.

Similarly, in many religious arguments, certain sources of answers (e.g., the Bible) are assumed, for the purpose of that kind of argument, to be decisive. There is nothing wrong with such arguments, as long as you are aware of how they differ from other kinds of inquiry (e.g., scientific investigation).

One reason it is important to realize that there are differences between certain kinds of argument is that one and the same oracle can sometimes be a reliable one in one type of inquiry but unreliable in another. A high-ranking public official may be a poor judge of scientific questions; a brilliant scientist may be simply confused when he or she ventures to discuss philosophical or religious questions; and so on.

ARGUMENTUM AD VERECUNDIAM

13.3 The Fallacy of Authority

The choice and the evaluation of oracles can be illustrated by considering some of the mistakes common in this area. Some of them have been recognized in the traditional literature and given names. One such label is "the fallacy of authority."

This fallacy can be looked upon in different ways. When someone is accused of committing this fallacy, what the accuser often has in mind is a truth-oriented inquiry. If you trust completely a certain oracle's answers in such an inquiry when in fact it is fallible, then you can be said to be a victim of "the fallacy of authority." You are, as we might put it, treating that particular oracle as an authority when it (he, she) does not deserve to be so treated. Notice that, on this interpretation, the fallacy of authority is a strategic mistake, not a violation of the definitory rules of the interrogative game.

One context in which the fallacy of authority is often committed is in discussions about the nature of science and scientific truth. Often what science says about this or that matter (e.g., evolution) is equated with what leading scientists say about it. As was noted in the preceding section, this is simply a mistake. In science, there are no authorities whose statements can be taken to represent the entire scientific community, let alone "science itself." It usually is sound advice to rely on what scientists claim to have discovered, but that does not mean that any one scientist's answers are infallible.

However, a perhaps more interesting situation entailing the fallacy of authority involves confusion between different types of arguments. For example, there need not be anything fallacious in a legal or religious argument to treat a certain oracle's answers literally as the last word on a subject, but in a scientific context there equally literally are no authorities. No scientist's pronouncements or even his or her experiments are taken to be conclusive; every single answer has to be confirmed by independent evidence. In such a scientific context, to rely only on some one authority's answers is indeed to commit a serious mistake.

For example, in 1989 a scientific team at the University of Utah claimed to have established experimentally the possibility of energy-producing nuclear fusion at room temperature. This announcement was surprising and caused a great deal of discussion in scientific circles and in the news media. One comment reported was that the scientists who claimed to have made the discovery were reputable. However, no scientist considered this an indication of reliability. Everybody was waiting for independent confirmation (or disconfirmation) of the discovery, thus illustrating the fact that character witnesses (so to speak) carry little weight in science.

△▼ EXERCISE 13-B

Review what was said in Chapter 10 (Section 10.12) about the fallacy of begging the question. Discuss how the issues involved in that fallacy relate to problems concerning the fallacy of authority—how, for example, begging the question is related to decisions about when and how to rely on authorities.

13.4 The Fallacy of Arguing *Ad Hominem*

Somewhat similar things can be said of another well-known—but not necessarily well understood—"fallacy," the so-called fallacy of arguing **ad hominem.** You are likely to have heard the phrase before. Maybe you have yourself been accused of the mistake of arguing *ad hominem.* But what is meant by this term?

The Latin phrase means that something is relative to or addressed to (i.e., is *ad*) some particular person. But what is wrong about addressing one's argument to one person rather than another?

A classical (though no longer accurate by contemporary usage) statement of what arguing *ad hominem* means is to say that it amounts to "pressing a man with the consequences drawn from his own principles or admissions" (John Locke). — *could be circumstantial* But if this is what arguing *ad hominem* amounts to, there does not seem to be anything fallacious about it. What Socrates did in his famous method of elenchus (recall what was said of it above in Chapter 10, Section 10.4) was precisely to examine the consequences drawn from his interlocutor's answers. Was Socrates committing the *ad hominem* mistake? Certainly not. There is nothing mistaken or otherwise wrong about the way Socrates conducted his inquiry.

In other walks of life, using someone's admissions against him or her seems to be equally acceptable. If you are arrested and a police officer reads you your Miranda rights and says, "Anything you say may be used against you," it will not help you very much if you reply, "But, Sir, you are committing the *ad hominem* fallacy." So what is the error here?

The answer, interestingly, depends on the kind of inquiry in question. In the types of arguments in which you are simply trying to refute your opponent's views, it is often entirely fair to argue *ad hominem* in the sense we are considering. Likewise, if you are trying to change someone's mind by means of your argument, it might very well be a good idea to base it on his or her own answers to your questions.

But in other contexts, especially in an inquiry which aims at establishing truth in some matter or other, it is simply bad strategy to trust any one oracle's answers too much, and even perhaps a bad strategy to address one's questions to that particular one in the first place. This is especially clear when we come to a search for scientific truth.

If you want to find out the scientific truth about some matter or other, it may be a bad strategy address your questions to some particular man (or woman) of science. You may even have to consult oracles other than human beings, that is, address your questions to nature herself. Hence the real mistake in arguing *ad hominem* in this sense is strategic in nature. It lies in confusing one kind of inquiry with another one.

There is some advice worth considering in connection with this (older) meaning of the *ad hominem* error. Sometimes, when our primary goal is to seek the truth, we nevertheless become so concerned to refute another person's position that we prematurely rest from our labors if only we manage to refute the opponent. But refutation of an opponent is not the same as establishing or arguing for the truth. Keeping ourselves from getting confused about our goals in argument and inquiry can be an important matter.

There is a more modern way, however, in which the phrase "*ad hominem* argument" is used. In a recent textbook it is explained as follows:

> The argument against a person is the fallacy of rejecting the claims a person advances simply on the basis of derogatory facts (real or alleged) about the person making the claim. Such a procedure takes for granted that the substance or content of a claim is essentially connected with the character or situation of the claimant. (From Stephan Toulmin, Richard Rieke, and Alan Janik, *An Introduction to Reasoning*, 2d ed. [New York: Macmillan, 1984], p. 144)

But, once again, it is not clear what is supposed to be fallacious about this so-called fallacy. Surely the character of a witness (who may be the accused person) in a court of law is relevant to the evaluation of his or her testimony. Otherwise the entire practice of calling character witnesses would be a colossal fallacy of arguing *ad hominem*.

Of course, not every derogatory fact about a witness is relevant to the reliability of his or her testimony. The witness may have unusual and offending political or religious views, but that fact does not by itself make his or her answers suspect. But if the label *ad hominem* is applied to such argumentative malpractice, which often amounts to little more than an appeal to the jurors' prejudices, then the correction of such a "fallacy" is no longer a matter of logic and reasoning. The way to counter such misuses of arguments is to discover how to disabuse people of their prejudices, not to put forward more finely calibrated arguments. The mistake is a moral rather than an intellectual one.

However, an intellectual mistake sometimes does lie at the bottom of what is called an argument *ad hominem*. Admittedly, the character of an oracle is relevant to the reliability of the answers given to the inquirer by that oracle. But a sharp distinction has to be made between the evaluation of the *answers* of an oracle, which are particular steps in an argument, and the evaluation of somebody's *entire argument*: The character of an oracle is relevant to the evaluation of his or her answers; the character of an arguer is *not* relevant to the effectiveness of his or her argument. Unfortunately, many accounts of the *ad hominem* error do not sufficiently distinguish between evaluating an oracle's claims and evaluating the inferences in an argument.

For example, if you are a defense attorney, it may be a good idea to discredit a witness's testimony by impugning his or her character. However, it is not only inadmissible but often bad legal tactics to try to discredit the opposing attorney's argument by challenging his or her character, intelligence, or professional integrity. Even if such accusations were true, they have to be shown to have affected some particular step in the argument in the light of actual evidence.

Hence, this variety of the alleged *ad hominem* fallacy is really due to a failure to distinguish from each other two different evaluative tasks, namely, the evaluation of an oracle's answers and the evaluation of some reasoner's argument.

△▼ EXERCISE 13-C

▶ 1. Your instructor may assign an editorial or other argumentative piece from the news of the day or perhaps a sketch from Appendix A. Study the piece for *ad hominem* elements and discuss whether these are being legitimately applied to the task of evaluating an oracle.

2. Analyze a controversial argument in the light of the considerations raised thus far in the discussion of strategies for evaluating oracles.

3. In the sixties, radical students used the slogan, "Never trust anyone over thirty." Discuss this principle in relation to various strategic mistakes concerning the reliability of different kinds of oracles. (What would you say about this principle if it had been put forward by somebody over thirty?!)

▶ 4. Your instructor may assign argument sketches from Appendix A. Discuss how problems with uncertainty of answers may arise in the interrogative moves and what strategies from Chapters 12 and 13 may be appropriate for coping with the uncertainty.

△ ▼ **EXERCISE 13-D**

Examine your argument construction and essay project for problems with the fallacy of authority and with the *ad hominem* errors. Continue to examine your argument to see how effectively you are handling problems with uncertainty of answers.

13.5   If You Know Your Oracles Well . . .

The idea of evaluating answers by evaluating answerers can be pushed further. The more you know about an oracle, especially about the way in which that oracle's responses are determined, the more you should attend to the fact *that* the oracle gives a certain answer rather than to *what* the answer is.

For instance, in an extreme case you may know that a certain oracle always lies. Then you can extract a great deal of information from that oracle's responses, not by believing them, but by using as a new premise the fact that the oracle gives such-and-such an answer.

△ ▼ THINK ABOUT IT

Some interesting logic puzzles are based on the insight imparted above about oracles. Here is one of the classic versions:

> A traveler comes to a fork in the road and does not know which way to go to reach his destination. There are two people at the fork. Both know the correct way, but one always lies while the other always tells the truth. The traveler cannot determine who is the liar and who the truth teller. Furthermore, the traveler is allowed to ask only one yes/no question and to address it to only one of the persons at the fork. What question should be asked and to whom should the question be addressed?

This puzzle can be solved, and we leave it to you to find a solution. Here are a couple of hints: The traveler simply does not have enough information to decide to whom the question should be addressed. The question will have to work with either oracle. One of the other things you need to notice is that either person at the fork is, in an important way, a reliable oracle. The problem is that the one is reliably honest and the other reliably false.

If you find the solution, try to write up your results in an interrogative table.

Another example of this kind of strategy is to be seen in number 11 of Exercise 2-A in Chapter 2.

Illustration   In detective stories it sometimes happens that the murderer betrays himself or herself by giving an answer to a question which shows that he or she knows something that only the murderer could. The content of the answer may otherwise be completely irrelevant to the investigation, but the fact that the murderer knows tells the investigator everything!

For example, in Josephine Tey's *Brat Farrar* the plot turns on the following scenario. A brother in a large family has disappeared and been gone for a long time. Someone outside the family, who resembles the long-lost brother, is trained by an intimate of the family to impersonate the lost sibling very effectively. This individual presents himself to the family as the long-lost brother and succeeds in fooling everyone—with one exception. One of the other brothers remains steadily convinced that the impersonator cannot be the genuine brother. What did this brother know that the others did not? Try to think of an explanation. The conclusion of the story provides a dramatic answer. (We will not spoil the novel for you by revealing it. Try to use your own ingenuity first and then read the book.)

△ ▼ **EXERCISE 13-E**

At this point you should be wrapping up your major argument construction and essay project. One last matter to consider is whether a discussion of the general reliability of your oracles can help strengthen a reader's confidence in the information your inquiry uses to support its ultimate conclusion.

13.6 Dialogues and Debates

So far we have been using the words "inquiry," "reasoning," and "argument" almost interchangeably. There are, however, differences between what these three terms suggest. In an inquiry a person or group of persons (e.g., an investigative reporter, a research group, a grand jury, an FAA crash investigation team, the entire scientific community, or whatever) is typically trying to find out the truth about some matter. The role of the oracle or oracles the inquirer consults in such inquiries is entirely passive. All that the oracles do is to answer the inquirer's questions.

Such interrogative games are sometimes referred to in game theory as "games against nature." The term does not mean that the only oracle is nature but signals that the other party (the oracle) is essentially passive. The oracle only answers questions, and does not ask them or otherwise initiate moves.

Notice that even such a passive oracle can be either cooperative or uncooperative. It can try to give the most helpful answer, or it (she, he, they) may try to impede the inquirer's investigation as much as possible. A case in point is what is known as a hostile witness in a court of law. Such differences in the oracles usually influence the inquirer's strategies. This difference can be represented in the games by assigning suitable costs and payoffs to the oracle.

However, sometimes questioning games of a different sort are played between two players who are both human beings and who are both taking an active role in an interrogative game; that is, both are asking questions.

In fact many different kinds of such interrogative games exist. They can be called *dialogical* games. Their rules differ from one game to another. Usually the players are allowed to put questions to outside oracles, which are the same for both players. However, over and above such questions, each of the players may also be allowed to address questions to the other player and use the answers (if any) as additional information, that is, as a new entry in the left side of their reasoning table.

Notice that in dialogical games questions play a somewhat different role than in the games of inquiry. In the latter, questions typically bring in new information which it is hoped will take the inquirer closer to the truth. In dialogical games answers to questions may serve the purpose of refuting one's opponent through his or her own admissions.

In an extreme form of this type of game each player is trying to prove his or her own ultimate conclusion, and each player starts with the other player's ultimate conclusion as an initial premise. Each answer a player gives to an opponent's question is added to the left side of the opponent's table and is conjoined with the initial ultimate conclusion on the right side of his or her own table. The players alternate making moves, and there are various other restrictions. It turns out that even such apparently antagonistic dialogical games can be partly cooperative, depending on the relationship between the two different ultimate conclusions. Some dialogical games are competitive rather than cooperative; these are called *debates*.

△▼ THINK ABOUT IT

In high schools and colleges there are often organized programs for competitive debating. Discuss how competitive debates are typically structured, and relate the structure of such debates to the interrogative model.

In other dialogical games the goal is not to refute one's opponent but to reach agreement or at least to get as close to agreement as possible. Many real-life negotiations can be thought of as dialogical games of this sort. Negotiations can be cooperative or antagonistic. As in most dialogical games, discovering the opponent's strategy is a key to shaping one's own.

13.7   Another Milestone

We have now completed our study of the basic elements of reasoning according to the interrogative model. The book has been designed so that, depending on the amount of time devoted to various topics, the first three parts could form the focus of an entire course. The more advanced topics in Part 4 are well worth studying, but the insights that have been gained in Parts 1 to 3 provide a good practical introduction to skills and strategies for reasoning. You are now well equipped to analyze, construct, and evaluate arguments.

Chapter 21 provides an overview and summary of the interrogative model. Despite mention of some of the more advanced topics, it can be read with profit by those who complete their study here at the end of Part 3. In Chapter 21 we draw together all the main insights our discussion of the interrogative model has given us about analysis, construction, and evaluation of arguments.

PART △ FOUR

Advanced Topics in Interrogative Reasoning

▲ 14 ▼

First-Order Predicate Logic

In our study of deductive logic in Part 2 we learned how to use some fairly simple technical methods to analyze the relation between premises and conclusions. In this chapter we will add several new powerful tools for analyzing logical inference steps. The methods of statement logic have shown us how to take premises apart into their simpler statement units. Our brief introduction to predicate logic will show how simple statements can be broken analyzed smaller parts which are no longer statements.

To illustrate what is meant, let us look again at how statement logic handles the following example about John and Mary and where they live. We shall take the following sentences to be premises.

p1. If John lives in Florida, then Mary lives in California. $F_J \supset C_m$

p2. John lives in Florida. F_J

p3. The tall girl over there is John's fiancee. E_{TJ} $T = M$

p4. John's fiancee is Mary. E_{mJ}

What conclusions can likely be drawn from these premises? Here are two possibilities:

c1. Mary lives in California.

c2. The tall girl over there lives in California.

Using our statement logic methods, we can represent these premises and conclusions as follows:

p1. $A \supset B$

p2. A

p3. C

p4. D

c1. B

c2. E

Before proceeding, make sure you agree that the way the statements have been represented breaks them down as far as statement logic will permit. Our next step is to check for validity using the table method. We will first check c1 and then c2.

Premises and Deductive Inferences	Conclusion
1. √ $A \supset B$ (prem)	7. B
2. A (prem)	
3. C (prem)	
4. D (prem)	
5. $-A$ $\vert$ B (from 1 by 5)	
6. x Bridge (from 5 to 7)	
(from 2 & 5 by 7) $\vert$	

This first table shows that B, our first conclusion, stands in a valid relation to the premises. If we assume the premises to be true, the conclusion also is forced to be true. Now we try c2.

Premises and Deductive Inferences	Conclusion
1. √ $A \supset B$ (prem)	E
2. A (prem)	
3. C (prem)	
4. D (prem)	
5. $-A$ $\vert$ B (from 1 by 5)	
6. x	
(from 2 & 5 by 7) $\vert$	

This table is finished, and it shows an invalid relationship. We leave it to you to see what the counterexample is.

Still, if you read c2 in English, it looks as though it should be true anytime the premises are true. The problem is that our statement logic is not getting at everything that is going on in these premise and conclusion statements. Information about California and Florida and John and Mary is being lost when we use statement letters to replace the English statements. In Part 2 we mentioned that in more complicated logic we would have to bring John and Mary and where they are living back into the picture. Now is the time to do that.

The first step is easy. We simply agree to continue using the symbols of statement logic in the way we have already learned. We will still be able to represent statements with uppercase letters if it suits our purposes, and our friends, the logical operators &, ∨, ⊃ and -, can continue to be used in the ways we have studied in the basic table method.

14.1 Representing Names and Predicates

The next step is to add a new way of representing statements. As we have seen, we sometimes need to be able to keep track of what is going on inside a statement. In predicate logic we do this by letting lowercase and uppercase letters take on new assignments. To understand these we need two new terms: "name" and "predicate." We shall first learn these terms in connection with relatively simple statements. For example:

1. Florida is a fast-growing state.
2. The tall girl over there lives in Florida.
3. John is tall.
4. Texas is between Florida and California.
5. Katie runs swiftly.

"Florida," "the tall girl over there," "John," "Texas," "California," and "Katie" are all names in predicate logic, as is any expression that is being used to designate a specific individual object. Notice that "the tall girl over there" is pointing out a specific object, so it is serving as a name along with the more obvious examples. This notion of name can get confusing and controversial, but we will usually be working with problems in which it will serve its purpose well enough.

In predicate logic we use lowercase letters from a through u to represent these (nonvariable) names. (The reason for the word "nonvariable" will be explained in a moment.) We have not used lowercase letters much yet, so this will give them a useful job. As you would expect, we use different letters as names of different objects, and we try to use the same letter to name the same object whenever it occurs.

In the examples note the following expressions: "fast-growing state," "lives in," "is tall," "is between," "runs swiftly." None of these is being used to designate an object but, instead, they indicate properties or relations of objects. *Florida* has the property of being a *fast-growing state*. *The tall girl over there* relates to Florida by *living in* it. *John* has the property of being *tall*. *Texas* relates to *Florida* and *California* by being *between* them. *Katie* has the property of *running swiftly*. In predicate logic, expressions indicating properties or relations of objects are called "predicates." Some predicates involve only one name; others relate two or more names together.

We use uppercase letters to represent predicates. We have already used uppercase letters in statement logic to represent statements. Using them also to represent predicates could cause a lot of confusion. We can avoid these confusions if you will carefully learn the following rule: **An uppercase letter standing by itself represents a whole statement, but when an uppercase letter is combined with a lowercase letter or letters, the uppercase letter now represents a predicate.** When uppercase letters represent predicates, we use different letters to represent different predicates, and we try to use the same letter to represent the same predicate whenever it occurs. It is also best not to take an uppercase letter that is already representing a statement to represent a predicate.

You should further note that just as uppercase predicate letters will not appear by themselves, so lowercase name letters will not usually appear by themselves. They will usually be combined with uppercase predicate letters.

▲
_____

Nonvariable Name: In predicate logic any expression that is being used to designate a specific individual object. We use lowercase letters from *a* through *u* to represent these nonvariable names.

Predicate: In predicate logic any expression that is being used to indicate properties or relations of object. We use uppercase letters to represent predicates. When an uppercase letter is representing a predicate, it will always be combined with at least one name. An uppercase letter standing by itself continues to represent whole statements, as in statement logic.

Always form whole statements. Carefully learning and using this rule will help us avoid serious problems. Our goal is to be able to form statements that are true or false. The name *John* by itself is neither true nor false; it is not a statement. The predicate *is tall* by itself is neither true nor false; it is not a statement. So we will not let lowercase name letters or uppercase predicate letters stand by themselves. But the combination of name and predicate in *John is tall* does form a statement. It can be used to say something true or false. Lowercase name letters and uppercase predicate letters must usually appear combined with each other.

△ ▼ EXERCISE 14-A

Indicate in the following sentences which expressions serve as nonvariable names and which are predicates:

▶ 1. The cat is on the mat.
2. Hamburg is in West Germany.
3. The Buick is to the left of the Ford.
▶ 4. Mabel heard the news and called Harriet on the phone.
5. Ben Franklin and David Hume were good friends.
▶ 6. Susan sings beautifully.

14.2 "Is Identical To"

Before we are prepared to go back to our problems with John and Mary, California and Florida, we will need one more tool—another logical operator to add to our symbols &, ∨, ⊃, and –. Our new logical operator uses a symbol familiar to you from math, the equal sign (=). In predicate logic, however, it will mean "is identical to." This gives us one way to write lowercase name letters without their being combined with uppercase predicate letters. For example, $a = b$ is a permissible use of lowercase name letters without an uppercase predicate letter: $a = b$ makes the statement that a and b both name the same object; this is either true or false, so $a = b$ is a statement. A lot of controversy surrounds the little symbol =, but for the time being we can ignore that.

___▲_____

> **Symbol for Identity:** In predicate logic = is the symbol for "is identical to." It can be used to make the statement that two different names designate the same object.

△ ▼ EXERCISE 14-B

Not all uses of "is" involve identity. Based on your understanding of identity, indicate which of the following uses of "is" indicate identity and which do not:

▶ 1. The tallest building in the world is in New York.
2. Ben Franklin is the inventor of bifocals.
▶ 3. The morning star is the brightest object in the dawn sky.
▶ 4. Venus is the morning star.

5. Venus is called the morning star. Cvm

6. Ari is a Greek. Ga

14.3 Putting Our Tools to Work

Now we are ready to put our new tools to work. We are hoping that they can help us with the conclusion statement logic claimed was invalid. Let us review the premises and the troublesome conclusion:

p1. If John lives in Florida, then Mary lives in California.

p2. John lives in Florida.

p3. The tall girl over there is John's fiancee.

p4. John's fiancee is Mary.

c2. The tall girl over there lives in California.

This conclusion sounds in English as though it will be true whenever the premises are all true, in other words, as if it were in a valid relationship to the premises. Predicate logic will show that the conclusion does in fact relate validly to the premises.

First we need to represent the statements. We will let a stand for John, b stand for Florida, c stand for Mary, and d stand for California. We will let L stand for the predicate "lives in." This give us

p1. $aLb \supset cLd$

p2. aLb

For p3 and p4 we can use e to stand for "the tall girl over there" and f to stand for "John's fiancee." ("Fiancee" does name a relationship, and we could let B stand for the predicate "fiancee of." This would give us eBa for p3. But we also know that in usual use "John's fiancee" picks out and names a specific individual. In predicate logic there is often more than one way to represent what is going on in a sentence. This example works more easily if we let f represent the name "John's fiancee.") This gives us the following:

p3. $e = f$

p4. $f = c$

c2. eLd

Notice that each premise and conclusion line is a simple or a complex statement. Each line is either true or false. (We have written "aLb" in p1 and p2, but we could have just as easily written "Lab." The important thing is to be careful and accurate in our representations.)

Now we turn again to the table method to check for validity:

Premises and Deductive Inferences				Conclusion	
1. √		$aLb \supset cLd$	(prem)	10.	eLd
2.		aLb	(prem)		
3.		$e = f$	(prem)		
4.		$f = c$	(prem)		
5.	$-(aLb)$	cLd	(from 1 by 5)		
6.	x			(from 2 & 5 by 7)	
7.		fLd		(from 4 & 5 by ??)	
8.		eLd		(from 3 & 7 by ??)	
9.		Bridge		(from 8 to 10)	

The finished table seems to show validity in the relation between the premises and the conclusion. Notice that Table Rules 7 and 8 are stated in such a way that they can easily be applied to the more complex statement representations in lines 6 and 9. The only problem is that a couple of steps in lines 7 and 8 need more careful justification. We used our understanding of "is identical to" to substitute f for c in line 7 and then e for f in line 8. We can put this understanding in a new rule. We already have eight table rules for logical inference, so this will be Table Rule 9.

As we turn to additional rules for logical inference it is important to remember that we are dealing with logical operators. In Part 2 we learned about &, ∨, ⊃, and –. In this chapter we have now added = and will soon add three more operators. As in Part 2, rules are formulated so that they are to be applied only when a logical operator is the *main* operator in the line.

9. **Rule for Substitutivity of Identity:** If an open path on the left side of a table contains a full line of the form $a = b$ and also another full line in which one of the names a or b appears one or more times, write at the bottom of the path a new statement line formed by replacing some or all of the occurrences of that name by the other name.

The rationale for this rule is that if a and b really are identical to each other, then anything true of one of them must be true of the other as well.

We can now go on to a related Rule 10. It is short and sweet.

10. **Rule for Path Closure by Denied Self-Identity:** Close any path on the left side that contains a full line of the form $-(a = a)$.

The rationale for this rule is that our lowercase letter names are chosen to represent specific objects. A letter must represent one and the same object in the table. If a line of thought leads us to conclude that an object is not the same as itself, then we have a line of thought in which not all the premises can be made true at the same time. Therefore we close the path.

Rule 10 has a right-side reverse image version:

10r. **Rule for Closure by Self-Identity on the Right Side:** Close any path on the right side that contains a full line of the form $a = a$.

The rationale for this rule is that in the right column we are testing whether every full line could be imagined to be false. But it cannot be false to say that an object is identical to itself.

△ ▼ EXERCISE 14-C

1. Represent the following sentences in predicate notation:
   ▶ a. Katie looks at the map and imagines flying to New Zealand.
   b. Willard prefers the desert to the jungle.
   ▶ c. President Reagan presented Frank Sinatra with the medal of freedom.
   ▶ d. Mike thanked Susan and Nancy, and opened the gift.
   e. President Reagan did not present Mick Jagger with the medal of freedom.
   f. Mandy misses misty mornings. *Mabe*

2. Construct tables for the following and test for validity:
   ▶ a. $aRb ⊃ Pb$
   $Pc ⊃ -Pd$
   Pc
   $b = d$
   Therefore, $-aRb$
   ▶ b. $-(aRb \& bRa)$
   $aRb ∨ bRa$
   $a = b$
   Therefore, aRb
   c. $(aRb \& bRa) ⊃ (a = b)$
   $-aRa$
   aRb
   Therefore, $-bRa$

14.4 Quantification

We have one more hurdle to get over, and then we will know all we need to about predicate logic. This hurdle is known as *quantification*. One of the most powerful features of our language is that it enables us to speak in an indefinite way about "somebody," "something," "somewhere," "sometime," "everybody," "everything," "everywhere," and so forth. We can talk about things and people and places and times without immediately pinning ourselves down to the names of specific individuals, objects, places, or times. We can also indicate in a rough way the "quantity" of whatever it is we are talking about. For example, sometimes we mean to talk about "everyone" in relation to whatever it is we are discussing, other times about "someone."

You will notice that in English we can also often indicate the "domain" in which we are operating. If we say "everyone," it usually means we are thinking of a domain made up of people. If we say "somewhere," it usually means we are thinking of a domain made up of places. The same happens with words like *sometimes* and *something*. In our study of predicate logic it will be useful for us to keep in the back of our minds some idea of what the domain is in which our words are operating. Sometimes more than one domain is involved. Someone might say, "Everybody has some place to call home." In this sentence "everybody" is operating on the domain of persons, and "some" is operating on the domain of places.

Variable Names

Predicate logic provides a way for capturing and clarifying what is happening in our use of these and related words. We will need to understand two things that are happening in these kinds of statements. First, instead of naming specific objects, these statements use "variable names" that do not immediately point out any specific object. We have reserved lowercase letters from the end of the alphabet to serve as these variable names. Following is an example.

1. Somebody stole my pickup truck.

"Somebody" does not name any specific person, but it is clearly holding the place where a regular name could go. For example,

2. Jack Rothals stole my pickup truck.

We can rewrite statement 1 to read

3. Somebody—x—stole my pickup truck. $\exists x \ S_{xp}$

You can still understand the sentence, and the x conveniently opens up a "hole" into which various regular nonvariable names might be placed. For example,

4. Somebody—my brother—stole my pickup truck.

We still have not dealt with everything that the word "somebody" is doing, but thus far predicate logic is showing us that one of the things the word "somebody" does is to open up a space where a variety of regular names might be filled in. We let lowercase letters from the end of the alphabet (w, x, y, z) serve to represent this function of opening a space for a variety of possible regular names. (Do be careful, however, to reserve ∨ for use as *or*.) Remember that lowercase letters from the beginning of the alphabet (a through u) serve to represent regular (nonvariable) names. The space-holding names are called variable names, because they hold open a space for a variety of regular names.

Consider again the example:

Somebody stole my pickup truck.

It will not be sufficient for us now to write it as

5. x stole my pickup truck.

Among other things, number 5 is not a statement. How could it be true or false when x is just a place holder? Number 5 means "_____ stole my pickup truck." Something else has to be done before we have a statement. We could, of course, put a regular name in the blank, but words like "somebody" and "everybody" make it possible to have a statement without putting in a regular name.

Quantifiers

Without naming names, the word "somebody" in the above example says that there exists someone who stole my pickup truck; for now let us just call that person "x." "Somebody stole my pickup truck" is a statement. It might be true or it might be false. Predicate logic represents this other part of what "somebody" is doing by introducing a new symbol: $\exists$ is a logical operator used to represent the phrase "there exists." $\exists$ is *always* used with a variable name letter like "x" or "y" so that we get $\exists x$ or $\exists y$. These expressions are read as "there exists x such that" and "there exists y such that." It is important to remember that the logical operator $\exists$ is to be used only with variable names like "x" and "y," *not* with uppercase predicate letters.

Such expressions need to be put together with other symbols to make a complete statement. Going back to the example above, we can use what we already know and let the regular name a stand for "my pickup truck." We then let S stand for the predicate "stole." Our example can now be symbolized by

6. $\exists x\ xSa$

This represents the statement "There exists an x such that x stole my pickup truck." This is rather more cumbersome than the normal English "Somebody stole my pickup truck," but it clearly indicates the two different things that the word "somebody" is doing. On the one hand it is saying "There exists" and on the other hand it is talking about an unnamed something, call it x. In the back of our minds we might also note that the domain in which x is operating seems to be persons.

This gives us the basic tool for dealing with words such as "somebody," "something," "somewhere," and "sometime." Words like "everybody" can be treated in a similar way. Let us try

7. Everybody loves my pickup truck.

Like "somebody," "everybody" opens up a variable place in a sentence. We could rewrite number 7 as

8. Everybody—x—loves my pickup truck.

Variable name letters serve the same function here as in the "somebody" case. The other job "everybody" is performing is that of saying "for every." We introduce the new symbol ∀ to represent the phrase "for every." This logical operator is always used along with a variable name letter like x or y. So we get ∀x or ∀y. These formulas are read as "for every x it is the case that" and "for every y it is the case that."

Such formulas need to be put together with other symbols to make a complete statement. To complete our statements we need to be able to represent the rest of what is going on in the English. For number 7 write a for "my pickup truck" and write L for "loves." That gives us

9. ∀x xLa

This represents the statement "For every x it is the case that x loves my pickup truck." This is rather more cumbersome than the normal English "Everybody loves my pickup truck," but it clearly indicates the two different things that the word "everybody" is doing. On the one hand it is saying "For every" and on the other hand it is talking about an unnamed something, call it x. In the back of our minds we should again note that the domain in which x is operating seems to be persons.

14.5 Partial Translation Rules for Predicate Logic

In Part 2 we learned that translating between English and a formal language is quite difficult. That is certainly the case with the powerful and subtle formal language of predicate logic. Before we tackle the problems of translation, we will do as we did in Part 2: We will first learn more about how the formal language works, and then in the next chapter we ask how to render some of the insights we have learned into English.

To learn more about the formal language, however, it will be helpful to examine some of the usual ways in which English is related to the formal logical language. As we have seen previously, translating from English into the formal notation of logic is an art, not a science, which has to be learned by means of examples rather than by rules. Strict rules are extremely hard to formulate for such a translation.

Instead of relying on rules, try to do what experienced translators do in translating from one natural language to another. Such translators do not rely on the form of words of the sentences to be translated. They try to grasp what the speaker or writer means and to express it in the other language, often by means of a different-looking sentence. Likewise, you should not try to translate English into formal notation word by word or phrase by phrase. In fact, English phrases are often destroyed in the translation and their parts separated from each other.

Here is an example of such a restructuring:

(Every Greek) is European

becomes

$\forall x \, [(x$ is Greek$) \supset (x$ is European$)]$

Here you can see how the noun phrase "Every Greek" is split into two parts, which are moved into entirely different segments of the translation. Furthermore, the variable x has no obvious counterpart in English. Also, the English word "is" is in effect expressed by a combination of two symbols in the formal notation.

The following is an example of an English sentence whose translation into the formal notation appears reasonably easy once you have seen it:

If Peter owns a donkey, he beats it.

The translation is, using Dx for "x is a donkey," xOy for "x owns y," xBy for "x beats y," and p for "Peter":

$\forall x \, [(Dx \ \& \ pOx) \supset pBx)]$

It would be very difficult, however, to formulate the precise rules that could take us from the English sentence to the symbolic translation.

In the following we formulate a number of rules of thumb for translating from English into the formal notation. In them, we shall assume that what is being talked about are human beings (persons). It is also assumed that —(s)he— is an expression which may contain a personal pronoun, while —x— is the same expression except that x has been substituted for all the personal pronouns referring back to the initial quantifier word. Instead of "she" or "he," we might for example have "herself" or "himself."

1. Someone (—(s)he—) translates as $\exists x$ (—x—).

For instance, ''Someone is talking to his or her brother'' is translated as

$\exists x \, (x$ is talking to x's brother$)$

2. Some A (—(s)he—) translates as $\exists x \, [Ax \ \& \ (—x—)]$

For instance, "Some boy is talking to his brother" is translated as

$\exists x \, [Bx \ \& \ (x$ is talking to x's brother$)]$

where B means "is a boy."

3. Some A who —— (—(s)he—) is translated as $\exists x \, [Ax \ \& \ x \ —— \ \& \ (—x—)]$

For instance, "Some boy who jogs is talking to his brother" is translated as

$\exists x \, (Bx \ \& \ x$ jogs $\& \ x$ is talking to x's brother$)$

As you can see, when we are making statements about *some*one or *some*thing, we join our various statements by using the operator $\&$. For situations in which we are making statements about *every*one or *every*thing, we have similar rules except that we have to join the statements by using the operator ⊃, instead of the operator &. The reason for this is that if we say, for example, that "Everyone who reads this chapter is learning predicate logic," we are not intending to say that "Absolutely everyone in the world is reading this chapter *and* learning predicate logic." Rather, we are intending to say that, "In every case *if* a person is reading this chapter, *then* that person is learning predicate logic." Here, then, are some rules for "every."

4. Everyone (—(s)he—) translates as ∀x (—x—)
5. Every A (—(s)he—) translates as ∀x (Ax ⊃ (—x—))
6. Every A who —— (—(s)he—) translates as ∀x [(Ax & x ——) ⊃ (—x—)]

Further translation rules include:

7. Nobody (—(s)he—) translates as ∀x -(—x—)

For instance, "Nobody talks to himself or herself" translates as

∀x -(x talks to x)

8. No A (—(s)he—) translates as ∀x [Ax ⊃ -(—x—)]

For instance, "No adult talks to himself or herself" translates as

∀x [Ax ⊃ -(x talks to x)]

where Ax reads "x is an adult."

9. No A who —— (—(s)he—) translates as. . . . (Try yourself to formulate a similar rule and provide an example.)

Translation rules similar to those for "some" can be formulated for the indefinite article "a" or "an." The following is an example.

10. An A (—(s)he—) translates as ∃x [Ax & (—(s)he—)]

For instance, "A donkey is owned by Peter" translates as

∃x (Dx & pOx)

in the notation used in the earlier example.

△▼ EXERCISE 14-D

What are the formal translations of the following English sentences:

▶ 1. Someone loves everyone. (Shorthand: xLy for "x loves y" or "y is loved by x.")
▶ 2. Everyone is loved by someone.
3. Everyone loves someone.
4. Someone is loved by everyone.
▶ 5. Every Greek is European.

6. Some Greek is European. $\exists_x (G_x \notin E_x)$

▸ 7. No Greek is Asian. $\forall_x (G_x \supset -(A_x))$ or $-\exists_x (G_x \notin A_x)$

8. Some Greek is not Asian.

$\exists_x (G_x \notin -A_x)$

9. Anything that glitters is gold. $\forall_x (G_x \supset G_{1x})$

$\forall_x (C_x \notin M_x \supset -J_x)$ 10. I wouldn't join any club that would have me as a member.

$\forall_x (M_x \supset \exists_y F_{xy})$ ▸ 11. If anyone is missing then someone will find him or her.

▸ 12. If Peter can find it, he will beat a donkey. $\forall_x [(D_x \notin F_{px}) \supset B_{px}]$

13. Peter will beat every donkey he owns.

$\forall_x [(D_x \notin O_{px}) \supset B_{px}]$

14.6   Rules for Quantifiers

To see what the other rules are that are needed in the more powerful formal language we now have at our disposal, let us go back to one of the examples used in Chapter 1 (Section 1.11), that of the notorious nonexisting Barber of Shave-ville. But to avoid getting bogged down in details, let us first get two out of the way.

First, let us agree to restrict our attention to the male inhabitants of Shave-ville. Thus, when we say "someone," we mean "some man living in Shave-ville," and when we say "everyone," we really mean "every man living in Shave-ville." This is a very common restriction. For instance, if the chair of a committee looks around and asks, "Is everyone here," she or he is not asking whether all human beings are there but merely whether all the members of the committee are present.

Second, we can simplify the example by introducing one more logical operator, the symbol ↔, to be read "if and only if." It can be thought of as shorthand, so that $A \leftrightarrow B$ really says the same as $(A \supset B) \& (B \supset A)$. Because it expresses a two-way conditional relationship between two statements, the complex statement $A \leftrightarrow B$ is called a "biconditional." We can handle biconditional statements in our tables simply by adding the equivalence between $A \leftrightarrow B$ and $(A \supset B) \&$ $(B \supset A)$ to Table Rule 6.

△ ▼ EXERCISE 14-E

1. The operator ↔ has been defined so that it is equivalent to two conditionals joined in a conjunction. Thus, we could always do without ↔ so long as we were willing to write the more cumbersome equivalent formula. The symbol is, however, quite handy, especially if we learn a table rule for taking apart a biconditional. We leave it to you to show that when a biconditional is found on the left side of a table, it splits the table, putting its two components together on separate lines in one path and the denials of each of its components together on separate lines in the other. On the right (conclusion) side there is also a

split, but on the right side of a table the denial of the left component together with the right component is put in one path, while the denial of the right component together with the left component is put in the other path. This is the result you should come to by putting the equivalent of the biconditional, $(A \supset B)$ & $(B \supset A)$, at the top of the left side or the right side of a table and applying the rules you learned in Part 2. These new rules will not have any numbers, but you can use them by referring to the rule for the biconditional.

2. Show that a table can always be closed by Table Rule 7 (Closure by Contradiction) if a statement of form $A \leftrightarrow -A$ occurs in its left column.

Let us now return to the Barber of Shave-ville. We want to show that the barber cannot exist. This can be done by putting a characterization of him at the top of a table and then closing it by means of Table Rule 7.

Now what is the Barber of Shave-ville like? He is supposed to shave all and only those men who do not shave themselves. Remembering the restriction of our attention to male Shave-villeans, we can express this by saying that for everybody it is the case that the barber shaves that person if and only if that person does not shave himself. The statement to be put at the top of the left column says that there exists such an individual.

This can be expressed in our formal notation by the following:

1. $\exists x \, \forall y \, [xSy \leftrightarrow -(ySy)]$

where aSb is to be read "a shaves b."

Now what can we do to derive a contradiction from statement 1? It is hard to argue about unspecified kinds of individuals. It is easier, as it were, to personify them; that is to say, take an imaginary example. In statement 1, individuals of a certain kind are said to exist. Hence we can choose in our imagination one of them, give it a name, and go on to argue about that individual.

This is what lawyers do all the time. When an unknown person is referred to, lawyers often assign a name arbitrarily to him or her, usually "John Doe" (sometimes "Richard Roe") or, as in the famous 1973 Supreme Court abortion case, "Jane Roe."

We, too, can introduce a name for one of the individuals said to exist in statement 1. Instead of "John Doe," we can use a special kind of lowercase letter to name this unknown individual. It is tempting to use the letters a through u, as we have already agreed to use these as names. This could be misleading, however, because the letters a through u are used to point to specific individuals. In this case we are trying to point to an unknown. All we know about this individual is he or she is supposed to exist. For this reason we will use lowercase letters from the Greek alphabet, that is, α, β, γ, and so forth.

This may look confusing, but all we need to remember is that these letters name an unknown individual whose existence is guaranteed by an existentially quantified statement. We might say that these special Greek letters are "dummy names" for the "arbitrary individual" introduced by an existentially quantified statement.

With this in mind, we can use α as a dummy name and move from statement 1 to

2. $\forall y \, [\alpha Sy \leftrightarrow -(ySy)]$

This statement is said to be obtained from statement 1 by *existential instantiation,* a rule whose formulation we shall return to in a moment.

Now what can we do with statement 2? If you still remember how we showed that there is no Barber of Shave-ville, you will remember that the trick is to ask whether he shaves himself or not. It is easy to see what this idea amounts to as applied to statement 2. This statement says that something is true of every individual. Hence it must be true of α in particular. In other words, we can move from statement 2 to

3. $\alpha S\alpha \leftrightarrow -(\alpha S\alpha)$

In other words, statement 3 can be inserted in the left column. But the presence of this statement in the left column is enough to show that the table can be closed by contradiction, as we showed in the exercise. Hence, there cannot be any Barber of Shave-ville (of the kind described). Notice that we were wise not to use a regular name for the barber, because it turns out there never was one! The step (move) from statements 2 to 3 is known as *universal instantiation.* We now proceed to give precise formulations of the rules of existential and universal instantiation.

Instantiation Rules

Our brief introduction to predicate logic will conclude with the learning of three more table rules for logical inference. These will give us more than enough tools for the logical inference steps in our interrogative inquiries. (By the way, this type of deductive logic is called "first-order" logic because the notions of "some" and "every" are being applied only to individuals, not to predicates. In higher-order logic the quantifiers are allowed also to range over predicates.)

The first two of our new rules give us a way to put names into quantified statements. Being able to do this can often help in attempts to test for validity. The two rules are precisely the ones suggested by the example of the Barber of Shave-ville. As we turn to the rules it is important to remember that we are dealing here with logical operators. In Part 2 we learned about &, $\lor$, $\supset$, and -. In this chapter we have now added =, $\leftrightarrow$, $\forall$, and $\exists$. As in Part 2, the rules are formulated so that they are to be applied only when a logical operator is the *main* operator in the line. The fact that $\forall x$ appears at the beginning of a line does not automatically mean that it is the main operator. For example, the statement $(\forall x \, Ax \lor \exists x \, Bx)$ has $\lor$ as its main operator. As we learned in Part 2, parentheses, brackets, and braces are often used to show which operator is doing what job in a given complex statement.

11. **Rule for Universal Instantiation:** Anytime a universally quantified formula appears with $\forall x$ as the main operator on a full line on the left side of a table, choose either a regular or a dummy name such as b or α and substitute the

chosen name for every occurrence of x in the original formula, writing the result in the open path (or paths) underneath the original formula. Do *not* put a check mark by the universally quantified line.

There is an important fact about this definitory rule: *In choosing names for universal instantiation, you can always restrict your attention to names that already occur in the subtable in which this universally instantiated line is found.* This restriction is optional in purely logical arguments, but in arguments that involve answers to questions it is necessary to maintain the restriction that we not introduce new names into a subtable by Rule 11.

Table Illustration for Universal Instantiation

Premises and Deductive Inferences	*Conclusion*
1. $\forall x \, (Ax \, \& \, Bx)$ (prem)	. . . .
2. . . . . (prem)	
3. . . . . (. . . .)	
4. $Cb \lor Cd$ (from . . . .)	
5. $Ab \, \& \, Bb$ (from 1 by 11)	
6. . . . . (. . . .)	

The rationale for Table Rule 11 is that $\forall x \, (Ax \, \& \, Bx)$ says A and B are true of every object in the domain. Therefore, we are free to say that A and B are true of any named object in the domain. This rule is most likely to help us if we pick names that are already in use in the path. We do not place a check mark by the line $\forall x \, (Ax \, \& \, Bx)$, because a universally instantiated line remains available for use over and over again, and it is sometimes essential to be able to reuse it.

Our next rule is similar to Rule 11 except for some very important differences.

12. **Rule for Existential Instantiation:** Anytime an unchecked existentially quantified formula appears with $\exists x$ as the main operator on a full line on the left side of a table, examine the path in which the formula occurs to see whether the path already contains a full-line version of the original formula with a regular or dummy name substituted for x. If so, nothing further should be written and the existentially quantified line should be checked off. If not, choose a dummy name such as α that has not been used anywhere in the subtable(s) in which the existentially quantified line occurs and substitute the chosen name for every occurrence of x in the original formula. Write the result in the open path (or paths) underneath the original formula. Put a check mark by the existentially quantified formula.

Table Illustration for Existential Instantiation

Premises and Deductive Inferences	Conclusion
1. √ ∃x (Ax & Bx) (prem)	. . . .
2. . . . . (prem)	
3. . . . . (. . . .)	
4. Cβ ∨ Cd (from . . . .)	
5. Aα & Bα (from 1 by 12)	
6. . . . . (. . . .)	

The rationale for this rule is that ∃x (Ax & Bx) says A and B are true of at least one object in the domain. Therefore, we are free to say that A and B are true of some arbitrary object in the domain. We cannot, however, assume that A and B are true of some object we have already named. It is for this reason that we must always use a new dummy name, unless we already know from some other occurrence of the formula what named object goes in it. This is different from Rule 11, where we are advised to use old names as often as possible. We place a check by the line ∃x (Ax & Bx) because this line can only be used once in the paths in which it appears.

In the light of these definitory restrictions in Rule 12, we can formulate another strategic rule: *It is often best carefully to apply Table Rule 12 first wherever possible.* Then we can apply Rule 11 to produce more statements using the same name. Actually, the situation is much more complicated than this. In Chapters 17 and 18 we shall discuss the strategic importance of and guidelines for existential instantiation in the detail it deserves.

14.7 The Significance of Existential Instantiation

You actually met existential instantiation (without this fancy name) in Chapter 1 in the example of Meno's slave boy. There Socrates took a square and drew three others next to it so that the slave boy could form a square with a side twice as long as the original square's side.

The ancient Greeks did most of their mathematics in this geometric way, and drawings such as these have come to be known as "auxiliary constructions" in geometric reasoning. What do these auxiliary constructions do? They do not tell us that other squares can be drawn in addition to the original one. We already knew that before Socrates said anything. What Socrates did was to select and name (point to, designate) certain especially helpful squares for the reasoning that is needed in this inquiry. It is not enough that we know that certain squares could be drawn; we need to have the squares actually named or indicated before we can reason about them or reason with their help. What Socrates did was to give an existential instantiation of some particular squares to aid us in our reasoning.

Notice also that the diagram Socrates introduced is a "dummy" diagram in much the same way that our variables for existential instantiation are "dummy" variables. Socrates was not inquiring into just the one specific square he drew in the sand over two thousand years ago. He was actually arguing about any arbitrary square. Hence, the symbols he used ought to have been lowercase Greek letters, our symbols for dummy names, rather than the Roman letters we use for proper names. (Come to think of it, there is a good chance that Socrates used Greek letters!)

△ ▼ EXERCISE 14-F

Construct tables for the following:

▶ 1. $\forall x \ \forall y \ (xRy \supset Px)$
   $\exists y \ aRy$
   Therefore, Pa

▶ 2. $\forall x \ \exists y \ xRy$
   $\exists y \ \forall x \ (-xRy \ \& \ yRx)$
   Therefore, aRb

3. $\forall x \ \forall y \ \forall z \ [(xRy \ \& \ yRz) \supset xRz]$
   $\exists x \ (aRx \ \& \ xRa)$
   Therefore, aRa

14.8 Table Rules 11r and 12r

The reverse-image right-side versions of Table Rules 11 and 12 are as follows:

11r. **Rule for Universal Instantiation on the Right Side:** Anytime an unchecked universally quantified formula appears with $\forall x$ as the main operator on a full line on the right side of a table, examine the path in which the formula occurs to see whether the path already contains a full-line version of the original formula with a regular or dummy name substituted for x. If so, nothing further should be written and the universally quantified line should be checked off. If not, choose a dummy name such as α that has not been used anywhere in the subtable(s) in which the universally quantified line occurs and substitute the chosen name for every occurrence of x in the original formula. Write the result in the open path (or paths) underneath the original formula. Put a check mark by the universally quantified formula.

Table Illustration for Universal Instantiation on the Right Side

Premises and Deductive Inferences		Conclusion
1.	(prem)	$\checkmark$ $\forall x\, Ax$
2.	. . . .	. . . .
3. $Cb \vee Cd$	(from . . . .)	. . . .
4.	(from . . . .)	$A\alpha$
		(From 1 by 11r)

The rationale for this rule is that $\forall x\, Ax$ says that A is true of every object in the domain. On the right (conclusion) side of our tables we are trying to imagine that the line is false. Therefore, when we instantiate we say that A applies to some arbitrary individual like α. Then we continue to try to imagine that $A\alpha$ is false. α needs to be a previously unused dummy name of some arbitrary individual, because we cannot assume that the false instance of Ax will involve a name that is already in use in the table. We check the line, because there is only this one arbitrary test case that will be used to try to maintain that $\forall x\, Ax$ is false. No more instantiations can be done on this right-side universally quantified line. Notice that on the right side it is the universally quantified statement that is very restricted in its instantiations. On the left side it is the existentially quantified statement that is restricted in its instantiations.

12r. **Rule for Existential Instantiation on the Right Side:** Anytime an existentially quantified formula appears with $\exists x$ as the main operator on a full line on the right side of a table, choose either a regular or a dummy name such as b or α and substitute the chosen name for every occurrence of x in the original formula, writing the result in the open path (or paths) underneath the original formula. Do *not* put a check mark by the existentially quantified line.

Table Illustration for Existential Instantiation on the Right Side

Premises and Deductive Inferences		Conclusion
1.	(prem)	$\exists x\, Ax$
2.	. . . .	. . . .
3. $Cb \vee Cd$	(from . . . .)	. . . .
4.	(from . . . .)	Ab
		(From 1 by 12r)

The rationale for this rule is that $\exists x\, Ax$ says that A is true of at least one object in the domain. On the right (conclusion) side of our tables we are trying to imagine that the line is false. Therefore, in order to imagine that this existentially quantified line is false, we must be able to say that it is false in respect to every possible instantiation. So, in attempting to write falsehoods on the right side, we are free to instantiate the existentially quantified statement as many times as we like, using either regular or dummy names as we need. For this reason we do not check the line. In arguments that involve answers to questions, it is necessary to add the restriction that we not introduce new names into a subtable by Rule 12r.

14.9 One More Rule

It is possible to have denials in which one of the quantifiers is the next main operator in the formula. In such a case none of our equivalences from Table Rule 6 in Chapter 7 will be appropriate. The rule for denied quantification is as follows:

13. **Rule for Denied Quantifications:** Anytime a denied quantifier ($-\forall x$ or $-\exists x$) occurs as the main and next main operator on a full line, check it and write at the bottom of all open paths in which that line occurs the same statement with $\exists x-$ in place of $-\forall x$ (or with $\forall x-$ in place of $-\exists x$) at the front.

Table Illustration for Denied Quantification

Premises and Deductive Inferences			Conclusion
1. $\checkmark$	$-\forall x\ (Ax \supset Bx)$	(prem)	. . . .
2. $\checkmark$	$-\exists x\ (Ax \& Bx)$	(prem)	
3.	. . . .	(prem)	
4.	. . . .	(. . . .)	
5.	$Cb \lor Cd$	(from . . . .)	
6.	$\exists x\ -(Ax \supset Bx)$	(from 1 by 13)	
7.	$\forall x\ -(Ax \& Bx)$	(from 2 by 13)	
8.	. . . .	(. . . .)	

The rationale for this rule is that "it is not the case that every . . . " tells us that "some are not. . . . " This explains the move from line 1 to line 6. "It is not the case that there exists . . . " tells us that "everything is not. . . . " This explains the move from line 2 to line 7. The line is checked, because we will not have any other rule for using it. Since we are dealing with an equivalence, the same reasoning applies on the right side of a table.

In studying statement logic we learned to be careful not to apply a rule unless it applied to the main connector of a statement line. In a similar way these new table rules are applicable only to quantifiers that are governing a whole line. As in statement logic, so here: Parentheses, brackets, and braces are used to help determine what is governing what. In a case in which two quantifiers are both governing a whole line, the leftmost quantifier is the one to which the rules may be applied. For example, if you have the line $\forall x \, \exists y \, Axy$, Table Rule 11 can be applied to it, but Table Rule 12 cannot.

△ ▼ EXERCISE 14-G

Construct tables for the following to determine which are valid arguments

1. $\forall x \, \exists y \, Rxy$
   Therefore, $-\exists x \, \forall y \, -Rxy$

▶ 2. $\forall x \, \forall y \, \forall z \, [(xRy \, \& \, yRz) \supset xRz]$
   $\forall x \, \forall y \, (xRy \supset yRx)$
   $\forall x \, \exists y \, xRy$
   Therefore, $\forall x \, xRx$

▶ 3. $\forall x \, \exists y \, xRy$
   $\forall x \, \forall y \, [xRy \supset \forall z \, (xRz \supset y = z)]$
   $\forall x \, xRx$
   Therefore, $\forall x \, \forall y \, (xRy \supset x = y)$

▶ 4. $\forall x \, \exists y \, Rxy$
   Therefore, $\exists x \, \forall y \, Ryx$

5. $\forall x \, \forall y \, (Rxy \supset Ryx)$
   Therefore, $\exists x \, \exists y \, Rxy$

14.10   Syllogisms

Our quantifier rules enable us to deal with the logical consequences known as **syllogisms.** Syllogisms were studied in detail already by Aristotle. The following is an example of a valid syllogism:

Every B is A
Every C is B
Hence: Every C is A

This can be formalized as follows:

$\forall x \, (Bx \supset Ax)$
$\forall x \, (Cx \supset Bx)$
Hence $\forall x \, (Cx \supset Ax)$

The validity of this argument can be shown by the table method as follows. Note that in this table the lines are numbered in the order in which the various logical inference moves have been made.

Premises and Deductive Inferences			Conclusion	
1.	$\forall x\ (Bx \supset Ax)$	(prem)	3. $\sqrt{}$	$\forall x\ (Cx \supset Ax)$
2.	$\forall x\ (Cx \supset Bx)$	(prem)		(conclusion)
7. $\sqrt{}$	$B\alpha \supset A\alpha$	(from 1 by 11)	4. $\sqrt{}$	$C\alpha \supset A\alpha$
8. $\sqrt{}$	$C\alpha \supset B\alpha$	(from 2 by 11)		(from 3 by 11r)
9.	$-B\alpha$ $\quad$ |10. $A\alpha$	(from 7 by 5)	5. $-C\alpha$	(from 4 by 5r)
11. $-C\alpha$ $\quad$| 12. $B\alpha$|Bridge	(from 6 to 10)	6. $A\alpha$	(from 4 by 5r)
Bridge| $\quad$ x $\quad$ | $\quad$ <(from 5 to 11)			<path closed 9 & 12 by 7	
(Lines 11 & 12 from 8 by 5)				

Syllogisms are inference relations in which there are precisely two premises and one conclusion. The premises and conclusion are of one of the following rather restricted types of the form:

First premise: Every B is A; Every A is B; No B is A; No A is B; Some B is A; Some A is B; Some B is not A; Some A is not B.

Second premise: Similarly for C and B instead of B and A.

Conclusion: Similarly for C and A instead of B and A.

Of course, in some syllogisms the inference relations are valid logical inferences as we saw in the above table, but others are invalid. For instance, the following syllogism is valid:

(*) No A is B

Some C is B

Hence: Some C is not A

The following is invalid:

(**) Some B is A

No B is C

Hence (?): Some C is A

△▼ EXERCISE 14-H

▶ 1. Show by means of the table method that (*) above is valid but (**) invalid.

2. Find another valid and another invalid syllogism form and show that they are valid and invalid, respectively.

14.11 A Surprisingly Complex Little Example

As another example of how the quantifier rules can be put to use, let us see how our old familiar sample argument, Sherlock Holmes's reasoning about "The Curious Incident of the Dog in the Night-time," can be analyzed by means of quantifiers and quantifier rules. The argument was analyzed less thoroughly in both Chapters 1 and 2 of Part 1. As was pointed out in Chapter 2, it suffices to consider the left side of the table only. The following abbreviations are used:

Wx = x is a watchdog

Sx = x was in the stable

xBy = x barked at y

t = the thief

m = the stable master

xMy = x is the master of y

The following formulation of Sherlock Holmes's argument should be compared with the verbal formulation in Chapter 2.

1. $\checkmark$	$\exists x\ (Wx\ \&\ Sx)$	Interrogative Move
2. $\checkmark$	$(W\alpha\ \&\ S\alpha)$	From 1 by 12
3. $W\alpha$		From 2 by 3
4. $S\alpha$		From 2 by 3
5. $\forall x\ [(Wx\ \&\ Sx)\ \supset\ -xBt]$		Interrogative Move
6. $\checkmark$	$(W\alpha\ \&\ S\alpha)\ \supset\ -\alpha Bt$	From 5 by 11

Two subtables branch here. The first has the following entry:

7a. $-(W\alpha\ \&\ S\alpha)$		From 6 by 5

This path immediately closes however by 7 from 2 and 7a. So we only need to consider the other path:

7b. $-\alpha Bt$		From 6 by 5
8. $\forall x\ \forall y\ [(Wy\ \&\ -yBx)\ \supset\ xMy]$		Interrogative Move
9. $\forall y\ [(Wy\ \&\ -yBt)\ \supset\ tMy]$		From 8 by 11
10. $\checkmark$	$(W\alpha\ \&\ -\alpha Bt)\ \supset\ tM\alpha$	From 9 by 11

Again our construction branches into two paths. The first path begins with:

11a. $\checkmark$	$-(W\alpha\ \&\ -\alpha Bt)$	From 10 by 5
11aa. $-W\alpha\ \vee\ --\alpha Bt$		From 11a by 6

And this in turn branches into two paths. The first path begins with:

11aaa. $-W\alpha$		From 11aa by 4

This closes from 3 and 11aaa by 7. The other path begins with:

11aab. $--\alpha Bt$ From 11aa by 4

But this closes from 7b and 11aab by 7. So we can go back to the other path branching from line 10. It begins with:

11b. $tM\alpha$ From 10 by 5
12. $\forall x\,(xM\alpha \supset x = m)$ Interrogative Move
13. $\surd\; tM\alpha \supset t = m$ From 12 by 11

Once again we have two branching paths. The first is:

13a. $-tM\alpha$ From 13 by 5

This path closes from 13a and 11b by 7. So all that remains is the other path, which begins:

13b. $t = m$ From 13 by 5

This, however, is the conclusion that the thief was the stable master, which was the conclusion to be proved. This last path bridges from 13b to the ultimate conclusion. Because all the other paths closed, we have a successful interrogative inquiry. The conclusion follows validly from the reasoning on the left side. And if the answers given in the interrogative moves are true, then the conclusion must also be true.

This analysis shows vividly how quickly a reasoner's mind can run through a large number of steps. Holmes's elementary-looking insight is seen to involve no fewer than nineteen steps. Yet, as Sherlock Holmes himself said on another occasion, "There were such steps, however."

Throughout the book we have seen that an argument that on the face of things looks simple can in reality involve several unexpressed interrogative steps. Now we can see that an apparently simple process of reasoning can involve a large number of tacit logical inference steps as well.

14.12 Undecidability

When we worked with statement logic, we could be confident that our table method would mechanically finish eventually. It can be proved that in statement logic the mechanical table method can always lead us to discover whether we have validity or invalidity and, in the case of invalidity, what could serve as a suitable counterexample. (We ignore here problems such as that the table for a big set of statements might use up all the available paper or that we might run out of ink or that our lives might end. The idea is that, given enough time and room, a statement-logic table can always be finished.)

The complications of predicate logic make it the case, however, that our table procedure for testing for validity can no longer always be counted on to finish. Sometimes we may end up with every path closed. Then, as in statement logic, we have a proof of validity. Sometimes we may end up with an open path to which no rule can be applied. Then, as in statement logic, we shall be able to formulate the counterexample that shows invalidity. (It helps when encountering these situations to use the strategic rules formulated in this chapter and in Part 2.)

But sometimes a path will go on generating itself infinitely. Moreover, it can be shown that there is no mechanical (computable) method of predicting how far we have to carry out the construction to be sure it can be carried all the way to infinity, that is, to be sure that no hidden possibility of closing the path is still lurking in the table. This means that no mechanical method allows us to recognize whether we have validity or invalidity. This is known as the *undecidability* of first-order predicate logic. Instead of proving this result, we shall simply include a table here to illustrate the problem:

Premises and Deductive Inferences			Conclusion
1.	$\forall x\,\exists y\,xLy$	(prem)	aLa
2. $\checkmark$	$\exists y\,aLy$	(from 1 by 11)	
3.	$aL\alpha$	(from 2 by 12)	
4. $\checkmark$	$\exists y\,\alpha Ly$	(from 1 by 11)	
5.	$\alpha L\beta$	(from 4 by 12)	
6. $\checkmark$	$\exists y\,\beta Ly$	(from 1 by 11)	
7.	$\beta L\gamma$	(from 6 by 12)	
8.	. . . .	(. . . .)	
9.	. . . .	(. . . .)	
10. and so on and on			

Because of the ways in which Table Rules 11 and 12 work, this table is guaranteed to go on forever. We might suspect that the relation between premise and conclusion is invalid, but the table will never reach a stopping point which provides us with a counterexample in the same way as in statement logic.

In this case, it is not hard to see that the construction can be carried on indefinitely and that no opportunities of rule applications will remain unused in the construction. In such a case the entire infinite path provides a counterexample in the same way as did the finite paths of statement logic that could not be carried any further.

However, in many cases it is not possible to decide whether a construction path can in fact be continued to infinity. Then we face the phenomenon of undecidability.

In Chapter 17 we shall see that **the most important strategic question in interrogative inquiry is how far an argument has to be carried (how far a table**

has to be constructed) to reach the desired conclusion or to discover a counter-example. What we have just seen about undecidability means that this strategic question does not admit of a mechanical answer which would apply to all cases. This is so, even in the case of purely deductive reasoning.

14.13 Proving Validity

(Note: This Section is for those who happen to be interested; it can be omitted without any loss of continuity.)

One of the most important distinctions made in the study of logical inferences is the distinction between *truth* and *validity*. It may be worth our while to have another look at this important distinction and its consequences.

The table method is a general way of keeping track of an inquiry aimed at showing that a conclusion is *true*. What the inquirer is trying to do is to show that the conclusion is true on the assumption that the initial premise lines and interrogative answer lines are true. When the table is closed, we know that the inquirer has established that the conclusion is true, subject to the assumption about the truth of the premises and the interrogative answers.

By *truth* we have meant truth in the world in which the inquiry takes place and to which the different oracles' answers pertain. This normally means *actual truth* (truth in the actual world).

However, in Part 2 and Chapter 14, we have restricted our attention to inquiries in which the only moves in the "game" of inquiry are logical ones. In this special case, when the table is closed, we are in a position to make a stronger claim than that the conclusion is actually true if the initial premises are actually true. We can conclude that in any imaginable situation ("possible world") the same relation between premises and conclusion holds. This is so because we assumed that the inquirer puts no questions to any oracle concerning what is true in the actual world. Hence it does not matter which possible (or actual) world the inquiry is designed to apply to. This is the reason for the general applicability of deductive logic in all inquiries. Valid logical conclusions hold in any imaginable situation or world.

When, in deductive logic, the table is closed, the conclusion is said to be a *valid* logical conclusion from the initial premises. Showing that there is a valid relation of conclusion to the initial premises requires more than just showing the truth of the conclusion in the actual world. The business of a professional logician includes studying relations of validity. A logician is, among other things, devising methods of obtaining an overview on all valid relations of logical inference.

Here we have an unanticipated gift in store for any who wish to be students of formal logic for its own sake. Our table method is principally designed to be a representation of the *quest of truth*. What we have seen in this chapter and in Part 2 is that as a by-product we also obtain a method of studying logical validity.

Many logicians nevertheless prefer methods that look somewhat different from our table method. What they would like to have is a more direct approach to logical validity. They would, first of all, like to locate a class of obviously valid relationships, perhaps indicating the valid relationship by an arrow. Such arrow configurations are sometimes called *sequents*. For instance, the following is a valid sequent:

$A, B, C \rightarrow B$

Such obviously valid sequents are often called *logical axioms*.

Logicians would also like to have a number of rules for obtaining other valid sequents, preferably all of them, by successive applications of the rules. Such valid derived sequents can be called *logical theorems*. The overall system can be called an *axiom system for logic*. Many textbooks of symbolic logic present such axiomatizations of logic (not necessarily in the sequent form, though) rather than logical tables. Why did we not do likewise?

There are two very good answers. The first is that we wanted to keep the distinction between truth and validity absolutely clear. In logicians' usual techniques, it is much more tempting to confuse them than in our table method.

The second answer is that the table method does in fact automatically provide a logician with an axiomatization of logic. To put the point directly, all we have to do is to turn the table method of logical inference around. By so doing, we obtain the kind of axiomatization of logic which is found in many textbooks of formal logic and which we have just now briefly described.

More explicitly, what we mean is this: Let us assume that you have closed a deductive table, that is, closed a table without any interrogative moves. Then consider the following way of rewriting it:

1a. For each of the steps in a subtable construction, form the following sequent:

$(*)$ $A1, A2, \ldots, Ai \rightarrow B1, B2, \ldots, Bj$

where $A1, A2, \ldots, Ai$ are all the statements on the left side of the subtable at the time and $B1, B2, \ldots, Bj$ are all the statements on the right side so far.

1b. Leave out all the checked statements from $(*)$.

The outcome is a sequent. Follow this procedure for all the steps in the subtable.

  2. Reverse the order of the sequents.

This method will provide you with a series of sequents that is a derivation of the conclusion from the premises. We provide an illustration of this process by means of a brief example. Consider the following closed table:

Premises and Deductive Inferences				Conclusion	
1.		−A	(prem)	5.	B
2. √		A ∨ B	(prem)		
3.	A		B (from 2 by 4)		
4.	x		Bridge (3 to 5)		(1 & 3 by 7)

We begin by forming the sequent consisting of initial premises on the left and the ultimate conclusion on the right:

–A, A ∨ B → B

The two subtables created by application of the rule for ∨ include the following two sequents:

–A, A → B

and

–A, B → B

Notice that A ∨ B is omitted since it has been checked by this stage.

This completes the procedure described in 1a and 1b above. The second stage is to reverse the order of the sequents that were created at each step. This gives us:

–A, A → B	–A, B → B

–A, A ∨ B → B

The horizontal line indicates that a rule of inference has been applied. In this case it is the rule based on disjunction. Notice that because the order of inferences is reversed, the table branches downward but the sequents branch upward.

A closed table analyzed in this way will not usually produce a series of sequents that immediately shows the final sequent to be a valid logical theorem. In fact, our illustration is not quite yet in such a form. Two more rules, however, provide all that is needed to permit tracing a derivation back to a set of three initial sequents that serve as the logical axioms in the system. Here are the rules:

3. Use as the only initial sequents the axioms:
   a. A → A
   b. A, –A → B
   c. B → A, –A

4. To turn a derivation into a proof, derive the top line of sequents emerging from the application of rule 2 from the axioms 3a–c, by the following rules:

   a. You may add any statement to the left side of a previous sequent.
   b. You may add any statement to the right side of a previous sequent.
   c. You may rearrange the order of statements on either side of a previous sequent.

In our illustration –A, A → B is of a form that is already one of the logical axioms of the system, so it may serve as an initial sequent according to rule 3b. –A, B → B is not of a form to be an initial sequent, but you can begin instead with B → B (of the form found in axiom 3a). Then use rule 4a to obtain –A, B → B. Now we can write our entire proof thus:

$$\frac{\cfrac{B \rightarrow B}{-A, B \rightarrow B}}{-A, A \rightarrow B}$$

$$\frac{-A, A \rightarrow B \qquad\qquad -A, B \rightarrow B}{-A, A \vee B \rightarrow B}$$

This series of sequents serves as a demonstration of the validity of the inference from $-A$ and $A \vee B$ to B, just as our original table did.

△▼ THINK ABOUT IT

What would a set of sequent calculus logical inference rules have to look like? Trying stating some of the rules, based on your knowledge of our Table Rules 1–13. Remember that because the order of inferences is reversed, the tables branch downward but the sequents branch upward.

▲ 15
▼

First-Order Predicate Logic in English

In Chapter 9 we noted how difficult the problems of translation between English and formal logic really are. These problems become even more difficult when we move from statement logic to first-order predicate logic. The problem is that English words are combined in ways that are much more complicated than the ways in which logical symbols are combined. Consequently, the task of translating from English to the logical notation is much more complicated than first meets the eye.

For instance, consider the English statement

1. If everybody comes to Sam's party, he will be surprised.

It fairly obviously means the same as

2. $\forall x$ (x comes to Sam's party) $\supset$ Sam will be surprised.

Likewise, the English statement

3. If anybody comes to Sam's party, he will be surprised.

can mean the same as

4. $\exists x$ (x comes to Sam's party) $\supset$ Sam will be surprised.

But statement 3 can clearly mean, instead of statement 4, the same as

5. $\forall x$ [(x comes to Sam's party) $\supset$ (x will be surprised)]

In other words, any guest who comes will be surprised. Yet the two English words "every" and "any" both mean, when taken alone, roughly the same as $\forall x$. Why, then, do statements 1 and 3 behave so differently?

For another example, consider the following English statement:

6. If Peter owns a donkey, he beats it.

This clearly means the same as

7. $\forall x$ {[(Peter owns x) & (x is a donkey)] $\supset$ (Peter beats x)}

Yet the English indefinite article "a" normally is an existential quantifier like $\exists x$. How then can it suddenly become (as it seems) a universal quantifier in statement 6?

If you are puzzled by these questions, you are not alone. The problem of translating between natural and formal languages is in fact so difficult that there is little hope for us to be able to explain here what is going on in examples 1, 3, or 6.

15.1   Simpler Statements and the Main Operator

In Chapter 9 you learned a technique for using the insights of formal statement logic while working primarily in natural English. We will now apply the same technique for using the insights of first-order predicate logic while again working primarily in natural English.

The technique involves calling on your natural ability to understand what is happening in complex statements in English. Instead of trying to translate an entire statement into the formal notation, your task is to ask yourself: What does the statement say? Are there simpler statements within the complex statement, and if so, what are they? Are the simpler statements being related to each other in the ways we studied in statement logic? Are there quantifier words, and if so, what is their meaning in the statement?

In statement logic you were concerned with four logical operators: -, &, ∨, and $\supset$. Predicate logic continues to use these operators in the same way, as well as three additional operators: =, $\forall$, and $\exists$. (We also learned how to use the operator ↔.) Whenever we discover that one of these new operators is the main operator in a complex statement, then we will be able to apply the appropriate Table Rules 9, 10, 11, 12, or 13 from Chapter 14.

We discussed how to determine what the main statement-logic operator of an English statement is in Chapter 9. But how do you tell whether the main operator of an English statement is an existential quantifier or a universal quantifier? Again, the procedure is simple and usually quite easy. Just ask yourself: Does the main statement say something about at least one object (individual) of a certain kind, but not about all of them? If so, the main operator is an *existential quantifier*. Does the main statement say something about every object (individual) of a certain kind? If so, the main operator in the statement is a *universal quantifier*.

In both cases, the application of a quantifier rule happens in principle in the same way as in a formal language. Of course, in English there are no variables of quantification that can be replaced by an instantiating name. What happens is nevertheless clear: The quantifier word ("something," "everything," "someone," "everyone," etc.) is replaced by the instantiating term, and so is every pronoun whose antecedent is that quantifier word.

Notice also that quantifiers in English do not include only "every" and "some," but also "any," "each," "all," the indefinite article "a" (or "an"), and "no." For instance, "nobody said that" means the same as $\forall x\ -(x$ said that).

△ ▼ EXERCISE 15-A

What is the main operator in the following statements? If denial is the main operator of the entire statement, indicate the main operator of a statement that is equivalent to the denied statement.

▶ 1. Jimmy cannot beat anyone.
▶ 2. Jimmy cannot beat everyone.
   3. Tom, Dick, or Harry spoke to everybody.
   4. Tom, Dick, or Harry spoke to each person.
▶ 5. No brain injury is too insignificant to be ignored. [A hortatory sign on the wall of the interns' lounge of a certain neurological hospital!]
   6. Everybody loves someone.
▶ 7. Someone is loved by everybody.
   8. Somebody loves everyone.
   9. Everyone is loved by somebody.
▶ 10. Everyone is loved by a certain person.
   11. On this dangerous street someone is hit by a car every month.

After you have learned to apply the quantifier rules to English sentences, you can use what you learned about formal logic to test the validity of different arguments conducted in English.

△ ▼ EXERCISE 15-B

Assume as your initial premise the (conceptual) truth

If you pass anyone on the road, he or she walks more slowly than you.

Which of the following statements can be validly derived from this premise? Do not translate it fully into logical notation, but do use tables to find the statements that are in a valid relation with it.

1. If you pass John on the road, John walks more slowly than you.
▸ 2. If you pass someone on the road, someone walks more slowly than you.
▸ 3. If you pass nobody on the road, nobody walks more slowly than you.
4. If you pass anyone on the road, anyone walks more slowly than you.

Restricted Quantification

In a formal language, as was explained, a domain of individuals is assumed as being specified independently of any particular statement. The terms you may insert for the variables of quantification include the names of each and every member of the domain. We can express this by saying that quantifiers *range over* the whole domain.

If you want to restrict your quantifier to some part of the domain, you have to do that separately. For instance, if you want to restrict your attention to individuals which have the predicate A, you have to replace the existential quantifier $\exists x$ prefixed to Sx, $\exists x\ Sx$ by $\exists x\ (Ax\ \&\ Sx)$. Similarly, the universal quantifier $\forall x\ Sx$ would need to be replaced by $\forall x\ (Ax \supset Sx)$.

In English, some quantifier words normally range over the whole domain. They include such words as "someone," "somebody," "something," "everyone," "everybody," and "everything." But usually we do not face such generic quantifiers. Usually in English, quantifiers come to you already restricted. They occur in such combinations as "some X," "every Y," "any Z," "a certain V," or "a W." In these expressions, X, Y, Z, V, or W is a (possibly complex) predicate of individuals. These expressions X, Y, Z, V, or W are not a part of the quantifier, logically speaking, and do not correspond to the variables of quantification used in formal languages. They mark restrictions on the range of the quantifier, necessitating the insertion of a new conjunction for existential quantifiers or of an antecedent of a conditional for universal quantifiers into the statement in question.

For instance, "everybody is mortal" is synonymous with $\forall x\ (x$ is mortal$)$. But "every man is mortal" must be expressed in our formal language as $\forall x\ [(x$ is a man$) \supset (x$ is mortal$)]$. Likewise, although "somebody is poor" says the same as $\exists x\ (x$ is poor$)$, the statement "some Scot is poor" has to be translated as $\exists x\ [(x$ is a Scot$)\ \&\ (x$ is poor$)]$.

Please notice (and keep in mind) that $\exists x$ goes together with $\&$ while $\forall x$ goes together with $\supset$, even though they are otherwise parallel.

Because quantifiers in English usually come to you already restricted, this fact has to be taken into account in applying the rules of logical inference. Usually, the intended restriction is obvious in the sense that it is part and parcel of our understanding of the quantified statement in question. Once you have found this restriction, you have to take it into account in your application of the quantifier rules.

For instance, suppose that you have established in your mind that an English statement is a universal statement restricted to individuals satisfying a certain condition Ax. (This may be shown by the fact that the expression "every A" is the main operator in the statement.) Then you can apply, for example, Table Rule 11 for universal instantiation almost in the same way as in formal languages, except that you have to add to the newly introduced statement an antecedent Ab, where b is the instantiating term you are using in applying Rule 11. This turns the new statement introduced by Rule 11 into a conditional statement.

In the same way, when you apply Table Rule 12 to an English sentence where the main operator is "some A," the new statement you insert into the left side must also contain the conjunct $A\beta$, where β is the new instantiating term you are using.

For example, assume that the following sentence occurs in the left side of a table:

Every man is mortal.

Then the result of applying Table Rule 11 to it might be, for example,

If Ari is a man, then Ari is mortal.

Since *every* is a universal quantifier, we are free to use any name we like in instantiating.

Now, assume that the following sentence occurs in the left side of a table:

Some Greek is a man.

Then the result of applying Table Rule 12 to it might be, for example,

John Doe is a Greek and John Doe is a man.

Note carefully that we had to use a dummy name, "John Doe," because existential instantiation cannot use a proper name.

Once more, assume that the following sentence occurs in the left side of a table:

No Greek is mortal.

Then the result of applying our rules might be, for example,

If Ari is a Greek, Ari is not mortal.

It is tempting for us to try to show you how various formal logic techniques handle the English in the statement "No Greek is mortal," but it actually is both simpler and more reliable for you simply to use your own understanding of the statement to appreciate the instantiation of it made here. (Question: Why is it permissible for us to use a proper name like "Ari" here?)

△ ▼ EXERCISE 15-C

Write out a possible result of applying quantification rules to the following English sentences.

1. No one is an island.
2. No vulgar tourist has yet discovered a certain Caribbean Island.
▸ 3. Everything that glitters is not gold.
▸ 4. If any girl comes to the party, Sue will be pleased.
5. If every girl comes to the party, Sue will be pleased.
▸ 6. If any girl comes to the party, she will be pleased.
7. If any reporter is untrustworthy, all reporters are untrustworthy.

Sometimes the restriction on the range of a quantifier is expressed, not by a simple or relatively simple predicate expression, but also by a relative clause. Then it is natural to unpack the relative clause when you apply a quantifier rule to an English sentence. The way of doing so is fairly obvious if you have understood the treatment of simpler quantifier expressions.

For instance, consider the statement

1. A boy who was fooling Mary kissed her.

Here the main operator is the complex existential quantifier

2. A boy who was fooling Mary

When statement 1 is treated as prescribed by Table Rule 12, it could yield a statement of the form

3. John Doe kissed Mary, John Doe is a boy, and John Doe was fooling her.

△ ▼ EXERCISE 15-D

▸ Show what a series of applications of the rules of logical inference (on the left side) to the following statement might be:

A boy who was fooling her kissed a girl who loved him.

(Hint: What are the quantifier expressions? Clearly there are two: "A boy who was fooling her" and "a girl who loved him.")

Summary

Our study of formal logic was meant to show us many of the details of logical inference. In practical use it is not wise to spend a lot of time translating everyday English into formal representations. This is both extremely difficult and unnecessary.

Instead, when you are working with a logical inference involving a complex English statement, ask yourself what the simpler statements are and what the main logical operator is in the statement. You do not need to do any other translating, because once you have identified the main logical operator in the statement, you will know which rule of logical inference to apply and how to apply it.

△ ▼ EXERCISE 15-E

Construct tables for the arguments contained in the passages. You may either translate fully into predicate-logic notation or simply identify the main operators and apply the rules in English.

▶ 1. Everyone loves a lover. John loves himself. Therefore, everyone loves John.

2. Everyone in the race is faster than everyone who is not in the race. Someone is not in the race. Therefore, the slowest person is not in the race.

▶ 3. Someone can solve the problem. Therefore, there is someone such that, if he or she can solve the problem, then anyone can.

15.2 Further Complications

An additional remark is needed here. It is important to realize that an English statement has a conditional as its main operator only if the antecedent and the consequent do not contain pronouns referring back to the other half. If we do have pronouns referring back to the other half, we do not have two complete statements linked with each other conditionally. The antecedent of the pronoun is then often a quantifier which is the main operator instead of the "if-then."

For instance, consider the statement

If anyone comes to the party, he will be surprised.

Its consequent contains the pronoun "he." (We assume that the context does not tell us who "he" is.) Accordingly, the consequent

he will be surprised

does not make any self-contained statement, for it leaves open the question: Who is that "he"? Hence the main operator in the "if-then" statement is not the conditional "if-then," but the quantifier "anyone." Accordingly, the statement is of the form

$\forall x \ [(x \text{ comes to the party}) \supset (x \text{ will be surprised})]$.

In other words, the main operator is $\forall x$ under the guise of "anyone." If "anyone" does not take precedence as the main operator over "if-then," we could not interpret the "he."

In contrast, the statement

If someone comes to the party, everyone will be surprised.

has the conditional as its main operator, for its two halves are free-standing statements. Both are understandable without the help of the other. Hence, the main operator is the "if-then," and the "logical form" of the statement is that of the conditional. Accordingly, its translation is

$\exists x$ (x comes to the party) $\supset$ $\forall x$ (x will be surprised)

Similar remarks apply to disjunctions and conjunctions.

This method of applying formal techniques to English arguments is a further elaboration of the method learned in Chapter 9. The summary provided just before Section 9.4 should be reviewed with these predicate-logic insights in mind.

△ ▼ EXERCISE 15-F

1. Identify the simpler statements (if any) in the following English sentences.
▶ a. Someone forgot to turn off the faucet and the oven.
   b. Not everyone managed to finish the race.
▶ c. If nobody comes to Sue's party, she will be surprised.
   d. A visitor is not allowed to step on the grass unless he or she is accompanied by a member of the college.
   e. Sue will be surprised if a Greek comes to her party.
   f. Sue will be surprised only if no independents come to her party.
   g. When it is raining you should carry an umbrella.
▶ 2. What is the main logical operator (if any) in the above English statements?
3. Apply appropriate left-side table rules to the above English statements if possible. Your task is *not* to translate but to identify the appropriate rule of logical inference that should be applied and to show what application of that rule would do on the left side of a table.
4. Apply appropriate right-side rules to the above English statements if possible. Your task is *not* to translate but to identify the appropriate rule of logical inference that should be applied and to show what application of that rule would do on the right side of a table.

15.3   What Is "Is" (Formally Speaking)?

There is one other respect in which our formal notation differs markedly from natural languages. This difference is illustrated by a puzzle which goes back all the way to Aristotle. The puzzle takes the form of an argument which is blatantly invalid but which seems to be of the same form as a valid argument. The invalid argument has as its premises p1. You are not Socrates.

p2. Socrates is a human.

And its conclusion is:

c1. You are not a human.

The argument is blatantly invalid. (You may very well be yourself a human different from Socrates, who definitely is a human.) Yet the following argument is valid:

p1. You are not Socrates.

p2. Socrates is Xanthippe's husband.

c1. You are not Xanthippe's husband.

What is going on here? The answer is that the innocent-looking little English word "is" corresponds to more than one symbol (or combination of symbols) in our formal notation. The English word "is" can express any one of the following four ideas:

1. Identity: For example, "Jack is John Blaupunkt, Jr."; "Socrates is Xanthippe's husband."

2. Predication: For example, "Jack is blond"; "Socrates is a man."

3. Existence: For example, "God is"; "There are white elephants."

4. Class inclusion: For example, "Whale is a mammal."

The difference between the four uses of "is" can be explained as follows:

1. In the case of identity, "is" expresses that two objects or persons are the very same object or person. For instance, Jack is in the first example the same person (is identical with) John Blaupunkt, Jr.

2. In the case of predication, "is" indicates that something or somebody has a certain characteristic. For instance, "Jack is blond" does *not* express an identity of Jack and blondness (even if Jack should happen to be the perfect example of a blond male) but states that Jack possesses a particular trait, viz., being blond. In old-fashioned terminology, "is" used to be called a *copula* when it is used in this way.

3. The use of "is" to express existence is fairly rare in English, except in the combination "there is" or "there are." In this use "is" does the same job as the existential quantifier $\exists x$. In certain other languages, for example, the ancient Greek, there is no separate verb to express existence. Instead, "God exists" was in the ancient Greek typically expressed by a sentence which literally translates as "God is."

4. In the case of class inclusion, what *is* expresses can only be captured by a combination of symbols. For instance, "Whale is a mammal" expresses neither an identity of whales and mammals nor any one object's having a certain property. Instead it says that "Each and every whale is a mammal." The way to express this in our notation is clearly $\forall x\,[(x\ \text{is a whale}) \supset (x\ \text{is a mammal})]$.

Now we can see what is wrong with our initial puzzle example. Its form is in reality the following:

p1. $-(a = b)$

p2. Mb

  c. $-Ma$

where a is "you," b = "Socrates," Mx = "is a human." In contrast, the valid argument had the following form:

p1. $-(a = b)$

p2. $b = h$

  c. $-(a = h)$

where h = "Xanthippe's husband." (Note that the argument assumes that the expression "Xanthippe's husband" picks out one and only one person.)

△▼ EXERCISE 15-G

1. Show by the table method that the first of the two above arguments is invalid but the second valid.

2. Give examples of the uses 3 and 4 of "is" in English.

▶ 3. In the following, which occurrences of "is" represent identity and which do not:

   a. Nobody is home.
   b. Two is the only even prime number.
   c. The elephant is the largest land animal.
   d. The victim is the innocent one.
   e. There is no Santa Claus.

.16

Presuppositions of "Wh-" Questions

We have come to the end of our basic study of the definitory rules of logical inference (deductive) moves. Part 2 and Chapters 14 and 15 were devoted to this study. Occasionally we examined strategic rules. We shall take up a more advanced study of strategic rules for logical inference in Chapter 17.

Meanwhile, we have some other unfinished business to transact. We have formulated a number of both definitory and strategic rules for questioning moves in our interrogative "games."

In Part 3 of the book you learned about the nature of information, about different sources of answers to questions, and about the difference between principal and operational questions. You also studied basic strategies for coping with uncertain answers. In Chapter 11 you learned how to identify two fundamentally different types of questions, and you studied the importance of establishing presuppositions for the questions you wish to ask in interrogative inquiries. You might wish at this point to review this material in Sections 11.2–11.4.

In Chapter 11 we were not able to study the formal representation of "wh-" questions, because we had not yet studied first-order predicate logic. Now that you are familiar with predicate logic, we can examine the formal representation of "wh-" questions. The distinction between statement questions and "wh-" questions is essentially the same as that between statements and names explained in Chapter 14. In ordinary use the alternatives involved in a statement question are specified by statements. In a "wh-" question, the alternatives are usually specified by names.

16.1   Review of the Form of Statement Questions

The questions we are studying can all be put into the form of a request:

Bring it about that . . . I know that. . . .

We have already studied the formal structure of statement questions. Consider again the example question:

Is Mary in class today?

If A represents "Mary is in class today" and $-A$ represents "Mary is not in class today" then the question can be analyzed as:

Bring it about that (I know that A or I know that $-A$).

What is desired in this question is what is in parentheses:

I know that A or I know that $-A$.

So this sentence is the desideratum of "Is Mary in class today?"
More generally, the form of a statement question is

Bring it about that (I know that $A \vee$ I know that $B \vee$ I know that $C \vee \ldots$).

Yes/no questions have the general form

Bring it about that (I know that $A \vee$ I know that $-A$).

The desideratum of the question is the part that follows the phrase "Bring it about that. . . . " This means that the desideratum of a statement question can be formed simply by putting "I know that" in front of each of the alternative statements suggested by the statement question and joining the resulting sentences with the word "or." (The word "whether" introduces such alternatives joined by "or," and this is why "whether" indicates a statement question rather than a "wh-" question.) So, the desideratum of a statement question will in general look like this:

I know that $A \vee$ I know that $B \vee$ I know that $C \vee \ldots$

The general form of the desideratum of a yes/no question will simply be

I know that A ∨ I know that $-A$.

Recall now that the presupposition of a question can be found simply by omitting all occurrences of the phrase "I know that" from the desideratum. So the general form of the presupposition of a statement question is

A ∨ B ∨ C ∨ . . .

and the general form of the presupposition of a yes/no question is simply

A ∨ $-A$

In general, then, the presupposition of a statement question is simply the statement letters joined by ∨. Whenever we want to ask a statement question, we can check rather easily to see what our presupposition is and whether we are in a position to make the assumption the question requires.

16.2 The General Form of "Wh-" Questions

Recall that "wh-" questions are questions that use words like "who" and "what." There are many different kinds of "wh-" questions, making use of all the familiar newspaper reporter words like "who," "what," "where," "when," "why," and "how." ("How" can be used to ask a "wh-" question even though it is not literally a "wh-" word. Remember also that "whether" looks as though it should introduce a "wh-" question, but it actually introduces statement questions.)

The techniques we learned in our brief study of predicate logic can help us here. As with statement questions the general form of a "wh-" question also begins with the request

1. Bring it about that . . . I know that . . .

In "wh-" questions the part that begins " . . . I know that" will, as before, be called the desideratum. The problem is how to represent what precedes and follows "I know that." There is more than one way to get at the meaning of "wh-" questions, but for now we shall focus on one of the simpler and more likely ways to handle them. Here is an example:

2. Who stole my pickup truck?

Putting this question in more general form we get

3. Bring it about that I know who stole my pickup truck.

The troublesome word "who" is still in the picture, but we can at least see that the desideratum here is

4. I know who stole my pickup truck.

Thinking back to our study of predicate logic, we can rewrite this 4 as

5. $\exists x$ I know that (x stole my pickup truck).

The crucial and tricky thing to notice here is that $\exists x$ *precedes* the phrase "I know that." This marks an important difference between statement questions and "wh-" questions. We can illustrate the difference by considering a potentially confusing type of statement question:

6. Will someone be ordering pizza?

This is a yes/no statement question, but it also involves a quantifier in the word "someone." We shall still, however, call this a statement question, because it does not explicitly ask us to think about *who* the someone might be. This question presupposes two alternatives and asks which is the case. The main logical operator involved is not the quantifier $\exists x$ but the disjunction $\vee$. The alternatives are:

7. Someone will order pizza or it is not the case that someone will order pizza.

Let P be the predicate "will order pizza." We can represent the alternatives as follows:

8. $\exists x\ Px$

or

9. $-\exists x\ Px$

In posing the original question we are simply asking which alternative is the case. We are not explicitly asking who will order the pizza. Thus, this example is not to be analyzed as a "wh-" question. Because question 6 is a statement question, its desideratum will be

10. I know that $\exists x\ Px \vee$ I know that $-\exists x\ Px$.

Even though quantifiers are involved in representing this question, it still functions as a statement question, because its purpose is to present alternatives and to ask which is the case. The presupposition of the question is

11. $\exists x\ Px \vee -\exists x\ Px$

Now we can return to our first example:

Who stole my pickup truck?

The desideratum here is

$\exists x$ I know that (x stole my pickup truck).

Note carefully how the question does not ask for a choice between alternatives but rather that I be brought to know a particular object (person) who fits a particular description. Thus, we have not analyzed question 2 as

12. Bring it about that I know that $\exists x$ (x stole my pickup truck) $\vee$ I know that $-\exists x$ (x stole my pickup truck)

Such a representation would stand not for the "wh-" question "Who stole my pickup truck?" but for the *statement question*, "Did someone steal my pickup truck?" You should examine these examples carefully to make sure that you understand the difference.

The presupposition of question 2 is thus not a set of alternatives, but

13. $\exists x$ (x stole my pickup truck).

Here is another example:

14. What is the capital of Indiana?

We shall rewrite this as

15. Bring it about that $\exists x$ I know that (x is the capital of Indiana).

The desideratum of this question is thus

16. $\exists x$ I know that (x is the capital of Indiana).

And the presupposition of the question is

17. $\exists x$ (x is the capital of Indiana)

△▼ EXERCISE 16-A

▶ Using predicate logic notation, analyze the question "Is there a capital of Wales?" and show exactly how it is different from the question "What is the capital of Wales?"

16.3 Definitory Rules for Interrogative Moves

Now we can state in formal notation Rule Q2 from Chapter 11:

Q2. **Rule for "Wh-" Questions:** If a statement of the form $\exists x\, Ax$ occurs on the left side of a table, the inquirer may ask one of the oracles who or what (more generally, which value of x) has the property A. If an oracle gives an answer, it is added to the left side of the table.

Normally, the oracle's answer is of the form Ab, where b is a real name (not a dummy name). Now the table will look rather similar to a table in which an existential instantiation is carried out.

Table Illustration for "Wh-" Questions

Premises, Interrogative Moves, and Logical Inferences	Conclusion and Logical Inferences
1. T　　(initial premise(s)) 2. . . . .　　(from . . .) 3. $\exists x\, Ax$　(from . . .) 4. . . . .　　(from . . .)	C　(ultimate conclusion) . . . .　　(from . . .)

This table might be continued by adding a statement of the form *Ab*:

Premises, Interrogative Moves, and Logical Inferences	Conclusion and Logical Inferences
1. *T* (initial premise(s)) 2. . . . . (from . . .) 3. ∃x *Ax* (from . . .) 4. . . . . (from . . .) 5. *Ab* (from 3 by Q8) ◄———————— 6. . . . . (from . . .)	*C* (ultimate conclusion) . . . . (from . . .) [Assuming the oracle answered *Ab*]

Of course, the addition has to be based on the oracle's answer (*if* any is given).

Notice that there is an interesting difference here between Rule Q2 and Rule 12 of Chapter 14 concerning the logical inference move of existential instantiation. In Rule 12, the instantiating term must be a dummy name. In Rule Q2 the result is always a regular (proper) name, provided that the oracle gives the inquirer an answer at all.

Rules Q1 (Chapter 11) and Q2 express the important requirement that a question should not be asked before its presupposition has been established. It is a mistake (breach of definitory rules) to ask a question whose presupposition has not been established. The reason for this is that if the presupposition is false, any answer that the oracle would likely give will likewise be false, and we are looking for truths in our inquiries. In Chapter 11 we discussed this kind of mistake under the traditional name "the fallacy of many questions" or our own suggestion of "leaping to a presupposition."

Further Observations

We are not quite yet done with Rule Q2. It needs a further restriction, caused by the use of dummy names. Dummy names are not names of real individuals or objects. They are names (if that is the word) of imaginary individuals you have decided to consider as a part of your logical argument.

So what? Why cannot such imaginary individuals be treated in the same way as real ones? One source of difference is this: Not only do you not know who or what is referred to by a dummy name, an oracle will not know that either. Hence, no oracle will answer a question which pertains to the bearer of a dummy name. *In other words, no answer by an oracle may contain dummy names.* This restriction must be added to our interrogative Rule Q2.

△▼ EXERCISE 16-B

1. Construct tables for the following arguments. By asking the right questions in the right way, you will be able to close the tables entirely. Assume that the

oracle will answer any statement question and any "wh-" question with any acceptable answer you think you need, so long as the appropriate presupposition is in place.

▶ a. $\exists x\ (Px \lor Qx)$
   $Qa \supset Ra$
   Therefore, Ra

▶ b. $\exists x\ (aRx \supset Px)$
   $\exists x\ -Px$
   Therefore, $\exists x\ -aRx$

   c. $\forall x \exists y\ -(xRy \lor yRx)$
   $\forall x \forall y\ (xRy \supset aRy)$
   Therefore, $-bRa$

16.4 Complex Questions

More complicated questions also exist. For example, perhaps the most important type is a question with an outside universal quantifier. An example of such a question might be

Whom does everybody admire most?

Its desideratum is

I know whom everybody admires most.

Such a question has three different possible readings, or interpretations. On the first reading, the universal quantifier is not really outside. An answer might accordingly be, for instance,

Everybody admires Albert Schweitzer more than anyone else.

On this reading, the desideratum is of the form

$\exists y$ I know that $\forall x$ (x admires y more than anyone else).

But the admired person may of course depend on the admirer. Even then we can have two readings. On one of them a conclusive answer specifies a function which for each person associates her or him with the appropriate admired person. Thus, on this reading, an answer (not necessarily a true one) might be

Everybody admires most his or her father.

On yet another reading, a conclusive answer takes the form of a list of all the people in the relevant domain of individuals together with the name of their admired ones. Such an answer can be called a *list answer*. List answers are very clumsy to give and hence a *function answer* such as the last statement represents is usually the expected one.

Sometimes a function answer is not possible; only a list answer is available. A case in point is the question

Who won the 5K Run at each of the Olympic Games?

An answer would have to give a list of all the Olympic Games paired with the name of the winner of the 5K Run at each of them. An entry in the list might thus be, for example, "At the Olympic Games in Paris in 1924 the 5K Run was won by Paavo Nurmi."

Complex questions involving an outside universal quantifier are important, because many of the questions a scientist puts to nature in a controlled experiment are of this kind.

16.5   Moving On

When we are engaged in significant pursuit of knowledge, it is important that we keep these insights about presuppositions of questions in mind. We are now prepared to turn to some of the most interesting questions about strategies for developing arguments. Some of these strategic aspects are closely related to what we have been discussing in this chapter. For example, soon we will see how paying attention to the presuppositions of questions not only helps us avoid mistakes but also helps us open up our range of attention so that we are able to find the really interesting questions that may make our inquiry more successful. Insight into other advanced strategies will be based on our study of first-order predicate logic.

.17

Advanced Strategies in Reasoning

What have you learned so far? Much of what has been discussed through Chapter 16 are definitory rules for the questioning games of which reasoning essentially consists. You have learned a number of rules for making logical inference moves—called, unsurprisingly, rules of inference. We have discussed other kinds of definitory rules as well, that is, rules for interrogative moves. Many of these are summarized on the inside covers of this book.

We have also, however, learned the difference between definitory rules and strategic rules, and we have studied a number of strategic principles, especially those in Chapters 12 and 13 for reasoning with uncertain answers. In this chapter we shall continue our study of advanced strategies for achieving excellence in reasoning.

17.1   Definitory and Strategic Aspects of Reasoning

Rules of Sportsmanlike Conduct

First, it may be observed that in some games there are rules of still another kind than definitory or strategic, namely, rules of sportsmanlike conduct. When a Britisher says of another player's behavior, "That's not cricket," she or he does not mean that the other player is not abiding by the definitory rules of a certain game. Nor is it being said that the other player is failing to employ an effective strategy in whatever pursuit he or she is engaged in. What that proverbial phrase means is that the person is not behaving in the way traditionally expected of the players of cricket, that most British of all sports.

Similarly in dialogue and debate situations rules govern the ethics and the etiquette participants are expected to follow. However, we are not studying these sorts of rules in this book. Instead, we are concerned with the rules for inference and questioning in reasoning games.

Overemphasis of Definitory Rules

In many textbooks on logic and reasoning, a lion's share of attention is devoted to definitory rules. Although readers of such textbooks do receive some training in strategic considerations, they gain little knowledge of the general principles according to which one can go beyond doing things merely correctly. Often the very distinction between definitory rules and principles of successful strategy remains unclear in these textbooks. This amounts to a serious neglect of strategic rules in the teaching of logic and reasoning.

An indirect indication of this overemphasis on definitory rules can be seen in a comparison between the teaching of logic and the practice of logicians. Research logicians practically never use in their own professional argumentation the definitory rules of inference listed in textbooks of deductive logic, certainly not when they are searching for an argument to prove a new result. The situation is not much better with studies of informal nondeductive reasoning. One can learn little about reasoning strategies from books on inductive logic or informal logic.

This excessive stress on definitory rules of reasoning means that students often become more concerned with avoiding or locating mistakes in reasoning than with reasoning well. The use of the term "fallacy" is sometimes indicative of this preoccupation with avoiding mistakes. In our time this word is usually taken to mean a mistaken inference (or inference-type). Originally it applied to other kinds of mistakes in interrogative games. In most textbooks of logic and argumentation you can find long discussions of various fallacies, but scarcely a word about strategies of reasoning.

This narrow emphasis on avoiding mistakes has not always been characteristic of logic. Instead, logic began its career in history in Aristotle's hands as a study

—frequently a rather down-to-earth study—of the tricks and pitfalls of the questioning games that were practiced among the followers and students of Plato and Socrates. We noted above in Chapter 1 the popular idea that the feats of reasoning by clever detectives like Sherlock Holmes are due to their superior strategic skills in logic.

A Comparison Between Logic and Ethics

In a way, logic has suffered a fate similar to what has befallen ethics. Originally, one of the main aims of ethical theory was the identification of various kinds of excellence in conduct and the giving of advice as to how one can develop such excellences in oneself. Descriptions of different kinds of excellence can be found, for example, in Aristotle's famous treatise in ethics, the so-called *Nicomachean Ethics*. It is not even clear whether all these different sorts of excellence he describes have anything to do with what we would in our day call morality. Yet they were all traditionally called virtues.

Illustration In the *Nicomachean Ethics* Aristotle describes a virtue he calls "magnanimity." Among other things, Aristotle tells us that a "magnanimous person" does not flaunt his superiority in relation to ordinary people. This sounds like one of our familiar rules of morality, until we read Aristotle's explanation. It is easy, he says, to be better than ordinary folk, so displaying such superiority is not an indication of any particular excellence. Therefore the person of excellence will not bother with this.

But a funny (or sad) thing happened on the way to contemporary morality. Somehow people's ethical preoccupations changed, and the emphasis on achieving excellence was replaced by an emphasis on avoiding moral mistakes. This development is reflected in the changes in the meaning of ethical terms. Virtues were originally thought of as kinds of moral excellence. A virtuous man was literally a moral virtuoso, a star performer on the stage of life. From that idea there is a long way to the Victorian meaning of a virtuous person as one who has preserved her or his moral purity. (In the most sexist meaning, a woman's "virtue" was almost identified with preserving her virginity.)

We may not agree with some of Aristotle's ideas of excellence, but we can lament the loss of emphasis on achieving excellence in living. Both in the theory of reasoning and in ethics we are dealing with a switch of emphasis from the achievement of excellence to avoidance of mistakes. In this book we are trying to reverse this unfortunate switch in the case of reasoning.

△▼ THINK ABOUT IT

In contemporary arguments about medical ethics there are significant discussions of the practice of "defensive medicine." It is alleged that the threat of malpractice suits is causing doctors no longer to pursue excellence in their medical practice but rather to pursue safety through "defensive" medical procedures. Some say that unnecessary tests and procedures are ordered, not to help the patient but to protect the doctor in case a charge of malpractice is brought. Fingers are pointed on all sides as to who is at fault in these matters.

We are not interested in pointing fingers, but we do think that this situation at least partly reflects a confusion over definitory rules as distinguished from strategic rules. It is tempting to think that a doctor's skills can be summed up by a set of rules. Such rules, so this line of thought goes, are taught in medical schools. They are definitory in character in the sense that one has to follow them to be a competent doctor. Following them may even be thought sufficient for achieving excellence as a doctor.

Indeed many people jump to the conclusion that a doctor is guilty of malpractice (i.e., has broken a definitory rule) as soon as he or she fails to bring about a cure. This conclusion is as mistaken as the idea that merely following the definitory rules of logical inference suffices to enable you to reason well. In fact, many of the rules that a doctor has been taught are strategic in nature. Failing to follow such rules does not necessarily constitute malpractice, and following them does not guarantee success.

In most significant human endeavors there is an important difference between doing things correctly and doing them well. Furthermore, although it is relatively easy to judge whether someone is pursuing her or his craft correctly, it is not at all easy to make foolproof judgments about the achievement of excellence. We suspect that the problems over malpractice and "defensive medicine" have arisen in part because too many in our society have confused strategic principles for excellence in medical practice with definitory rules for correctness.

17.2   Game Theory and the Concept of Strategy

Admittedly, strategic rules for reasoning are incomparably more difficult to find and to formulate than definitory rules. It is not even clear whether, and if so in what sense, there can be a regularly applicable set of strategic rules of reasoning. Yet quite a few things can be said about them.

A clue is offered here by the leading idea we are pursuing in this book: *to understand reasoning as an interrogative game.* This is useful, for the idea of strategy is most happily at home precisely when applied to games. Indeed, as we have previously mentioned, there exists a mathematical theory called "game theory" or "the theory of games" which is, in effect, the most general existing theory of strategies and strategy selection. Its applicability extends in fact beyond competitive games to strategies of cooperation. (Hence the name for this discipline, "game theory," may not be entirely appropriate. Perhaps "strategy theory" would be a more accurate designation.)

Game theory does not offer ready-made, ready-to-use rules of strategy for reasoning. But it does provide some useful tools for studying strategies and strategic rules.

First, the concept of strategy receives a precise definition in game theory. This definition does not quite match what the word "strategy" conveys in ordinary life, but it is not very far from the familiar usage of the word. According to game theory, a strategy for a given player is a rule which specifies what that player is to do in any conceivable situation which may arise in the course of a play of the game. The concept thus defined will be called *strategy in the strict sense*. (We shall continue to speak sometimes of strategies also in a looser, everyday sense.) In a two-person game, a strategy of the first player is said to be a winning strategy if it results in his or her win no matter which strategy the other player is following.

There are many activities to which the strict concept of strategy defined above does not apply. For instance, it applies to chess, bridge, or poker, but not to the familiar ball games. Games in which the strict definition of strategy makes sense are sometimes called games of strategy. However, in a looser sense, we can speak of strategies in connection with almost any game.

One reason why the strict concept of strategy is important from the standpoint of theory is that a strict strategy can in principle be chosen by each player before the game is actually played. If all players choose a strict strategy, the course of the game is completely determined, and there is, in theory, no need for the players to go through their moves. They can all divulge their strategies to an impartial umpire, who can then calculate, on the basis of them, what must happen in the game.

In actual practice, strategies are too complicated for such prior choice to be feasible. But even in real life, partial choices of strategy sometimes take place. Ordinary chess players create their strategies "over the board," that is, move by move during a game. But a chess-playing computer follows a strict strategy. Furthermore, in championship chess matches, you will sometimes find that the grandmasters make their first six to ten moves without spending much of their clock time. What that shows is that they have in effect decided ahead of time which opening and which opening variants they will use. In other words, they have decided on a partial strategy before the actual play.

Game theory does not usually tell you what the best strategy is in a given game. It nevertheless yields useful clues as to what determines the value of a strategy. In general, game theory tells us, we can assume that, at the conclusion of playing a given game, each player is faced with a definite outcome determined by the rules. This is called by game theorists the "payoff" of that game. A payoff can be positive (a relative win) or negative (a relative loss).

Several things are useful to know about such payoffs. First, we cannot always speak of victory and loss. These concepts have a clear meaning only in what are known as two-person, zero-sum games. In these, either the one player has a fixed positive payoff and the other player the same negative payoff, or vice versa. In other words, what one player wins, the other one loses. There are games, however, in which both players can win. Such games are known as (partly or totally) cooperative games. Thus there can be strategies of cooperation as well as competitive strategies.

Second, the payoffs do not usually depend only on the situation reached by players at the end of the game but on the entire history of the game. In an interrogative game the inquirer's payoff can depend on whether the table she or he has managed to close has a true ultimate conclusion or not. In another type of interrogative game it may depend on whether or not the inquirer has refuted his or her opponent's claims. But the payoff can also be thought of as depending on the different steps of the game.

For instance, in some games it will cost the inquirer a certain amount to ask a question, depending on the kind of question. Think again, for example, of the expense of designing an experiment to answer a question put to nature or a research project to answer a historical question. Even if the inquirer closes the game table, his or her payoff is reduced by the cost of such questions. Logical inference steps themselves may be thought of as involving a cost, for example, that of computer time to work through complex logical calculations.

Third, the reason we have mentioned payoffs here is that the choice of strategies in a game depends essentially on its payoff structure. It clearly makes a difference to your argument, for example, whether you are trying to find the truth or merely to refute someone else's claims. Whether the interrogative moves you need to make are expensive, or whether or not ultimate success in the inquiry means a large positive payoff for you. One needs carefully, as they say, to "calculate the cost." In inquiry as in other aspects of life there is such a thing as "winning the battle but losing the war." If the ultimate payoff fails to be worth the cost of inquiry, it may be because not enough attention was paid to strategic considerations.

In Chapter 13 we found that certain common mistakes in reasoning are due to a confusion between different kinds of interrogative games. The concept of payoff helps us specify precisely the differences between different kinds of reasoning situations. Different kinds of interrogative games are typically games that have different payoff structures.

—▲ _____

Strategy (in the strict sense): According to game theory, a strategy for a given player is a rule which specifies what that player is to do in any conceivable situation which may arise in the course of a play of the game.

Games of Strategy: Games to which strategies in the strict sense may be applied.

Winning Strategy: A strategy which results in a win no matter which strategy the other players are following.

Partial Strategy: A strategy which falls short of specifying what is to be done in every conceivable situation but which still gives guidance for achieving excellence in the game.

Payoff: The outcome, whether positive or negative or zero, of a completed play of a game. Because the choice of a strategy in a game depends essentially on the game's payoff structure, it is important to have a clear understanding of the ultimate payoffs one is seeking. In interrogative inquiry this means, among other things, that we need to keep in mind what it is we are trying to accomplish in our inquiry.

Illustrations

1. The concepts of payoffs and strategy figure into everyday activities in a variety of ways. For a simple example you might consider two people playing a game of Scrabble. At least two different strategies present themselves in that game. One is to choose words in such a way that the board shows increased possibilities for a variety of high-scoring plays for both players. Another strategy is to choose words so that fewer high-scoring opportunities are offered to your opponent. Which is the best strategy? It all depends—on a number of factors.

   The most interesting factor for our purposes right now is the one having to do with payoffs. What payoffs do the players seek? Some players, not surprisingly, say that the payoff is, of course, to have the highest score and win the game. They will try to choose whichever strategy promises to put their score ahead of their opponent's. Other players, however, show by their behavior that for them the payoff lies in striving for the highest scores possible, no matter who happens to have the highest score at the end. Clearly, the latter will choose words which open up the board as much as possible. Those, on the other hand, whose goal is to win, may find it important to limit scoring in a number of situations. The point is that strategies for excellence in playing depend in important ways upon what the player considers the payoff to be.

2. An understanding of the complex issues raised in the study of strategic principles can also help clarify some interesting questions that arise about business ethics. Too often ethics in business is taken to mean merely the avoidance of incorrect actions, such as price fixing and other illegal activities. Here again we see the impulse to reduce strategic questions about excellence to definitory questions about correctness.

   But people do recognize that there is also a sense of "business ethics" in which ethical behavior is taken to be not merely a matter of correct behavior but rather to require more positive action in the fulfillment of duties, such as those to the customer, the employee, or the community at large. The distinction between definitory and strategic rules helps to put this situation into perspective.

   Definitory rules prescribe necessary conditions upon the operations of businesses; transgressions of these rules constitute a violation of the definitory rules of the business "game." Strategic rules, however, go on to characterize methods for achieving success. One need not abide by them in order to remain within the boundaries of correct business behavior, but following them may lead to a positive payoff.

The fascinating question, however, is: What makes for a positive payoff? Is a positive payoff to be measured in terms of dollar profits? Does a positive payoff involve doing what you do better than others do it? Better in what way? Does it involve a sense of having contributed to the community? The strategy you should adopt in business depends upon your answers to questions like these.

Notice that once we get beyond questions of correctness, questions about excellence can become quite complex. We can achieve reasonable agreement about what is illegal business practice, but there is wide-ranging disagreement about what is successful business practice—what makes for a positive payoff. Different people will define success differently. Some will see it in terms of dollar profits; others will speak of self-satisfaction; still others will think in terms of contributions to society. Sorting out these disagreements is difficult, but the really interesting questions about business ethics lie in this area of strategic considerations about achieving excellence in the world of business.

17.3   Strategies vs. Particular Moves

One general insight game theory offers is that when it comes to better or worse strategies, the only game elements that in the last analysis can be evaluated are strategies in the strict sense. This may not sound like much of an insight, but it amounts in reality to an important truth. For what other candidates are there? It might seem that we could tell of particular moves in a game whether they are strategically right or not. It is true that often we appear able do so. For instance, in annotated records of chess games, particular moves are typically marked when they are considered good, very good, "iffy," mistakes, or serious mistakes. But it is important to realize that such an evaluation of particular moves is not always possible. *What can always be evaluated are entire strategies.* Even when particular moves can be rated good, bad, or mediocre, this typically depends on considering them as a part of some tacitly assumed overall strategy.

Thus, strategic principles normally cannot be formulated so as to be applicable move by move. Or, strictly speaking, they cannot always be exhaustively expressed in terms of particular moves but can only be expressed in terms of overall strategies.

In this respect, strategic principles (strategic rules) differ from definitory rules. In most games all the definitory rules can be formulated to describe what is permissible for a player in a given situation. What has happened earlier in the game and what will happen later in the game do not usually play a role in their formulation.

In reasoning games, all definitory rules concern particular moves admissible in certain situations. In contrast, there is no realistic hope of formulating strategic principles for reasoning and argumentation in the form of one-move rules. Thus a study of strategies of reasoning will inevitably look quite different from existing textbooks of logic. The most striking difference is that there will not be many rules in the strategic study that would look like a deductive logician's beloved "rules of inference."

This fact is not difficult to understand. Suppose I ask you, "How do I get from here to the airport?" and you answer, "Turn right at that intersection." Was that advice good or not? It is not clear that one can tell. For whether I get to the airport, or whether I get there speedily, may depend on my later "moves" in the "game" of finding my way round. It does not create a happy ending if I make the right turn you advise me to make but make a mistake in a later intersection. Furthermore, I might be able to reach the airport by turning left, contrary to your suggestion. Which way is better (e.g., quicker) will normally depend on what I do later. Even when taking one turn rather than another "has made all the difference," as Robert Frost once said, making this difference has not been inevitable. It is more likely to have been a result of a strategy than to have created a strategy.

What this illustrates is the fact that in the last analysis only complete overall plans can be evaluated. Yet attempts have been made time and again to formulate strategic rules in terms of one move (e.g., one decision) at a time. In the final analysis, let us not forget the following important principle: **Strategies for reasoning games (interrogative games) are more fundamental than individual moves in the game. They typically assess individual moves in terms of the overall plan for the game.**

17.4   Coherence of a Line of Inquiry

One consequence of the crucial role of strategies in argument evaluation concerns whether an argument makes good sense, or is *coherent*, to use a term often employed by linguists. Speaking somewhat loosely, we can say that an argument or inquiry is coherent if it leads toward some well-defined goal. Questions about the coherence of an inquiry cannot be answered by considering the particular steps of the argument one by one, in isolation from each other. (Notice that one can go step by step if one is examining the validity of the argument.) *The coherence of an argument can only be judged on the basis of the strategy the arguer is pursuing.*

The steps in an argument may appear perfectly in order, and yet the argument as a whole does not make much sense because it does not lead anywhere. In such cases, the overall argument is not a coherent one in spite of the naturalness of the individual steps.

Illustrations   The importance of a well-defined goal might perhaps be illustrated by certain computer programs which have been designed to simulate a doctor's questions in a psychiatric interview. Each question the computer asks sounds reasonable enough but, unlike a real psychiatrist's questions, the program has no direction. The computer never "adds the answers together," as Socrates would have said. Conversely, even an absurd-sounding step in a line of inquiry might suddenly make sense when we realize what strategy the reasoner is following.

For instance, in the story "Silver Blaze," in which the "Curious Incident of the Dog in the Night-time" takes place, Sherlock Holmes asks, apparently out of the blue, of a shepherd whose flock is grazing near the stables, "Have any of your sheep gone lame lately?" This question may appear so irrelevant as to be nonsensical until we realize what it is that Holmes is trying to prove, that is, what there is in the right side of his logical table. Holmes has formed a conjecture he is trying to test. He suspects that the stable master stole the horse Silver Blaze (temporarily, for a part of the night) in order to lame it so slightly that no one would notice but so severely that it would lose its next big race. Such an operation, Sherlock Holmes reasoned, is so delicate that the stable master very likely practiced it on some other animal before daring to attempt it on the famous horse. The sheep grazing nearby provided possible practice animals. And, as it happened, Holmes turned out to be right. Some sheep had in fact turned up lame. Holmes's question becomes understandable only when we realize what overall strategy he has in mind.

— ▲ _____

Coherence of a Line of Inquiry: An argument or inquiry is said to be coherent if it follows a reasonable strategy designed to lead toward some well-defined goal.

17.5   Reasoning as World Making

As was noted, it is difficult to formulate clear-cut strategic principles for the "games" of reasoning in the everyday sense, let alone in the strict sense, of strategy. Most of the rest of this chapter and the next will be devoted to making various suggestions as to what a good reasoner is well advised to keep in mind.

In this section, a general perspective on strategy selection for reasoning games will be presented, based on the way they proceed. As was explained above in Chapter 2, when the inquirer is trying to derive the conclusion from the initial premise (or set of premises), his or her enterprise can be viewed as a sort of thought experiment. The inquirer tries to construct in his or her thought (or, in our regimented form of reasoning, in the interrogative table) a description of the world as it would have to be if the initial premises were all true but the ultimate conclusion false. This imagined world will be called a *countermodel*, more explicitly, a countermodel to the claim that the conclusion can be derived interrogatively from the initial premise(s). The thought experiment we are envisaging here can thus be viewed as an attempted countermodel construction. The search for counter-examples in deductive logic is a special case of such a construction process.

Because this thought experiment pertains to the real world, everything the inquirer can establish to be true about it can be included in the constructed world model. That is, all the answers which the inquirer receives from the oracle and which have not been bracketed by Rule Q3 are entered into the left side of the table. But beyond that the construction depends only on the inquirer's imagination.

What the inquirer hopes to end up with is a situation in which the entire logical table is closed, that is, in which the entire thought experiment is eventually frustrated in all possible directions. For then the hoped-for ultimate conclusion cannot fail to be true in the real world if the initial premise(s) and answers to questions are all true. Moreover, as was noted previously, the rules for constructing a logical table are set up in such a way that, if the inquirer manages ultimately to close the table, he or she can automatically interpret it as a valid argument from the initial premise(s) and the interrogative moves to the ultimate conclusion.

— ▲

Countermodel: A scenario in which the initial premises (and answers to questions) are all true but the ultimate conclusion false.

△ ▼ EXERCISE 17-A

 1. Analyze the following invalid argument, and describe in outline a countermodel that shows invalidity.
    a. Assume that all couples who have had children have always been more distantly related to each other than first cousins. (premise)
    b. It is the case that you and each of your ancestors have had two natural parents and four natural grandparents. (premise)
    c. Therefore, for the nth generation back you must have had 2^n natural ancestors, which means that about forty generations ago, there must have been nearly a trillion people on the face of the earth.
2. Return to Exercise 14-G at the end of Section 14.9 in Chapter 14. Give counter-models for any of the arguments in that set which are invalid.

17.6 Strategies for Countermodel Construction

From the interpretation given above of what happens in an interrogative game, we can derive some rough-and-ready rules as to how to play the "game" well, that is, how to reason well. What is needed is to be able to anticipate the course of an attempted countermodel construction and to be able to guide it to its desired conclusion (if that is possible), that is, to a dead end.

How does one anticipate the course of an attempted countermodel construction? Your experience with deductive table construction shows you what to expect in general. What the inquirer hopes to do is to close every subtable. To do this, the construction process will have to be carried out to a certain level of complexity. The attempted countermodel must have a certain minimal complexity before its impossibility (its closure) can be seen.

Illustration Consider the task facing the inquirer trying to prove that the sum of the three angles of a triangle (a plane Euclidean triangle) equals 180 degrees or two right angles. We can think of this task as showing that from the initial premise

ABC is a plane triangle.

The inquirer can derive the ultimate conclusion

The sum of the three angles *ABC*, *BCA*, and *CAB* equals 180 degrees.

The interrogative game approach is to look for a countermodel. Can the conclusion be false while the initial premise is true? If you imagine the triangle *ABC* as being drawn, there is apparently little you can say about the sum of its angles. Indeed, if *ABC* were a triangle drawn on the surface of a sphere rather than a plane, the conclusion could easily be false.

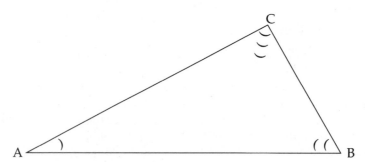

What our reasoner has to do is to consider a more complex geometric configuration. For instance, the reasoner might realize that there is a line through C parallel to *AB*:

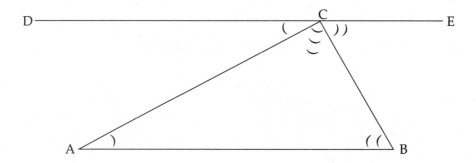

Once the line *DE* is considered, it becomes possible to see that, based on previous information about parallel lines, the angles *ACD* and *CAB* are equal. Also, the angles *BCE* and *ABC* are seen to be equal. But, angles *ACD*, *ACB*, and *BCE* all together make up a straight line or 180 degrees or two right angles. Therefore, it becomes impossible to imagine that our ultimate conclusion is false. So,

The sum of the three angles *ABC*, *BCA*, and *CAB* equals 180 degrees.

In this case we became able to see the impossibility of a countermodel only by considering a configuration more complex than the initial configuration of the triangle *ABC*. This is a standard "move" in the geometer's reasoning, and it is also characteristic of all interrogative arguments. Before a subtable in a table construction can be closed, the world construction in that subtable must have reached a certain level of complexity. In our illustration it sufficed simply to introduce one new line into the construction. In many cases, indeed typically, we have to introduce a great many individuals into the attempted countermodel construction before it can be closed. Thus, **the crucial strategic consideration in interrogative inquiry is to anticipate the level of complexity needed to close each of the subtables.**

17.7   The Importance of New Individuals

Consider the following definitions:

— ▲ ─────────────────────────────────────

Individual: A basic idea of the logic we are studying is that we start from a given domain of entities and then study their properties and relations. Any one of these entities is called an individual. In formalized representations, individuals are represented by lowercase letters (for example, lowercase Roman letters *a* through *u* and lowercase Greek letters). In first-order predicate logic, quantifiers are used only with reference to this basic set of individuals.

New Individual: An individual that has not yet been mentioned in a table construction.

Real Individual: An individual actually known to the inquirer. In formalized representations real individuals are named by lowercase Roman letters.

Imaginary (Arbitrary) Individual: An individual imagined to be in the domain but not known to the inquirer. Imaginary individuals can be introduced by existential instantiation on the left side of tables and by universal instantiation on the right side. They are often important for enabling us to reason about what is happening in a given table construction. In formalized representations imaginary individuals are named by lowercase Greek letters. These are sometimes called dummy names.

We can now ask how the minimal complexity required to close a table is related to the rules of countermodel construction. The key insight is that the number of individuals in the construction is the main determinant of the complexity of the configurations reached in it. When new individuals are introduced into the construction, it can become more complex.

But how are new individuals introduced into the countermodel construction? Among our definitory rules of interrogative games precisely three of them can accomplish this: Rule Q2, the rule for "wh-" questions (Chapters 11 and 16); Table Rule 12, the rule for existential instantiation on the left side (Chapter 14); and Table Rule 11r, the rule for universal instantiation on the right side (Chapter 14). As indicated in Chapter 14, Table Rules 11 and 12r are not allowed to introduce new individuals into a subtable in interrogative reasoning.

When Is an Individual New?

A countermodel construction is represented by a subtable. Remember that a subtable consists of an open path on the left side of a table paired with an open path on the right side. The question whether an individual is *new* or not is decided subtable by subtable. If the individual has not previously appeared in a subtable, then it is new to that subtable.

Introducing New Individuals

Rule Q2, the rule for "wh-" questions, always introduces real individuals into the construction whenever an answer to a "wh-" question is given. Often these are also new individuals. Table Rules 12 (Existential Instantiation on the Left Side) and 11r (Universal Instantiation on the Right Side) always introduce new, imaginary (or "arbitrary" as some logicians call them) individuals.

Summary It is clear that the way the rules for introducing new real and imaginary individuals are applied is the most important strategic consideration in interrogative inquiry. This is so because it is only by an appropriate application of these rules that you can reach a sufficiently complex configuration (stage in an attempted countermodel construction) to enable you to close your argument table.

Arguments Not Requiring New Individuals

In some cases a subtable can be closed without introducing new individuals. In such a case, the line of thought represented in the subtable is, in a certain sense, noncreative. The inquirer did not have to extend his or her imagination beyond what was already being talked about in the premises and the conclusion. In such a case all that is needed is to see clearly what is said in the premises and in the conclusion.

Of course, arguments that do not involve new individuals need not be trivial. They may involve a number of steps of logical inference and perhaps even a number of interrogative moves, but at least in the deductive case, we could almost say that the reasoner need only free himself or herself from the mental blocks that might cloud his or her mental vision to carry out such an argument.

One partial exception to this point is that it sometimes requires considerable research to find the answers to questions needed in this kind of argument. Such research may require much ingenuity on the part of the inquirer.

Arguments Requiring New Individuals

It is the introduction of new individuals that typically makes an argument interesting and creative. You may have noticed this in constructing deductive arguments in Chapter 14. The same role of new individuals is also illustrated by our geometric example, where the crucial parallel line is a geometric individual that makes all the difference to the argument.

In a different way the "Curious Incident of the Dog in the Night-time" is also a case in point. Before Holmes called attention to the incident, the good inspector had been concerned with the main individuals in the case: the horse that disappeared, the unknown thief, the slain stable master, a suspicious passer-by, and the unknown killer. The questions he was unsuccessfully trying to answer concerned the relationships among these individuals. He was not able even to determine in all cases how many of these were uniquely different individuals.

What Holmes does is not unlike what the geometer does when introducing a new line into a figure. Holmes introduced a new individual into the inquiry: the watchdog. (The dog had been mentioned before, but it had not played any role in the inspector's reasoning.) And, as in the geometric example, this step served to clear up the situation dramatically. Thus, the "secret" of Holmes's "deduction" (reasoning) was precisely the introduction of a new individual into the inquiry.

But how can the inquirer anticipate which introductions of new individuals are likely to further the argument? No completely exceptionless rules are possible. However, the inquirer's familiarity with the subject matter of the argument can play a crucial role in her or his strategy selection. For if the inquirer knows what kinds of configurations of entities are likely to be possible and impossible (among the objects the inquiry deals with), she or he can steer the countermodel construction away from the possible configurations and toward the desired impossible situations.

For instance, if the inquirer is arguing about people, he or she is likely to have some idea of what kinds of situations are likely to be possible and impossible for human beings. If the inquirer is a skillful reasoner, he or she will use this knowledge in guiding the countermodel construction.

Illustration: Strategy in Geometric Reasoning A geometer normally has a good intuitive idea as to what geometric configurations are possible and can use this intuitive knowledge to guide his or her reasoning. This is in fact the reason why figures are practically indispensable in geometric reasoning. Geometric reasoning itself being purely logical, its conclusiveness is completely independent of any appeals to figures, either actual ones or those conjured up in one's geometric imagination. However, figures or other similar visual aids may be indispensable for finding and carrying out an argument. The dependence of geometric reasoning on figures is therefore a matter of strategic rules, not definitory ones.

In Chapter 1 we studied the interrogative game played by Socrates and the slave boy. The most important contribution Socrates made to this game involved his introduction of geometric figures that illuminated the relationship between the original square and the one twice its area. Here the choice of the right configuration of individual lines to introduce was the whole key to success.

Another Illustration Consider again the argument found in question 3 of Exercise 14-F, in Section 14.7 of Chapter 14. It had the following premises and conclusion:

$\forall x \, \forall y \, \forall z \, [(xRy \, \& \, yRz) \supset xRz]$

$\exists x \, (aRx \, \& \, xRa)$

Therefore, aRa

Recall that in order to determine the validity of this inference it was essential to consider a new individual, one whose existence is implied by the existential quantifier in the second premise. Notice that once we consider an individual with this property, say α, the conclusion follows immediately from the first premise. But a crucial step in the reasoning process was introducing this individual.

In more complicated examples this point is underscored; here there was but one such individual we had to introduce, but in other situations literally an infinite number of candidates may present themselves, and success depends upon making the correct choice among them.

△ ▼ EXERCISE 17-B

1. Questions about the relationships between the authors of the New Testament Gospels, Matthew, Mark, and Luke have fascinated scholars for centuries. These three books are known as the "Synoptic Gospels," and they have the curious property of "telling different stories in nearly the same words." This has led to much speculation about possible sharing of materials among the authors. One of the more popular solutions to this so-called "synoptic problem" involves the suggestion that we should expect to find that additional documents were involved in the writing of these books. Find someone in your school's department of religious studies who can fill you in on this topic or find a reference work in the library, and then discuss what you have learned in the light of the strategic importance of introducing new individuals into the solution of a problem.

2. Examine the proof of a theorem in Euclidean geometry, and discuss how the introduction of auxiliary constructions provides the key to finding a successful proof.

3. Your instructor will provide an example for you to analyze. Your task is to discover and explain the significance of the introduction of new individuals into this inquiry.

17.8 The Two Different Stages of Inquiry

We are now in a position to give you some rough-and-ready strategic advice for interrogative inquiry. The most important first stage in an inquiry is to reach a configuration of individuals in each subtable which is sufficiently complex to enable you to close it. Before that stage is reached, rules other than those that introduce new individuals should be used only in so far as they are needed to put us in a position to introduce new individuals.

What this means is that, in your rule applications *before* the sufficient number of individuals has been introduced, you should concentrate on adding to the left side (in one step or several) existentially quantified statements of the form $\exists x\, Sx$ and to the right side universally quantified statements of the form $\forall x\, Sx$.

For instance, if you have on the left side a statement which contains no existential quantifiers, no negation signs, and no conditionals, then there is no point in applying any rule to it at this stage of the game, because such applications cannot ever produce an existentially quantified statement.

Now observe how important it is to anticipate when a sufficiently complex configuration has been reached. For *when a sufficiently complex configuration has been reached, a reasoner is well advised to change her or his tactics*. In this second stage of the inquiry you should not try any longer to introduce suitable new individuals by means of applications of the rule for "wh-" questions and other quantifier rules (including rules preparatory to their use). Instead, a good strategy now calls for applications of the other rules. And the aim in the second stage is the closure of the subtable in question, not the introduction of new individuals.

Illustration It may help you to understand the nature of the problem of introducing new individuals if you will compare it to the challenges involved in putting together a jigsaw puzzle. The job in such a puzzle is to relate and connect the pieces to each other. Sometimes you carefully examine an individual piece to see where it might fit. This is done especially with edge pieces and with pieces that have a distinctive color or pattern. Other times, a configuration of pieces that you have already put together helps you decide what sort of piece you need to look for next. Eventually you get enough of the pieces together so that you are able to find a place for everything and to complete the puzzle.

If you have a defective puzzle, a couple of different things could be going wrong. On the one hand, a piece may be missing; then the overall pattern of the puzzle tells you what you need, but unfortunately it cannot be found and the puzzle cannot be solved. On the other hand, there may be an extra piece that does not belong to the puzzle. It may take quite a bit of studying before you discover that there is no way to relate it to the other pieces. More significantly, you will usually need to have put much of the puzzle together before you learn that a piece does not belong or that one is missing. Similarly, you must usually carry an argument construction out to a significant level of complexity before you see that it closes and is valid or that it cannot close off all possible countermodels, that is, that it is invalid.

In many cases in real-life inquiry we run into all of these problems. On the one hand, there seem very often to be more pieces around than we really need. Determining which need to be introduced into the inquiry and which should not be is a difficult task. On the other hand, there come times when we think we know exactly what sort of individual is needed to complete the argument, but we seem unable to locate this finishing piece. Yet again, we may think we have all the right pieces, but it turns out they do not fit together in the way we had hoped.

There are no mechanical and automatic ways of learning how to find the right pieces to complete an inquiry. We can, however, see that the first stage of inquiry often involves sorting out the pieces and determining which ones are needed to make the argument sufficiently complex. The second stage involves taking the appropriate pieces that have been introduced and relating them in the ways that show the validity of our argument.

△ ▼ EXERCISE 17-C

1. Analyze the following argument by filling in the missing steps, and check for validity:

   Alex is Beth's full brother.

   Alex is Chris's first cousin.

   Therefore, Beth is Chris's first cousin. (Hint: It will be necessary to formulate what "full brother" and "first cousin" mean in ways that will relate them to each other. Which new individuals and which predicates can be introduced to accomplish this task?)

2. Discuss how the preceding exercise illustrates the two stages of inquiry.

▶ 3. Go back to question 1 in Exercise 17-A at the end of Section 17.5 and discuss how a countermodel for that invalid argument could not be described until a sufficient number of individuals had been introduced into the argument.

17.9 Looking for Patterns in the Construction Process

One help in trying to decide when an argument is ready to be closed and in general to guide it is to keep an eye on regularities in the construction process.

For instance, applications of previous interim results to new cases can create a pattern which repeats itself as the table grows. Spotting such patterns is an important part of a reasoner's skill.

An inquirer's ability to anticipate patterns, especially recurring ones, is enhanced by experience with the subject into which one is inquiring. This helps explain why familiarity with a subject and background knowledge about it can assist in a specific inquiry. We note, however, that sometimes this same background knowledge can hinder us if we are confronting genuinely new phenomena. For then our past experience is likely to tempt us to overlook the most important pieces in the new puzzle.

This skill is not unlike the skill of an experienced chess player who has learned to anticipate certain often occurring configurations of pieces. Among the differences between the two cases is that such a configuration is likely to occur only once in each play of the game of chess, whereas the same type of application of old information to new cases can occur repeatedly in one and the same inquiry. Also, chess usually begins with the same initial configuration of pieces, whereas the initial configuration is different in different inquiries.

Here again it may help to think about the comparison with jigsaw puzzles. Familiarity with the puzzle and its patterns can sometimes be a great help for the process of reconstructing the overall picture.

Experienced teachers often improve with age partly because they become better at recognizing a particular pattern of problems that may be hindering a student. Counselors in many different fields gradually accumulate considerable background information that enables them to recognize patterns in their clients' problems. Recognition of patterns can show the way to effective solutions. Scientists and engineers constantly rely on their knowledge of typical patterns in investigations of the material world.

17.10 Analogical Reasoning

Another related strategic insight involves the role of analogies in reasoning. Two cases might at first seem quite unlike each other. However, on closer examination they may be analogous; that is, features A and B in one case may bear the same relation to each other as features C and D of the other case. Analogy is thus a little like a proportionality in geometry or arithmetic, as in

$A:B::C:D$

In an analogy A and C and B and D may be quite different from each other, but the *relationship* between A and B and its similarity to the *relationship* between C and D is what is at issue.

If you can find an analogy between different cases, and if you are familiar with reasoning about one of them, it is often a good strategic idea to try techniques from the known case in your reasoning about the new case. Even if both cases are unfamiliar to you, the discovery of an analogy may suggest fruitful lines for effective interrogative moves.

Illustration (We have invented this example in order to illustrate analogical reasoning, but it is similar to many everyday examples.) A psychologist might discover a characteristic behavior pattern in a number of persons she or he has observed. Let us assume that the behavior pattern is a desirable one and that the psychologist becomes interested in what it may be related to.

The persons in whom this pattern has occurred might be quite unlike each other. Some are women; some are men; some are young; some are well educated; others have little formal education; and so on. The psychologist is puzzled. With what is the behavior connected?

Finally, she or he discovers something: All the people in question are youngest children from large families. They are not similar to each other in other ways, but they all exhibit the behavior in question and they all have a particular relationship to their childhood families. In other words, they are connected with each other by analogy.

After discovering this analogy, the psychologist can use it in a variety of ways. When she or he comes upon the same behavior pattern in a new patient, the psychologist may want to frame some questions suggested by the possibility that the new patient is also the youngest child of a family. This may help the psychologist more quickly grasp what is happening in the new patient's life.

The psychologist may also, however, want to use the analogy as a guide for an inquiry into what causes the particular pattern of behavior that has been observed. In this case the analogy would suggest that likely new individuals to introduce into the inquiry would involve persons and situations uniquely encountered in large families.

Many textbooks treat analogical reasoning as a type of inductive reasoning. In Chapter 19 we discuss the limitations involved in inductive reasoning generally. At this point we simply point out that the power of reasoning by analogy has more to do with strategies for finding and asking fruitful questions than with the employment of some sort of nondeductive inference. Theorists have encountered many difficulties in formulating sharp definitory rules for analogical inference. The reason is that analogies have more to do with strategies for questioning than with rules for inference.

17.11 Anticipating the Oracles' Answers

Another way in which an inquirer's guiding background knowledge can manifest itself is to be able to anticipate the oracles' answers—whoever or whatever those oracles happen to be. Obviously, being able to foresee what answers one is likely to receive is a mighty help in guiding the course of one's line of questioning (reasoning). We may, for example, think of one's intuitive geometric knowledge as a means of anticipating answers to geometric questions.

Ability to anticipate answers one is likely to receive is, for another example, also important in lawyers' reasoning and questioning. A somewhat cynical rule of thumb exists for lawyers conducting cross-examinations in a court of law: "Never ask a question if you do not know what the answer will be." Whatever the merits of this particular old saw are or may be, it certainly is true that ignorance of the answer one is likely to elicit in cross-examination creates major hazards for a lawyer.

Here again, teachers and counselors often find themselves able to anticipate the direction in which a problem with a student or a client is going, and this can help them formulate remedies for the problem. Scientists are often quite confident that they know how an experiment will turn out before they ever perform it.

Always, however, because we are dealing with strategic matters, there is an element of the unpredictable. Sometimes our inquiries confront us with new configurations and surprising answers. In such situations we must be prepared also to let ourselves see what is new. If we try always mechanically to assimilate new inquiries to old patterns, then we risk missing some of the most creative and interesting insights we may come upon.

17.12 Form and Content in Good Reasoning

A considerable controversy has raged as to whether skills in logical reasoning and reasoning in general are transferable from one subject matter to another. We can now see that the answer to this question depends on the kind of skills and subject matter involved. We have seen that background knowledge concerning the subject matter greatly facilitates strategy selection in reasoning. In that sense, a large part of one's actual reasoning abilities may be tied to specific subject contents.

Sherlock Holmes puts the point this way concerning his knowledge of crime: "There is a strong family resemblance about misdeeds, and if you have all the details of a thousand at your finger ends, it is odd if you can't unravel the thousand and first." (From Sir Arthur Conan Doyle, "A Study in Scarlet," p. 24 in *The Complete Sherlock Holmes* [New York: Doubleday, 1905]).

However, the way a reasoner puts background knowledge to work is a skill which is independent of the subject matter. That is the kind of skill this book seeks to develop in its readers along with the awareness that there is always need for openness to original, unanticipated, and creative insight. In reasoning well it is often the surprising and the unexpected that can make all the difference. We shall return to this theme in the next chapter.

.18

Strategic Parallels Between Deduction and Interrogation

In this chapter we will examine how connections between logic in the narrow sense and logic in the "Sherlock Holmes" sense give us insight into how to develop reasoning skills in "observation and deduction."

18.1 The "Sherlock Holmes" Sense of Logic

Where can we find strategic rules for interrogative argumentation? Or, if strict rules are unobtainable, where can we look for strategic advice? The traditional answer to these questions is: logic, in the sense of what we called earlier the "Sherlock Holmes" sense of logic, according to which logic is thought of as the science of reasoning well. In this section, we shall investigate what truth, if any, there is in this old idea.

Deductive and Interrogative Moves

At first sight, an easy answer seems possible. The study of logic in the narrow sense is, so it seems, a part of the science of good reasoning, but it is only a part. At this stage of our study of the interrogative model, the relation of logic (deduction) to reasoning in general can be given a preliminary formulation.

The relationship in question is one of a division of labor. Interrogative inquiry involves two kinds of steps, interrogative steps and logical inference steps. Deduction (logical inference) and interrogation therefore appear as two separate but equal components of inquiry. Neither is dispensable. Questions are needed to bring in substantially new information, and deductions are needed both for the purpose of spelling out the consequences of such information and for the purpose of paving the way for new questions by establishing their presuppositions.

As we have seen, one impetus to the deductive component in inquiry is thus presuppositions, whose role in the logic of interrogative games can help us understand the nature of inquiry in general. Not surprisingly, important thinkers have considered the logic of questions an important aspect of inquiry and have paid special attention to presuppositions.

The interactive relationship between logical inferences (deductions) and interrogative moves deserves a few further comments. First, as the interrogative model shows, logic (of the kind codified in the rules of inference you have learned) is an indispensable component of reasoning. There is no such thing as a completely informal logic of argumentation or reasoning.

Furthermore, there is no sense in which one of the two intertwined components of interrogative inquiry, deduction and questioning, is more important or more difficult, absolutely speaking. Such judgments can only be made on the basis of particular assumptions concerning the "cost" of different kinds of moves in the interrogative games of inquiry. A game theorist would codify such assumptions in the "payoffs" of the game. There is no unqualified reason an interrogative inquiry could not contain long chains of nontrivial logical inference moves of the kind discussed in Chapter 17.

It is also important to realize that the role logic plays in the form of deductive (logical inference) moves in the overall process of inquiry cannot in general be separated from the others. Deductive moves are needed in the first place for the purpose of establishing presuppositions for interrogative moves. Thus the order of the two kinds of moves cannot in general be changed so as to segregate them from each other. Only in those rare special cases in which presuppositions are not needed or are trivial can we hope to rearrange the applications of the two kinds of rules, for example, in such a way that all interrogative moves precede all deductions.

Deductive and Interrogative Moves: A Parallelism

Our discussion has not yet touched on the most important insight about the relationship of deductive logic to reasoning in general. This insight begins to unfold for us when we note certain important facts about the relationship of logical inference steps to interrogative moves in the "games" of inquiry outlined above.

Suppose that there occurs on the left side of a logical table (or subtable) an existential statement

1. $\exists x\ Sx$.

What this situation amounts to is, of course, one in which the inquirer has either proved that $\exists x\ Sx$ is true or assumed it to be true. How can the inquirer try to exploit such a situation? In two different ways.

First, the inquirer can apply the logical inference rule of existential instantiation to the statement in question. The output (statement added to the left column) is of the form

2. $S\alpha$.

Here α is not a name of any known member of the domain of discourse. As discussed in Chapter 14, it is sometimes called, aptly, a "dummy name." If it is thought of as standing for something, that something has to be thought of as an "arbitrary individual"—whatever such an animal is or may be. A concrete consequence of this status of α is that the inquirer cannot ask any questions in which the term α occurs, for an "arbitrary object" does not have any definite properties about which one could inquire.

A completely satisfactory interpretation of the role of dummy names can only be obtained by means of the original idea on which the method of logical tables is based. A table construction means an attempt to construct in imagination a countermodel, that is, to construct an imaginary situation in which the initial premise T would be true but in which the hoped-for conclusion C would not be true. Even though dummy names like α stand for individuals in the attempted imaginary counterexample, they do not stand for objects in the real world.

But the inquirer can try to exploit the presence of statement 1 on the left side of a logical table in another way. The inquirer can use the statement as a presupposition of a "wh-" question. Because the presupposition has been established, the inquirer may ask the question. Whether an answer is forthcoming depends on the restrictions that have been placed on the oracle's responses.

Let us assume, for the sake of argument, that the oracle answers the question. The answer will be of the form

3. Sb

where b is a proper name of an element in the domain of individuals of the "world" or "universe of discourse" in relation to which the interrogative game takes place.

The Importance of Asking Questions

The outcomes 2 and 3 above are similar in structure. How do they compare with each other as far as the rest of the interrogative game is concerned? Everything the inquirer can do by means of answer 2 he or she can do by means of answer 3. But not vice versa, for the inquirer may very well be able to use answer 3 as a basis for further questions, whereas answer 2 was seen to be incapable of serving in that role.

Hence, when it comes to a choice between the deductive move and the interrogative move, the inquirer is well advised to make the latter, provided that the oracle will answer the question and that the "cost" of the question is not too great. At the very least, the inquirer is doing as well if she or he asks the question (and obtains an answer), and normally he or she is doing better in the rest of the interrogative argument on the basis of answer 3 than on the basis of answer 2.

Similar observations can be made when a disjunction

4. $A \vee B$

is present in the left side of a logical table. Again, the inquirer has two options: either to apply the relevant logical inference rule for disjunction to statement 4, which results in splitting the logical table construction into two further paths, each of which has A or B, respectively, as its sole new formula, or to use statement 4 as the presupposition of a statement question, to which the answer, if the oracle is forthcoming, is A or B.

Which course of action is more advantageous to the inquirer? If the oracle actually responds with an answer, the inquirer is better off with the interrogative move. For then he or she has to try to close only one of the two table construction paths which the inquirer has to worry about if a logical inference move was made.

Once again, therefore, it is never advantageous for the inquirer to make a logical inference move if he or she can ask a parallel question and have it answered. This observation constitutes an interesting strategic rule. It is unfortunately applicable only if you know ahead of time whether the question you are thinking of asking will be answered by the oracle.

Furthermore, the two types of deductive moves, existential instantiation and the splitting of a table construction into several paths, are the only nontrivial deductive moves as far as the left side of a logical table is concerned. The other rules (governing universal instantiation and conjunctions) can only be applied a finite number of times in any one situation. They can never open up essentially new opportunities of rule application or split up the attempted countermodel construction into several parts.

Hence, *all important logical inference steps of interrogative reasoning can be (and should be) replaced by corresponding questions, provided that these questions are answerable.* This result throws light on the reasons for which deductive logic sometimes seems to play a relatively small role in actual everyday reasoning and argumentation.

Vindication of the "Sherlock Holmes" Sense of Logic

Our observations open an important perspective on the role of logic in the general process of reasoning. As was noted above, at first sight the interrogative model assigns to logic a status of "separate but equal" in relation to the rest of interrogative reasoning. It might even appear possible to study the other components of reasoning independently of the principles of deductive logic. This is not the whole story, however. What we have seen shows that logic is integrated into the mainstream of inference much more firmly than that.

A more superficial consequence can be formulated as a vindication of the old usage in which "logic" is thought of as a label for any old inference. We have called this usage the "Sherlock Holmes" sense of "logic." A similar usage is found with words like "deduction," "inference," and so forth. This vindication can be explained as follows.

What we have seen means essentially that, in so far as answers are forthcoming to the inquirer's questions, it is advantageous for him or her to ask a question instead of performing the corresponding deductive move. Thus interrogative moves can do the same job as deductive inferences, normally even better (provided that an answer is actually available). Hence, it is eminently natural also to call the interrogative step a "deduction" or "inference," for it serves the same purpose, after all, as a deductive step in the logicians' narrow sense of "deduction." But this is precisely the usage we have called the "Sherlock Holmes" sense of "deduction," "inference," "logic," and so forth. Far from being a play on, or a misuse of, these words, it can now be seen to be but a slight extension of the use of these terms in deductive logic. What could be a more complete vindication of Sherlock Holmes?!

It is to be remembered, of course, that the parallelism between deduction and interrogation holds only in so far as the inquirer's questions are actually answerable. This answerability assumption is usually not satisfied for all the relevant questions. It can be argued, however, that it is more likely to be satisfied in the kind of inquiry Sherlock Holmes was engaged in than in many other types.

18.2   Deductive Strategies and Interrogation

The most important observation concerning the role of logic in interrogative argumentation nevertheless still remains to be made. In deductive reasoning, it is known that one of the crucial determinants of good strategy is the choice of the right existential formulas of the form $\exists x \, Sx$ to instantiate. Even if you are not familiar with the studies of mechanical theorem proving in which this fact emerges especially clearly, the point is easy to understand on the basis of what was said in Chapter 17. For it is precisely existential instantiations that introduce new individuals into deductive reasoning and thereby make the total arguments nontrivial. They are the steps of the inquirer's imaginary counterexample construction which introduce new objects. Such steps obviously determine the course of the inquirer's thought experiment. The proper choice of these instantiating steps is thus obviously of crucial strategic importance in deductive reasoning.

Historically, an important example of this fact is the deductive argumentation used in elementary geometry, where existential instantiations are known as auxiliary constructions. Perceptive analysts of geometric reasoning have known since antiquity that success or failure depends on the right choice of auxiliary constructions.

Now it was just seen that existential instantiations are parallel to answerable "wh-" questions. Clearly, on the interrogative side too, it is the choice of appropriate "wh-" questions to ask that essentially determines the chances of success of a line of interrogative inquiry. Indeed, it was this very possibility of guiding the course of inquiry by a judicious selection of questions that first prompted Immanuel Kant to compare the experimental reasoning of physical scientists to "putting questions to nature." Thus in interrogative inquiry too, the selection of the appropriate existential sentences as a basis of the next move is one of the crucial strategic considerations.

Moreover, and most crucially, the general parallelism which we have seen to obtain between interrogation and deduction obviously means that the strategic principles governing this choice of the existential sentence to try to instantiate are roughly the same in interrogative inquiry and in deductive logic.

Deductive Logic as a General Theory of Reasoning Strategies

Even though the strategic parallelism between deduction and questioning is not quite complete, it brings to light the true role of deductive logic in reasoning in general. The relation of deductive logic to the rest of inquiry is not one of "separate but equal" roles. Or, rather, this is the idea one receives if one only looks at the definitory rules of reasoning, that is, looks only at inference in deductive logic and at the rules defining how one can put questions to one's source of new information.

If we turn our attention to strategic rules instead of definitory rules, we see that the strategic rules are largely (but not completely) the same in both cases. This means, among other things, that the study of deductive strategy selection largely amounts to a study of strategy selection in inquiry (reasoning) in general: **The strategic rules of deductive reasoning are very nearly the strategic rules of inquiry (reasoning) in general**.

Again, this result is a striking vindication of the traditional conception of logic as an important ingredient, perhaps as the most important ingredient, in the art of reasoning in general. This fundamental (but partial) identity has often been obscured by concentration on the so-called rules of inference, that is, on definitory rules of the "game of logic," at the expense of strategic rules of deductive reasoning. This failure was noted earlier in Chapter 17. Now we can see how important the consequences of this distinction can be.

Here, then, we have an answer to the question concerning the role of logic in argumentation and inquiry. We can see that logic plays only a modest supporting role in the total drama of reasoning on the level of particular steps of inquiry. *But when it comes to questions of strategy, logic suddenly assumes a new function. It* is as if a supporting actor were at the same time the director of the entire play. On the strategic level, the principles of deductive strategy selection are a major part of the principles of strategy in the entire process of reasoning.

A qualification needed here is that the parallelism between deduction and interrogation does not help us decide when to bracket or unbracket any answer (or an initial premise) (Rules Q3–Q6). Such decisions are needed when not all the answers are certain. In a sense, deductive logic is therefore more useful strategically in finding out what the truth is than in proving it true when premises or answers have been called into question.

△▼ EXERCISE 18-A

Write a brief essay in which you summarize the key points concerning the role of logic (narrow sense) in inquiry.

18.3 Looking for New Questions and New Concepts

Even though it is impossible to find foolproof strategic rules for interrogative argumentation, it is possible to locate principles useful for planning one's strategy. Such principles do not tell you what to do in a particular type of situation but what to keep an eye on in making your moves.

In the rest of this chapter we shall identify two directions in which you are well-advised to look in constructing arguments. Not surprisingly, the two principles tell you to look for something new, either for new questions to ask or for new concepts to use.

Looking for New Questions to Ask

We shall begin with new questions. In order to raise a new question, the inquirer needs new presuppositions. Hence a new look at the presuppositions of interrogative moves is in order. (You may wish to review the material on presuppositions of questions in Chapter 11 [Sections 11.2–11.4] and in Chapter 16.)

Presuppositions of Yes/No Questions

You have learned that before a statement question may be asked, its presupposition must have been established. For instance, if you want to ask, "Is it the case that A, B, C, . . . , or E?" you must have established the truth of the statement

1. A or B or C or . . . or E

This applies also to yes/no questions, for they are a subclass of statement questions. To ask the question "Is it the case that B or is it the case that not B," the disjunction

2. *B* or not-*B*

must be true. In the formal version of interrogative arguments the expression

3. $B \vee -B$

must occur in the left column of the game table.

Here you might very well be surprised. The disjunction 3 cannot fail to be true. If B is false, then $-B$ is true; if $-B$ is false, B must be true. In either case, statement 3 is true. It is the simplest case of what philosophers call a *tautology*. It is apparently an empty statement. Its truth does not tell anything about what the world is like. And if so, there does not seem to be any reason to require the presence of statement 3 in the table before the question "*B* or not-*B*?" may be asked, for statement 3 is known to be true anyway.

Several things can be said in response to this legitimate worry. First, in Chapter 11 we examined in detail the fallacy of many questions which we are inclined to call "jumping to a presupposition." You will recall that the error of jumping to a presupposition involves asking a yes/no question that presupposes more than a simple tautology like $B \vee -B$. The requirement that the presupposition of a question always appear in a table before the question is asked helps us guard against jumping to an illegitimate presupposition.

Introducing Tautologies

This possibility of a hidden, shared presupposition in what looks like a statement and its denial is useful to keep in mind when you are examining an argument expressed in ordinary colloquial language and rewriting it in logical notation. However, the possibility of such shared presuppositions has not any bearing on what can be said of statements whose presuppositions genuinely are of the form

$(\ast)$ $B \vee -B$

Why should we require that even authentic yes/no questions should have presuppositions of the form $(\ast)$? Is not the inquirer free to ask such a question without further ado? In a certain sense, yes. The presuppositions of yes/no questions highlight something different from the presuppositions of other questions. In other cases, the inquirer must first establish a certain substantial fact before he or she can ask the question. In the case of yes/no questions, there is no fact that has to be established first.

However, there *is* something else that the inquirer must do: The inquirer must raise the question. It must occur to the inquirer that this is a question that might be raised. The inquirer, in other words, must *become aware* of the question that needs asking.

We are here dealing with an important matter. One way of incorporating it into our interrogative model is to go on requiring that the presupposition (∗) must be present in the left column before the yes/no question "Is it the case that B or not?" is asked. That is the bad news for the inquirer. The good news is that the inquirer will now have the opportunity of introducing statements of the form (∗), which may be used, if need be, as presuppositions of yes/no questions. Thus we must add the following simple rule to the earlier ones:

14. **Rule for Tautology Introduction:** At any stage of the game, the inquirer may introduce a statement of the form $B \lor -B$ into the left column.

Uses of the Rule for Tautology Introduction

Several comments are in order here:

1. To avoid misunderstandings, it is useful to recall that normally further restrictions are present. By introducing tautological statements, the inquirer may become able to ask more yes/no questions. However, there is no reason in general to expect that these questions are all answerable. They are often made unanswerable by restrictions other than the need for presuppositions.

   For example, in mathematics and in many sciences, it may be a considerable achievement simply to formulate an interesting problem. For instance, a famous seventeenth-century mathematician is best known for a problem he posed, generally known as Fermat's problem. Posing such a problem may be considered as an interrogative move relying on a presupposition introduced by the rule for tautology introduction. Typically, such questions concern the behavior of all numbers or all objects of some other sort. Typically, too, there is no "oracle" that can provide an answer to such questions, even though it is not only permissible but laudable to ask them.

2. The introduction of tautological statements does not only open new opportunities of asking yes/no questions. It may also help the effective application of logical inference rules. It can be shown that in deductive logic whatever can be proved to be valid by means of auxiliary premises of the form $B \lor -B$ can also be proved without their help. This is one of the basic results in contemporary logical theory.

   However, even in deductive reasoning it may be helpful in another sense to introduce tautological disjunctions of the form $B \lor -B$. Even though they do not open any doors for proving new consequences, they often make it possible to prove the same results more quickly (in fewer steps).

3. In contrast to logical inferences, when it comes to interrogative arguments, adding tautological premises of the form $B \lor -B$ may open possibilities for establishing new consequences which would not have been possible to establish without them. In this sense, the rule of tautology introduction is more important in interrogative inquiry in general than in deductive logic.

Over and above enabling the inquirer to reach new conclusions, tautological disjunctions $B \lor -B$ also make it possible for the inquirer to prove old conclusions more quickly and more easily. The rule for tautology introduction is a definitory rule, but it opens possibilities for effective strategies.

Illustration   To explain how it is that the introduction of tautological disjunctions can help in deductive logic, we may first note that they justify the following additional rule:

Rule for Existential Generalization: If a statement of the form Sb is present in the left side of the logical table, then the statement $\exists x \, Sx$ may be added to the left side.

Here is the rationale: Put Sb as the initial premise in the table. The rule for tautology introduction allows us to introduce $\exists x \, Sx \lor -\exists x \, Sx$ into the table. Then the path is split into two. In one path, we have $-\exists x \, Sx$. By Table Rule 13 this becomes $\forall x \, -Sx$. Then we may introduce $-Sb$ into it by Table Rule 11, and we close the path by Table Rule 7. What remains is therefore the one path with $\exists x \, Sx$ in it. So, whenever a statement of the form Sb is present in the left side of the logical table, then the statement $\exists x \, Sx$ may be added to the left side. (Be sure you see how the steps work here.)

Rule for Creating Conjunctions (another rule brought to you by way of tautology introduction): If A and B occur in the same path on different lines in the left side of a table, add $A \, \& \, B$ to the path.

△ ▼ EXERCISE 18-B

1. Show how the rule for creating conjunctions above can be justified by means of the rule for tautology introduction without using any right-side table rules.

▶ 2. Show that the following statements are inconsistent:

$\forall y \, [aAy \, \& \, -\exists x \, (bAx \, \& \, xAc)]$
bAa

Show this first without the help of tautological disjunctions and hence without the two additional rules we have just examined. Then show how these two additional rules, made possible by tautology introduction, can simplify the argument.

Tautology Introduction: Important, but Not Always Possible

Even if the introduction of tautologies is always possible, it need not always be the best strategy. Applications of the rule for introducing tautologies may carry a "cost" in our interrogative games; that is, they may reduce the inquirer's eventual payoff.

The Problem of Range of Attention or Awareness   Sometimes there can even be restrictions on which tautologies may be introduced by the inquirer. What do these restrictions mean? What is the meaning of the rule for introducing tautologies anyway?

An answer was indicated above. In carrying out an inquiry, a crucially important strategic consideration obviously is which questions to pose. Usually, the inquirer has initially in mind a number of questions he or she is prepared to raise. They may be thought of as being represented by the corresponding number of statements of the form $B \lor -B$ in the left column of his or her logical game table. But it can happen that it does not suffice to raise the questions whose presuppositions are already present in the left column. Sometimes new tautological presuppositions have to be introduced.

What this means is that the inquirer is extending his or her range of attention. This is what it means in practice to open the door for asking new yes/no questions through establishing presuppositions by the rule of tautology introduction. Because of the importance of extending the range of one's attention in conducting an inquiry, it is important to recognize when such an extension takes place. In the interrogative model such extensions can be recognized, for they will be applications of the rule for introducing tautological statements. And restrictions on this rule represent restrictions on the inquirer's range of attention.

Having a wide range of attention and being able to extend it are clearly useful for successful inquiry. This fact has naturally been noted before. For instance, the American psychologist and philosopher William James (1842–1910) writes:

> And now we can see why it is that what is called sustained attention is the easier, the richer the acquisitions and the fresher and more original the mind. In such minds, subjects bud and sprout and grow. . . . geniuses are commonly believed to excel other men in their power of sustained attention. (*The Principles of Psychology*, Vol. 2 [New York: Henry Holt, 1890], p. 423.)

Now we also know how to recognize steps of inquiry (moves in the interrogative games) in which the inquirer is extending his or her range of attention. These are applications of the tautology introduction rule formulated above. One of the reasons for having this rule is precisely to call attention to such extensions of one's range of attention.

Needless to say, not all new questions will help one's inquiry. Choosing the right applications of the rule for tautology introduction can be a crucially important strategic consideration. The principles for choosing the right presuppositions (which could later enable the inquirer to ask the corresponding question) are the same as the principles of choosing the right questions to ask.

Illustrations   All this can be illustrated by means of real-life examples.

1. The importance of coming up with new questions was implicit in our very first illustration of reasoning as questioning (inquiry as inquiry). This was the "what if" example in Chapter 1. In it creative reasoning was represented essentially as asking new, previously unthought-of questions.

2. A real-life example from a past time also illustrates the importance of extending the range of one's attention. A young physician is working in a rural community. He is examining a patient, a vigorous young woman from a farm,

who has a minor complaint. In the course of the examination, it turns out that the woman has sharply elevated blood pressure. The doctor is puzzled and wonders what might be the cause of this alarming condition. Should he order further tests? At that point a wise old nurse whispers into the doctor's ear: "Why don't you ask her how she got here." It turns out that the woman had just bicycled ten miles from her farm to the doctor's office, an exercise likely to raise the blood pressure of the most healthy person.

3. The third example does not deal with the consequences of raising a new question, but with the consequences of not raising a relevant one, and by so doing significantly restricting the reasoners' range of attention. In this real-life case the reasoners are members of a jury. The example is quoted from J. H. Phillips and J. K. Bowen, *Forensic Science and the Expert Witness* (Sydney: The Law Book Company Ltd., 1985), pp. 3–5 (with omissions). The term "forensic science" refers to the science of criminal investigation.

> On a cold winter morning in December 1972, the body of an Aberdeen housewife, Mrs. Helen Will, was found in a wood just to the south of the Scottish border. She had been strangled. A lorry driver named John Preece was later charged with the murder, and was convicted by the majority of a jury after an eight day trial at Edinburgh in June 1973. He was sentenced to be imprisoned for life. The conviction of John Preece was to set in train a sequence of extraordinary events that would ultimately lead to a searching examination of the role of forensic scientists in the criminal justice system and their ethical obligations to the law courts.
>
> It was scientific evidence that brought about Preece's conviction. Scientific evidence of biological fluids, hairs, fibers, grass seeds and other material was said to link Preece to the victim. This evidence was principally given by a Dr. Alan Clift and was corroborated, to an extent, by the opinions of a junior colleague who had himself not actually undertaken any of the scientific work. Dr. Clift was no Johnny-come-lately to forensic science. At the time of this trial he had been a forensic scientist with the Home Office for nearly 20 years. Dr. Clift was a founding member and treasurer of the prestigious Forensic Science Society. Small wonder that the majority of the jury appear to have accepted his evidence and convicted.
>
> Dr. Clift's evidence covered three main subjects, biological fluids, hairs and fibers, but its most significant aspect was his evidence that the deceased had stains from an individual—who was both blood group "A" and a secretor—on her clothing. A secretor is a person who secretes some of the ingredients of blood into body fluids. About 40 per cent of the population have blood group "A", and the prosecution was able to show that not only was the accused blood group "A", but also a secretor. However, the jurors at the trial did not hear all that Dr. Clift knew on this topic. Dr. Clift did not tell the court that the deceased was also blood group "A", and most probably a secretor. Nobody asked him. There is no doubt that he knew this to be so, because he had included this information in his initial report made to the English police. He did not include it in a subsequent report he made for the Scottish authorities. He did not tell the Crown Prosecutor about it.

Preece, the lorry driver, was to remain in prison for several years before questions were raised in Parliament and elsewhere as to the quality of the forensic evidence at his trial, and more particularly, the scientific detachment of Dr. Clift. In 1977 Dr. Clift took a brief holiday in France and, while he was away, what was later described by the Home Office as a "routine control check", was carried out. A search of his desk drawers produced, according to the Home Office, disturbing evidence which led to his immediate suspension on full pay. He was to stay thus suspended for four years. Senior Home Office cases in which Dr. Clift had given evidence were reopened for new investigation.

One of the earliest to be investigated was the Preece case. His lawyers quickly got wind of these events, and successfully applied for a reference under Scottish criminal procedure by the Secretary of State to the High Court of Justicary of Scotland.

In June, 1981, the court considered the reference. Dr. Clift was required to attend at the hearing, and some six other leading forensic experts also gave their evidence. Some were called on behalf of Preece and others on behalf of the Crown. Dr. Clift repeated the evidence that he had given at the trial, and was subjected to very prolonged cross-examination during which his competence, honesty, and scientific detachment were exhaustively probed. At the end of the day the court's judgment upon him was a personal disaster. The court found that it had been established that at the trial Dr. Clift had failed to give in evidence that the victim was blood group "A", and probably a secretor, and had similarly failed to inform the Scottish authorities of these facts.

This example raises, as the authors of the quoted book note, important questions as to role of an expert witness in the entire criminal procedure. We are not concerned with the details of these questions except as illustrations of the importance of questions and, more specifically, of the importance of choosing the right questions in legal reasoning.

Leaving aside for the moment the problem of intentional non-disclosure of material matters, courts may receive in any given case insufficient or unsatisfactory evidence about forensic science matters because, under our adversary system, it is left to the parties—largely if not entirely—as to what witnesses of an expert nature are to be called. There is also the lack of formal definition of an obligation of an expert witness to indicate to the court what his or her evidence does not prove or suggest to be likely. Allied to this is the problem that evidence is taken in court—at least in criminal cases—by question and answer means. Should the expert simply answer the questions put, or should the expert consider them to be relevant? What are the ethical obligations in this respect? This leads to the further problem that if the expert decides to take the initiative in the witness box, the expert may unwittingly enter into inadmissible areas and cause the trial to mis-carry.

In court room the witness is very largely a captive of the questioner. It is not an exaggeration to assert that a satisfactory result depends just as much on the skill of the questioner as on the skill of the witness. The manner of the questioning conditions the form and often the content of the answers and when, as sometimes happens, the questioner does not really understand the subject matter, questions may be put in ways which either confound or restrict the witness. Questions are sometimes asked which are unanswerable because, to a scientific witness, they have no rational basis, and not infrequently, the wood is lost in the trees. (Op. cit., p. 5)

△ ▼ EXERCISE 18-C

Construct or find from the literature an example in which raising a new yes/no question marks a breakthrough in an argument or inquiry.

Getting New Answers to Old Questions

It is important to keep in mind that the information which may be obtained from an oracle is not fixed once and for all; advances in technology may enable us to receive answers to questions which we were unable to receive before. This point is perhaps most clearly illustrated in the case of scientific inquiry, where great ingenuity is often required in the design and construction of experiments in order to have certain key questions answered.

Consider, for instance, how the microscope has extended the range of information available from nature. How much of our current medical knowledge has resulted from the use of this instrument in the course of conducting research? Questions concerning the nature of many ailments, the reactions of the body to certain treatments, or the structure and composition of our component parts could only have received answers by means of the use of microscopes.

We see the same phenomenon in connection with astronomical research, or research into the composition of subatomic particles. In both of these cases progress depends upon the development of more powerful tools, so that information not currently obtainable from nature will be accessible to researchers in the future.

Introducing New Concepts

The word "concept" is related to the word "conceive" and is used in a variety of ways. For our purposes we can think of a concept as a particular way of organizing our thoughts about the qualities and relations that may characterize an object. When I point toward you and say, "There's a human being," I am using the concept "human being" to bring together a number of different things that might be said about you. In our formal notation concepts are usually indicated by uppercase predicate letters. For example, W was used in a previous example to replace "watchdog."

Introducing a new concept into an inquiry involves introducing a new way to organize the information. Somewhat the same things can be said of the introduction of new concepts as have been said of the introduction of new tautological premises of the form $B \vee -B$. In deductive logic, new concepts do not open any possibilities of deriving conclusions which could not be derived without them. At the same time, new concepts can simplify and shorten deductive arguments.

In contrast, in interrogative inquiry in general, new concepts can open the possibility of deriving ultimate conclusions which otherwise could not have been derived. Furthermore, new concepts may help to shorten and to simplify interrogative arguments. Whether they do depends on precisely which questions are answerable and which may be asked.

No special additional rule is needed to allow the introduction of new concepts. They may be introduced in two ways:

1. By the oracles' answers to questions. This happens typically in answers to complex questions of the kind discussed in Chapter 16 (Section 16.4).
2. By tautological premises. If no restrictions are imposed on them, they may contain expressions for new concepts (i.e., concepts not so far occurring in the argument).

Illustration As an example of the usefulness of new concepts, a true story can be told which illustrates the nature of new concepts. Often, the use of what is in effect a new concept means ordering the facts of a case in a new way.

Our illustrative story takes place in an elementary school in Germany in the eighteenth century. A tired schoolmaster wants to keep his little students out of mischief for a while and tells them to add all the numbers from one to one hundred. Most of the students begin adding $1 + 2 = 3, 3 + 3 = 6, 6 + 4 = 10$, and so forth. At the end of the class hour, all the students were still calculating or had a wrong answer, with one exception. One of the students had simply written one number down. It was 5,050, which is the right answer. The name of the boy with the right answer was Carl Friedrich Gauss (1777–1855). He was later to become one of the greatest mathematicians of all times. But how had he got hold of the right answer? By imposing a new order on the problem he had been given. Instead of thinking of it as the addition

$1 + 2 + 3 + \ldots + 100$

Gauss had reordered the task mentally to look like this:

$(1 + 100) + (2 + 99) + \ldots + (50 + 51)$

This can be seen to equal

$50 \times 101 = 5,050$

Reordering the data of the problem was tantamount to the introduction of a new concept.

18.4 Summary of Advanced Strategic Considerations

In this and the preceding chapter we have learned some of the different strategies the inquirer should keep in mind in reasoning. What are some of these crucial insights?

Among other things, we found that strategy selection in the whole project of interrogative reasoning (inquiry) is governed by the same principles as strategy selection in deductive (predicate) logic. We have pointed out that in deductive logic the one crucial strategic question is the choice of the new individuals which can be introduced by existential instantiation. In other words, the crucial strategic consideration is which existential statement to instantiate first. Because of the parallelism of deduction and questioning, in rational inquiry the crucial strategic principle the inquirer should keep in mind is which "wh-" question to ask. This means in effect: Which existential statement already established should I use as a presupposition of a "wh-" question?

The importance of this consideration is not hard to understand. In any reasoning task, obviously one of the crucial strategic questions the inquirer is faced with is this: Which individuals (objects and/or persons) do I have to consider in my argument to carry it out? This question is to all intents and purposes the same as the question as to which "wh-" question to ask.

But how can the inquirer tell which "wh-" question to raise? It has been indicated that no completely general strict strategic rules are possible. Some rules of thumb can nevertheless be formulated. One important factor is the set of restrictions imposed on the oracles' conclusive answers. Questions which will not be answered by the oracles are of course useless to the inquirer. As was indicated earlier, different restrictions on the oracles' answers characterize different types of inquiry. The principles of strategy selection are therefore likely to be different in different types of reasoning (e.g., observational, experimental, clinical, etc.). There is little that we can say here by way of strategic advice that would apply to all situations.

It may nevertheless be useful to recall what was learned in Chapter 17. You learned there that before an inquiry has reached a situation of sufficient complexity, it is important to introduce suitable new individuals into the argument. Hence, in the early stages of an inquiry the best questions are, by and large, those whose answers introduce as many new individuals into the argument as possible. These answers are the ones having the greatest permissible logical complexity. Thus one piece of strategic advice that you will want to keep in mind is: *In the early stages of an inquiry, try to ask more complex questions in preference to simpler ones.*

For instance, a scientist is usually better off if she or he can perform controlled experiments (that is, ask logically complex questions of nature), than if the scientist merely makes observations (that is, puts simple questions to nature). This is why excessive concern with inductive reasoning may be strategically misleading. As we will study in more detail in the next chapter, inductive reasoning tends to rely on simpler questions and does not highlight the importance of formulating logically complex questions.

As indicated previously, this strategic advice about introducing new individuals applies only to that part of an inquiry in which the table construction has not yet reached the complexity needed to close the table. But this is typically the most difficult part of the argument.

Another partial version of the same advice of choosing which individuals to introduce into one's reasoning is the old cynical question: "Who's the woman?" The idea underlying this proverbial question is that whenever there is something wrong, surprising, or mysterious in a man's life, it is due to his relationship to some woman or other. Hence the best strategy in trying to draw conclusions concerning his life is to introduce that woman into one's reasoning, for example, by asking questions about her identity.

18.5 The Role of Surprises in Reasoning

Another strategic viewpoint is revealed by considering the presuppositions of questions. Such presuppositions represent information you have already gained. By asking a question, you are trying to add to that information. One strategic clue here is the fact that often the information an answer yields is the greater the greater the information its presupposition gives. This is especially the case with "why" questions. Now what does the informativeness of a statement mean in down-to-earth terms? It means that the fact the statement tells us about is a surprising one. This suggests a strategic principle which is in fact observed by many real as well as fictional reasoners: Look to see whether there is something strange or unusual about the facts of the case, and inquire into it.

Illustration Out of an abundance of examples, here is a description of the methods of a fictional private investigator, Jemima Shore:

> Jemima Shore, for her part, wished she could feel so totally convinced about the guilt of James Roy Blagge. It would have made life so much simpler. Instead, her instinct was troubling her; that famous instinct, merrily castigated by both Cy Fredericks . . . and Pompey of the [Scotland] Yard. . . . But Jemima knew by experience that this instinct was not to be derided.
>
> The single word "instinct" drawing the fire of such quizzical males as Cy Fredericks and Pompey, was in fact not quite accurate. It was more that Jemima possessed a very strong instinct for order. This would not let her rest so long as the smallest detail was out of place in the well-regulated pattern of her mind. On this occasion the small detail which was troubling her, and would continue to do so naggingly until she resolved it, was Christabel's distress at the televised rehearsal and her continued nervous state since Mr. Blagge's arrest. . . . [T]here could be no question of Mr. Blagge attacking anyone while he was in the cells at Beauport. What then was frightening Christabel Cartwright? (From Antonia Fraser, *Cool Repentance* [London: Methuen, 1983], pp. 163–164)

Notice how Ms. Shore's puzzlement about a disorderly fact leads her to ask a question about it.

△▼ EXERCISE 18-D

1. Find and discuss an example in which the asking of a logically complex question has played an important role.
2. Find and discuss an example in which puzzlement about a disorderly fact has guided the inquiry.

.19

Models of Scientific Reasoning

One of the most crucial factors influencing the course of inquiry is the set of restrictions which limit the oracles' answers. It is very difficult to get a general view of all these restrictions. There is one set of partial restrictions, however, whose effects can be understood and which are related to issues in scientific reasoning.

19.1 The Atomistic Assumption

Let us start from one specific possible restriction. Consider the kind of inquiry in which an empirical scientist is engaged. In empirical science the answerer (the oracle) is nature. Now what kinds of answers can nature give to the scientist's questions? Apparently the answer is easy: Nature, it seems, cannot tell a scientist what the case is or is not, always and everywhere but merely how things are in one particular case, namely, in the particular situation in which the scientist is making his or her observations.

What does this restriction amount to in logical terms? If you remember what was said in Chapter 14 about the logic of quantifiers, the answer is clear. Nature's answers to a scientist's questions cannot contain any quantifiers. For to talk of what happens "always" and "everywhere" is to talk of all the members of one's domain of discourse, that is, to use quantifiers. This restriction is called the *atomistic assumption* or the *atomistic postulate*.

19.2   The A-Assumption

The atomistic assumption is at one end of a long line of possible restrictions. The next possible type of restriction also allows answers which say something about all objects in the scientist's domain of discourse, but only something about each of them taken alone, not in relation to other objects. For a logician, such answers have the following form: $\forall x \, S[x]$, where $S[x]$ does not contain any quantifiers (expressions like "every" and "some") or equivalent expressions. Such answers will be called *A-answers*, and the restriction of the oracles' answers to them is known as the *A-assumption*. More generally, A-answers may be of the form $\forall x_1 \, \forall x_2 \ldots S[x_1, x_2, \ldots]$.

19.3   The AE-Assumption

The next restriction also allows answers of the form $\forall x \exists y \, S[x,y]$, where $S[x,y]$ does not contain any quantifiers or equivalent expressions. Of course, A-answers and quantifier-free answers are also allowed. This restriction is known as the *AE-assumption*, and answers of the $\forall x \exists y \, S[x,y]$ form are called *AE-answers*. More generally, AE-answers may be of the form $\forall x_1 \, \forall x_2 \ldots \exists y_1 \, \exists y_2 \ldots S[x_1, x_2, \ldots, y_1, y_2, \ldots]$.

Whenever you state a law expressing a *functional dependence* of one variable on another one, you are making an AE-statement. For what a functional dependence means is that for each value of the one variable ($\forall x$) there corresponds a certain value of the other ($\exists y$).

Clearly, we can similarly define AEA, AEAE, . . . answers and corresponding assumptions. We thus obtain an infinite series of less and less strict restrictions. In each case, there may be other restrictions to which the oracles' answers are subject.

Illustrations For instance, if the oracle says "All humans are rational," then the oracle is giving me information about each human being taken individually. Hence, this is an A-answer. But if the oracle says, "Every human has a mother," then the item of information relates each human being to one other who is asserted to exist. Hence, we are dealing with an AE-answer, not with an A-answer.

△ ▼ EXERCISE 19-A

Test your understanding of the distinctions outlined above by trying to decide what kind of answers each of the following might be.

▶ 1. No bachelor has a wife.

2. Where there is smoke, there is fire.

▶ 3. All humans are mortal. (Suggestion: Think about what the word "mortal" means.)

4. "No man is an island, entire of itself; every man is a piece of the continent" (John Donne, *Devotions upon Emergent Occasions*, Meditation XVII).

▶ 5. All whales are mammals.

19.4 Unrestricted Inquiry

There can even be types of inquiry not subject to any of the A, AE, AEA, . . . restrictions. Consider, as an example, the reasoning of a physician who is attempting a diagnosis of a patient. The doctor may put questions to the patient and have clinical tests performed. But the doctor can also consult a medical handbook or a treatise of physiology for the purpose of diagnosis. The "answers" she or he is likely to receive from such books do not concern particular matters of fact. They normally concern the general laws governing human biology. And in principle there does not seem to be any limit as to how complex such laws might be, logically speaking. Thus clinical inquiry can be taken to exemplify inquiry with unrestricted logical (quantificational) complexity.

The same can be said of the reasoning employed by real or fictional detectives. Their reasoning, too, can in principle invoke any type of available information, however great its logical complexity.

To return once more to the "Curious Incident of the Dog in the Night-time," one of Sherlock Holmes's questions was seen to receive a general answer. He was in effect asking, "Who is it that *any* trained watchdog does not bark at in the middle of the night?" In Chapter 14, therefore, the answer to this question was expressed as an A-statement, not as an answer concerning a particular dog.

19.5 Where Do General Scientific Truths Come From?

Different restrictions of the AEA . . . type necessitate different strategies on the part of the inquirer and in general give rise to different types of inquiry. For instance, consider the atomistic assumption.

Let us assume that the inquirer would like to establish through his or her argument a *general* conclusion C, that is, a conclusion with universal quantifiers and perhaps even with existential quantifiers governed by universal ones. Normally, such a conclusion cannot be derived logically from answers that are quantifier-free statements ("particular propositions," as they are sometimes known), except with the help of a strong initial premise T which already contains quantifiers.

Because scientific theories normally are general truths or at least general claims about how things are, they in effect contain general quantifiers. Because they typically express dependencies between variables, scientific theories normally have at least AE complexity and so cannot be derived from atomistic (quantifier-free) answers without the help of strong initial premises T. But if the only answers empirical scientists can hope for from nature are atomistic, how can they hope to establish general claims?

In view of this problem situation, how are we to understand the nature of empirical scientific reasoning? How is it that scientists manage to set up general theories?

Four main answers to this question have been offered by different philosophers.

1. Some philosophers argue that, even though you cannot derive general theories from quantifier-free answers alone by means of truth-preserving (deductive) logical inference rules, there may be other kinds of inference rules, known as *rules of inductive inference,* which can do so. We shall return to the idea of inductive inference later in this chapter.

2. As we have already mentioned, restrictions on available answers can be partly compensated for by strengthening the initial premises T. Some philosophers have accordingly suggested that the success of empirical science is based on suitable general premises, such as the assumption of the uniformity of nature.

3. One of the most popular answers to our problem is to say, in the words of the story of a local character advising a tourist, "You just can't get there from here." In other words, according to this view general theories of empirical science are not arrived at by rule-governed inquiry, but are of the nature of hypotheses. Such hypotheses can be made more dependable by deriving conclusions from them and comparing them with the atomistic answers nature can give to the inquirer.

   This view is known as the *hypothetico-deductive conception* of the scientific method. The name is misleading, for the conclusions the inquirer derives from a theory need not be deductive conclusions only but can also involve answers.

4. Strategically speaking, a promising response to the problem situation is to deny that empirical inquiry is subject to the atomistic restriction. This solution can be backed up by distinguishing *observational inquiry* from *experimental inquiry.* Observational answers are atomistic (quantifier-free). However, in a controlled experiment a scientist studies the dependence of the observed variable on the controlled variable. The answer nature gives to a scientist's experimental question is therefore a statement of how the one variable depends on the other. Such an answer is not quantifier-free, but an AE-answer.

If this is the case, there is nothing impossible about deriving general theories from nature's answers, for these answers already are general propositions.

△▼ EXERCISE 19-B

The great scientist Isaac Newton, whom you met in Chapter 1, claimed that he had "deduced" from the "phenomena" some of the laws and theories he had discovered. How is such a claim to be looked upon from the vantage point of the four different characterizations of scientific reasoning given above?

19.6 The Inductive Model

The first of the four answers above requires further discussion. For this purpose it is useful to look back and see what we have done in this chapter from a bird's-eye perspective. We have been discussing the most general problem situation any inquirer—at least any inquirer who is not interested only in logic and mathematics—must face. As we have emphasized, logical inference steps do not give the inquirer any information not already present before the logical inference. Such an inference simply spells out the information which is contained in the statements the inquirer has already established. You have learned that such inferences are known as *deductive inferences*.

But how then can the inquirer get new information? The answer we have been giving to you is: by putting questions to the oracles and using the answers as additional premises. There may be situations in which the oracles' answers are not thought to be entirely reliable, but this does not spoil the interrogative approach. In Part 3 you learned how to sift and to compare different answers and oracles so as to establish which answers to trust.

But if we assume that the only answers we can get from nature are atomistic answers, how can we establish any general conclusions about nature? At this point, the inductivist would suggest an approach different from the interrogative approach. The inductivist would say that the deductive logical inference rules do not do the whole job. Instead of resorting to questions whose (nonatomistic) answers are uncertain, why could we not equally well (and perhaps even better) add to the deductive rules of inference further rules whose conclusions do not simply spell out the information we already have but go beyond it? Such inferences could be called *inductive inferences*.

As we saw in Chapter 5 of Part 2, inductive inferences go beyond the given information, and consequently they are not always truth-preserving. They may lead to false conclusions from true premises. But then, answers to questions can also be false. So why do we not formulate some inductive rules of inference and use them instead of asking questions?

Many different patterns of reasoning are discussed under the heading of "induction." An important type of inductive inference is concerned with establishing causal relationships. As it is often very important to be able to determine in what way significant properties of our environment are related to each other, scientific reasoning involves such study. The philosopher John Stuart Mill (1806–1873) analyzed a number of the ways in which we discover causal relationships and on the basis of this analysis offered inductive rules for reasoning which have come to be known as "Mill's Methods."

Mill's Methods are concerned with how properties are seen to be necessary and/or sufficient conditions. A property A is said to be a *sufficient* condition for the property B if and only if the following is true:

1. $\forall x \, (Ax \supset Bx)$

Formula 1 also gives us a way to characterize a *necessary* condition. A property B is said to be a necessary condition for the property A if and only if statement 1 is true.

A number of interesting rules can be formulated to help us find what is and what is not a necessary or a sufficient condition. The inductivist way of looking at such rules involves asking questions to which there are atomistic answers. Mill's Methods then give guidance as to what kinds of individual cases to ask questions about to show what is or is not a necessary or sufficient condition for what. For instance, if we ask of an individual b whether it is an A and whether it is a B, we might receive the atomistic answer that

2. Ab & $-Bb$

If this answer is true, it tells us that A cannot be a *sufficient* condition for B. The reason for this is that the definition of a sufficient condition, statement 1 above, tells us that for every individual, if it is A it must also be B, in order for A to be a sufficient condition for B. But answer 2 says that there is an individual which is A but is not B.

Similarly, the same answer, statement 2 above, tells us that B cannot be a necessary condition for A. The reason in this case is that the definition of a necessary condition tells us that for every individual, it will be the case that the individual will be A only if it is B, in order for B to be a necessary condition for A. Therefore, if an individual is not B while it is A, as in answer 2, it must be that B is not a necessary condition for A.

We see, then, that a couple of true atomistic answers can sometimes give us sufficient information to determine with certainty that one property *is not* a sufficient (or necessary) condition for another. The problem, however, is that we are often more interested in discovering when one property or combination of properties *is* a sufficient and/or necessary condition for another. To show that there *is* such a relationship requires, as statement 1 shows, that we be able to say something about *every* individual. In simple and artificial situations there may be a limited number of individuals and properties, and we may actually be able to enumerate all the cases and discover what is a necessary and/or sufficient condition for what. But when we are dealing with the complexities of everyday life and of the study of nature, we are often faced with an unlimited or indeterminate number of cases. How to determine whether the general requirements in the definitions of sufficient and necessary conditions are met is the difficult problem that inductive inferences are meant to solve.

The underlying idea in inductive inference is that if we observe a sufficient number of individual (atomistic) cases concerning a possible causal relationship, we can, with growing confidence, hope to discern whether the general causal relationship does in fact hold. In the simplest case one might simply observe that in a very large number of cases it is always seen that whenever an individual is characterized by C, it also turns out to be characterized by D. This could lead us to think that perhaps

3. $\forall x \, (Cx \supset Dx)$

and/or perhaps

4. $\forall x \, (Dx \supset Cx)$

We might, however, further observe that sometimes we find an individual characterized by D which is nevertheless not characterized by C. This would lead us to reject our idea number 4. In other words D is not a sufficient condition for C nor is C a necessary condition for D. Still, if in thousands of cases we never find that an individual is characterized by C but not by D, we might *inductively infer* that formula 3 is true and that therefore C is a sufficient condition for D and D is necessary for C. Mill's Methods give detailed advice about how to look for appropriate evidence of necessary and sufficient conditions.

Mill's Methods can be formulated so as to look somewhat like our other rules of table construction. For example, the first three methods, which involve what Mill called *agreement and difference,* can be illustrated by the following example:

Assume that we suspect that the necessary condition of property C is to be found among the properties $D_1, D_2, \ldots, D_k$. Now, assume that we have observed three individuals a, b, and c with the following results:

5. $D_1a, D_2a, \ldots, D_ka, Ca$
6. $D_1b, -D_2b, \ldots, -D_kb, Cb$
7. $-D_1c, D_2c, \ldots, D_kc, -Cc$

Individual a is characterized by all the properties $D_1, D_2, \ldots, D_k$ and is also characterized by C. Individual b is characterized by C and otherwise only by the property D_1. Individual c is *not* characterized by C, nor by D_1, but is characterized by $D_2, \ldots, D_k$. Observation of individual b (number 6) eliminates the possibility that any but D_1 might be the necessary condition for C. Both observation of a (number 5) and of c (number 7) give us instances that support the conclusion that D_1 is the necessary condition for C. If we were able to make a "sufficient" number of further observations, we might be able to make up our mind that D_1 *is* a necessary condition for C.

As we have said, however, reasoning which follows this sort of inductive pattern does not always yield a true conclusion, even if all the premises are true. The problem is that we cannot observe every case, and the possibility remains that some other case would have shown that, for example, D_1 was *not* after all a necessary condition for C. We can never be sure we have observed a "sufficient" number of cases in order to make it impossible to imagine our conclusion about a causal relationship false.

19.7   Induction vs. Interrogation

Here we can see clearly what the difference is between the idea we are pursuing and the inductivists' idea: They are studying uncertain inferences from what they take to be certain (indubitable) premises. We are studying certain (deductive) inferences from uncertain premises. The inductivists advise you to rely on indubitable atomistic answers combined with possibly fallible inductive inferences. We advise you to rely on indubitable, deductive inferences combined with logically complex but possibly fallible answers.

Sometimes it is said that inductive inference differs from deductive inference in that induction yields only probable conclusions, whereas deductive conclusions can be established with certainty. This characterization of the difference has to be approached with caution, however. It can, for example, be shown that a definite probability can be assigned to an inductive conclusion only if the "prior probability" (probability before evidence) of the inductive conclusion is known. This prior probability cannot always be established inductively. Furthermore, deductive reasoning can also yield conclusions that are only probable, namely, when the premises of the deductive inferences are not certain but only probable.

Here we shall not study inductive inferences much further. Their significance as an element of the scientific enterprise is often exaggerated. A basic reason why we must be at least somewhat wary about inductive inference is easy to see. A step of inductive inference goes beyond the information previously gathered in the inquiry, but it gives the appearance of relying only on the information we already have. A step of inductive inference does not sufficiently alert us that we are, in such a step, introducing new information into the inquiry. We are not given the right perspective for devising strategies to cope with the uncertainty that enters as we introduce new information.

In contrast, in putting a question to an oracle and getting an answer, the inquirer normally does get some new information and recognizes that she or he is getting it. Even if the inquirer cannot trust the answer to be true, it is a new item of information that goes beyond the data the inquirer had before the question was asked. For this reason, rules for questions and answers are more basic than rules of inductive inference. For the same reason, what looks like inductive inferences should often (perhaps always) be replaced by deductive inferences from uncertain premises.

We note also that the inductive approach quite often requires making strong initial assumptions about where to begin to look for causal relationships. This has led some philosophers to offer theories 2 and 3 (above, beginning of Section 19.5) as alternative accounts of the scientific method. They say it is better to construe scientific reasoning as involving strong initial premises rather than as involving inductive inferences. These approaches, however, focus our attention on initial premises rather than encouraging us to look for interesting and new questions along the way in our inquiries. Thus, we come back to the interrogative account of scientific reasoning and of reasoning in general.

Illustration Here is a real-life example of reasoning that can be construed in several different ways, from *The Evidence Never Lies: The Casebook of a Modern Sherlock Holmes* by A. Lewis and H. MacDonell (New York: Holt, Rinehart and Winston, 1984, pp. 1–3, 22).

The background of the evidence is this:

> It was 4:45 P.M. on Tuesday, December 7, 1965. In the early winter dusk, the long shadows of the trees striped the woodland. Only fifteen minutes remained of the deer hunting season. On this last day, a hunter was permitted to shoot a doe as well as a buck, which meant that he did not have to waste precious time looking for a pair of antlers.

> Bob Ferry could not believe his luck when he spotted a doe moving down into the gully. He lifted his shotgun, took careful aim at her, and pulled the trigger. It was not the howl of a wounded animal that reached his ears but the astonished cry of another hunter.

> Ferry did not understand what had happened. He had spotted a deer. He had taken aim at a deer—not a man. He could not have hit a man. His pulse was racing, and he was paralyzed in place. The empty shell still lay at his feet marking the spot from which he had fired. A low wire fence separated him from the action that sped around him like a fast-motion movie. The other members of the hunting party were converging on a spot about 155 feet in front of him and to the right. Somebody was shouting, "Roxbury! It's Roy Roxbury! He's been shot in the throat." . . .

> Schuyler County Sheriff Maurice Dean took charge of the still dazed Robert Ferry. When none of the other hunters admitted to having seen a deer, Dean became convinced that Ferry had not seen one either. Dean was a hunter and, from his own experience, was certain that Ferry had heard a noise and, without looking, had fired at it. On the last day of the season, some men were known to become trigger-happy.

The crucial argument takes place in the witness stand during the ensuing trial.

> MacDonell was sworn in and, after establishing his credentials as a forensic scientist and expert in the field of firearms, Tillman began a line of questioning relating to the specifics of the Ferry case. He asked MacDonell if he was familiar

with the type of Remington Peters ammunition that Ferry had been using. The reply was in the affirmative, and the criminalist was then asked to describe a piece of this ammunition to the jury.

"The firing mechanism, called a primer, is at the base of the shell. Inside the shell, above the primer, is gunpowder, then wadding, and finally, the slug. After firing, the expended shell may be ejected and fall to the ground, which is admittedly what has happened in the case of Ferry. The wadding freely follows the slug and doesn't separate and fall away until within eighteen and thirty-six inches and usually travels freely not more than twenty-five feet after that."

"How can you be so certain of these measurements?"

"On the morning of April 30, 1966, in the backyard of my home, I test-fired a variety of shotguns, including the model of Ithaca Deerslayer that Ferry was using. In every instance, the separations took place within the distances I've just given." He smiled. "I happen to have all these weapons around the house because I'm a gun collector."

MacDonell's reasoning can be looked upon in at least three different ways. He might be thought to be drawing an inductive inference based on his observation ("In every instance . . . "). Or, alternatively, he might be taken to be assuming, as an initial premise, the uniformity of shotguns or at least of shotguns of the kind Ferry had been using. This alternative is related to theories 2 and 3 above (beginning of Section 19.5).

But we can also look upon MacDonnell's test as establishing (or trying to establish) the uniformity of different shotguns of the relevant make through experiments, that is, through logically complex questions put to his collection of guns. This is the interrogative approach.

Which of these accounts of his reasoning would MacDonell likely recognize? There is no way of telling. However, what we can say here is which account of his reasoning cuts deeper into the realities of the situation. The reliability of the inductive inference in question obviously depends on the uniformity of the objects (in the case in point, shotguns of a certain make) with which it deals. If the uniformity is merely assumed, the uncertainty in question still persists. But if, by suitably complex questions in the interrogative approach, one can ascertain that there indeed is the uniformity (regularity) needed, one has in effect bypassed one source of the uncertainty in the other approaches. (By the way, Bob Ferry was acquitted.)

What is seen in this example can be applied more generally. For instance, many of the rules that statisticians have formulated can be looked upon in different ways. They can be viewed as inductive rules of a certain kind. If so, they would presumably have to be considered as definitory rules for inductive inferences. They would tell us how to make inferences of a certain kind.

Often, however, it is a good idea to look upon the rules of statistical inference in a different way—not as rules defining certain types of nondeductive inference, but as *strategic rules*, advising us when to accept (at least for the time being) certain logically complex answers nature seems to be offering to the inquirer.

It does not make strategic rules any less useful if they are not infallible. Also, because they deal with entire strategies of inquiry, it is perfectly understandable if the acceptance or rejection of a logically complex answer given by nature is later reversed. Such reversals can take place in the best of strategies.

What we are seeing then is that inductive rules, such as those formulated in Mill's Methods, can be thought of as rules concerning what kinds of questions to ask rather than as rules for inductive inference. For example, Mill called his fifth rule *the method of concomitant variation*. This method is closely related to the idea that an experiment, or some other situation where we can study the mutual dependence of two variables, can yield an answer which is not atomistic. The answer is not atomistic because it says that for *each* value of the one variable there corresponds (*there is*) such-and-such a value of the other one. Hence, the answer contains an existential quantifier governed by a universal quantifier and is of AE complexity. Mill's discussion of such situations illustrates the important role that answers of AE logical complexity play in scientific inquiry. Such complex answers are typically what is sought in a scientific experiment.

Mill's Methods illustrate more generally the fact that many of the techniques of inquiry which in the past have been dealt with under the heading of "induction" can be more effectively discussed in terms of the interrogative approach to inquiry. There is no need to add to the interrogative model any new rules for inductive inferences.

▲ 20 ▼

Definition and Identification

Our knowledge of the interrogative model of inquiry provides both a familiar method for approaching the issues of definition and identification and a complex account of what is happening. This chapter seeks to explain the familiar method and to give some indication of the complex account.

20.1 A Method for Definitions and Identifications

A request for a definition can be thought of as a request for information about what a word means—that is, about what it stands for or represents, or how it is used. (Throughout this section we will speak of defining "words," but what is being said can equally be applied to defining phrases, special symbols, or any other linguistic expression that has a use about which we can inquire. We will also speak of *identifying* what a word represents. What the difference is between definition and identification will be discussed later in the chapter.)

We can meet the request for a definition in several ways. If there are appropriate synonyms of the word in question and if we can confidently expect that the person asking for a definition is familiar with what the synonymous word means, then providing a synonym may do part or all of the job of defining. (A synonym is simply a word whose meaning in the relevant context is sufficiently similar to that of the word we are trying to define.)

Say, for example, that some people familiar with deductive logic but unfamiliar with the early chapters of this book ask what we mean by a "logical inference." We might be able to tell them all they need to know about our use of the phrase by saying that we use it to mean the same as the phrase "valid deductive inference."

Unfortunately, in many cases, there are no suitable synonyms available for the word we are being asked to define. In such cases we need another approach.

Suppose that we are trying to define "logical inference" for someone who does not know what a valid deductive inference is. Then we could approach our task as in Chapter 1, where we tried carefully to describe the circumstances in which it is appropriate to use the phrase. This required that we explain how the word "inference" is used, and that in turn required introducing the words "premise" and "conclusion" into the picture. We then tried to make sure that everyone understood what it would mean to "imagine the premises to be true" and to try to "imagine the conclusion to be false." We then took all of the pieces and put them together in a way that indicated quite specifically when an inference could be called a "logical inference" and when it could not.

It begins to look as though our method for giving definitions is not very simple. The problem, however, deserves a closer look. The preceding discussion of how we went about defining "logical inference" points up several basic principles.

1. Even though there are many different ways and means of conveying the meaning of a word to someone, we can always try to do so with the help of interrogative inquiry. This is so because the explanation of the meaning of a word involves leading people to a true statement of what the word means or what it is that the word applies to in the relevant context. Such a statement can often be established by means of interrogative arguments. In brief *you can search for definitions by means of questions.*

2. The interrogative model suggests we should first think of the process of defining as one of answering questions about what a word means. If we are in dialogue with the person asking for the definition, that person can help by asking questions about the word's uses. Otherwise we can try to anticipate the kinds of questions that a person would need to ask in order to learn how the word is used.

3. There are many ways to answer questions about the meaning of a word. We have already mentioned using synonyms. Sometimes we can physically or verbally point to the item or situation that the word names. Sometimes we can simply show the word at work in a typical sentence or paragraph, and those who are seeking the definition begin to grasp how it is used.

4. When we cannot answer the questions so simply, it is then especially helpful to think of the definer's task as an interrogative inquiry. The aim of the game is to answer a "wh-" question, namely, "What does this word mean?" This

question can typically be paraphrased as: "What does this word apply to?" The point is that we have a "wh-" question before us. Later in this chapter we will examine in more detail how an interrogative inquiry enables us to search for an answer to a "wh-" question even when we cannot anticipate what the answer will be.

△▼ THINK ABOUT IT

You are perhaps familiar with the game of "twenty questions" (Appendix B offers a brief discussion). The game requires attempts to identify a thing or person by means of questions. Experienced players, who know certain rough strategic rules, find for instance, that it is usually a good idea to divide the field into a few roughly equally large classes and to ascertain which the object to be identified belongs to. This will be more efficient than asking questions about particular persons or objects or small classes.

△▼ EXERCISE 20-A

▶ You have been given 30 coins and told that one and only one of them is clearly heavier than the others, but you cannot tell which is the heavier without weighing them. You have a simple balance scale. What is the minimum number of weighings that will guarantee your finding the heavier coin? In other words, how do you arrange the inquiry in the most efficient way? (The same number of weighings will also guarantee discovering the odd coin even if you do not know whether it is heavier or lighter. You will, however, need a more sophisticated weighing scheme. Can you work it out?)

5. Notice that we are not usually being asked to explain all of the many meanings of a word. Instead, it is usually the use of the word in a specific context or in a specific way that is of current interest.

6. Often we are being asked to *report* how a word is used in a certain community. Then our task is to give an accurate account of the way people in that community use the word.

7. Sometimes, however, we are in a situation where we have had to make a more precise set of specifications for using a word than is found in ordinary usage. Or perhaps we need to apply a word to a new situation. Then our task is to give an account of the way *we* have chosen to use the word. We might also want to explain why we use the word the way we do, especially if our meaning differs from ordinary meanings.

So far we have said that giving a definition involves explaining how a word is used and that this is to be done by answering appropriate questions about how the word is used. We can now go further by suggesting that in complicated cases we might think of the task of defining a word as an inquiry centering on the word's use. The word "define" suggests the notion of setting boundaries, and that means eliminating uses of the word that might have been thought possible. Our interrogative notion of "information" as that which enables us to eliminate alternatives is well tailored to the task of "defining."

In an inquiry aimed at defining a word, our ultimate conclusion will specify how it is used. We may or may not be able to state the ultimate conclusion at the beginning. Even if we can state the ultimate conclusion, it is likely that those who are seeking a definition will be helped to better insight if we make available some of the key inquiry steps that lead up to the definition.

Our initial premises would be information which we think we have in common with the people for whom we are providing the definition. From this initial situation we then proceed by making logical inference moves and interrogative moves that lead us to a closed table. The general skills we have learned in the interrogative approach to reasoning turn out to be directly adaptable to the specific task of providing definitions.

△ ▼ EXERCISE 20-B

Use your insights into the interrogative model to help you find and write definitions for the following words.

1. *Deciduous*
2. *Climacteric*
3. *Logic*
4. *Inertia* (in an everyday context)
5. *Inertia* (in physics)
6. *Denouement*
7. *Dialectic*
8. *Opportunity Cost*
9. *Selling Short*
10. *Medicare DRGs*

20.2   Definitions Help Resolve Ambiguity and Vagueness

In this section we examine more closely some of the problems definitions are meant to solve. If you are asked to define a certain word you are using, you are being asked to spell out what you mean by that word. Defining one's words is an important part of being clear about what you say and about what you mean.

One reason why definitions are important is that words and phrases are often used incorrectly. For instance, "momentarily," properly speaking, means "for a moment," not "in a moment." One can only hope that an airline pilot is not meaning his words literally when he or she announces to the passengers that the aircraft will be airborne "momentarily." One also hopes that the pilot is more careful with his or her words in communicating with air traffic controllers.

△ ▼ THINK ABOUT IT

As more and more people "misuse" a word, it is likely to take on a new meaning. You might check a dictionary to see if "momentarily" includes the pilot's meaning. You might also discuss old and new uses for the word "hopefully."

The meaning of words sometimes is not sufficiently clear for us to be able to use them effectively. This problem involves what is called *vagueness*. Words sometimes suggest multiple uses in a given context, and it may not be clear which meaning is intended. This problem involves what is called *ambiguity*. The giving of definitions is meant to help us with these difficulties.

Words and expressions convey information, enabling us to eliminate from our thinking certain alternative situations we otherwise might have thought possible. Sometimes words and expressions seem to convey information but do so in ways that do not clearly or unmistakably indicate what situations are being eliminated from the inquiry. Sometimes the meanings of the words we are using do not allow us precisely to eliminate situations as we at first thought they might.

We have run into this problem from the beginning. In even the simplest analyses of arguments we have often found it necessary to supply "between the lines" information to spell out precisely that which the inquirer has in mind. "Between the lines" information helps us to pin down more precisely how and why the inquirer is eliminating certain otherwise imaginable situations from the inquiry.

Both the word "ambiguous" and the word "vague" are rooted in ancient words that meant "to wander." These words are used to indicate occasions when words and expressions are liable to wander in ways that confuse our attempts to specify what kind of information is being provided.

Ambiguity

Words and expressions are said to be "ambiguous" when they communicate more than one possible piece of information, that is, when it is unclear what set of alternative situations we are meant to eliminate. For example, a bumper sticker may say that "Nurses are patient people." Here the word "patient" may mean to eliminate the possibility that nurses have short tempers and are unwilling to see a difficult problem through to the end. "Patient" would be the opposite of "impatient." But nurses are also those who often work with people who are ill. We say that one who is ill in a hospital is a patient. The bumper sticker may mean to suggest that the situations most relevant to the nursing profession are situations in which hospital patients are found.

Because this is a bumper sticker slogan, both pieces of information are intended, and we are alert to look for more than one meaning. Part of the game of bumper stickers is to try, in a short expression, to communicate a double (or multiple) message. There is nothing wrong with this game, and we derive a certain measure of enjoyment from it.

Ambiguity can be a problem, however, whenever we are not alert to the ways in which an ambiguous expression confuses our thinking. If, in a given context, the meanings of a word create ambiguity, then we risk spelling out the information in an unintended way. Worse still, we may use the ambiguous expression one way part of the time and another way in another. Our bumper sticker game with "patient" can illustrate the problem.

p1. All patient people are trained in health care.

p2. Tom certainly is a patient person with his children.

c. Therefore, Tom must be trained in health care.

The premise p1 can be made plausible only by making use of the playful sense of "patient person," "one who works with hospital patients," whereas p2 uses the more usual sense of "someone who is slow to get angry and who is willing to bear with others who may be difficult to deal with." The conclusion erroneously attempts to combine the information in the premises to eliminate the possibility that Tom would fail to be trained in health care.

Interrogative analysis of such an argument advises us to ask questions in order to pin down more precisely what the information is that is provided in the meanings of a word or phrase. This enables us to be alert to occasions when ambiguous words and expressions are tempting us to come to conclusions that are not actually warranted.

△ ▼ EXERCISE 20-C

Explain how ambiguity infects the following argument. What interrogative move would help expose the confusion?

p1. Everything that runs has feet.

p2. The Mississippi River runs to the Gulf of Mexico.

c. The Mississippi River has feet.

Irony involves a special type of ambiguity, sometimes defined as "saying one thing but meaning something contrary." The effect of irony comes from the double meanings. For example, an instructor might say, "As you've known for two weeks, your paper is due next week. No doubt you all have already written an outline and two preliminary drafts." In the usual college or university context both the instructor and the students would recognize this as irony, because no one thinks any student has gotten going so early and so thoroughly on the assignment. The instructor is probably having some fun while trying to urge the students to get with it. Someone might, however, miss the playfulness and conclude that the instructor is awfully naive about student work habits.

In Plato's dialogue *Meno,* to which we have referred several times, Meno begins the conversation by asking "Can virtue be taught?" Socrates replies that people like Meno must really be smart to be able to ask such a question. For his own part Socrates says he doesn't even know what virtue is, let alone whether it can be taught. Meno might be flattered, but people who are well acquainted with Socrates know that he in no way thinks Meno to be smart, but rather thinks him to be uncareful in his thinking.

Notice that, as with any case of ambiguity, confusion arises whenever we fail to notice the multiple meanings that are in play. The cure for the confusions is to ask more questions, that is, make more interrogative moves, until the way the multiple meanings work has been clearly defined.

Vagueness

Ambiguous and ironic words and expressions create problems, but they at least have clear uses. The problem is that their multiple uses can confuse us as to which piece of information is intended. Vagueness involves a different kind of problem.

Words and expressions are said to be "vague" when they resist having *any* clear and consistent use in the context. Ambiguous information clearly eliminates two or more sets of possible situations but fails to tell us which set is intended. Vague information fails clearly to demarcate what the situations are that are to be eliminated. When confronted with vague information, we may be tempted to draw a logical inference to clarify what is intended. But because the original information lacks clarity, we inevitably introduce further new information as we try to clear things up.

There is nothing wrong with introducing further information so long as we are aware of what we are doing. Problems with vagueness arise when the inquirer is unaware or unclear about how vague expressions are at work in the argument.

For example, someone might argue as follows:

p. This novel is pornographic.

c. Therefore, this novel should be banned from our high school library.

An analysis of this argument would quickly show that at least one between-the-lines piece of information needs to be supplied, perhaps through an interrogative move such as

i. Should pornographic novels be banned from our high school libraries?

Depending on how a person understands the word "pornographic," she or he may be more or less willing to answer yes to the supplied interrogative move, but that would still not finish the analysis of the argument. It would be very important to check whether the use of "pornographic" that led to a yes answer in the supplied interrogative move, matches the use that is involved in the original premise, "This novel is pornographic."

The word "pornographic" in this context is a vague expression because there are no clearly agreed criteria for its use in our conversations. If we are entangled in an inquiry that makes use of this expression, it is very important that we check each occasion of its use. If it is not being used in similar ways throughout the argument and we fail to notice this fact, we may think we can draw logical inferences when in fact none would guarantee the truth of the conclusion.

△ ▼ EXERCISE 20-D

▶ 1. Discuss the following two arguments in terms of problems with vagueness. What interrogative moves might help clarify the situation?

   a. I just read in this magazine that the Babylonian civilization was much older than the Roman. So the Babylonian civilization must have begun several years before the Roman.

   b. I just read in this magazine that my type of computer is much older than yours. So my type must have been designed a millennium or more before yours.

2. Review the material on conclusive and partial answers in Chapter 10 (Section 10.2). Write a brief discussion of how ambiguity and vagueness contribute to the mistake of thinking one has a conclusive answer when only a partial answer is actually available.

Further Illustrations

The words we have been using in this textbook are often used in several different ways. Here are a few words relevant to argumentation and inquiry that are often used loosely or imprecisely or, in some cases, merely in a way different from the one in which we have been using them: "imply," "infer," "argue," "refute," "logic," "theory." What are some of the multiple ways in which they are sometimes used? Here are a few brief explanations:

1. We have used the word "imply" to indicate valid logical consequence. A statement B is said to be implied by A if and only if it is a valid consequence of A.

   However, the word "imply" is often used in a different way. A speaker is said to "imply" something he or she is not stating explicitly but which seems to follow from what is said. For instance, suppose that you ask, "Could Kasparov have made a mistake?" If I answer, "Anybody can make a mistake," I am not *saying* that Kasparov could have made a mistake, but I am *implying* it by saying something on the basis of which a simple interrogative argument could be built.

   There is nothing wrong about such usage, but sometimes it is extended to cases in which what one says could not easily be made the basis of an interrogative argument leading to what is being suggested. In other words, "imply" comes to mean the same as "suggest." This use, whether we want to call it mistaken or not, is somewhat loose and can be misleading.

2. "Infer" is often used in the same way as "imply" in the loose usage just described. For instance, "Are you inferring that I am not telling the truth?" is likely to mean merely, "Are you suggesting . . . ?"

3. "Argue" is often used in the sense of "quarrel," as in "Jack and Jill argue constantly about their family finances." This unfortunately is not likely to mean that Jack and Jill are constantly trying to construct lines of reasoning about their family money management.

   Sometimes "argue" is used to mean "contradict" or "deny." This is an especially dangerous misuse, because it can lead to misunderstandings. For instance, a headline in early 1990 in *USA Today* declared that "new research makes long-held view that lead can lower child's IQ unarguable." In the correct sense of "arguable" as "capable of being argued for" or "defensible," *unarguable* would mean that the link between lead poisoning and lowered IQ can no longer be defended in the light of new research.

   A perusal of the actual news story, however, revealed that the opposite was actually meant by the reporter who wrote the story. By *unarguable* the reporter misleadingly meant "incapable of being argued against" or "undeniable."

4. "Refute" is used correctly only when something is proved to be wrong. Nevertheless it is often used merely in the sense of "contradict," as in, "He sharply refuted the suggestion and implied that the accuser was merely covering up his own mistake."

5. We met earlier (in Chapter 1, Section 1.10) the "Sherlock Holmes" sense of such words as "logic" and "deduction." This broader use of such words is not objectionable, and in fact in Chapter 18 we saw that this sense is a fact firmly rooted in the nature of interrogative inquiry (Sections 18.1 and 18.2). Still, in thinking about reasoning and inquiry, you should be aware of these possibly misleading uses of the key terms you are using.

6. In science "theory" denotes a body of well-established general claims capable of explaining a number of facts about some given subject matter. In common usage, however, the word often means little more than a hypothesis or a conjecture. In this book we have been using the word "theory" in its scientific sense, in which there need not be anything conjectural suggested. In Chapter 19 (Section 19.5) we saw that a theory can sometimes even be derived deductively from nature's answers to experiments.

The Importance of Being Unambiguous

One can go seriously wrong in reasoning if one uses an ambiguous word in different ways in one and the same argument. For instance, the following argument can be fallacious:

1. Nelson owns a bank.

2. Whoever owns a bank is rich.

3. Therefore Nelson is rich.

This argument may fail because the word "bank" is ambiguous in English. It can mean either a kind of financial institution or else a strip of land bordering a river. If the latter is meant in statement 1 but the former in statement 2, the argument will be fallacious: Its premises can be imagined true while its conclusion (statement 3) is imagined false.

What was said in Chapter 15 (Section 15.3) about "is" is often expressed by saying the English word is ambiguous. Accordingly, there will be a danger of fallacious inference involving "is" if its different senses are not kept separate from each other.

The following type of example goes back all the way to Aristotle.

1. Socrates is not Plato.

2. Plato is a man.

3. Therefore Socrates is not a man.

One way of explaining the fallacy of statements 1–3 is to say that in statement 1 "is" is an "is" of identity, whereas in statements 2 and 3 it is an "is" of predication. Hence, this attempted inference is fallacious.

The claim that the English word "is" is ambiguous has to be taken with a caution, however, for there may be other ways of dealing with those fallacious arguments which, like the one we just discussed, are normally blamed on the alleged ambiguity of "is."

△▼ EXERCISE 20-E

▶ Represent the argument above in the logical notation explained in Chapter 14 and show that statement 3 does not follow logically from statements 1 and 2.

Ambiguities Created by Historical Changes in Usage

A kind of ambiguity can come about when a word changes its meaning in the course of history. Sometimes it can be hard to tell which meaning is intended, and sometimes contemporary readers may even be unaware of the earlier meaning.

We have noted, for example, in Chapter 13 (Section 13.4) that the phrase *ad hominem* has changed in use since the time of John Locke. If we were to use today's meaning in trying to understand Locke's, we would miss his point.

In another instance, "conscious" originally meant what its Latin root literally means, namely, "sharing knowledge." If you did not know that, you might very well be puzzled by some relatively recent uses of the word. In Jane Austen's novel *Northanger Abbey* (Ch. 30), Henry Tilney is introduced to Mrs. Morland "by her conscious daughter." Does Jane Austen mean that the daughter was not asleep or in a coma? Of course not. But what is the meaning then? It is precisely the old meaning. As one scholar explains the situation: "She was *conscious* in exactly the classical sense; knowing much which her mother did not know about Henry and her own relations to him, she was in a secret, shared knowledge with him" (C. S. Lewis, *Studies in Words* [New York: Cambridge University Press, 1961], p. 186).

Much of what can be said about "conscious" can also be said of "conscience." What it originally meant was simply one's awareness, knowledge shared with oneself, of one's own moral mistakes. Only later did the word come to refer to an internal source of moral advice.

△ ▼ EXERCISE 20-F

1. Do further research on the meaning of "conscience" (or of the corresponding verb) in the New Testament, including 1 Cor. 1:4; 1 Tim. 1:5, 29; Acts 23:1; 1 Cor. 8:7; I Pet. 2:19. (Suggestion: In the book by C. S. Lewis just referred to, see the chapter "Conscience and Conscious," or consult a dictionary of biblical usage.)

2. Using dictionaries, formulate an explanation of what the word "classical" means in present-day usage. Then compare that meaning with what "classical" or its Latin counterpart meant in the earliest known occurrence wherein a young writer is told to emulate authors who are "classical, not proletarian." Note the relation between "classical" and "class" and consider the different meanings of "class." (Suggestion: Use for ideas information in Harry Levin's *Contexts of Criticism* [Cambridge: Harvard University Press, 1957], the chapter "Contexts of the Classical.")

Definitions

By defining a word in an appropriate way, we can often eliminate ambiguity and vagueness. For the definition must apply to only one of the meanings of an ambiguous word, and a good definition will attempt to provide clear criteria for use of a word which threatens vagueness in a given context. As we have noted, the words used in discussing argumentation and inquiry can be understood in several ways. We do not need to declare certain uses mistaken, but we do need to be clear about how these words are used in discussing the analysis, construction, and evaluation of arguments.

Structural Ambiguities

Ambiguity and definition can relate to problems that go beyond the uses of single words. Sometimes a whole statement admits of more than one meaning even though it does not contain any single ambiguous word. Such sentence-level ambiguity is sometimes called *amphiboly*. Sometimes it is due to the structure of the statement in question. Such structural ambiguities, as they may be called, are often quite subtle and hard to explain. One reason is that structural ambiguities cannot be resolved by giving a correct definition of some one word. It is instead necessary to find ways of discussing the possible uses of the whole statement.

Consider an example of structural ambiguity: The following sentence can be taken in two ways even though it is not easy to see why:

Mary is not the only woman who loves her husband.

△ ▼ EXERCISE 20-G

Express the two readings of this sentence about Mary in our logical notation. (Use the representations Wx for "x is a woman," Hxy for "x is y's husband," Lxy for "x loves y," and m for "Mary." Here's a little help to get you started: One of the readings is

$$-\forall x\ \forall y\ \{[(Hxm\ \&\ Wy)\ \&\ Lyx] \supset y = m\}$$

▸ What is the other reading?

20.3 Dictionaries and Ostensive Definitions

How can one define a word or a phrase? How can one explain to another person what one means by a word? As we have seen, there are many different ways of explaining the meaning of an expression, and the interrogative model gives us a general method for providing definitions.

Here we focus our attention on defining new or foreign words. When you are in doubt as to precisely what a word means, one thing you can do is to look it up in a dictionary. However, you have to know a lot of meanings before you can consult a dictionary successfully, for in a usual English dictionary English words are explained by means of other English words. If you are trying to explain the meaning of an English word to a foreigner, you could use a bilingual dictionary. It sometimes gives you the translation of the English word to the foreigner's own tongue. But the foreigner understands the translation only because he or she already knows that language.

There are in fact a bewildering variety of explanations of meaning. You can even try to explain what a new dance step or gymnastics movement is by performing it. Such an explanation of meaning can be considered an instance of what are called *ostensive* definitions. In general, an ostensive definition consists in presenting an instance of what is being defined. To define "red" you might point at something bright red and say, "That is red!"

Ostensive definitions can be effective tools in teaching other people meanings of new words, but they are not without their problems. For instance, suppose I am trying to teach you a word of Finnish and point, for the purpose, to a table on which there are three round blue plates. What is the word supposed to be used for? Does it mean the same as "blue," "round," "three," "plate," "object," or perhaps even "table"?

Furthermore, even if you can resolve that problem, you will face further ones. What happens when you define, for instance, a color word, say, "punainen," ostensively? You are in effect saying: "A color like this or sufficiently similar is called 'punainen.' " But how do you know what counts as sufficiently similar (and similar in what respect)? For instance, if someone teaches you ostensively the meaning of the actual Finnish color word "punainen" by pointing to a red object, you might go away thinking that "red" and "punainen" mean the same. Yes, they do, but only roughly, for "punainen" applies also to pink objects.

20.4 Definitions as a Tool of Inquiry

Earlier we saw that questions can play a double role in an argument or inquiry. Often the aim of the inquiry is to answer a principal question, and the means of doing so involves answers to smaller, or operational, questions.

Somewhat in the same way, definitions can play a double role in an argument or inquiry. We have seen that an inquiry can aim at a definition. But definitions can also serve as tools in an interrogative argument and can become important steps in an interrogative inquiry. Definitions are in fact commonly introduced into various kinds of serious arguments such as those found in legal, scientific, and mathematical contexts. Such introductions of definitions into an interrogative inquiry can be called *defining moves*.

Defining moves must satisfy certain conditions. First, in order not to create unnecessary uncertainties, the definition must specify completely and explicitly when the defined word applies and when it does not. Such definitions are called *explicit definitions*. What they look like in logical detail will be explained in the next section.

Second, because only answers by an oracle are allowed to introduce new information into an argument, defining moves must not do this. Philosophers sometimes express this requirement by saying that a definition must not be "creative." The consequences of this requirement depend on whether the word to be defined already occurs in the argument or whether it is a new word.

If the word to be defined already occurs in the argument, we are entitled to introduce a definition for it only if this definition is seen to follow from what we know, that is, if the definition can be established through interrogative inquiry based on the preceding lines. If it can be thus established, there is no new rule needed to justify the definition's introduction.

If the word or other symbol to be defined is a new one in the inquiry, we can introduce an explicit definition for it without running the risk of smuggling new information into the argument. But to be entitled to do so, we need a new rule for our interrogative games.

Rule for Defining Moves: At any stage of an interrogative game, the inquirer may choose to make a *defining move.* A defining move consists in adding an explicit definition of a new word or symbol to the left side of the game table.

Why is it useful for the inquirer sometimes to make a defining move? A partial answer is that such a move helps to simplify the statements that are made in the course of an inquiry. This can in turn make it easier to discover good arguments. For example, recall the case of the "Barber of Shave-ville" in Chapters 1 and 14. Formally, in that argument we are talking about an individual x who satisfies the condition

$\exists x \, \forall y \, [xSy \leftrightarrow -(ySy)]$ (xSy is to be read "x shaves y".)

It is helpful, however, for thinking through the problem in English to introduce a name, "the Village Barber," for this rather complicated person x. The name helps us to fix our thoughts more firmly and to think of useful questions to ask, such as whether the Village Barber shaves himself.

20.5   An Advanced, Logical Account of Definitions and Definability

So far we have discussed how statements are established through interrogative inquiry and how new statements, in the form of answers to the inquirer's questions, contribute to an inquiry. In this section, we shall discuss in greater detail how concepts are "established" in the sense of being defined or identified through interrogative inquiry. Remember that in Chapter 18 (Section 18.3) we defined *concept* as "a particular way of organizing our thoughts about something. A concept organizes our various thoughts about the qualities and relations that may characterize an object."

Explicit Definitions

We will now examine the interrogative method of giving definitions in more technical detail. In doing so, it will be useful to recall the symbol introduced in Chapter 14 (Section 14.6), the biconditional sign $\leftrightarrow$, read as "if and only if." A kind of shorthand notation, it enables $A \leftrightarrow B$ to say the same as $(A \supset B) \, \& \, (B \supset A)$.

For the purpose of understanding what definitions are all about, we can then ask: What is the best possible type of definition? To make our ideas clear, let us assume that we are trying to define a new symbol, for instance, a one-place predicate letter P, in terms of other known symbols. This is done by telling to which individuals P applies or does not apply, using a statement of the following form:

Def: $\forall x\ (Px \leftrightarrow D[x])$

Here $D[x]$ is an expression, usually a complex one, which satisfies the following conditions:

1. P must not occur in $D[x]$.
2. $D[x]$ must not contain any other variables than x.

The reasons for these requirements are as follows. If P occurred in $D[x]$, the attempted definition would be circular: P would be defined by reference to P. If condition 2 were not satisfied, there would be another variable, say y, in $D[x] = D[x,y]$. Then the attempted definition would not tell whether P really applies to a given individual b. All that the definition would say about whether P applies to b is

$Pb \leftrightarrow D[b,y]$

But this does not convey any definite information, for the right-hand side depends on the unknown individual y.

If the definition satisfies the conditions 1 and 2, then it is said to be an explicit definition of P in terms of the concepts (symbols, words) which occur in $D[x]$. In the definition, P is called the *definiendum* and $D[x]$ the *definiens*.

Closely similar things can be said of the definitions of other kinds of symbols, for example, names and relation symbols. For instance, the explicit definition of a two-place relation Rxy on the basis of $T[R]$ is of the form

$\forall x \forall y\ (Rxy \leftrightarrow D[x,y])$

where $D[x,y]$ satisfies the same conditions:

1. R must not occur in $D[x,y]$.
2. $D[x,y]$ must not contain any variables other than x and y.

The explicit definition of a name b is of the form

$\forall x\ (b=x \leftrightarrow D[x])$

where $D[x]$ satisfies the conditions we have already mentioned and also satisfies the condition that the following can be established through interrogative inquiry:

$\forall x \forall y\ (D[x]\ \&\ D[y] \supset x=y)$

Definitions and the Availability of Answers

You will recall from Chapter 19 that the oracle's answers often are restricted according to their logical complexity. One possible form of such restrictions is the atomistic assumption, which restricts available answers to quantifier-free statements. What happens to such restrictions when an explicit definition is introduced? Consider

Def: $\forall x \, (Px \leftrightarrow D[x])$

In this definition P is a new one-place predicate symbol and $D[x]$ is an expression, usually a complex one, which does not contain P or any free individual variables other than x.

If the same rules are used as before, the definition may in important ways change the prospects of an interrogative inquiry. For instance, suppose that $D[x]$ is a complex formula such that answers of the form $D[b]$ or $-D[b]$ were not available to the inquirer, because only atomic sentences and their negations are available under the atomistic assumption. After the introduction of the explicit definition, answers of the form Pb or $-Pb$ *will be* available. But because such answers are equivalent to answers of the form $D[b]$ or $-D[b]$, this latter class of answers has now been made available by the definition.

Hence, a defining move must be carefully scrutinized to see whether important preconditions for it have been satisfied. For even though such a definition does not introduce new information directly, it may do so indirectly, by making new answers available that were not available before the definition. Such a defining move will be admissible only if the inquirer has in fact managed to make the newly available questions answerable.

Such a defining move may be the indication that the inquirer has accomplished a change in his or her answer-extracting methods. In the case of a natural scientist, this may for instance mean that she or he has improved on the experimental or observational techniques.

Using an old pair of philosophical terms in a partly new sense, we may say that when a definition in a defining move does not make new answers available under the rules of the game, the definition is a *nominal definition*. When, however, a definition does extend the range of answerable questions under the rules of the game, then it might be called a *real definition*. A real definition is only justified when an extension of the class of available answers has in fact taken place in the inquiry.

Explicit Definitions in Real Life

Many definitions one encounters in real life can be expressed in roughly the same form as we have been examining. For instance, many legal definitions are of this kind.

Examples of Legal Definitions

Murder: Criminal homicide constitutes murder when

a. it is committed purposely or knowingly; or

b. it is committed recklessly under circumstances manifesting extreme indifference to the value of human life.

This definition of murder can be thought of as saying the same as the following statement:

For any act x, x is an instance of murder if and only if x is a criminal homicide, x is committed purposely or knowingly, and x is committed recklessly in circumstances manifesting extreme indifference to the value of human life.

So expressed, this definition is seen to be of the form of an explicit definition. The following definitions can likewise be brought into the same form:

Burglary: A person is guilty of burglary if he enters a building or occupied structure, or separately secured or occupied portion thereof, with purpose to commit a crime therein, unless the premises are at the time open to the public or the actor is licensed or privileged to enter.

Citizen: One who, under the Constitution and laws of the United States, or of a particular state, is a member of the political community, owing allegiance and being entitled to the enjoyment of full civil rights.

Agent: A person authorized by another to act for him, one interested with another's business.

Rape: Unlawful sexual intercourse with a female without her consent.

Notice that these legal definitions are like logical ones in that precise and careful formulation is required if they are to serve their purpose without causing unnecessary confusion. Note also that definitions can form chains in the same way as inferences may in interrogative inquiry. For instance, in the definition of rape, the word "consent" is to be taken in its legal meaning, not in its everyday sense of saying "yes." In the legal meaning, the person giving his or her consent to something must be legally capable of doing so. For example, to give consent in the legal sense the person must be of a sufficient age as defined under the law.

More Examples If the intended values of our variables are natural numbers 1,2,3, . . . , then the definitions of odd number (Ox) and even number (Ex) can be expressed in the form we have been examining as follows:

$$\forall x \; [Ox \leftrightarrow -\exists y \; (x = 2y)]$$
$$\forall x \; [Ex \leftrightarrow \exists y \; (x = 2y)]$$

△▼ EXERCISE 20-H

1. Express in the form we have been discussing the legal definitions we have given above. You might go on to define the following concepts: first-degree murder; homicide; libel; statutory rape. Use dictionaries, encyclopedias, legal handbooks, and so forth.

▶ 2. Define the following arithmetical concepts (for natural numbers): x is a prime (i.e., indivisible) number; x is a power of some number.

When Is a Concept Definable?

Some of the most important questions concerning definitions still remain to be asked. They concern the definability of a concept occurring in the initial premises of an inquiry. One of them is the following: When is such a concept definable? We can now sharpen this question and ask: When does a symbol, say, a one-place predicate P, admit of an explicit definition of the form we have been examining?

   We restrict our attention to concepts occurring in the initial premises because we cannot hope to define P without knowing something about it. We have to know something about how it is related to the other concepts in terms of which it is to be defined. Let us suppose that this knowledge is summed up in an assumption (or a set of assumptions) T. (Because T must contain P, we might write it also as $T[P]$.) Then the question whether P is explicitly definable in terms of the other symbols of T on the basis of T assumes an interesting form. What is being asked is: Does an explicit definition of the form we have discussed (satisfying, of course, conditions 1 and 2) follow logically from T? If the answer is yes, we shall say that P is *explicitly definable on the basis of* T.

   The reason why this approach to definability is useful is that it enables us to use the logical tools explained in Part 2 and in Chapter 14 for the purpose of testing questions of explicit definability.

Example Consider the following theory T:

$[\forall x\ (Px \leftrightarrow Qx) \vee \forall x\ (Px \leftrightarrow -Qx)]\ \&\ \exists\ (Px\ \&\ -Qx)$

Then P is definable in terms of Q, in that the following is a valid consequence of T: $\forall x\ (Px \leftrightarrow -Qx)$

△▼ EXERCISE 20-I

Consider what you know about different family relationships. On the basis of that knowledge, which is like a theory T, you can work out all kinds of definitions. We will not try to write out the theory explicitly, but we can use what we need from it. In doing so, we might use the following abbreviations:

$Mx = x$ is male; $Lx = x$ is female

$Hxy = x$ is y's husband; $Wxy = x$ is y's wife

$Pxy = x$ is a parent of y

$Fxy = x$ is y's father; $Oxy = x$ is y's mother

$Cxy = x$ is y's child; $Sxy = x$ is y's son; $Dxy = x$ is y's daughter

$Gxy = x$ is y's grandparent

$Bxy = x$ and y are siblings; $Uxy = x$ and y are cousins

$Rxy = x$ and y are married to each other

   You can define many of these concepts in terms of others in the form we have been using, for instance

$\forall x\ \forall y\ [Sxy \leftrightarrow (Pyx\ \&\ Mx)]$

$\forall x\ \forall y\ (Cxy \leftrightarrow Pyx)$

$\forall x\ \forall y\ [Bxy \leftrightarrow \exists z\ \exists u\ (z \neq u\ \&\ x \neq y\ \&\ Pzx\ \&\ Pzy\ \&\ Pux\ \&\ Puy)]$

▶ 1. Try to define *G* in terms of *P*. Try to define *H* and *W* in terms of *R* and *M* and *L*.

▶ 2. Show that all the other terms listed, except for *M*, *L*, *H*, *W*, and *R*, can be defined by means of any of the following pairs of terms:

    a. *P* and *M*
    b. *P* and *L*
    c. *C* and *M*
    d. *C* and *L*
    e. *P* and *S*
    f. *C* and *D*

△▼ EXERCISE 20-J

Show the following: Assume (1) that a one-place predicate *P* can be defined on the basis of a theory *T*[*P*] by using a number of concepts which do not include *P* or *Q*. Assume also that (2) *Q* can be defined in terms of the same concepts plus *P*. Then *Q* can be defined on the basis of *T*[*P*] in terms of the same concepts as *P*.

    The result stated in this exercise enables us to build chains of definitions. You can start from a set *S* of concepts, and define *P* in terms of the members of *S*. Then whatever you define in terms of the members of *S* plus *P* could also have been defined in terms of the members of *S* directly. In other words, chains of definitions preserve definability in terms of the given initial concepts.

    So far we have given you only examples of concepts that are definable in terms of others. But what would be an interesting example of a concept that is not definable in terms of certain related ones?

    Consider the following: Think of the family relationships mentioned in the exercise above. You can define a grandparent in terms of the relation *P* of parenthood. An individual *x* is a grandparent of *y* if and only if there is *z* such that *Pxz* and *Pzy*. Formally this can be written as

$$\forall x \forall y\ [Gxy \leftrightarrow \exists z\ (Pxz\ \&\ Pzy)]$$

    But can you define the general concept of *ancestor* in the same way? By "the same way" we mean without being forced to use the concept of number. The answer is that you cannot define the general concept of ancestor in this way.

    The problem is that you would have to say that there must be some natural number k and individuals $z_1, z_2, \ldots z_k$, such that *x* is a parent of z_1, z_1 is a parent of z_2, z_2 is a parent of z_3, and so on up to z_k, who has to be a parent of *y*. It can be shown that the definition of ancestor cannot be made in the kind of logic you have learned in this book without using the concept of number unless there is an upper bound to k.

Implicit Definability

Suppose you are given a theory *T*[*P*] and asked to find out whether *P* is definable on the basis of *T*[*P*] in terms of its other concepts. If you consider what you are asked to do, you will find that you are at a disadvantage in that the notion of explicit definability does not tell you *what* the explicit definition in proper form might be. By means of the techniques you learned in Part 2 and in Chapter 14, you can only examine whether a given proposed explicit definition really follows from T or not. You cannot by means of these techniques look for an explicit definition or try to establish whether there is one.

We can say more than this, however. Let us note, first, that apparently explicit definability is not the only game in town. For, if we know T, we may very well ask whether it perhaps determines the interpretation of P as soon as the interpretation of all the other symbols of T is fixed, even if no explicit definition is a valid consequence of T.

But how can we understand this idea of "determining the interpretation of P"? The basic idea is clear: Let us express T also as $T[P]$ and let $T[Q]$ be the statement (or set of statements) obtainable from $T[P]$ by replacing P everywhere by a new one-place predicate Q. Then, if $T[P]$ determines the interpretation of P, $T[Q]$ will likewise determine the interpretation of Q, and *in the same way*. Hence, if $T[P]$ and $T[Q]$ are both assumed, they must have as a valid logical consequence

$$\forall x\ (Px \leftrightarrow Qx)$$

If this is the case, then P is said to be *implicitly definable* on the basis of $T[P]$. (A word of warning: The term "implicitly defined" is often used in other ways, too, by philosophers.)

Beth's Theorem

But now we seem to have confused the situation seriously. We seem to have two different kinds of definability on our hands—explicit definability and implicit definability. Which is the right one? How are they related to each other? Fortunately, the ghost of an eminent Dutch logician and philosopher, E. W. Beth, rushes to our rescue. For Beth established the remarkable result that *implicit and explicit definability coincide*.

We are not in a position to prove this subtle and important result here. It is easily seen that explicit definability entails implicit definability, but the converse relation is far from obvious. This result is known as Beth's Theorem. One reason the theorem is important is that it helps to extend the use of the techniques of deductive logic to questions of definability.

For instance, suppose that you are given a theory $T[P]$ and asked whether P is definable in terms of the other predicates and names. What can you do? Apparently very little. For you do not usually know what the definiens $D[x]$ is or might be. Therefore, you cannot use the logical techniques you have learned to derive the explicit definition from $T[P]$.

Here Beth's Theorem (and its proof, which we have not given to you here) helps crucially. For what you can do is to try to derive logically

1. $\forall x\ (Px \leftrightarrow Qx)$

using as the only initial premise the conjunction

2. $T[P]$ & $T[Q]$

This is the kind of task you learned to do in Part 2 and Chapter 14. It can be done by trying to construct a closed logical table which begins with statement 2 on the left side and statement 1 on the right side.

Such a table construction can yield other information. For instance, suppose that you have successfully derived statement 1 from statement 2 deductively. It can then be shown (we will not try to prove it here) that on the basis of this argument one can actually find the definiens $D[x]$ for an explicit definition of P on the basis of $T[P]$—in other words, find an explicit definition of P.

Thus Beth's Theorem shows how the techniques of logical inference can be used not only in testing proposed explicit definitions but also in looking for them.

Padua's Method

A logical proof of statement 1 from statement 2 can be viewed in a different light as well. In Chapter 14 we learned that sometimes a logical table construction produces an actual counterexample to the alleged logical consequence relation. In the present case of a table construction starting from statements 1 and 2, such a counterexample would be one in which all the other symbols in $T[P]$ except for P have a fixed interpretation, but in which P and Q have different interpretations, even though they both are related to the other concepts in the same way, that is, in the way $T[P]$ prescribes. Such a counterexample is a vivid way of showing that the interpretation of the other symbols of $T[P]$ does not determine the interpretation of P. This is usually expressed by saying that P is *independent* of the other concepts. Showing independence by constructing a counterexample in which P and Q have different interpretations is known as Padua's Method. Beth's Theorem shows that independence can always be tested by trying to construct a logical table, one of whose products could be a Padua-type counterexample. In the light of what was said in Chapter 17 (Section 17.5) about argumentation as attempted "world construction," this means that independence can be proved by constructing through logical inference a Padua-type counterexample to definability.

△ ▼ EXERCISE 20-K

▶ Show by Padua's Method that one cannot define "niece" and "nephew" in the sole terms of "parent" and "sibling."

Identifiability

At this point an interesting perspective is opened to us. Earlier we saw that logical proofs (deductive arguments) are merely a special case of interrogative arguments.

Now that we have seen how we can try to find explicit definitions by means of logical inferences (deductive arguments), is there perhaps a similarly wider notion of definability, related to interrogative argumentation in the same way as explicit definability is related to deductive argumentation?

The answer is that indeed such notion does exist. It is called *identifiability*. Identifiability in fact plays an important role in many actual sciences, including statistics, econometrics, and systems theory.

Identifiability differs from definability in one respect: It is relative to that particular scenario (world, or model, situation) to which oracles' answers pertain. But otherwise the analogy is very close. In fact we can define counterparts to explicit and implicit definability for this new notion.

A one-place predicate P is *explicitly identifiable* in M on the basis of $T[P]$ if and only if a statement of the following form can be derived interrogatively from $T[P]$ in M:

$$\forall x \ (Px \leftrightarrow D[x, a_1, a_2, \ldots, a_k]$$

Here $D[x, a_1, a_2, \ldots, a_k]$ satisfies the same conditions 1 and 2 as $D[x]$ in our definition formula, and $a_1, a_2, \ldots, a_k$ are proper names of individuals in M.

Example

Let $T = [\forall x \ (Px \leftrightarrow Rx) \lor \forall x \ (Px \leftrightarrow -Rx)] \ \& \ Pb$

Let us also assume that the oracle will tell the inquirer whether Rb or $-Rb$. Assume, for the sake of argument, that the oracle would give the latter answer, $-Rb$. Then

$$(*) \ \forall x \ (Px \leftrightarrow -Rx)$$

is derivable by means of an interrogative argument from T. In other words, P is identifiable in M on the basis of T.

△▼ EXERCISE 20-L

▶ 1. Construct the interrogative argument which leads from T and the answer $-Rb$ to $(*)$. What would the result be if the oracle gave the answer Rb?

▶ 2. Show that P is not definable on the basis of T.

Example Let us assume that we have a genealogical "theory," $T[C]$, which says that any descendant of a member of the clan C is always a member of the clan. If D is the relation of being a descendant, then this can be expressed formally as

$$\forall x \forall y \ [(Dxy \ \& \ Cy) \supset Cx]$$

This "theory" alone will not enable us to define membership in the clan C, not even jointly with some suitable "theory" of family memberships.

Assume, however, that in fact there is a founder f of the clan, in the sense that the clan members are all his or her descendants. If the oracle answers a sufficient number of questions, membership in the clan may very well be identifiable (in the actual world). The identifying formula will then be

$$\forall x\ (Cx \leftrightarrow Dxf)$$

△▼ EXERCISE 20-M

▸ What are the simplest questions our oracle would have to answer in order for us to be able to derive this identifying formula from the given theory?

Example Let the theory T consist of some suitable set of arithmetical truths plus the following equations:

$$\forall x\ \forall y\ (ax + by = 1)$$
$$\forall x\ \forall y\ (cx + dy = 1)$$

Then a, b, c, d are not identifiable on the basis of T unless $a = c$, $b = d$. If these equalities do hold, our two equations coincide. Let x_1, y_1 and x_2, y_2 be two different pairs of values (individuals) satisfying

$$ax_1 + by_1 = 1$$
$$ax_2 + by_2 = 1$$

where $x_1 \neq x_2$, $y_1 \neq y_2$.

By solving this pair of equations with respect to a and b we can show that they are identifiable in the domain of real numbers on the basis of T.

This example shows you how identifiability problems can come up in actual science. The theory T of our example might be a simple economic "model" (theory) where x and y are variables like the price of a certain commodity and the quantity of it. In such a theory, $a, b, c,$ and d are unknown parameters which have to be determined from observations. But no economist can determine them unless they are identifiable by means of actually observed pairs of corresponding values of x and y.

Implicit Identifiability

In analogy with implicit definability we can define a kind of implicit identifiability. In this sense, P is implicitly identifiable in M on the basis of $T[P]$ if and only if one can interrogatively derive from $T[P]$ & $T[Q]$ in M the following statement:

$$\forall x\ (Px \leftrightarrow Qx)$$

where Q and $T[Q]$ are as before: Q is a new one-place predicate and $T[Q]$ is like $T[P]$ except that Q replaces P.

Beth's Theorem can be extended to identifiability in the sense that implicit identifiability, in the sense explained, can be shown to coincide with explicit identifiability.

Identifiability and "Wh-" Questions

In Chapter 10 (Section 10.6), we saw that interrogative inquiry means answering a "big" (i.e., principal) question by means of a number of answers to "small" (i.e., operational) questions. It was explained how yes/no questions can be answered in that way. However, it was not explained how one might find an answer to a "wh-" question by means of interrogative inquiry. Now we are in a position to see how principal "wh-" questions can be handled.

Suppose we are given a principal premise $T[P]$ and ask the question: Who or what are all the individuals x such that Px? Clearly an answer to this principal question would have to be an identification of P on the basis of $T[P]$. But how can we find out if P is identifiable? And how can we find out how P can be identified?

The answer is obviously given by the definiens of P. But how is the definiens found? This question is the same as: How can one look for the identification formula, which is of the form

(∗) $\forall x\ (Px \leftrightarrow D[x, a_1, a_2, \ldots, a_k])$

where $D[x, a_1, a_2, \ldots, a_k]$ is the definiens.

Our extension of Beth's Theorem yields an answer to the first of our questions. In order to try to decide whether or not P is identifiable on the basis of $T[P]$ we can try to derive interrogatively

$\forall x\ (Px \leftrightarrow Qx)$

from $T[P]$ & $T[Q]$, where $T[P]$ is the given initial premise and Q is a new one-place predicate.

Thus the theory of identifiability occupies a central position in the entire theory and practice of interrogative inquiry. It shows how "wh-" questions can be answered by means of interrogative inquiry. In other words, it shows how we can finally pose principal "wh-" questions and try to answer them by means of interrogative and logical inference moves.

Conclusion

.21

Argument Analysis
and Evaluation

In this concluding chapter we sum up the techniques you have learned in this book for argument analysis and evaluation.

21.1 Principles of Argument Analysis

Our guiding model for understanding argument and reasoning has been the interrogative model. Our rules and methods have involved the interrogative tables with which you have by now become so very well acquainted. But, as you have discovered, when working with your own and other people's arguments, you will rarely find them set out in table form. They will also, like most everyday arguments, not mention certain "obvious" steps that are nevertheless involved in a successful argument. These omitted steps must be made explicit when the argument is analyzed in table form.

The job of argument analysis involves finding ways to put your own and other people's arguments into the interrogative table form. In other words, we can approach any argument given to us by trying to distinguish what the initial premises are, what the ultimate conclusion is, what the interrogative moves are, and what the logical inference moves are. We may not need to get every last detail into precise interrogative form, but the goal is to analyze arguments by distinguishing their various parts. With this in mind we can provide a list of questions to ask ourselves as we begin to separate an argument into its parts:

A1. **What is the ultimate conclusion the inquiry is trying to establish?** What kind of *principal question* is the inquiry trying to answer? Is it trying to establish a single predetermined conclusion C or to answer a question such as "B or not-B"?

A2. **What are the explicit initial premises of the inquiry?** Notice that only explicitly formulated statements count as initial premises. Other kinds of background information that may be needed but unstated will be handled in terms of interrogative moves, that is, as information brought in by putting questions to one's sources of tacit, background information.

A2.1. At which steps, if any, has the inquirer questioned (by means of bracketing) the reliability of any of the initial information?

A2.2. Has the inquirer noted how bracketing of any suspect initial premise information would affect later lines?

A2.3. Does the inquirer discuss how to restore confidence in any initial premise information that has been called into question?

A3. **What are the steps of the inquiry?** Usually it is not a difficult task to recognize the ultimate conclusion of a real-life inquiry. The key, initial premises are also likely to be reasonably easy to spot. We have discovered, however, that some important steps in an inquiry are likely to involve answers to questions addressed to one's background knowledge. These are often not explicitly stated as initial premises.

A difficulty, then, in trying to understand a line of inquiry lies in identifying the different steps of the argument. Your experiences in dealing with examples and exercises in this book will have helped you appreciate the nature of this difficulty. In almost every simple inquiry you have encountered, an apparently simple argument has turned out to involve a surprisingly large number of steps, many of which were left unspoken in the verbal or written formulation of the argument.

For instance, when Sherlock Holmes's line of reasoning in "The Curious Incident of the Dog in the Night-time" was converted into table form in Chapter 14, it was seen to involve a surprising number of steps.

It is important to realize that the task of spelling out the tacit steps of an argument is not simply a textbook exercise. It is an important task because we cannot evaluate an argument without knowing what steps it actually involves. This is especially important with regard to the steps that are not explicitly spelled out in the written or verbal account of the argument.

For example, consider again the argument about the war on drugs analyzed in Chapter 3 (Section 3.4). The conclusion, if true, would have very important practical consequences for the allocation of funds to different aspects of the war on drugs. It is therefore important to be able to evaluate it. Is it really true that the major suppliers of drugs would not let their profits drop? Is it really true that the only source of extra money that addicts have is crime? Such questions are crucial for the evaluation of this argument. However, before the relevant steps are brought out into the open, these questions cannot be raised.

It lies in the nature of inquiry that we cannot always be sure what tacit steps the arguer took. For this reason, argument analysis and evaluation is not an exact science but requires creativity and empathy. We need to try to understand what the inquirer had in mind by putting ourselves mentally into the inquirer's own position.

Another way of stating the same point is this: When we look at an account of a real-life argument from the viewpoint of the interrogative model, our first impression is usually that the argument is full of holes. But most of the holes have been left in the argument intentionally. Evaluation of the argument depends on how the holes can be filled. In trying to fill in apparent gaps, you have several different possibilities to choose from. For instance, as we learned in Part 3, you have a choice of filling in more steps (interrogative and/or logical inference steps) or of supplying crucial information from a lower-level inquiry.

This makes a real difference. If you simply add steps into one and the same argument, you are operating with the same initial premises and the same ultimate conclusion. If, however, you are trying to fill the gap by means of a lower-level inquiry, then this lower-level argument has its own initial premises, conclusion, and perhaps even oracles, different from those involved in the higher-level inquiry.

This leads us to formulate a couple of further questions for argument analysis:

A3.1. Which steps of the argument should be understood as involving suppressed intermediate steps, and how can we make these suppressed steps explicit?

A3.2. At which points in the argument table does the inquirer seem to be relying on answers that come from a lower-level inquiry, and what must that lower-level inquiry look like?

It can be difficult in analysis to know how charitable to be to the inquiry we are analyzing. Certainly, we intend to find the more important suppressed steps and lower-level inquiries upon which the inquirer has depended. There is nothing wrong with an inquirer's skipping the simpler "obvious" steps and concentrating on the most important. But if too much is missing, we begin to suspect that the inquirer has also suppressed some of the essential steps. *If our attempt at analysis convinces us that some of the crucial moves have been suppressed, then our evaluation of the argument is likely to be negative.*

A4. **Which steps or moves are interrogative moves?** Notice that this question can only be raised after the argument has been divided into as many steps as are needed. For what looks like a single step in the original line of thought often turns out to involve several different steps, some of which can be interrogative steps and others logical inference steps. Hence, the original, undivided step cannot be called either an interrogative or a logical inference move. It is a mixture of both. For instance, when Sherlock Holmes in effect asked, "Who is it that a trained watchdog does not bark at in the middle of the night?" and answered, "Its master, the stable master," he was in reality asking two questions linked to each other by a logical inference step. (See Chapter 14, Section 14.11.)

A4.1. For each interrogative move, what is the precise question?

A4.2. Who or what is the "oracle" (source of information) to whom or to which the question is addressed?

It is especially important to try to identify the main source or sources of tacit information presupposed by the arguer. Often, of course, the interrogative steps involving tacit information will not be explicitly brought out in the everyday statement of the argument. Part of the job of analysis is to make the more important of these steps explicit.

Appeals to tacit knowledge are sometimes indicated by such phrases as "it is generally known that," "of course," "naturally," "clearly," "obviously," and so forth. You now know the importance of being alert to how this tacit information is coming into the inquiry and of subjecting the interrogative moves involved here to the same critical examination to which you subject other moves.

Interrogative moves are not always or even often indicated in everyday inquiries as questions. Still, as we have learned, it increases our insight to examine them as interrogative moves. For example, understanding the introduction of new information as an answer to an interrogative move explains the importance of references—parenthetical notes, footnotes, endnotes, and so on—in scientific and scholarly writing. These references identify the oracle to which the author is referring, and such references give the reader an opportunity to examine for himself or herself how reliable it may be. You are asked to provide such references in much of your academic work, and the reason is that you are being taught to become aware of the oracles you are using, to be more critical of them, and to allow others also to assess the reliability of your sources of information.

A4.3. What is the presupposition of the question, and where, if anywhere, in the inquiry has the presupposition been established?

A4.4. Is the answer to the question a partial or a conclusive (complete) answer, and what makes it partial or conclusive?

A4.5. At which steps, if any, has the inquirer called into question (by means of bracketing) the reliability of any of the answers to interrogative moves?

A4.6. Has the inquirer noted how bracketing of any suspect interrogative-move information would affect later lines?

A4.7. Does the inquirer discuss how to restore confidence in any interrogative moves that have been called into question?

A5. **Which moves are logical inference moves, and what rule(s) of logical inference justify them?** In trying to answer this question it is useful to keep in mind that what obviously is a logical inference step in a verbal argument typically is a sequence, sometimes a long one, of logical inference steps of the kind we studied in Part 2 and in Chapter 14. For many purposes, such inferential shortcuts do not have to be filled in, as long as their status as valid logical inferences can be defended when called into question.

For instance, in the Smith-Jones-Robinson puzzle in Chapter 5 you drew logical inferences which were not instances of the rules you later learned in Part 2 and in Chapter 14. Some elementary arithmetic was needed in the puzzle, but such mathematical reasoning involves logical inferences we have not discussed.

It may happen, however, that the validity of a purported logical inference is not obvious. To evaluate an argument containing such an attempted inference, you therefore have to find out whether the inference is in fact valid. To do this, you must split the inference up into a series of "smaller" inferences, each of which is sanctioned by an explicit rule of logical inference, for example, by one of the rules we have formulated or by the fundamental definition of validity.

In practice you will find that there are many more logical inferences than those we have discussed. Many of them depend on the meaning of different words or phrases. For instance, in the Smith-Jones-Robinson puzzle, you had to use rules that depended on the meaning of such English words and phrases as "precisely half the distance between," "precisely three times as much," "the nearest," and so forth.

Even when a rule is used that depends only on the meaning of the logical words we have studied, the inquirer may not be relying on the same basic set of rules as we have formulated. Nevertheless, if the rule is correct, it can be understood and employed in ways similar to what we have learned in our study of formal deductive logic. Thus one part of the task of argument analysis is to see how the logical inference rules the inquirer is explicitly or implicitly using can be shown to be valid—if they are valid.

A5.1. Which logical inference steps split the interrogative table into different branches? (For example, see the rules for "or" and "if-then" statements in Chapter 7.)

A5.2. At what stage of the inquiry is a particular path or subtable closed and by what rule? (For example, see Table Rules 7 and 8 in Chapter 7.)

In first-order predicate logic (quantification theory), more questions arise:

A5.3. In each step that involves quantifiers ("some" and "every"), what is the intended domain or universe of discourse? (In other words, which individuals are acceptable as values of the quantifiers?)

A5.4. What counts as the same individual? (In particular, what assumptions is the arguer making as to when individuals figuring in two different scenarios are the same or different?)

A5.5. Which moves introduce new individuals into the argument, and by what rule?

These various principles of argument analysis cannot be separated completely from the principles of argument evaluation, which we will discuss in a moment, but even at this stage we can note the following.

First, as we try to analyze some other person's inquiry and arguments (or our own!), we may discover so much confusion that we cannot begin to get the necessary basic answers to the analytical questions listed above. This is surely a sign that the inquiry has not gone well, and our evaluation of it will likely be very negative.

Furthermore, it frequently happens in everyday inquiry that some of the steps do not seem to be justified by any known rule. Does that mean the arguer made a mistake? Not always. Often the arguer is simply skipping some of the intermediate steps. Then the right attitude on our part, as we analyze the argument, will be to try to find the missing steps rather than too quickly give a negative evaluation of the inquirer's work.

△ ▼ EXERCISE 21-A

Appropriate arguments from Appendix A will be assigned for analysis.

21.2 Principles of Argument Evaluation: Correctness

The preceding rules are primarily concerned with argument analysis; they help us take apart an inquiry or argument into its various steps. Once an argument or inquiry has been analyzed, we are then in a position to evaluate how well it supports the ultimate conclusion.

Following are the key questions we need to ask ourselves as we evaluate an argument or line of inquiry.

E1. Has the argument table closed? If the table has not completely closed, then we know that the argument in its current state is unfinished. We are not likely to accept or be persuaded by an inquiry that has not in some way dealt with all the alternative paths it has opened up.

E2. **Have the logical inference moves been made correctly?** Here we begin from our basic knowledge of the definitory rules for logical inference moves and check to see whether the logical inferences made in the inquiry are indeed truth-preserving. We have already noted several times that there are many more ways in which legitimate logical inference moves may be made than those we studied in Part 2 and in Chapter 14. Nevertheless, our study of the fundamental idea of logical inference gives us a basis for checking most common logical inferences for correctness. If mistakes have been made, they would have to be corrected, and this may make it no longer possible to bring the inquiry to successful closure.

E3. **Have the interrogative moves been made correctly?** Here we work from our knowledge of the definitory rules for interrogative moves. We check to see whether the appropriate presuppositions were available for the questions. We make sure that we have some idea what oracles are being used as the sources for answers. We note how the inquirer has handled problems with uncertainty in the answers. Have the bracketing and unbracketing of answers (and premises) been handled correctly? Have reasonable attempts been made to discover possible inconsistencies in the information that has been accepted into the left side of the interrogative table for the inquiry?

△ ▼ EXERCISE 21-B

Return to your analyses of the arguments in Exercise 21-A, and evaluate these for validity and correctness of moves.

21.3 Principles of Argument Evaluation: Excellence

At this point our approach to evaluating inquiries begins to cross the line from evaluating for correctness on the basis of definitory rules to evaluating for excellence on the basis of strategic rules. From the beginning we have noted that there is more to inquiry than correctly following definitory rules. There is an art to reasoning well that cannot be captured by mechanical rules. In this section we touch on some of the features of argument evaluation that are involved in achieving excellence.

E4. **How is the problem of uncertainty of premises and answers handled in the inquiry?** Definitory rules tell us how to bracket suspect lines, but determining the reliability of a given piece or source of information is a difficult matter. We might check whether appropriate strategies have been used for dealing with suspected random and systematic errors. Have lower-level inquiries been used to support suspect moves in the main inquiry? Have strategies for evaluating oracles been employed? If an inquiry involves a large number of uncertain answers (or premises), then (other things being equal) it is less reliable than an argument involving few uncertain answers.

E5. **If our evaluation of the inquiry has exposed weaknesses in it, can we find strategies for improving it and will it be worth further effort to improve it?** The answer to this type of question will depend on how many and what kinds of weaknesses we have found. If there are problems with the logical inference moves, attending to these may be relatively easy or nearly impossible on the basis of the available materials in the argument. If there are problems with the interrogative moves, again they may be more or less easy to remedy. The same goes for problems with uncertain answers and premises.

We have noted that there are often gaps in a typical argument. If the original inquirer has not indicated how to fill the gaps, are we in a position to do that for him or her? Are we willing to? An amusing example of the concerns here is provided by the story of a famous mathematician who said in presenting a difficult mathematical paper, "Now it obviously follows that so-and-so." But then he stopped, hesitated, asked aloud, "Well, is it really obvious?" Then he stood and thought for a while, rushed out of the lecture room, came back ten minutes later and said, beaming, "Yes, it is obvious!"

The decision about whether further work on the inquiry will be worthwhile also depends on our own goals and purposes. How important is the subject of the inquiry to us? How much time and other resources can we afford to devote to improving the arguments? Can we see how a more appropriate strategy might make for success where the current inquiry failed? For example, could strategic insights from Chapters 17 and 18 be of help? The important point to notice is that these are the sorts of questions that need asking when we are seriously concerned about evaluating arguments and inquiries.

E6. **Is it possible and useful to move beyond the conclusions of a (successful) inquiry and would we criticize the inquirer for having failed to go further?** Here we are asking whether the inquirer has made the most effective moves, either logical inference or interrogative moves. Could a stronger, more informative conclusion have been established? Was the oracle prepared to answer some questions that the inquirer simply failed to ask? Should the inquirer have tried to learn more about what the oracles and logical inferences could have told him or her?

E7. **Could the argument have been made shorter, less confusing, more concise, or more economical?** In some cases we might think that the inquiry has been successful but that it could have been accomplished in a more efficient or straightforward way. The considerations taken up here are partly practical. Usually, a simpler, more direct argument helps us do a better job of teaching or persuading others. Perhaps more powerful use of questions rather than logical inferences could have brought us to the conclusion more simply. Perhaps some of the material brought out in the argument was not really needed.

But here we also begin to consider matters which may have to do with what we call style and cleverness. Sometimes we are interested not simply in a solution to our puzzles and principal questions but in an "elegant" solution. It is possible to evaluate arguments on these grounds as well. Perhaps such considerations indicate as well as motivate increasing interest in how the inquirer's mind works.

△ ▼ EXERCISE 21-C

Return to your analyses and evaluations of the arguments in Exercises 21-A and 21-B, and evaluate these arguments for excellence.

△ ▼ THINK ABOUT IT

The German mathematician Georg Cantor (1845–1918), founder of set theory, once said that elegance is a concern of tailors and shoemakers, not of mathematicians. What do you think he meant by this statement? Do you think he was right?

General Comment It may not be accidental that these principles of argument analysis and evaluation are naturally formulated as questions. Some scholars have in fact tried to interpret the very process of reading as a kind of dialogue between the reader and the text, in which the reader all the time puts questions to the text.

21.4   Argument Evaluation: Strategies vs. Moves

Earlier we pointed out that in the last analysis it is not particular moves that can be said to be more or less excellent, only entire strategies. This fact has to be kept in mind in evaluating an argument. Even though in practice we can often, perhaps usually, speak of good and bad moves, this talk makes sense only on the assumption that the players in question are following a reasonable game plan. Strictly speaking, only strategies can be evaluated for excellence, not individual moves.

This leads to an interesting conclusion. As we pointed out earlier, a strategy (in the strict sense) is a rule that tells a player what to do in every possible situation that might come about in a play of the game in question. In evaluating a strategy, we therefore have to consider *merely possible* situations. This may sound strange and unrealistic. Yet it is a very real fact of life not only to game theorists but to game players.

The game of chess again offers nice examples. Often the people observing a given game are not so much interested in the final conclusion—who won? Rather they are interested in what kinds of reasoning, what strategies, were being pursued both by the winners and by the losers. In this connection a book dealing with the strategies of the famous Russian chess player Kasparov has this to say:

> Two kinds of positions are shown: those that really occurred, designated as Actual Position, and those that might have occurred if either White or Black had chosen different moves from those actually played. Each of the latter is designated as Possible Position, followed by the hypothetical moves that inspired the tactic and the hypothetical result. . . .
>
> I have included many Possible Positions because they are usually far more instructive than what actually transpired. They highlight interesting pitfalls that were avoided by both players—those brilliant and valuable moves buried in the analysis, eluding ordinary observation. They tell us what would have happened if so-and-so had played such-and-such. Thus you can truly appreciate the meaning of the grandmaster's actual moves through study of the moves he avoided—the obvious isn't necessarily the best.
>
> Basically, chess is a game of ideas. Actual moves, possible moves, analysis, strategy, tactics, threats, plans, whatever—all for the master are equal in the realm of thought and deserve equal time on their individual merits.
>
> Masters tend to be more interested in the analysis of a game than in its actual moves, which may be incorrect or inexact. A move that is actually played is not necessarily superior to the alternative moves that were not, or to the reasoning guiding their selection. Many actual moves, in fact, are blunders, worthy of limited study. Nor does a victory mean that it was won with the best moves.
>
> Analyzing alternative possibilities and their consequences brings us closer to the truth. Analysis may find a defense that would have saved the game for the loser. Comparing reasonable alternatives to the moves actually played uncovers the objectively best ideas. (Bruce Padolfini, *Kasparov's Winning Chess Tactics* [New York: Simon & Schuster, 1986], p. 9)

This emphasis on possible positions illustrates what we have said. Moreover, what is said here about the evaluation of a chess player's line of reasoning applies to the evaluation of reasoning in general. Usually, there is no unique best strategy. Strategy evaluations have to be comparative.

21.5 When Do I Know Something?

One particular form of argument evaluation deserves a separate examination. Often the evaluation of a line of reasoning takes the form of asking: Does the inquirer, as a consequence of his or her argument, now *know* the conclusion?

First, philosophers have discussed this problem at great length but without any definitive, clear-cut answer. It is often posed as a problem of *defining knowledge*. Some ingredients of such an attempted definition are clear. Suppose the inquirer claims to know that she or he knows that *S*. What is needed to make this claim true?

First, the inquirer presumably believes that *S*. Second, *S* must be true. No one can be truly said to know what is not the case.

So much is uncontroversial. It is also uncontroversial that something more is needed. The two requirements just formulated characterize mere *true belief* rather than knowledge proper. Hence something more has to be added to any possible definition of knowledge. The difficult problem here is to find out what else must be added. The suggestions as to what more is needed for knowledge than mere true belief include the following:

1. What is needed is a justification of the true belief.
2. What is needed is evidence that makes the belief more probable than some minimum standard of probability.
3. What is needed is evidence that puts the belief beyond all "reasonable doubt." This is the standard of proof used in criminal cases tried before a jury.

All three suggestions can be shown to be unsatisfactory as a general characterization of knowledge. For instance, we will soon see that it is sometimes reasonable to say we know something that nevertheless cannot be proven in a court of law.

△ ▼ THINK ABOUT IT

1. Read Agatha Christie's short story "The Under Dog." On the basis of the story, answer this question: To the best of your own judgment, did Lady Astwell know who the murderer was? Be prepared to defend your answer by reference to the story.
2. Can you see reasons why some or all of the characterizations of knowledge just given are unsatisfactory? Be prepared to explain what your reasons are.

The question of whether someone knows or merely has a true belief is not a concern of philosophers only. It can come up in an interesting way in real life too.

Illustration Here is a summary of a situation in which the question of knowing comes up in an important way. A patient with a gunshot wound in his head is brought to the emergency ward of a hospital in California. The physician on duty had served in Vietnam and had seen similar wounds there. On the strength of his experience, he makes a diagnosis of the injury which implies that the patient is indubitably beyond any hope. Accordingly, the patient is not put on maximum life support systems and dies. His family sues the hospital and the physician. An autopsy reveals that the doctor's diagnosis was in fact correct. The lawsuit is nevertheless continued. The family's lawyer claims that because the physician on duty had not specialized in neurology, he could not have *known* what the patient's injury was like. He was lucky enough to have had a *true belief* in the matter, but since he did not *know*, he was culpable of negligence in not putting the patient on full life support systems.

△ ▼ EXERCISE 21-D

In your opinion was the doctor culpable? Write a brief argument defending your answer.

How can knowledge claims be evaluated? Even though no sharp answer can be given, a number of considerations can be put forward. Indeed, they are, by and large, the same ones that were listed in connection with argument evaluation above.

1. It is fairly clear that there is no single definite meaning of the words "knowing" and "knowledge." On different occasions, for different people, in the light of different purposes, these words will mean different things.

2. The question as to whether an inquirer knows something is often taken to be merely about the logical relationship between the information the inquirer has so far received and his or her knowledge claim. In other words, in this sort of situation what matters is whether the knower's initial premises and interrogative moves can be put together into a closed table with *S* as the ultimate conclusion.

Consequently, whatever the justification relation is, the inquirer should spell it out through something like interrogative reasoning. For instance, when a trial lawyer sums up the case for his or her client, what is summed up is not just the totality of testimony that has been presented in favor of the client but also the reasoning through which the testimony is brought to bear on the jury's decision.

But, concentrating on this kind of justification relation introduces not only questions about correctness of steps in the inquiry but also questions about strategy and excellence.

This, however, will mean that, as the word "knowledge" is actually used, often what justifies its application is *not* any binding or even particularly strong evidence that the inquirer has already found. Instead, what is offered as a justification of the knowledge claim are indications of the strategy the inquirer has used and will use. Hence, in evaluating knowledge claims, the section on argument evaluation: excellence (Section 21.3) will be highly relevant.

Illustrations We present below some examples of situations in which someone is said to know something, even when he or she cannot produce a proof or even evidence that could, for example, be presented in a court of law. They are from mystery stories of different kinds.

These examples suggest that what is accepted as knowledge depends on the reasoning strategy which led an inquirer to the conclusion which she or he is said to know. For instance, a clever sleuth like Hercule Poirot or Nigel Strangeways is sometimes said to "know" something that he cannot put "beyond reasonable doubt" in a court of law.

> He [Superintendent Henry Tibbett of Scotland Yard] was pretty sure by now that he knew the identity of the murderer, but he had arrived at the answer by a combination of small clues and the instinct which he called his "nose." This did not give him anything like the solid proof he needed, and besides, there

were gaps that he could not fill in. (From Patricia Moyes, *Murder a la Mode* [New York: Holt, Rinehart and Winston, 1983], p. 163.)

This example (we might want to call it "the nose knows" example) illustrates several things which have been said in this chapter. For one thing, the concluding comment on gaps in Henry Tibbett's line of thought illustrates what was said about the difficulty of deciding whether all apparent gaps in an argument can be filled and about the difficulty of filling them even when they can in fact be filled.

What we are doing here is to interpret Tibbett's "nose" as an almost unconsciously applied strategy of reasoning. This strategy enables him to weave together his "small clues" (answers to small questions) into a line of argument. This he can do even before ascertaining that these answers are all so reliable that the overall argument can be said to give "the solid proof he needed."

The role of strategy is not quite as obvious in the second example as in the first.

"John Wadsworth could have been the man she [Jane Austen] loved" said the Professor of English Literature. "All the evidence—what there is of it—fits. It's just the proof that's missing. . . ."

"It happens to us, too, Miss, sometimes, down at the station," said Detective Inspector with fellow feeling. "What's evidence is one thing, and what's proof—that's different altogether. Sometimes . . . " He paused.

"Yes?"

"Sometimes," he said awkwardly, "you just have to make do with knowing." (End of the book by Catherine Aird *Parting Breath* [New York: Bantam Books, 1983], p. 164)

We suggest that Ms. Aird's—or, rather, the good Inspector's—"evidence" which supports his knowing includes the reasoner's strategy in using the evidence.

Another example indicates that this sense of knowing is not the only one. Superintendent Armstrong addresses a question to Nigel Strangeways, the private investigator who is the hero of the novel:

"Now, sir, what's all this about your knowing who the murderer is?" Nigel was a little rattled by the aggressive manner of the question.

"Just that," he said, "but it's not for publication yet."

"Come, come, Mr. Strangeways. . . . If you have proof about the murderer, I must ask you to hand it over to me at once."

"I never said I had proof. I said I knew who the murderer was. You have all the facts in your possession that I have. . . . "

"I'm afraid I don't understand you, sir. You say you know who did the murder, but have no proofs. It sounds silly to me."

"Not the sort of proof that would satisfy you; or a court of law," added Nigel hastily. (From Nicholas Blake, *A Question of Proof* [New York: Harper & Row, 1979], p. 164.)

Here we can see the contrast between Nigel Strangeways's and the good inspector's respective conceptions of knowledge. It is fairly obvious that what sets Nigel Strangeways apart from Superintendent Armstrong is his strategy of drawing conclusions from evidence and of asking tacit questions concerning the subtler aspects of the case. In Strangeways's own words, they yield "clues . . . of the invisible, intangible sort." They are obtained in part by expert questioning of human witnesses. A little earlier, a friend had noted Strangeways's "skillful questioning" (op. cit., p. 151). This skill is obviously of the strategic kind.

△ ▼ EXERCISE 21-E

Find (or invent) a situation which illustrates the two different conceptions of knowledge that come up in the Strangeways example.

A P P E N D I X ▲ A

▼

Argument Sketches for Exercises in Argument Analysis, Construction, and Evaluation

△▼ Short sketches for practice in identifying premises and conclusions and for studying what is required for an inference to be a logical inference.

1. Cats are smarter than dogs. You can't get eight cats to drag a sled through arctic snow.

2. Perhaps an argument for the existence of a supreme being is that nobody except a supreme being could have made it so difficult to decide whether or not there was a supreme being!

3. The state of California has a government that is so large and complex that it is among the top ten largest government operations in the world. Thus, anyone who has successfully governed the State of California has demonstrated her or his ability to be president of the United States.

4. "[Laws against drugs] are indicators of what a society considers important. We consider the quality of individual human life worth fighting for." (From *Christianity Today*, quoted in *Religion and Society Report*, February 1989, p. 6)

5. I have never held a position in the federal government. For this reason I think I have the independence to do a good job of cleaning out the corruption and inefficiency that characterizes Washington today. I encourage you to support my campaign.

6. Where the press is free and every man able to read, all is safe. —Thomas Jefferson

7. Did Eve have a navel? No, because a navel is only needed for normal pregnancy and birth.

8. But Professor O'Connor, if I don't get a B in this course, I will lose my scholarship and will not be able to return to school.

9. Barbara Grizzuti Harrison: "One of the things that makes God God is that he knows everything (before I know myself, he knows me); so when I have wishes in regard to other people, I just say their names. I let him fill in the rest." (*Context*, April 15, 1989, p. 4)

10. From the article "Astrology Angst": "The chairman of a German astrological society, in one of the most voluminous and scientifically rigorous tests to date, failed to find astrology better at determining personality than random guessing, but said in February that he was not deterred. 'The desire for astrology to be true,' he said, 'is much stronger than all rational counterproofs.'" (*Context*, April 15, 1989, p. 4)

11. To be visible is to be able to be seen. So, to be desirable is to be able to be desired. There are people who desire pleasure. Therefore, pleasure is desirable. (J. S. Mill)

12. Some Christian groups have never baptized naturally aborted fetuses, though they baptize prematurely born infants. It seems that they do not regard them the way they regard prematurely born infants. Thus, they should be willing to accept therapeutic abortions.

13. We must defend the institution of property. No freedom is possible without it.

14. "All human beauty reflects God's beauty, human beauty that involves passion reflects God's passion. So, a beautiful and passionate woman or man is a wonderful metaphor for God." (Andrew Greeley, quoted in *Context*, January 15, 1990, p. 6)

15. Some biologists are government employees. If you are a botanist you are a biologist. Therefore, some botanists are government employees.

16. It just is not the case that some industrial workers fail to be covered by social security. Furthermore, some industrial workers need more adequate retirement pensions. Therefore, there are some people who need more adequate retirement pensions even though they are covered by social security.

17. Only a pantheist would believe that God is physical. But Spinoza was a pantheist, so he must have believed it.

18. Wherever the soil is very acid, flowers will not grow. But flowers grow in your garden, so the soil cannot be very acid there.

19. You cannot convict someone of murder just on circumstantial evidence. There is nothing but circumstantial evidence against the mayor. Thus the mayor cannot be convicted of murder.

20. Delilah detergent is stronger than dirt; that is why it is so effective in your wash.

21. The policy is effective; it does what it sets out to do.

22. Since blunders are forgivable, drug dealing also is.

23. Where there is love, there is no quarreling; I see no quarreling, hence?

24. Sarah is a good swimmer, so she must be Californian.

25. Chocolate must be fattening, because things I like always are.

26. Raw fish is nourishing; it has protein.

27. No elves are dwarves. All twickets are elves. Therefore, some twickets are not dwarves.

28. All students are eligible. Cheryl is a student; therefore she is eligible.

29. Only students are eligible. Charles is a student; therefore he is eligible.

30. There are no popular classical ensembles. The Arden trio is a classical ensemble; hence, it is not popular.

△▼ Somewhat more complicated sketches for practice in argument analysis

1. Research is going forward to produce better artificial hearts in the next ten or twenty years. "Some critics are already worrying that they'll work—and that the nation's overextended health-care programs will lose a precious $2.5 billion to $5 billion a year providing them for a relatively few dying patients. If such expenditures cut into funding for more basic care, the net effect could actually be a decline in the nation's health." (*Newsweek,* January 22, 1990, p. 53)

2. Eve to Adam as they were sent out of the Garden of Eden: "We never had a chance—coming from a single-parent home."

3. "Now they are not going to get paid for unwanted treatment, and that is going to carry a lot more weight with the facility than abstract patients' rights" —Rose Gasner, attorney for the Right-To-Die Society, after a court ruled in favor of a Long Island, N.Y., man who refused to pay a $105,000 nursing home bill for keeping his comatose wife alive against family wishes (*Vidette Messenger,* January 19, 1990, p. 4)

4. AIDS is just one of many viruses we can look forward to in the future. As the population of the earth increases, nature will find a way to get rid of a sufficient number of us. Because AIDS wipes out the immune systems, all

the infectious diseases (except smallpox) that were declared curable before the emergence of AIDS have come back.

5. The U.S. educational system is facing a grave crisis. Literacy rates here are surpassed by those of some nonindustrialized countries. Dropout rates are rising at a time when the workplace needs better-educated workers. A solution to this crisis can only come through a change in the priority of education for the average citizen. Education needs to be considered a necessity, an end in itself, by the average American if the crisis is to be resolved.

This requires having the best-qualified individuals possible in the teaching profession. But as our experience with the professions of law and medicine has amply demonstrated, a larger share of the best-qualified individuals will become teachers and, more importantly, remain teachers, only if teaching's importance in society is acknowledged through salaries that afford some measure of financial security.

6. If you want an explanation for declining literacy rates in the U.S., look no further than the boob tube. Before the popularity of television skyrocketed in the fifties, reading was a genuine entertainment alternative for most Americans. But for the generations since—who have been raised on instant, no-effort everything—instant, no-effort entertainment is the only choice. Why read a book, which requires the active participation of the reader, when electronic opium is a remote-control button away? And you don't have to be a sociologist to recognize that the prime motivation for virtually everything Americans do is entertainment; remove the entertainment motive, and you make the prospect of learning to read resemble an exercise in stoicism. Spend all the money you choose on studies in an attempt to address the problem, but if you want my advice, you'd be better off unplugging the TV set.

7. The government has no business trying to keep people from doing things that harm no one but those who voluntarily take part in the activity in question. But this is just what antigambling laws attempt to accomplish. Nobody forces people to gamble; it is something the participants freely choose to do. As long as they engage in this activity in private, the effects of the vice are felt only by the ones who actively take part. Moreover, such legislation is clearly ineffective. From penny-ante poker to bookie-backed betting, gambling continues in spite of the efforts to stop it. Now I don't have to tell you that legislation which doesn't accomplish what it sets out to is bad legislation, and as with all bad legislation, steps need to be taken to change these measures and to ensure that the government never again oversteps its proper bounds in this regard. The only way to permanently change the situation, however, is by means of a constitutional amendment. It is for this reason that I am supporting the proposal to this effect introduced by my distinguished colleague, Senator Jack Chance.

8. "Although to the best of our knowledge no substantial studies that would prove or disprove this theory exist, a number of observers suspect that one factor contributing to the rise in and acceptability of male homosexuality is the

spreading false impression that male sexuality has little or nothing to do with babies and families. . . . " (*Religion and Society Report*, January 1990, p. 7)

9. It had been three days since Cindy had seen the bear, her only companion since she had taken the job as a park ranger in September. What was more, the treat she had left on the old stump was still there, a sure sign that her ursine friend had not recently paid a visit to the camp. What could have happened? She turned her collar as another blast of cold air reminded her that the first snow was soon due. As this thought passed, another took its place, and she smiled. "Not even my left-over pancakes were enough to keep Ursula from finding a cozy spot for her winter's nap," she concluded. But where does a five-hundred-pound bear sleep? Just then she remembered the small cave she had spotted on her first day in the park, just up the hill from camp. Quietly, she crept up to the entrance, and peered inside. There, against the back wall, was the familiar outline of her friend.

10. Bach certainly is the greatest composer in European history. He was a terrific innovator, as many of the forms of music he pioneered became the standards for generations to come. He was the most prolific of composers, with a career that spanned decades that saw him create hundreds of works. Moreover, a composer whose works continue to be performed centuries after his death must be counted among the giants of his field.

11. Euthanasia is sure to become an issue of increasing importance as our population ages and the leading causes of death become long-term debilitating illnesses rather than accidents or infectious diseases. Too often the debate is clouded by emotion and irrational thought. However, turning one's attention to the following points may serve to clarify the situation. We consider it a duty, not a moral transgression, to end the life of a suffering pet. Why do we balk at providing the same service to willing humans? Is it not crueler to condemn these individuals to weeks, perhaps even months, of suffering? Besides, it is a greater injustice to squander precious medical resources on the terminally ill when so many others, particularly infants, could benefit from them instead; and frequently this is the only alternative to euthanasia. When these points are considered, it becomes clear that the present legal prohibitions against euthanasia ought to be lifted.

12. When I was poor I tithed, but now that I am more well off, I can't afford it!

13. The effects of the computer revolution are beginning to touch the lives of nearly everyone in the world. In developed countries, computers are becoming a standard feature of everyday life. They are found in virtually every business and an increasing number of homes. They are changing the way we learn, shop, drive, and entertain ourselves. Even in the nonindustrialized nations the effect of computers, while not as obvious, is just as profound. Improved weather forecasting, for instance, not only aids in the production of agricultural products but also saves lives by providing early warning of impending disasters such as typhoons and floods.

14. American foreign policy in the eighties was misdirected. The policy makers did not understand their adversaries' ways of thinking. History shows amply that the Russians have always been very much concerned with what happens close to their own borders. That's why they suppressed anti-Soviet movements in Hungary in 1956 and Czechoslovakia in 1968, just as they had crushed independence movements in Poland in the nineteenth century. On the other hand, Russians are not nearly as much concerned with promoting their cause far from their own sphere of interests. They failed to support the loyalists in the Spanish Civil War as strongly as they could have done, and they dismissed Khrushchev because of his "adventurism" in placing Soviet missiles in Cuba in 1962. For this reason, the foreign policy of the United States should have aimed at the reduction of Soviet support of Cuba and other communist movements in Latin America. In return, we could have stopped the support of Afghan rebels. The Soviet presence in Afghanistan was not aimed at the United States or Western interests anyway. It was aimed at Moslem fundamentalism, which is hostile toward both Russia and the United States. Hence, it would have been easy to negotiate a deal which would have significantly reduced communist influence in the part of the world where it is most clearly contrary to United States interests, namely, in Latin America.

15. It is a testament to humanity's continuing insensitivity that people still go to bed hungry. I say insensitivity rather than cruelty because most people don't realize that the resources are currently available to end world hunger. It would take a slight change in our lifestyles, but the millions of starving people worldwide would be given a chance actually to have a lifestyle as a result. One change alone, a switch from eating meat to a vegetarian diet, would free up enough grain to provide for the nutritional needs of virtually every starving person on earth. The grain fed to a cow to provide a human with one day's worth of protein would provide a week's worth of protein for the same person. Now I ask you, is that steak really worth it? Is your morning bacon so important as to justify depriving others of sustenance? There are no good excuses for the continued consumption of meat as long as people are dying of starvation.

16. There used to be a saying that if OPEC kept raising the price of petroleum, then they could try to eat their oil rather than the farm products of this country. But these days a better response might be that we will start putting corn into our gas tanks. In a land blessed with the agricultural capacity to produce more food than its inhabitants can possibly use and with the technology to turn excess grain into fuel for our autos, this seems to be the ultimate solution to our continuing economic dependence on the OPEC nations. Moreover, ethanol, the form of alcohol used as a fuel additive, produces fewer environmentally hazardous by-products. All that is needed is the support of the government, and the days of the economic blackmail practiced by OPEC will be history.

17. "As the late Hannah Arendt pointed out in her brilliant essay *On Violence:* 'It has become rather fashionable among white liberals to react to Negro

grievances with the cry, "We are all guilty" . . . Where all are guilty, no one is: confessions of collective guilt are the best possible safeguard against the discovery of the culprits, and the very magnitude of the crime the best excuse for doing nothing.'" (*The Religion & Society Report*, February 1990, p. 4)

18. The use of animals in laboratories is one of the greatest scandals of modern society and in all but the rarest cases should be prohibited. In the first place these animals are treated cruelly; little or no consideration is given to their well-being. Secondly, the experiments which involve the use of laboratory animals are largely unneeded. Many of the results gained through the use of these animals may be obtained through more humane methods, such as the use of computer models or dead human tissue. What's even worse, scientists are now finding out that the results thus obtained are not reliable. So not only is the practice of experimenting on animals cruel and unnecessary, it makes for bad science as well.

19. Well-meaning but sentimental animal lovers have suggested that we need more bureaucracy to police research involving animals. Don't these people realize that no scientist would act cruelly to laboratory animals? The current treatment of laboratory animals is as humane as is possible, given the important business of scientific progress.

20. Karl Barth on animal rights: "We should not do things that are inappropriate to the dignity of our *humanum*. The cruelty of gratuitous injury and pain inflicted on animals is wrong not because animals have rights, but because it is unworthy of who we are and are called to be. . . . The campaign against 'speciesism' is a campaign against the singularity of human dignity and, therefore, of human responsibility. It is a great conceptual confusion and strategic mistake when animal rights activists deny that singularity. The hope for a more humane world, including the more humane treatment of animals, is premised upon what they deny." (*Religion and Society Report*, May 1989, p. 3)

21. People do not identify with their future selves. A twenty-year-old will take up smoking hardly knowing or caring that his or her future self may suffer severe consequences several decades later. If a young person is wrong in not identifying with his or her future self, then taking up smoking will be irrational. If, however, it is rational not to identify with one's future self, then taking up smoking is immoral. It is immoral because it is wrong to do harm to someone else. (After D. Parfit, *Reasons and Persons* [New York: Oxford University Press, 1986], pp. 319–320)

22. It is clear to anyone who seriously considers the question that there can be no life after death. This would require that our minds, or souls if you prefer, continue to exist after our bodies have stopped working. This is because life after death is taken to imply a continued psychical or mental existence. But modern science tells us that this aspect of our personhood is just one feature of our bodies rather than a ghostly entity capable of an independent existence. Thus, when our bodies die, so do our souls.

23. The French Revolution, not the American, is the true ancestor of the democratic reforms sweeping the world today, in spite of the fact that the American Revolution was first. The American Revolution was not fought to gain equality for all citizens of the colonies but to better line the pockets of the wealthy colonists who balked at the taxes imposed by the King. The Americans were not starving to death, but as it is popular to say now, they wanted to succeed, not merely survive.

    The French, on the other hand, were motivated by considerations of survival to throw off the shackles of nonrepresentative government. While the nobles were less than happy with the king themselves, the revolution succeeded because the will of the people prevailed.

    Also, the French Revolution was a true civil war, not some small dispute in a faraway corner of the world. Only such an event could be the inspiration for the similarly revolutionary happenings of our time.

24. "Collange sees a major difference between the French and the American quest for human rights in the fact that the French were concerned with economic prosperity, the Americans with the pursuit of happiness. Since economic prosperity can be measured and quantified, while what makes a person happy is a matter of individual judgment, the American quest has produced greater freedom, the French enterprise greater government paternalism. As an incidental or not-so-incidental by-product, the situation in America has also produced greater economic prosperity than that in France." (From review of Jean-Francois Collange, *Theologie des droits de l'homme,* in *Religion and Society Report,* October 1989, p. 6)

25. John Henry Jowett (1912): "No sermon is ready for preaching, nor ready for writing out, until we can express its theme in a short, pregnant sentence as clear as crystal. I find getting that sentence the hardest, the most exacting, and the most fruitful labor in my study. To compel oneself to fashion that sentence, to dismiss every word that is vague, ragged, ambiguous, to think oneself through to a form of words which defines the theme with scrupulous exactness—this is surely one of the most vital and essential factors in the making of a sermon; and I do not think any sermon ought to be preached or even written until that sentence has emerged, clear and lucid as a cloudless moon." (*Context,* February 1, 1989, p. 1)

26. "In America, there is abundant survey research indicating that the great majority of workers find their jobs very satisfying. There is now a new Gallup poll indicating that nearly nine out of ten women of childbearing age are satisfied with their lives. There is a very close connection between satisfaction, marriage, and family. Fifty-three percent of married women, but only twenty-eight percent of the unmarried, say they are 'very satisfied.' And the frequency of 'very satisfied' rises dramatically among women with children. Overall, eighty-three percent of the women surveyed believe they will be able to meet their life goals." (*Religion and Society Report,* January 1989, p. 6)

27. "George Annas, an ethicist and health lawyer at Boston University, said, 'I don't even think there's a body of ethical thinking that thinks there's anything wrong with [transplantation of organs from an aborted fetus]. If it was a dead child and not a dead fetus, it would be OK for the parents to donate its organs. There is no reason in principle to treat a fetus differently than a child.' The last sentence is exactly right, of course. It is striking that the likes of Mr. Annas can recognize its truth when it comes to scavenging organs, but deny its truth when opposing those who would protect the fetus from being aborted in the first place." (*Religion and Society Report*, January 1989, p. 7)

28. Ronnie Gunnerson, the stepparent of a defiant teenage mother, says, "Parents have no rights. We cannot insist on either adoption or abortion." Her controversial solution: "If the pregnant teenager's parents are ultimately responsible for the teenager and her baby, then give those parents the right to decide whether or not the teenager keeps her baby." ("My Turn," *Newsweek*, March 2, 1987, pp. 10–11)

29. Tony Campolo: "The best way to handle sin in this particular age is through ridicule. . . . We are socialized to react to condemnation by becoming defensive. [But] we react to the ludicrous nature of our unchristian behavior by repentance. Strange as it may seem I think that, at this particular stage in history, pointing out the idiocy of sin rather than its diabolical nature—both of which are true—has the most effect." (*Context*, February 15, 1989, p. 1)

30. "Once more, let's rehearse. If we are Madisonians, we will oppose efforts to *establish* religion, *privilege* particular religions, and so on. But we will also oppose efforts to *inhibit* individuals or groups from putting their religion to work in their ethics and the like. Smart politicians, religiously formed, won't flaunt or taunt or swagger or presume when they *do* put their faith to work. But when they are on their own time, not on public space, they have as much right as any one else to 'go public' with their faith; and in public life, one cannot expect them to park their faith at the door. They have terrible responsibilities to be cautious and respectful. And we have terrible responsibilities to let them be who they are." (*Context*, February 15, 1989, p. 6)

31. Grant Gilmore: "Law reflects but in no sense determines the moral worth of a society. A reasonably just society will reflect its values in a reasonably just law. The better the society, the less law there will be. In Heaven there will be no law and the lion will lie down with the lamb. An unjust society will reflect its values in an unjust law. The worse the society, the more law there will be. In Hell there will be nothing but law, and due process will be meticulously observed." (From "The Storrs Lectures: The Age of Anxiety," *Yale Law Journal* 84(5) [1975]: p. 1044)

32. "Why is it that in the present day funerals are of much less significance than in earlier times and in other cultures . . . ? . . . . Today funerals have so much less work to do. . . . The lack of *communitas*, of *Gemeinschaft*, the growth of individualism, involves a certain withdrawal from each other's problems

including their deaths and their dead. . . . " (From J. Goody, *Death and the Interpretation of Culture*, quoted in *Context*, June 15, 1989, p. 5)

33. "Nothing surpasses, in felt intensity, the flushed radiance of this first night of marriage. But after the first night are many others which will require the quotidian, common rites of constancy—and therefore a more subtle and demanding version of the original ardor. . . . There remains to be mentioned only one last and critical reversal. The anticlimax of living at home an utterly ordinary life is anticlimactic only to those who pull back, in terror, from living it. The few, among whom I so wish I could include myself, who do not recoil from it are utterly at home with such a life, surrounded by children with their teeming demands and reckless laughter, by friends and their divorced companions, sometimes by homeless vagrants, and others of the world's delinquents. Pledged never to leave home or its endless tasks, they have chosen the hardest road; no journey is harsher than that which leads us to live in the place we spend our lives avoiding. But, for them, suffering keeps disappearing into celebration. If they are able to work this daily miracle, it is, they tell us, because they keep receiving, in small, unnoticed ways, the harsh stroke of divine mercy. To speak more of the joys of their suffering would require an essay on the geography of a real and lasting paradise." (From Jerome A. Miller, *The Way of Suffering: A Geography of Crisis*, quoted in *Context*, November 15, 1989, p. 3)

34. Kristine Beyerman Alster asks "Is it possible to care for the whole person?" You can be concerned, can try to address, "but certainly no one provider can care for the whole person as identified by the holists." Paul Tillich: "In order to speak of health, one must speak of all dimensions of life which are united in man. And no one can be an expert in all of them." She quotes a letter by someone named Friedlieb from a medical journal: "Where in the name of everything holy does it say that a physician is to be more than a healer of sickness? Why in the world are we expected to be all things to all people and take care of all of everyone's problems? Certainly no one expects a clergyman to do appendectomies or a sociologist to treat acute glomerulonephritis." (From *The Holistic Health Movement*, quoted in *Context*, July 15, 1989, p. 6)

35. The Bishop of Salisbury, John Baker, is saddened: "We should think about death far more, because it sharpens one's priorities as very few other stimuli can. It makes you say, 'What are the really important things I should be doing with my life, not just selfishly but also for other people? Are there quarrels I'd like to heal, relationships I should mend, something I'd like to do for somebody but kept putting it off?' " He argues that what we're doing by pushing the power of death away is robbing ourselves of its power "to make our lives what they are meant to be." (From *World Press Review* reprint, quoted in *Context*, August 15, 1989, p. 2)

36. Cynthia Thero: Believers "urgently need to take responsibility for the ways they live out their faith, or they're going to lose it. I see an incredible amount

of wasted lives due to lack of spiritual development. People go through the motions, and they're exhausted at night; but they don't experience any significant degree of pleasure or pain during the day. They experience nothing. People have been throwing their lives away spiritually. . . . " (*Context*, October 1, 1989, p. 3)

37. "Jacob Needleman was interviewed by D. Patrick Miller. What about the marketing of spirituality? Needleman doesn't like it but sees it as inevitable. You have to take on something of the environment. 'There's a story of a king who ruled a country where the water was poisoned. The poison made the people insane, but the king had pure water brought to him. Gradually he came to realize that he wasn't able to rule his people because he wasn't crazy; he couldn't understand his people. So he asked to have just enough of the poisoned water mixed in his own to make him a "little" crazy. Then he could rule more effectively.' Which may explain things in American spirituality." (*Context*, November 1, 1989, p. 3)

38. "Postman, who wrote *Teaching as a Subversive Activity* and *Amusing Ourselves to Death*, says that 'religion doesn't play well on television. In order to be on television, religion has to adopt the values of show business, and what plays well on television is not dogma or theology or history or tradition. What plays well on television is charisma. Of course, all the evangelicals know this very well, and they become celebrities. I regard this as a form of blasphemy.' Why? Because 'on television, people end up loving the preacher more than they love God. The Catholics eventually pulled pioneer Fulton Sheen because they feared this was happening, so evangelicals filled the void.' Mainstream Protestants asked Postman's counsel: 'I told them to stay off television. It would only lead to blasphemy.' He quoted two of the first three commandments. Interviewer: 'You sound like an evangelical.' Postman: 'I think you mean that as a compliment, but I'm not. I'm Jewish.'

"Television is *too* concrete. Postman: 'All I know is that there is tremendous importance in the vagueness of language. The great thing about the Bible— *and* the Constitution, for that matter—is that they are both vague in important parts. That keeps the document living.' " (*Context*, February 15, 1990, p. 6)

39. Robert M. Veatch, PhD, Professor of Medical Ethics, Kennedy Institute of Ethics, Georgetown University, Georgetown, Md.: "We don't have a good sense of what the role of the clinician ought to be in making inevitable social, ethical, and allocational choices. That's the problem that has dominated the discussion in the 1980s and will continue into the 1990s. We know fairly well what the parameters of that debate are.

"The new problem emerging for the 1990s shifts to the level of meta-ethics. It has to do with the nature of moral authority and what kinds of questions medical experts legitimately can answer. We are moving in the direction of a recognition that there really is no such thing as a medically correct course for a patient, independent of social and ethical value judgments.

"That will mean many of the standard procedures in medicine will be questioned. The notion of a standard treatment, medically indicated treatment, or treatment of choice will be essentially seen from an evaluative stance—and an evaluation about which physicians have no particular expertise. We'll increasingly discover that the normal functions assigned to a physician involve ethical and other value judgments about which physicians are not experts." (*Medical Ethics Advisor,* January 1990, p. 2)

40. The hedonist says that the question of what is good morals and what is bad must ultimately come down to a question of pleasure. For, he says, suppose we desire anything other than our own pleasure. Then whatever it may be that we desire, we take satisfaction in; and if we did not take satisfaction in it we should not desire it. But this satisfaction is that very quality of feeling we call pleasure; thus the only thing we can ever desire is pleasure, and all deliberate action must be performed for the sake of our own pleasure.

41. Florida State University will receive between 5 and 10 million dollars next year as a direct result of the efforts of some 75 or so student athletes. This figures to be about right, assuming that next year's football team is even somewhat successful, what with ticket sales, TV revenue, and a fat bowl paycheck.

Perhaps the greatest benefits to the university are less tangible than this cold, hard cash, however. Note, for instance, that since the football team's amazing success on the gridiron over the past three years, FSU has become the university in the state system with the most qualified freshman class, due to an increase in the number of applicants which is clearly tied to the football team's performance. Also note the unprecedented success of private fundraising efforts on behalf of the university. Since last September, over 6 million dollars has been raised by the University Foundation, already making this academic year by far the most successful ever in this respect. And this money will go directly to improve the quality of education available at FSU, allowing the construction of much-needed buildings and the hiring of top-notch faculty.

Put all this together and it's not hard to see that the well-being of the university is largely dependent upon the success of the football program. But what about the student-athletes themselves? How do they fare, given the dependence of the university upon their performance on Saturdays? The student-athletes are being treated fairly only if their status as students is not adversely affected by their status as athletes and they are receiving adequate financial compensation for their contribution to the welfare of the university.

But, first of all, any student-athlete who is required to practice as much as the football players do and is required to miss class as the football team does when playing away games, is adversely affected by his athlete status. Every minute on the practice field, and every minute on the team plane, is a minute which could be spent preparing for class.

Secondly, and perhaps most importantly, in exchange for the tremendous benefit to the university, football players are, from a financial standpoint, treated like chattel. Sure their basic financial needs are met, but this amounts to peanuts in comparison to their actual worth to the university. One Deion Sanders does more for FSU than a dozen university presidents, but would we consider paying the president so poorly that he was forced to find a summer job or was unable to afford a new car? Of course not. And if this were inappropriate compensation for the university president, isn't it inappropriate for our weekend gladiators as well?

Let's face it—when it comes to fair treatment of the football players at FSU, give this school an F.

42. Traditional grading systems (those with letter grades, pluses, and minuses) serve many valuable functions. Grading systems give students information on their academic achievement; they provide students with motivation for studying; and they supply a measure of students' relative performance which can be used to determine class rankings.

    Proponents of the elimination of grades in favor of such radical options as a satisfactory/unsatisfactory evaluation or a credit/no-credit system have contended that grades do not provide information about academic achievement and that they do not motivate greater studying or greater learning. However, these advocates of radical changes have not indicated how they would find an alternative means of ranking students. Class rankings are the means by which scarce resources are allocated. For example, they are the basis for deciding which students meet the academic requirements for financial aid; they are the basis for deciding which students will be able to go on to graduate or professional schools, and they are used in business recruiting.

    The demand for admission to the better graduate and professional schools far exceeds the number of places available. And if these sought-after slots are not allocated purely on the basis of grades, they will be allocated purely on the basis of personalism—on the basis of recommendations or string-pulling by professors to place those students whom they favor. Critics of traditional grading systems claim that grades threaten students and increase tension. But without grades, the situation in which admission to graduate or professional schools is based on personalism surely will neither reduce tension nor encourage learning. Because the number of letters of recommendation a graduate or professional school will require is relatively small, students would concentrate their energies on cultivating a few professors who appear favorably disposed to them.

    The only alternative to such a situation would be a drastically increased emphasis on various national entrance examinations. But these are hardly an adequate substitute for several years of course grades, and such exams are likely to cause greater anxiety than traditional grading systems, which distribute the risk over a large number of examinations.

    Critics of traditional grading systems often assert that grades are directly related to coercion and that only secondarily do they stimulate learning. But without traditional grading systems, learning might well take third place, behind apple polishing and the irresistible temptations of leisure, in the lives of most university students.

43. There is no such subject as philosophy. This is because, in order for a problem to be truly philosophical, it must be a problem which has no solution, and hence not really a problem at all. But there can be no area of investigation whose objects of study do not exist.

44. All knowledge requires justification. But in order for the conclusion of an argument to be justified, its premises must be justified. Obviously one cannot go on giving arguments for every premise in this way, as this would require an infinite number of arguments, something which we cannot provide. So there is no knowledge after all.

45. Evolution is only a theory; it cannot be proven on the basis of the fossil evidence. Because scientific creationism is also a theory about how animals and plants came into existence, a person should be able to decide which of these two views to accept. So schools should present both options to their students.

46. The basic principles of an area of knowledge must be subject to scientific confirmation in order for the subject to be a legitimate source of knowledge. Science itself is not such a source, however, as its basic principles may not be so confirmed.

47. The only feature of a being relevant from the standpoint of a right to life is the capacity for experiencing pleasure and pain. Now one fact that is immediately evident to all who have ever had the opportunity to spend time with farm animals is that cows, pigs, and even chickens share this capacity with men. So from a moral standpoint, even if not from the standpoint of etiquette, there is no appreciable difference between a veal dinner and a dinner of tender roast toddler. Both are indefensible.

48. Mark Twain somewhere says: "In the space of 176 years the lower Mississippi has shortened itself 240 miles. This is an average of a trifle over one mile and a third per year. Therefore, any calm person, who is not blind or idiotic, can see that in the Old Oolitic Silurian period just a million years ago next November, the lower Mississippi River was upward of one million three hundred thousand miles long and stuck out over the Gulf of Mexico like a fishing rod.

"And by the same token, any person can see that 742 years from now, the lower Mississippi will be only a mile and three-quarters long, and Cairo and New Orleans will have joined their streets together, and be plodding comfortably along under a single mayor and mutual Board of Aldermen.

"There is something fascinating about science. One gets such wholesome returns of conjecture out of such a trifle investment of fact."

△▼ Short sketches for practice in statement logic

1. God exists if God is omnipotent. God can do everything if God is omnipotent. If God can do everything, God can make a stone too heavy for God to lift. But if God can make a stone too heavy for God to lift, then it is not true that God can do everything. Therefore, God does not exist.

2. God exists only if God is omnipotent. God can do everything if God is omnipotent. If God can do everything, God can make a stone too heavy for God to lift. But if God can make a stone too heavy for God to lift, then it is not true that God can do everything. Therefore, God does not exist.

3. If Bush doesn't know about CIA wrongdoing, then he is either stupid or incompetent. But he isn't stupid. So if Bush isn't incompetent, then he knows about CIA wrongdoing.

4. If the lottery is a good idea, then the profit is going to a good cause. If the profit goes to increase education funding, then the profit is going to a good cause. But the profits are not going to increase education funding. So the lottery is not a good idea.

5. If either unemployment or interest rates rise, then we will have a recession and the national debt will increase. But interest rates will rise if unemployment does not rise. So we will have a recession and the national debt will increase.

6. If the economy is to be saved, we must take serious action on the deficit. But this requires a tax hike, something which the governor has promised to veto. So the health of the economy rests on the ability of the legislature to override this expected veto.

7. Evolution is either a theory or a fact. If it is just a theory, then it has no business in science, which by its very nature must deal only with fact. But if it were a fact then no one would be arguing about it in the first place. So evolution's claim to scientific status is illegitimate.

8. The fetus, even in the case of pregnancy resulting from rape or incest, is an innocent human being. Because abortion is the killing of the fetus, this is never a morally permissible option.

9. If universities charge no tuition, everyone will enter. If universities charge tuition, there is not equality of opportunity unless deserving students get scholarships. But universities must either not charge tuition or charge tuition. Moreover, it is false that everyone will enter universities. Accordingly, if there is equality of opportunity, then deserving students get scholarships.

10. Ginger is the sort of gal who if she marries a handsome man will be jealous and if she marries a rich man will be discontented. But if she is either jealous or discontented, she is not liberated. Moreover, if she marries a liberated man, she'll be happy. Ginger will marry either a handsome man, a rich man, or a liberated man. Hence, if she is liberated, she will be happy.

11. Stoic logician Chrysippus said that even dogs are capable of reasoning according to the disjunctive syllogism, for he had seen a dog chasing after an

animal come to a threefold division in the path. The dog sniffed at the two paths that the animal hadn't taken and without sniffing raced off down the third path.

△▼ Short sketches for practice in predicate logic

1. If an artist wants to eat, then she or he doesn't paint abstract art. Pete is an artist who wants to eat; therefore, he doesn't paint abstract art.

2. No biophysicists are untrained in chemistry. Some geneticists are untrained in chemistry. Therefore, some persons who are not biophysicists are geneticists.

3. Dash Outman is honest, hardworking, and experienced, all traits it is important for our next city commissioner to have. So Dash should be our next city commissioner.

4. All companies that have recently gone public are speculative to invest in. Only companies that are not blue chips have recently gone public. Therefore, no blue chips are speculative to invest in.

5. No republics are dictatorships. Not all republics are democratic. Therefore, some nondemocracies are not dictatorships.

6. If a group plays rock and roll, then it is loved by everyone. The How are loved by everyone; hence, they play rock and roll.

7. No composer lacks musical talent. Gerald Ford was not a composer; thus, he lacked musical talent.

8. A deficit in the federal budget is an inflationary influence. No inflationary influences are helpful to the balance of payments. Thus, at least one factor that is not helpful to the balance of payments is the deficit in the federal budget.

9. Every drink containing alcohol is an intoxicant and each drink which contains alcohol is a stimulant. So intoxicants are stimulants.

10. Many foods are not protein and chocolate bars are all food; hence, chocolate bars are not protein.

11. Some obscure and confused thinkers are philosophers; every sincere and intelligent person is a philosopher; so, there are intelligent people who are confused.

12. No mammals are parasites. All tapeworms are parasites. Therefore, no tapeworms are mammals.

13. All computers are machines. No computers are persons. Therefore, no persons are machines.

14. All lizards are reptiles. Some lizards are marine creatures. Therefore, some marine creatures are reptiles.

15. All Christian Scientists are believers in the power of prayer. Some social scientists are not believers in the power of prayer. Therefore, some social scientists are not Christian Scientists.

16. No humanists are nihilists. Some nihilists are anarchists. Therefore, some anarchists are not humanists.

17. Some disease germs are bacteria. Some viruses are disease germs. Therefore, some viruses are bacteria.

18. No furry mittens are stylish. Some stylish mittens are expensive. Therefore, some furry mittens are not expensive.

19. No ancient writers were interested in economics. Some writers interested in economics are writers who explained the economic history of their times. Thus no ancient writers explained the economic history of their times.

20. All toads are repulsive. Some members of Congress are repulsive. Therefore, some members of Congress are toads.

21. The only good insect is a dead insect. This insect is dead. Therefore, it is good.

22. Only good insects are dead. This insect is dead. Therefore, it is good.

△▼ Sketches that can serve as thought starters for projects in construction of arguments

1. "The worst thing is that we are living in a decayed moral environment. We have become morally ill, because we have become accustomed to saying one thing and thinking another. We have learned not to believe in anything, not to care about one another, and only to look after ourselves. Notions such as love, friendship, compassion, humility, and forgiveness have lost their depth and dimension, and for many of us they represent merely some kind of psychological idiosyncrasy or appear as some kind of stray relic from times past, something rather comical in the era of computers and space rockets." (From a speech by Vaclav Havel on New Year's Day in Czechoslovakia, quoted in *Newsweek*, January 15, 1990, p. 42)

2. "W. H. Auden said, 'Any marriage, however prosaic, is more interesting than any romance however passionate.' " (*Context*, January 1, 1989, p. 5)

3. The father of palimony, Marvin Mitchelson: "I never saw a prenuptial that didn't end in a divorce." (*Chicago Tribune*, Sunday, February 18, 1990, p. C4)

4. Heinrich Boll: "To regret big things is child's play: political errors, adultery, murder, anti-Semitism—but who forgives, who understands the little things?" (*Context*, March 1, 1989, p. 3)

5. "The only place outside Heaven where you can be perfectly safe from all the dangers and perturbations of love is Hell." (C. S. Lewis, *The Four Loves* [New York: Harcourt, 1960], p. 169)

6. "In *in re Ruiz*, an Ohio court ruled that the definition of 'child' in state child abuse statutes applies to a viable fetus, thereby allowing the state to prosecute a heroin-addicted mother for her child's symptoms of drug withdrawal." (*Midwest Medical Ethics* 3 [Summer 1987]:3)

7. G. K. Chesterton: "In modern discourse every superstition is admitted except the superstition of religion." (*Religion and Society Report*, May 1989, p. 4)

8. William Pfaff: "When people's lives are sterile, they consciously or unconsciously welcome war. Mild-mannered, sensible Harold Macmillan, though gravely wounded and disabled in World War I, was in North Africa in 1942 and '43 and said, 'I enjoy wars. Any adventure's better than sitting in an office.' Churchill's relish of war was notorious; he sought liberation there from the boredom of life." (*Context*, July 1, 1989, p. 4)

9. Pasteur, 1822–1895: "In the fields of observation, chance favors only the mind that is prepared."

10. "The trouble with liberalism, liberal Congressman Barney Frank (D-Mass.) recently observed, is its penchant for multiplying 'not-sa-pos-tas.'" (*Religion and Society Report*, May 1989, p. 2)

11. Augustine (*Confessions*): "Great is this force of Memory, excessively great, O my God; a large and boundless chamber! Who ever sounded the depths thereof? A wonderful admiration surprises me, amazement seizes me upon this. And men go to admire the heights of mountains, the mighty billows of the sea, the broad tides of rivers, the expanses of the ocean, and the circuits of the stars, and pass themselves by." (*Context*, May 1, 1989, p. 1)

12. Thomas A. Kempis: "At the day of judgment, we shall not be asked what we have read but what we have done." (*Context*, August 15, 1989, p. 5)

13. Prof. Leon E. Rosenberg, M.D., of Yale University Medical School: "I maintain that concepts such as humanness are beyond the purview of science, because no idea about them can be tested experimentally." (*Religion and Society Report*, August 1989, p. 4)

14. "Open as Lutherans have been to later scientific discovery, their original massive assault on what Catholics call 'artificial birth control,' a stand that lived on into the middle of the twentieth century in American conservative Lutheranism, disappeared almost without a trace a mere two decades later." (Martin E. Marty, *Health and Medicine in the Lutheran Tradition* [New York: Crossroad, 1986], p. 146)

15. Paul Ricoeur: "If we were to remove the suffering inflicted by people on other people, we would see what remained of suffering in the world, but to tell the truth, we have no idea what this would be, to such an extent does human violence impregnate suffering." (*Context*, July 15, 1989, p. 4)

16. "To poke fun at philosophy," Pascal once said, "is to be a true philosopher." (From Howard DeLong, *A Profile of Mathematical Logic* [Reading, Mass.: Addison Wesley], p. 227)

17. James Madison: "Religion flourishes in greater purity without than with the aid of government." (From his "Memorial and Remonstrance," quoted in *Context*, July 1, 1989, p. 1)

18. "Here is what some advertisers spent for sports advertising on American television last year: 'General Motors, $581,000 per day; Anheuser-Busch, $396,000 per day; Philip Morris, $374,000 per day.'" (From *Chicago Tribune*, quoted in *Context*, July 1, 1989, p. 3)

19. "A strikingly consistent statistic is that about 75% of Americans oppose abortions obtained for the reasons that 99% of abortions are obtained." (*Forum Letter*, May 31, 1989, p. 1)

20. "Old Left, New Left, New Old Left; history is one dream thing after another." (*Religion and Society Report*, June 1989, p. 5)

21. "Brian Berry, Rochester Institute of Technology sociologist, finds that today's young folks no longer agree with the old college slogan, 'Live high, die young and leave behind a good-looking corpse.' When surveyed, they told what they think of death. They'd like a heart-attack exit most and AIDS, syphilis, or fire deaths worst. Most wanted to die in their own homes. 'It also surprised me that women are more apprehensive about death than men.' So says Sarah A. Kass." (From the Education Supplement of the *New York Times*, quoted in *Context*, February 15, 1990, p. 5)

22. Read Ayn Rand's *Night of January 16th*. On the basis of the play provide an argument as to what conclusion the jury should come to.

23. Employers of today are unanimous in voicing this one complaint: The recent emphasis on vocational training has, contrary to the expectations of those seeking it, resulted in a work force less able to understand the complex features of today's workplace. This is why more and more captains of industry are hiring employees with a traditional liberal arts education rather than those whose training is more specialized.

24. "In 1988 Don Colburn reported the following in the Washington Post National Weekly Edition: 'Roman Catholic women in the United States are 30 percent more likely than Protestant or Jewish women to undergo abortions, a new national survey reports.' But the women who described themselves as 'born again' or 'evangelical' Christians, says Colburn, 'accounted for about one out of six abortions last year.' If people in traditions that oppose abortions would stop having abortions, two-thirds or more of the abortions would end." (*Context*, January 1, 1989, p. 5)

25. "From a medical perspective, patients who do not comply with the doctor's orders are usually seen as deviant and deviance requires correction. But many chronically ill people view their behavior differently, as a matter of self-regulation. In this light noncompliance supports people's desires for independence and autonomy, desires that align closely with the therapeutic goals of caregivers." (From Peter Conrad, *The Noncompliant Patient: In Search of Autonomy*, reviewed in *Hastings Center Report*, August 1987, pp. 15ff)

26. P. Porter, reviewing *Heaven: A History* by C. McDannell and B. Lang: "The authors compare theocentric and anthropocentric heavens. 'In the first, the souls of the blessed have no profile compared to God's: their joy is to be in His presence. Consequently even brilliant visionaries with a theocentric bias, such as Augustine and Calvin, have nothing much to say about Heaven. Being with God will be enough.' In the second category, everything is confusion. 'God is still present but He has a supporting cast ranging from the angels

to resuscitated household pets.' . . . Porter: 'Good Taste will always come down on the side of the theocentric Heaven.' Observe: 'Hell has done better at the hands of painters: its iconography gives them something to work with. However, God continues to get the best tunes.'" (*Context*, March 1, 1989, p. 6)

27. "In The Federalist No. 10 James Madison offered an enduringly serviceable definition of a faction. 'By a faction, I understand a number of citizens, whether amounting to a majority or minority of the whole, who are united and actuated by some common impulse of passion, or of interest, adverse to the rights of other citizens, or to the permanent and aggregate interests of the community.' Madison understood that the new republic was not designed to cope with ultimate truths. Factions may be right or wrong, but the divisive effect of contending factions must be contained not by resolving their truth claims but by letting them balance one another out through the process of countervailing forces." (*Forum Newsletter*, February 5, 1989, p. 5)

28. John Updike on why he supported the Vietnam War: "My undovishness, like my battered and vestigial but unsurrendered Christianity, constituted a refusal to give up, to deny and disown, my deepest and most fruitful self, my Shillington [boyhood hometown] self—dimes for war stamps, nickels for the Sunday-school collections, and grown-ups maintaining order so that I might be free to play with my cartoons and Big Little Books. . . . In all varieties of the Christian faith resides a certain contempt for the world and for attempts to locate salvation and perfection here. The world is fallen, and in a fallen world animals, men, and nations make space for themselves through a willingness to fight. Christ . . . came not to bring peace, he distinctly said, but a sword." (From *Self-Consciousness: Memoirs*, quoted in *Context*, May 1, 1989, p. 2)

29. Michael Harrington: "The atheistic humanist and the committed religious person have the same enemy, that slack, hedonistic and thoughtless atheism which, often embellished with a sentimental religiosity, is the real faith of contemporary Western society." He criticizes "faddish relativism" for producing people who "no longer know what they believe" but desperately want to believe in something. He wants a "united front of believers and atheists in defense of moral values." (*Context*, May 1, 1989, p. 5)

30. "No, the romance and beauty were all gone from the river. All the value any feature of it had for me now was the amount of usefulness it could furnish toward compassing the safe piloting of a steamboat. Since those days, I have pitied doctors from my heart. What does the lovely flush in a beauty's cheek mean to a doctor but a 'break' that ripples above some deadly disease? Are not all her visible charms sown thick with what are to him the signs and symbols of hidden decay? Does he ever see her beauty at all, or doesn't he simply view her professionally, and comment upon her unwholesome condition all to himself? And doesn't he sometimes wonder whether he has gained most or lost most by learning his trade?" (Mark Twain, "Old Times on the Mississippi," in *The Literary South*, compiled and edited by Louis D. Rubin, Jr. [Baton Rouge, La.: Louisiana State University Press, 1979], p. 306)

31. Leon Kass of the University of Chicago draws a parallel between the multiplicity of nations and the fact that there are two sexes. "The emergence of multiple nations, with their divergent customs and competing interests, challenges the view of human self-sufficiency. . . . God's dispersion of the nations is the political analog to the creation of woman: instituting otherness and opposition, it is the necessary condition for national self-awareness and the possibility of a politics that will hear and harken to the voice of what is eternal, true, and good." (*Context*, June 15, 1989, p. 2)

32. Today, to accede in the promotion of the myth that abortion is psychologically safe, even in the short run, is a deceit, no matter how well intentioned. The German-language literature is extensive and has been accumulating for some time. For example, Basel psychiatrist Markus Merz, who defends maintaining the right to abortion with certain restrictions, believes that even in the cases where he would professionally endorse the abortion, there is a "psychic injury to the affected woman and the destruction of unborn life, but sometimes these appear as the 'lesser evil.'" (Sean Donovan, *Human Life Review*, Spring 1989, p. 5)

33. In their interview of Dr. Richard Selzer, author of *Confessions of a Knife*, Bill McNabb and Mike Yaconelli describe Selzer as "a surgeon . . . a poet, a philosopher, a 'priest' whose parish is the sick, the lame, and the dying. He is a lover . . . of medicine," and more. Selzer: "Science has become the religion of our time for a great many people." The ex-Yale Medical School teacher likes to visit medical schools, where students often are "exhausted, grungy-looking, depressed, overworked" with souls that are starved; and he tries to offer these people some sort of transcendence of the merely technical. To improve education he would rule out students who get A's in organic chemistry, assuming that they "had already been destroyed," and would seek out the humanistically trained to deal with the "spirit." More reform? Selzer is for socialized medicine, but don't hold that against him, Doctors, if that blocks out other things he has to say.

    When it comes to tough medical decisions, for example, abortion and fetal research, is surgeon/teacher Selzer ready to let the clergy decide issues? "Ah yes, the clergy. Since we are not an Islamic country where everyone has the same religion, which clergy do we listen to? We live in a pluralistic society, as far as religion goes, and there are many churches, each of which insists that it has found the right path to God and dismisses all other churches' viewpoints." He illustrates: He admits that he once let a Jehovah's Witness child die. "I have to respect the Jehovah's Witness belief that if I force blood on someone, they would be kept out of the Kingdom of Heaven and be dammed for eternity. These people see things in terms of eternity, not just life." (*Context*, September 15, 1989, pp. 2–3)

34. "Two Christian Scientist parents, David and Ginger Twitchell, were convicted of manslaughter in a Massachusetts trial court in the April 1986 death of their 2½ year old son. The parents relied on prayer to treat the boy, who died of

a bowel obstruction after a five day illness in 1986. The parents were sentenced to ten years probation and ordered to take their three remaining children for regular medical examinations. . . . The Twitchell case raises serious First Amendment issues concerning free exercise of religion in life-threatening situations. Prosecutors, however, maintain that the religious claims must be rejected when children are involved." ("Christian Scientists Convicted," *LegalEase,* August 1990, p. 5)

35. Nietzsche: "The spread of the towering sciences has grown enormous and with it the likelihood that the philosopher will grow tired, even as a learner, and will take refuge somewhere and specialize; so that he will no longer reach his proper height—his superspection, circumspection, and 'despection.' Or he climbs aloft too late, when the best of his maturity and strength are gone, or when he is on the downgrade, coarsened and spoiled; so that his view of the world, his general estimate of things, is no longer of much importance. It is no doubt his intellectual conscience that makes him hesitate to be a dilettante, a centipede, a creature with a thousand antennas." (*Context,* July 15, 1989, p. 1)

36. Christopher Lasch: "The problem isn't how to keep religion out of politics but how to subject political life to spiritual criticism without losing sight of the tension between the political and the spiritual realm. . . . A complete separation of religion and politics, whether it arises out of religious indifference or out of its opposite . . . religious passion . . . condemns the political realm to 'perpetual warfare,' as Niebuhr argued in *Moral Man and Immoral Society.*" (*Context,* July 15, 1989, p. 3)

37. "Hadley Arkes, professor of jurisprudence at Amherst, reviews a recent casebook in constitutional law in the *Michigan Law Review.* The book is *American Constitutional Interpretations* by Walter Murphy et al., and Arkes thinks it is distressingly blind to the presuppositions underlying the conventional wisdoms that it endorses. For instance, the authors have nothing but scorn for the 'reactionaries' who opposed the New Deal in defending the 'freedom of contract.' But Arkes suggests that those 'reactionaries' had a firmer sense of moral right than do many of today's 'progressives' who discover putative rights, such as privacy, without even attempting to ground those rights in something like a natural or rational right. Arkes continues: 'This much may be said of the difference between the old apostles of "freedom of contract" and the new partisans of "autonomy": The judges who spoke seriously about the "freedom of contract" were alert to the moral ground from which that freedom arose. For that reason, they were alert to the fact that the freedom of contract could never encompass "the right to do a wrong; or to contract for immoral things." The same premises that established the rightful freedom of contract established an understanding, also, of the things that one could not claim in the name of one's "freedom to contract."

"But that same understanding does not seem to be present in the claims of "autonomy." The writers of the casebook evidently find the notion progressive and liberal. And yet, they do not even attempt to suggest the ground in which it is rooted: From what does it derive? What proposition, what axiom or truth, makes the claim to autonomy valid? What makes it "good" or "desirable"? Is it "good" merely because we stipulate it to be good, as a matter of our own, arbitrary insistence? Or do we stipulate it as good because there is something that makes it in principle good? These questions all had compelling answers when the claim to freedom was rooted in the nature of beings who had access, through their reason, to the standards of moral judgment. The answers could be made irresistible when it was shown that these same beings would fall into a hopeless contradiction when they resorted, as Kant said, to that perverse maneuver of "[proving] by reason that there is no reason." " (*Religion and Society Report*, June 1989, p. 7)

38. E. M. Forster: "Personal relations are despised today. They are regarded as bourgeois luxuries, as products of a time of fair weather, which is now past, and we are urged to get rid of them, and to dedicate ourselves to some movement or cause instead. I hate the idea of causes, and if I had to choose between betraying my country and betraying my friend, I hope I should have the guts to betray my country. . . . Probably one will not be asked to make such an agonizing choice. Still, there lies at the back of every creed something terrible and hard for which the worshipper may one day be required to suffer, and there is even a terror and a hardness in this creed of personal relationship, urbane and mild though it sounds. Love and loyalty to an individual can run counter to the claims of the State. When they do—down with the State, say I, which means that the State would down me." (From the *Times Literary Supplement*, quoted in *Context*, July 1, 1989, p. 4)

39. "The vast majority of Americans (in the Period of Formulation) assumed that theirs was a Christian, i.e. Protestant country, and they automatically expected that government would uphold the commonly agreed on Protestant ethos and morality. In many instances, they had not come to grips with the implications of their belief in the powerlessness of government in religious matters held for a society in which the values, customs and forms of Protestant Christianity thoroughly permeated civil and political life. The contradiction between their theory and their practice came only later, with the advent of a more religiously pluralistic society, when it became the subject of a disputation that continues into the present." And that's how we got so mixed up. (From *America in Theory*, quoted in *Context* [Editor's comment follows quoted passage], July 1, 1989, p. 5)

40. John Garvey: "But to say that death is terrible is not to say that the best alternative to it is life as we know it, or that this life is the only alternative. In fact this life is so saturated with death that we are often unable to see the fact, until some profound experience—perhaps of love or grief or joy, or most rare of all real stillness—reveals the ordinarily inert, nearly comatose, nature of ordinary consciousness." (*Context*, August 15, 1989, p. 3)

41. "The Eastern Straussians see America as fundamentally 'modern' by which they mean that America stands for the renunciation equally of the wisdom

of classical political philosophy and of Biblical revelation. . . . [They] assert that America is fundamentally Hobbesian. In other words, America was conceived in hedonism, atheism, and materialism and dedicated to the pursuit of comfortable self-preservation. However glorious the Founding may have been, the nation organized on this founding principle had sooner or later to abandon all glory in favor of a descent into the life of self-interestedness. As George Will, profoundly influenced by this line of analysis, puts it, America was 'ill-founded,' doomed to moral and political decay by the logic of its own principles.

"In contrast, the Western Straussians see America as broadly continuous with the classical and Biblical traditions. Indeed, in some respects they see it as perfecting these traditions, giving due public regard for the first time in history to the 'laws of nature and of nature's God'—i.e. both to the moral common ground and to the moral and theoretical disagreements between the great defining principles of the West: Reason and Revelation, Athens and Jerusalem." If Berns best states the Eastern case, Thomas Pangle and Kesler himself do best for the West—in case you want to look up the authors.

"More West: 'In the magnanimity of Washington and the other great statesmen of the Founding, . . . [they] find a practical wisdom that is better explained by Aristotle than Hobbes—and that informed the deliberations of the Founders at every step.' Yes, they had read Locke; but Algernon Sidney and Richard Hooker and, yes, Tacitus, Cicero, and the Bible were there, too.

"The East thinks America is 'solid but low' and that 'interest-group pluralism' is the best America can hope for. The West of Straussdom thinks that since 'America stands for something noble, for constitutional and moral principles transcending private appetites and public entitlements, then one ought to hope and to labor for a genuinely conservative restoration of American self-government.'" (*Context*, October 1, 1989, p. 2)

42. Oswald Spengler in *The Decline of the West:* "He foresaw a time in which moral discourse will become impossible, and instead of arguing moral questions, people will debate questions of alcohol and diet." He published this in 1918. See how much easier it is to get a dinner-table conversation moving happily along in 1989 on cholesterol or fiber in the diet than on abortion or poverty. (Quote from *Religion and Society Report*, July 1989, p. 6)

43. As the 1980 LCA statement on "Economic Justice" put it, justice takes place "at the intersection of serving love and enlightened self-interest." (*Forum Letter*, September 21, 1989, p. 3)

44. According to the *Journal of the American Medical Association:* "Authorities who have worked on stopping STD [sexually transmitted disease] spread for years said [that] the situation is now nearly out of control" [and warned that without a reversal in this trend] "We're going to have an entire infertile cohort [population age group under study]." The incidence of gonorrhea in the U.S.A. is ten times that in Sweden, and numbers of other STDs are prevalent, several

of which lead to irreversible sterility. Although AIDS is by far the most dramatic and menacing of the STDs, the total impact of the others on individuals and society is greater. (*Religion and Society Report*, October 1989, p. 8)

45. "Nietzsche, in *Thus Spake Zarathustra*, imagined a future race of beings who had abandoned the pursuit of happiness for the pursuit of health. He called these diminished denizens of the future 'the last men,' and he said of them that 'they have their little pleasure by day and their little pleasure for the night: but they respect health.' He could see them jogging toward him: bright faced creatures in their tracksuits, hearts beating, lungs dilating, heads brimming with the music on their Walkmen. These last men and women would convert sex into recreation; the asceticism of religion into the asceticism of athletics; the regimens of introspection into the power of positive thinking; the human good—in all its tragic complexity—into the glow of physical well-being.

    "When polled, Americans commonly list health at the top of their preoccupations, ahead of love, work, or money, and identify good health ahead of any other alternative, including love, as the chief source of happiness. . . . The medicalization of American individualism has made it only more evident that pursuing the American dream is a punishing marathon.

    "The message modern culture is likely to take from the new immunology is exactly the one Descartes took from his model of human nature: man's will will make him master of his fate. . . . The upbeat message of Siegel's book [*Love, Medicine and Miracles: Lessons Learned About Self-Healing from a Surgeon's Experience with Exceptional Patients*] is Promethean: you can cure yourself. The downbeat message is punitively Puritan: if treatment fails, you have nobody to blame but yourself. . . . Susan Sontag's *Illness as Metaphor* was the first to point out the accusatory side of the metaphors of empowerment that seek to enlist the patient's will to resist disease.

    "Hypochondria is indicative of modern individualism's persistent difficulty with reconciling itself to Fate, to its insistence that all dysfunction is a curable condition. As Baur [S. Baur, *Hypochondria: Woeful Imaginings*] points out, we present modern doctors with a range of minor disorders that premodern man would not have even considered illness, and we expect cures where no cure is either known or possible. . . . The 'last men' of modernity have jettisoned a culture of endurance for a culture of complaint." (Michael Ignatieff, "The Soul Returns to the Sickbed," *The New Republic*, December 26, 1988, p. 28)

46. G. K. Chesterton: "Despair does not lie in being weary of suffering, but in being weary of joy." (*Context*, November 1, 1989, p. 6)

47. "Removal of Gastrostomy Tube—McConnell v. Beverly Enterprises, 553 A.2d 596 (Conn. Sup. Ct., 1989): A Connecticut statute that authorizes the removal of life support systems only in specified circumstances was construed to permit the removal of a gastrostomy tube, even though the statute excludes nutrition and hydration from the definition of 'life support systems' that may be withdrawn. The Connecticut Supreme Court found it reasonable to distinguish

between artificial means of providing food and water, such as a gastrostomy tube, and normal means. The patient had suffered a severe head injury that left her in an irreversible persistent vegetative state. Her attending doctor determined that her condition was terminal and her family, acting in accordance with her express wishes, sought removal of the tube." (*LegalEase*, June 1989, p. 4)

48. "In its first decision on a patient's asserted 'right to die,' the U.S. Supreme Court held that a person whose wishes are clearly known has a constitutional right to the discontinuance of life-sustaining treatment. In its precedent-setting decision, eight Justices held that 'a competent person has a constitutionally protected liberty interest in refusing unwanted medical treatment.' The Justices, however, differed over how specific people must be in making their wishes known. In the *Cruzan* case [Cruzan v. Missouri 100 S. Ct. 2841 (June 25, 1990)], the Court ruled 5–4 that the state of Missouri can sustain the life of a woman, comatose for more than seven years, because her family had not shown by 'clear and convincing evidence' that she would have wanted the treatment stopped. Where a permanently unconsious person has left no clear instructions, the Court found a state is free to carry out its interests in the 'protection and preservation of human life' by denying a request by family members to terminate treatment. . . . Doctors have said that Ms. Cruzan could live 30 more years in her present unconscious condition. There are 10,000 people in the U.S. who are in the same type of coma as she is." (*LegalEase*, August 1990, p. 1)

49. Today's college students are indulging "premature affluence." "Campuses have come to resemble giant youth preserves where students are relatively free to do as they wish." (*Newsweek*, Fall/Winter Special Edition, 1990, p. 60)

50. Polybius (ca. 150 B.C.E.): "As men had fallen into such a state of luxury, avarice, and indolence that they did not wish to marry, or, if they married, to rear the children born to them, or at most but one or two of them, so as to leave these in affluence and bring them up to waste their substance—the evil insensibly but rapidly grew . . . and by small degrees cities became resourceless and empty." (P. Carrick, *Medical Ethics in Antiquity*, p. 106)

51. Jerome Miller "criticizes the 'modern therapeutic consciousness' here when it causes death to 'lose its capacity to devastate us. . . . We are never more unaware of what death really entails than when we speak of it without reserve. Because it fails to recognize that death's power to shatter our world cannot be accommodated within it, the new ethic of therapeutic openness avoids death as effectively as the most heartlessly scientific observation.'" (From Jerome A. Miller, *The Way of Suffering: A Geography of Crisis*, quoted in *Context*, November 15, 1989, p. 5)

52. "Peter Singer, the philosopher and defender of animal rights, writes: 'If we compare a severely defective human infant with a nonhuman animal, a dog or pig, for example, we will often find the nonhuman to have superior capacities, both actual and potential, for rationality, self consciousness, communication, and anything else that can plausibly be considered morally significant.'

"Francis Crick, who won a Nobel Prize in biology, argues that we should wait a certain period after children are born before legally declaring them to be persons. During this period they could be examined and tested; if found worthy, they could be allowed to live and be cared for; otherwise, permitted or helped to die.

"The idea of separating human personhood, with attendant rights, from biological humanity is a heavy weapon in the arsenal of defenders of abortion on demand. In a major work written in defense of abortion, one theologian writes: 'Many have argued that the term *person* should be reserved to designate those who *actually belong* to the moral community by virtue of criteria derived from our understanding of living human beings. In a notable defense of this position, philosopher Mary Ann Warren has proposed the following criteria for "personhood": "I suggest that the traits which are most central to the concept of personhood, or humanity in the moral sense, are, very roughly, the following:

1. consciousness (of objects and events external and/or internal to the being) and in particular the capacity to feel pain;

2. reasoning (the developed capacity to solve new and relatively complex problems);

3. self-motivated activity (activity which is relatively independent of either genetic or direct external control);

4. the capacity to communicate, by whatever means, messages of an indefinite variety of types, that is, not just with an indefinite number of possible contents, but on indefinitely many possible topics;

5. the presence of self-concepts, and self awareness, either individual or social, or both."'

"Consider the ideas of an even better-known and more influential thinker on the same subject: When a child is born, it is therefore not really 'in the world.' It takes several months before it reaches the point where it can actually move by itself and also absorb and express impressions other than the mere sensation of hunger, which is the pure expression of the will to live, just as it already exists in the fetus, simply taking on new form after the umbilical cord is cut and the previous form of food intake has been broken.

"But if that is so, then the infant does not actually take its place in human society until several months *after* its birth. So the question arises whether it runs counter to the basic principles of humaneness and the divine laws if one refuses to rear a newborn infant, which is clearly unviable when it emerges from the womb, but imposes on it the fate that would probably have befallen it anyway if the human gestation period, corresponding to natural requirements, had been longer. . . ."

"The writer who chose the quotation from Mary Ann Warren is Professor Beverly Wildung Harrison, a Presbyterian who teaches at Union Theological Seminary in New York. The second speaker was the late Adolf Hitler, a layman who subsequently became German Chancellor from 1933 to 1945. For 'The Criteria for Humanness,' see Francis Crick, in *Nature*, November 2, 1968; Peter Singer, 'Sanctity of Life or Quality of Life,' *Pediatrics*, July 1983, p. 129; Beverly Wildung Harrison, *Our Right to Choose* (Boston: Beacon Press, 1983), p. 219: Otto Wagener, *Hitler: Memoirs of a Confidant*, ed. by Henry Ashby Turner, Jr. (New Haven: Yale University Press, 1985), p. 146." (The whole passage is taken from *The Religion and Society Report*, November 1989, pp. 5–6.)

53. "In 1987, the latest year for which figures are available, the U.S. health-care tab rose 9.8% to 55.3 billion, or about 11.1% of the gross national product. . . . By 1993, it is expected to devour 12.5% of the GNP; by 2000, a whopping 15%.

"That isn't necessarily bad. Britain spends only about half as much per capita on health care as the U.S. does, but its citizens often spend years on waiting lists for high-tech palliatives Americans get for the asking. In Britain, patients sometimes have to wait years to receive artificial hips; every step during the wait causes excruciating pain.

"The U.S. system, though, has grown fat and unhealthy on its rich diet of high-tech goodies. Studies during the past few years indicate a fourth or more of our health dollars go for unneeded or questionable tests and treatments. Blue Cross and Blue Shield Association estimates $6 billion to $18 billion is wasted annually on tests alone. Meanwhile, some 37 million Americans don't have health insurance and struggle to get even minimal care.

"[Boston, a] city, known for its three medical schools and a wealth of prestigious hospitals, is also known for its physicians' costly style of practice—some doctors refer to patients who died after a plethora of heroic, high-tech measures as having suffered 'the Boston death.'

"A single liver transplant can cost $250,000 or more, and several U.S. children have had four of them. A premature baby can run up bills of $500,000 or more. As for the Boston death, don't ask." (David Stipp, "A Two-Edged Sword: Technology Offers Medical Miracles, but Miracles Cost Money," *Wall Street Journal*, November 13, 1989, pp. R19ff)

54. "Limiting use of technology is likely to reduce incomes of doctors, who derive fees from performing high-tech procedures. It could chill development of new technology that promises even better diagnosis and treatment. And it raises disturbing, ethical questions about access to technology, particularly among the poor and the very ill.

"Two years ago, the death of a seven-year-old Oregon boy whose family couldn't pay for a bone-marrow transplant provoked anger and anguish nationwide because the state Medicaid program had refused to pay for the surgery. But Oregon is nevertheless resolved to follow through on a crucial trade-off: To extend Medicaid insurance to more than 400,000 uncovered residents, it won't pay for some high-risk or high-cost procedures. 'We have a utilitarian ethic that says the greatest good for the greatest number,' says

John D. Golenxki of Bioethics Consultation Group Inc., a Berkeley, Calif., concern working with Oregon officials on the policy.

"Colorado, Maine, Washington and New Mexico are among states contemplating a similar approach. In some others, rationing is already a de facto condition. 'They ration care by setting rigorous standards about who gets covered in the first place,' says Daniel Callahan, director of the Hastings Center, a Briarcliff Manor, N.Y., think tank.

"In Texas, for instance, people qualify for Medicaid only if they earn less than 34% of the poverty-income level established by the federal government. That amounts to 958,000 people, says Donald Kelley, the state's deputy commissioner for health-care services. If Texas raised the threshold to 100%, an additional two million people would be eligible for Medicaid coverage. They are among the state's three million working poor and uninsured.

" 'What it is, is triage,' Dr. Kelley says. 'You've only got so much money, you can only do certain things. They [Oregon], may cover a lot more people, but their services aren't as broad as ours. We have chosen the people that we can cover and we cover them very well, though we're not extravagant.' " (Ron Winslow, "Rationing Care: Third Parties Step in to Perform Health-Care Triage," *Wall Street Journal*, November 13, 1989, p. R24)

55. "Of 503 patients over 70 years of age for whom resuscitation efforts were attempted, only 112 initially survived. But of those, only 19 regained enough health to eventually leave the hospital. Worse, only eight of the 19 returned home. The remainder were discharged to a nursing home or rehabilitation hospital. . . . In only 8% of the cases had doctors and the families even discussed what to do about resuscitation." (Michael Waldholz, "A Death in the Family," paraphrasing from *Annals of Internal Medicine* [August 1989], in the *Wall Street Journal*, November 13, 1989, p. R26)

56. "There is a staggering amount of waste in our health-care system, not in the sense of fraud so much as in the failure to apply technology to a stage of illness where it does the patient the most good. There are huge amounts of acute care that are unnecessary, not because patients don't need it, but because there was no one to help them early in the disease process, before they became acutely ill. I think that is the most serious problem that we face as a society.

"The idea that we have a limited amount of health-care dollars isn't controversial. But that we should seek to maximize the value of those dollars is a relatively new idea and it's long overdue." ("Taking Aim: An Expert Says the Health-Care System Puts Too Much Emphasis on Acute Care" [Interview with Jeff Goldsmith, national health-care adviser to accountants Ernst & Young and a lecturer at the University of Chicago's graduate school of business], *Wall Street Journal*, November 13, 1989, p. R29)

57. "Residents are so preoccupied with the problem of disease that they fail to think much about the patient who *has* the disease. And they forget (or never learn) how often the doctor himself must become part of the treatment, and

that in so doing, the doctor can often improve patient outcomes." (David Rogers, "Out of Touch: Is Technology Widening the Emotional Moat Between Doctors and Their Patients?" *Wall Street Journal*, November 13, 1989, p. R38)

58. Peter Laslett reviews Roderick Philips's important *Putting Asunder: A History of Divorce in Western Society:* "The 1950s and '60s are revealing themselves as the time of the Grand Climacteric in the family life of Western societies. It was then that consensual unions began to be widespread, abortion to be exceedingly common, contraception to be universal and numbers of births to fall so far that is now doubtful if many Western populations can maintain their numbers in the long term." The trend is so strong that "Roderick Philips finds himself wondering whether the time will come for the West when every marital union will be strictly temporary." (*Context*, December 1, 1989, p. 1)

59. Henri Poincaré (1854–1912) defined mathematics as follows: "Mathematics is the art of giving the same name to different things." (From Howard DeLong, *A Profile of Mathematical Logic* [Reading, Mass.: Addison Wesley], p. 88)

60. "What was remarkable about the Gettysburg Address, modern presidents please note, is its universalist vision. It posits no Satan. The only evil it understands—with a singleness of purpose that is appalling and sublime—is the evil of incompleteness. Thus Lincoln ensured that the Gettysburg battlefield would become a genuinely sacred place for the American republic . . . Lincoln's religious vision of a Union inhabited by free and equal citizens gave way to the coarse reality of Gilded Age America, built largely on the backs of exploited working men, women, and degraded blacks. Lincoln's principles may still prove impossible to realize as the foundations of a civil society. It was his political and literary genius, however, to have once compelled Americans to embrace them, even at the cost of nearly a million dead. Read Lincoln." (From the *New Republic*, quoted in *Context*, January 1, 1990, p. 2)

61. "[Ms. Evans] points out—the first time that this has been so strikingly brought to our attention—the degree to which infertility has become more common because of widespread contraceptive measures, including surgical sterilization, and of course abortion, which sometimes imperils a woman's subsequent ability to conceive and bear a child. Contraceptive technology permits the indefinite postponement of child bearing within marriage. It also facilitates sexual promiscuity, which often results in the sexually transmitted infections which reduce fertility. The contraceptive mentality tells women and their husbands that having children should be delayed, and when it is long delayed, problems of infertility are both more common and harder to treat. All this results in further alienation and exploitation of women—and, although Evans does not stress it, of the men who love them." (From the review of D. Evans, *Without Moral Limits: Women, Reproduction and the New Medical Technology* in the *Religion & Society Report*, February 1990, p. 7)

62. "While Gorbachev was conferring with the Pope, America's intellectual and artistic elite were demonstrating for 'anything goes' and more condoms. Divine

liturgy was celebrated in the Kremlin and only Frosty the Snowman remains for the ox and the ass to contemplate in the Chicago suburbs." (*Religion & Society Report*, February 1990, p. 8)

63. Stuart Westbury, Jr., PhD, FACHE, President, American College of Healthcare Executives, Chicago: "Our biggest problem in the '90's will be balancing ethics with resources. The major, medically-related ethical issues are all going to be finance driven. We'll deal with resource allocation and questions related to rationing, or assuring that rationing doesn't occur.

   "Issues like genetic engineering, in vitro fertilization, and other somewhat controversial programs still will not reach the top of the list in terms of major issues to deal with because they will be replaced by financial problems. Any ethical issue that has a significant financial component is going to take precedence over those that do not. I personally see a great deal of finance in right-to-die decisions." (*Medical Ethics Advisor* 6, no. 1 [January 1990]: 1)

64. Norma G. Calhoun, Administrator, Jesse Holman Jones Hospital; Springfield, Tenn.: "We significantly increased the cost of health care by trying to prolong life. Decisions in the 90s will be made based on economics. Who gets the transplant? Who gets dialysis?" (*Medical Ethics Advisor* 6, no. 1 [January 1990]: 1)

65. Arthur L. Caplan, PhD, Director, Center for Biomedical Ethics, University of Minnesota, Minneapolis: "In the '90s, there will be an extensive debate over national health insurance and what minimum benefits should be. We'll also see more attention paid to the relevance of personal responsibility for illness in allocating health care resources. Will smokers, drinkers, and people who don't wear their seatbelts be excluded because they failed to show the proper virtue to deserve medical care?" (*Medical Ethics Advisor* 6, no. 1 [January 1990]: 4)

66. Gordon Nary, Executive Director, AIDS Medical Resource Center, Chicago: "Essentially, we're going to be facing an ethical issue of health care rationing during the next decade.

   "If you take a look at the statistics for HIV infection; the fact that those infected are living longer; the amount of money it is costing to keep them alive; and some of the newer complications, such as an increase in dementia, and average cost of treatment for a patient is going to double over the next few years. It is around $55,000 now. It will be up over $100,000 soon.

   "The economy can't handle it. Without federal intervention, New York City's entire health care system is ready to go under very soon." (*Medical Ethics Advisor* 6, no. 1 [January 1990]: 5)

67. Ronald E. Cranford, MD, Associate Physician in Neurology, Hennepin County Medical Center, Minneapolis, Minn.: "In the 1990s, we will have to confront the issue not just of stopping treatment and letting patients die comfortably, but of active euthanasia.

   "You'll see a lot more suicides among the elderly, and there will be more grassroots movement towards euthanasia through lethal injections and other means. I honestly don't know where that will go. I don't know where I want it to go.

"I would hope that physicians and others can develop policies for more humane care of the dying and better treatment of pain and suffering. Withdrawing fluids and nutrition will become—and should become—commonplace and a more fully recognized practice in the 1990s.

"When the prognosis is uncertain, you treat. When you know there's no hope for recovery, then you're willing to aggressively stop treatment. That's a beginning, and we have a long way to go." (*Medical Ethics Advisor* 6, no. 1 [January 1990]: 5)

68. Moore vs. The Regents of the University of California: John Moore had a type of cancer called Hairy-cell Leukemia. It enlarged his spleen to 14 pounds from the 1 pound it should be. Moore received surgery to replace the spleen and when it was tested, the doctors found that it had a mechanism that attacked viruses and regulated the immune system. Through several years of research his physician isolated the attack cells. He received a patent for his new discovery and a sum of more than $2 million. When Moore was called to sign release forms to remove all rights to his spleen, he became suspicious and found out what the physician had done. He then filed suit saying that he should receive part of the profits. The Court ruled against Moore saying that recognizing ownership of body parts would open the way for lawsuits over frozen embryos, eggs and sperm, fetal tissue, and abortion. This case became the basis from which the National Transplant Act, preventing the sale of organs, came into effect. On appeal the California Surpreme Court concurred with the lower court in July, 1990, that a patient does not have property rights over body tissue that may be used to develop new drugs or medicines. The majority of the court argued that letting patients sue for rights in research would threaten incentives to conduct important medical research. The Court, however, did say that physicians have a "fiduciary duty" to tell a patient if researchers had an economic or personal interest in using or studying such tissues. The Court held that, if the fiduciary duty is not fulfilled, a patient may sue for breach of the duty of informed consent. ("Who Owns John Moore's Spleen?" *Chicago Tribune*, February 18, 1990, p. E1, and "Patient's Right to Tissue," *LegalEase*, August 1990, p. 4)

69. "It's thundering, lightning, hailing, storming, blowing at the closed gates to Eden; and the hand of the Lord is pointing Adam and Eve into exile from the Garden. Eve to Adam, smiling in exit: 'Well, at least we'll probably be able to get a book out of it.' " (From *Publishers Weekly*, quoted in *Context*, December 1, 1989, p. 6)

APPENDIX ▲ B

▼

Recreational Questioning Games

The interrogative "games" we have described can be compared with certain familiar games that are played for fun. Some years ago on television there was a program called *What's My Line.* In this game a celebrity panel would try to determine the occupation of a guest by asking a series of questions. In the game known as "twenty questions," you are allowed twenty questions to help you determine the object being thought of by your opponent. These sorts of games provide useful illustrations of some of the important features of interrogative inquiry.

For example, in these games the rules are constructed in such a way that you are usually prevented from solving the whole problem with a single question. In rational inquiry we are often prevented by the difficulty of the problem from solving it with but one question. The mistake in reasoning called "begging the question" involves trying to get the conclusive final answer by asking a big question you are not in a position to ask. Similarly, in these games participants are prevented from asking too big a question at the beginning. Instead, they must approach the solution step by step, using a series of questions.

These games also illustrate the two different roles questions and answers can play in inquiry. Sometimes a question leads directly to the conclusive answer that completes the inquiry. Often, however, questions have a more modest role. Many are designed to lead to intermediate answers. These intermediate answers, in turn, often open up the possibility of asking yet another question that may bring us closer to the conclusive answer.

"Botticelli"

Another recreational game, called "Botticelli," can illuminate these and several other features of the interrogative process. It will be useful to describe this game in detail.

"Botticelli" is best played with four or more people. One person is "it." For convenience we will use the name *Askee* for this person. The Askee chooses some historical figure either living or dead. The historical figure should be someone with whom everyone participating in the game is already definitely acquainted.

The goal of the game is for the others to identify the historical figure by means of a prescribed method of questioning. Initially, the only kind of question that can be asked of the Askee is a question of the form, "Are you the person who . . . " In the game these are called "stump questions." The part following the word *who* is filled in with some sort of description that would identify one or more historical persons. For example, "Are you the person who was president at the beginning of the War Between the States?" If the Askee has, in fact, chosen to be Abraham Lincoln, then she or he must admit this and the game is over. More likely, the Askee has chosen someone else, but she or he is still required to try to indicate who is being described in the stump question. In this case, if the Askee can successfully answer "Abraham Lincoln," then another stump question must be tried. Another stump question would be, "Are you the person who painted 'Venus Rising from the Sea'?" Perhaps the Askee won't know the answer to this one! (It happens to be the Italian Renaissance painter Sandro Botticelli, after whom this game is named.) In order to keep these stump questions somewhat fair, it is often agreed that when the Askee is "stumped," that is, fails to give the right answer, then at least one other person in the game must know the answer in addition to the person who posed the question. Otherwise the question is disqualified. If the Askee has been stumped, then the person who asked the stump question has earned the right to ask a different kind of question.

In the game this new kind of question is called a "direct question." Direct questions must be formulated so that the Askee can answer either "yes" or "no." Direct questions are chosen so as to narrow down the range of persons under consideration. For example, the Askee might be asked, "Is your person living?" The Askee must answer truthfully "yes" or "no." (You can see that the Askee should choose someone with whom he or she is reasonably familiar.) Notice that the answer to a well-chosen direct question will usually help focus the search in a more narrow area. If the Askee answers "no" to "Is your person living," that will eliminate a lot of people. Perhaps in the next direct question we would ask, "Was your person born after the year 1500?" Such a question would again help us narrow our search. Many different kinds of direct questions are useful, about gender, about occupation, about homeland, and so forth. The goal is to be able to ask enough direct questions until we finally come upon the chosen person. Unfortunately, the right to ask a direct question has to be earned each time by posing a successful stump question. By the way, as we mentioned before, if a stump question happens to zero in on the chosen historical figure, the Askee is required to answer truthfully and end the game.

One other rule must be noticed. Stump questions have to be chosen from within the boundaries of what we know about the person. For example, assume that we have asked the direct question, "Is your person female?" Assume further that the Askee has answered "yes." Now all further stump questions must be about women. This makes it harder to find stump questions, but it also forces all participants to focus their attention more closely on the area where the chosen historical figure will ultimately be found.

We note in passing that this game can also be played with fictional characters rather than historical characters. Participants can also agree to begin in a more limited area. For example, it could be decided to play the game thinking only of living persons, or only of women, or only of sports figures, or whatever.

Learning from "Botticelli"

This game has been described in detail, because it will help us grasp some important features of interrogative inquiry. Like the other games, it illustrates how we often are prevented in one way or another from asking the big question. In Botticelli we are forbidden to ask "Who are you anyway?" That would be "begging the question." Instead we must construct a series of questions that will lead us step by step toward the final answer.

Botticelli also can illustrate the difference between question-answer steps and logical inference steps. Assume that we have earned the right to ask a direct question and that we ask "Is your person's native language English?" Assume that the answer is "yes." This question-answer step gives us both direct and indirect information. Directly it tells us the person's native language is English. But by simple logical inference we can now rule out many people we might have been wondering about. The answer allows us to infer that the person is not an ancient Greek philosopher, or an Old Testament prophet, or the current leader of Mainland China. It would be a waste of questions to ask about any of these. In interrogative inquiry question-answer steps interact creatively with logical inference steps to move us toward our goal. This game can give us practice in looking for strategic direct questions whose answers will maximize the information we can get. It can encourage us to look for questions which not only give direct information but also set up a variety of logical inference steps. Here we see some of the difference between merely following the definitory rules and having an effective strategy for playing the game.

Botticelli also illustrates the notion of a "range of possibilities." As the game progresses our questions must be chosen from an increasingly narrow range of possible persons. If we know that the person is living, then the range of our possibilities is limited to living persons. If we know that the person is male, then the range of our possibilities is limited to men. Keeping track of the range of possibilities as we pursue a topic helps us focus our efforts more effectively. This is directly related to our understanding of "information" as "that which makes it possible to eliminate from an inquiry certain alternative situations that otherwise might have been thought possible." (See Section 1.8 in Chapter 1.)

There is one other important matter that Botticelli illustrates. We need to analyze the relationship between questions and answers very closely. For this it is necessary to distinguish between different kinds of questions. Botticelli illustrates one of the main differences very well. This little game has both stump questions and direct questions. The difference between these is that stump questions are an example of what logicians call *"wh-" questions*. The basic form underlying a stump question is "Who. . .," making use of one of the famous newspaper reporting words *who, what, when, where, how,* and *why.* The direct questions in our game are an example of what logicians call *statement (or propositional) questions,* of which yes/no questions are among the simplest. Here we simply notice the difference between these kinds of questions. In Chapters 11 and 16 we study this difference in much more detail.

Relaxing Exercise: Get together with some friends and play a questioning game.

A P P E N D I X ▲ C

▼

Puzzles, Problems, and Mistakes in Inquiry

Our approach to inquiry has been to discuss definitory rules for correctness in reasoning and strategic rules for excellence in reasoning. From time to time we have commented on mistakes in reasoning, but our focus has been on how things can be done rightly rather than on how they are so often done wrongly.

We are now at a point where we can reinforce much of what we have learned by looking at some of the mistakes, problems, and puzzles that crop up in inquiry. Many of these mistakes are discussed in traditional textbooks under the term "fallacies." In this appendix we will examine many of the traditional fallacies and also look at some interesting puzzles about reasoning.

C.1 An Overview of Different Ways to Make Mistakes

Our approach to inquiry as inquiry enables us to provide an overview of different kinds of fallacies and an understanding of their true nature. It is sometimes said, or assumed, that fallacies are mistaken inferences or inference patterns. This is far too narrow a view. By now you are thoroughly accustomed to distinguishing between interrogative and logical inference moves. You also know that mistakes can happen in either kind of move. Hence not all fallacies are mistakes committed in making logical inference moves. Fallacies also occur when interrogative steps are carried out.

For instance, it is a mistake to ask a question whose presupposition has not been established. As was pointed out above in Chapter 11 (Section 11.3), such a mistake is traditionally labeled a "fallacy," namely, the "fallacy of many questions." Such a fallacy is not, however, a mistake in inference. It is a mistake in questioning.

Furthermore, you are by this time familiar with the distinction between *definitory* rules of inquiry (reasoning) and *strategic* rules of inquiry. Mistakes in reasoning can involve an offense against either type of rule. Most of the mistakes traditionally called "fallacies" in philosophical books are violations of the definitory rules of reasoning. However, some fallacies are strategic mistakes rather than breaches of definitory rules. One simple example of strategic fallacies goes back to Aristotle. It amounts to moving in a circle in one's argument. One could call it (even though Aristotle does not) the fallacy of circular reasoning.

For instance, we might start with a simple argument represented as follows: Q is true because P is true and we know that $P \supset Q$. But somebody might ask how we can claim that P is true, and we might say that P is true because R is true and $R \supset P$. They might then want to ask how we can claim that R is true. If we were to say, "R is true because Q is true and we know that $Q \supset R$," our interlocutor might begin to worry. For she or he might rightly suspect that if we were once again asked how we can claim that Q is true, we would go back to the top of this paragraph and start over. In such circumstances we could be accused of "reasoning in a circle."

Reasoning in a circle in this way need not involve any violations of the definitory rules of reasoning. No mistake has been made in logical inference, and there is nothing incorrect about bringing in new information through interrogative moves. What is wrong with such circular arguments is that they do not lead us to a successful conclusion. If our hearers are at all careful in what they accept, they will want something outside the circle before they will accept all the interrogative moves that are currently within the circle. Or, if they accept all the interrogative moves as they stand, it must mean that the little circle of inferences was unnecessary. Either we have failed to convince, or we have wasted time and effort. Reasoning in a circle illustrates a problem with strategy rather than with definitory rules. While correct, either the interrogative or the inference moves have been ill-advised.

The contrast between definitory fallacies and strategic fallacies applies both to logical inference mistakes and mistakes in asking questions. We thus have the following fourfold classification of fallacies:

1. Definitory logical inference fallacies.
2. Strategic logical inference fallacies.
3. Definitory interrogative fallacies.
4. Strategic interrogative fallacies.

Strategic fallacies, however, cannot always be classified as mistakes in influence or mistakes in interrogation. The reason is that a strategy usually involves both kinds of moves and so a strategic error may involve both inference and interrogation.

C.2 Puzzles, Problems, and Mistakes in Logical Inference Moves

Inclusive and Exclusive "Or"

Our first topic is not much of a problem. It involves simply reminding ourselves that in working with statements containing "or," we must be careful not to read too much into the "or." In everyday English we sometimes use "or" in a way that says of the component statements: "One or the other is true but not both." On other occasions we use "or" to say: "One or the other or possibly both of the component statements are true." There is nothing wrong with our having these two uses. The first is called the *exclusive* use of "or," and the second is called the *inclusive* use.

Some languages provide two distinct words to mark this difference. For example, in Latin the exclusive disjunction is indicated by *aut* and the inclusive by *vel*. Our English "unless" and "or else" sometimes indicate exclusive disjunction, but not always. As we discussed in Chapter 9, this can be a source of misunderstanding.

Problems arise in logical inference if we are not careful to note which use of "or" is intended. In the deductive logic we learned back in Chapters 6 and 7, we tried, as a matter of strategy, to minimize the problems by agreeing always to interpret "or" as an inclusive "or." The reason for this is that the inclusive use of "or" conveys somewhat less information, and we are perhaps on safer ground to take only the minimum information from it. We devised the definitory table rules for "or" on the basis of this strategy.

That is not always an entirely satisfactory solution. Sometimes we know that an exclusive "or" is intended, and when this is the case it can be helpful to use the additional information provided. It is not difficult to show the additional information provided by exclusive "or." If we want to say "*A* or *B*," and mean exclusive "or," we could write $(A \ \& \ -B) \vee (B \ \& \ -A)$. The main point for the careful reasoner is that we need to be alert to how much information is being given by the "or" in everyday English and to use only as much information as is clearly available to us.

Exercise: Find or construct an argument which is valid if "or" is taken in the exclusive sense but invalid if taken to be inclusive. (Hint, review the discussion of "or else" in Chapter 9.)

Three Common Mistakes with Conditionals ("If-Then" Statements)

In Part 2 our definitory rule for conditionals (Table Rule 5) told us to split our logical table into two subtables with the denial of the antecedent (left component) in one subtable and the consequent (right component) in the other. This meant that if we happened also to know or discover that the antecedent was in fact true, then we could close the subtable that contained the denial of the antecedent (by Table Rule 7). In other words we would know that the subtable with the consequent in it is the one where the truth lies.

Or again, if we happened to know or discover that the denial of the consequent is true, then we could close the subtable with the consequent in it (by Table Rule 7). This would mean that the subtable with the denial of the antecedent in it must be the one where the truth lies.

As you learned in Exercise 7-C, people sometimes give Latin names to these inferences and indicate them in the following way:

Modus Ponens: $A \supset C$

$\underline{A}$

Therefore, C

Modus Tollens: $A \supset C$

$\underline{-C}$

Therefore, $-A$

This way of looking at how we reason with conditionals is correct, but it can mislead people. You might think that the following three inferences would also work:

Fallacy of Denying the Antecedent: $A \supset C$

$\underline{-A}$

Therefore, $-C$

Fallacy of Affirming the Consequent: $A \supset C$

$\underline{C}$

Therefore, A

Fallacy of Conversion: $\underline{A \supset C}$

Therefore, $C \supset A$

As you learned in Exercises 7-C and 8-C, all three of these patterns of reasoning are invalid and mistaken.

These mistakes in inference come about because people tend to read more into a complicated "if-then" statement than is actually there. One way to avoid such mistakes is simply to mark and avoid them as we are now doing. Once you have memorized that affirming the consequent, denying the antecedent, and conversion are all errors, you will be alert to avoid them.

Another approach is to review once again for yourself what is involved in valid deductive inference. A valid inference is one in which there is absolutely no way to imagine the conclusion false while imagining the premises all true. The table method gives a systematic way for doing the imagining, but you can also test a trial English sentence in your mind and see whether the inference is valid. For example, I might say that, "If it is raining, I will get wet." We might further imagine that "It is not raining." Does this mean there is no way to imagine that "I will get wet"? Of course not. But the fallacy of denying the antecedent claims that there is no way to imagine that "I will get wet." It is clearly a mistake. This same example can help you see the mistake in the fallacy of affirming the consequent and in the fallacy of conversion.

Exercise: Use the table method to show that the following inference pattern is valid:

Transposition: $\underline{A \supset C}$
Therefore, $-C \supset -A$

(Note very carefully how similar this is to conversion and yet how different. Conversion is invalid; transposition is valid.)

An Interesting Puzzle about Conditional, "If-Then," Statements

In Part 2 we were introduced to one way of analyzing "if-then" statements. "If-then" statements were represented by $\supset$, and they were said to be false only when the antecedent (left component) was true while the consequent (right component) was false. This is the standard truth-functional analysis of conditional statements. Conditionals understood in this way are sometimes called "material conditionals."

We mentioned, however, that this analysis does not always capture all the meaning of "if-then" statements in ordinary English. The analysis is used because it seems to get at the minimum meaning of "if-then," and our strategy was not to overinterpret the conditional. Unfortunately (or fortunately, if you like puzzles and tricks), this introduces some tricky puzzles. In this section we will explore some of the interesting problems that arise in understanding conditional statements.

Already in ancient Greece there were people who disagreed about how best to understand "if-then" statements. Some thinkers took the truth-functional approach that we took in Part 2, but others argued that we must be aware of several other ways to look at conditional statements.

The quickest way into the problems is to notice the dangerous side of the strategy of letting $\supset$ stand for the minimum meaning of our various "if-then" statements in English. We say $A \supset B$ is false only when the antecedent (A) is true while the consequent (B) is false. But this must mean that $-(A \supset B)$ is true only when the antecedent (A) is true while the consequent (B) is false. This is, in fact, what our Table Rule 6 in Part 2 was telling us. Here is the table:

Premises and What Follows from Them	Conclusion
1. √ −[(A ∨ B) ⊃ C] (prem)	. . . .
2. (A ∨ B) & −C (1 by 6)	
3. (A ∨ B) . (2 by 3)	
4. −C (2 by 3)	

Notice how the rule tells us that both the antecedent and the denial of the consequent are in fact true. An example, however, will show that this gives us some troubles. Try this conditional statement:

(∗)   If John writes his social security number on his examination paper, I will fail him in the course.

That seems pretty drastic! So, we can probably say that

(∗∗) It is not the case that if John writes his social security number on his examination paper, I will fail him in the course.

Let A stand for "John writes his social security number on his examination paper." And let B stand for "I will fail him in the course." This will mean that we have

(∗)   A ⊃ B

and

(∗∗) −(A ⊃ B)

Now I claim that I can prove from (∗∗) both that John *will* inescapably write his social security number on his examination paper and that I *will not* fail him in the course. Look at the table:

Premises and What Follows from Them	Conclusion
1. √ −(A ⊃ B) (prem ∗∗)	5. A & −B
2. (A & −B) (from 1 by 6)	
3. A (from 2 by 3)	6. A | −B
4. −B (from 2 by 3)	| (from 5 by 3r)
7. Bridges in both subtables	

This is too much! It seems quite plausible to assert the statement in (∗∗). But when I assert (∗∗), I certainly do not mean also to assert that it is true that John *will* write his number and that I *will not* fail him. The problem is that because we decided to interpret the truth of a conditional in a relatively weak way, we thereby are forced to interpret the denial of a conditional in a strong way.

Several different suggestions have been made about what may be going wrong here. One suggestion is that in everyday language we sometimes use conditional, "if-then," statements to assert a *causal* relationship between the antecedent and the consequent. When I say "If John writes his social security number on his examination sheet, then I will fail him," it sounds as though I am saying that John's writing his number will *cause* me to fail him. That's what also sounds implausible, so we are ready to say that it is not the case that John's writing his number will cause me to fail him.

The minimum analysis of "if-then" that we use in formal logic does not capture all of what we are saying when we assert a causal relationship. The minimum analysis only guarantees that if the antecedent is true, then the consequent will also be true. This captures part of what we mean when we assert a causal relationship but not all of what we mean. Thus, it is not surprising that when we deny $A \supset B$ in order to deny a causal relationship we get some unexpected results.

Sometimes "if then" statements made in ordinary or philosophical discourse express a logical connection, namely, that the consequent is a valid logical consequence of the antecedent. In this case "if-then" is expressing a connection between the antecedent and the consequent that is even stronger than that of a causal link. Truth-functional treatment of logical consequence falls even more short of capturing the full meaning of the original "if-then" than does truth-functional treatment of causal relations.

An attempt to provide a truth-functional treatment of valid logical consequence amounts to confusing the relationship between truth and validity. Truth-functional "if-then" permits any and all consequent statements to follow a false antecedent. Logical consequence, by contrast, requires showing that there is no way to imagine the consequent false while imagining the antecedent true. (See Chapter 5, Section 5.9, for a review of this relationship between truth and validity.) Use of truth-functional "if-then" should thus be avoided in discussions of valid logical consequence in reasoning and argumentation. The words "entails" and "implies" are often used in English instead of "if-then" to indicate the relationship of valid logical consequence.

To have noted this, however, is not to have decided what to do about the problems. Over many centuries different suggestions have been made. For our purposes, the most important lesson is again that we must be very careful as we try to think through what we are doing in our reasoning. We cannot simply rely on mechanical definitory rules but must always try to be clear about what reasoning strategies justify the moves we make in our inquiries.

Exercises

1. It is not the case that if you read this appendix you will pass the course. So, it must be that you will read this appendix and you will not pass the course. What does the table method say about this little argument? What do you say?

2. It is false that if you live in Tallahassee then you live in Atlanta. It is also false that if you live in Jacksonville then you live in Atlanta. Does this mean that you live both in Tallahassee and in Jacksonville? What does the table method say about this? What do you say?

3. If you neglect your studies you will fail. But you do not neglect your studies. So, you won't fail. What does the table method say about this? What do you think?

4. If you neglect your studies you will fail. And you failed. So, you must have neglected your studies. What does the table method say about this? What do you think?

5. If you neglect your studies you will fail. So, if you did not fail, then you did not neglect your studies. What does the table method say about this? What do you think?

6. If you neglect your studies you will fail. So, if you fail, then you neglected your studies. What does the table method say about this? What do you think?

7. Statement logic will show that the following complex statement cannot be imagined false: "If water freezes, then it is the case that if the temperature goes above 100 degrees Celsius then water freezes." The way to check this statement by the methods of statement logic is to put the complex statement into a formal representation. Then put the complex formula on the right (conclusion) side of a table and apply right-side table rules. Only one path will develop and it will close by Table Rule 7. What is happening here?

8. Use the approach taken in exercise 7 to see what statement logic does with the following complex statement: "Either Mary is taller than John if John is taller than Mary, or Mary is taller than John only if John is taller than Mary." Can the complex statement be imagined false according to statement logic? What is happening here?

C.3 Puzzles, Problems, and Mistakes in Interrogative Moves

The philosopher Aristotle said that there are many ways to do things wrongly and only a few ways to do them rightly. This is certainly true when it comes to interrogative moves in inquiry. In Part 3 we focused mainly on the ways in which interrogative moves can be rightly and effectively made. Now we look at some of the most commonly made mistakes in interrogative moves.

One way to avoid mistakes is to study them and name them, so that we are more alert to them when they occur. For more than two thousand years people have been studying and naming common mistakes in inquiry. In the following we will examine what are sometimes said to be "material fallacies." They are given this name to distinguish them from errors in logical inference which are sometimes called "formal fallacies." This also distinguishes them from errors having to do with ambiguity and vagueness (see Chapter 20) which are sometimes called "linguistic fallacies."

We would prefer, however, to speak of logical inference fallacies and interrogative fallacies, and to keep an eye out for when definitory rules are being broken and when strategic problems are emerging. We now turn our attention to mistakes in interrogative moves.

Begging the Question (*Petitio Principii*)

The famous mistake of begging the question was discussed in detail in Chapter 10 (Section 10.12). There the error was explained as an interrogative fallacy involving an attempt to ask the big, principal question in an inquiry too soon. Begging the question was said to be a matter of taking questioning shortcuts that are not available to us. Whenever we sense that considerable interrogative and logical inference work needs to be done to support a conclusion, we resist people's attempts to take shortcuts by claiming that the oracle will answer the big, principal question immediately, without need for further work.

Exercise: One form which the fallacy of begging the question takes is sometimes referred to by business consultants as "trying to manage the results instead of the activities that produce them." This error in business is further described as follows: "A baseball player never hits .300. He swings the bat. What happens next is beyond his control. Good ballplayers concentrate on their swing and accept their batting averages. . . . It is the same in business." (*Fortune*, July 30, 1990, p. 248) Explain how this error in business management can be seen to be a form of begging the question.

Circular Reasoning

Earlier in this appendix (Section C.1) we briefly discussed the problem of reasoning in a circle. This problem is similar to begging the question, because it seems to make the ordinary work of making interrogative and logical inference moves unnecessary. But in many cases such work *is* necessary, and we resist the attempts that some make to take unconvincing shortcuts.

Neither begging the question nor reasoning in a circle involves an obvious breach of any definitory rule. Instead, both come into play when we suspect that the strategy someone is employing takes too much of a shortcut on the way to the conclusion. We say they are mistaken, not because we dislike shortcuts, but because we think that a truly effective strategy for attacking the problem under discussion will require more reasoning than they are offering.

Many Questions

The interrogative fallacy of many questions, unlike the preceding fallacies, *does* involve a breach of a definitory rule. In Chapter 11 (Section 11.3) we discussed this error and suggested that it might better be called "jumping to a presupposition."

A key definitory rule of interrogative moves requires that we check to be sure that the presupposition of a question has been established before we ask or answer a question. Errors can be introduced into our reasoning when we permit interrogative moves based upon presuppositions that have not yet been established.

Interrogative Fallacies Involving the Reliability of Answers to Questions

You have learned that it is very important to assess the reliability of answers to the interrogative moves we make in inquiry. You also know that it is important to look for suppressed questions that may be hiding unreliable answers. A number of the interrogative fallacies described below involve common ways in which people are tempted to accept unreliable answers to their questions.

Appeal to Illegitimate Authority **(Ad Verecundiam)**   We often must rely on experts as authorities to answer questions involved in our inquiries. *Verecundiam* means "modesty," and in many cases there is nothing wrong with the modesty that defers to a legitimate authority. The error of appealing to illegitimate authority occurs whenever we lack good reasons for trusting our authorities.

There are many ways to illustrate this error. Some people are so impressed with successful entertainers that they also are tempted to trust these people in matters that have nothing to do with entertainment. They choose a car because a favorite actor endorses it, or they adopt a view about marriage simply because a singer they admire says that is what she thinks about marriage.

Even when we have good reason to trust our authorities, it remains a good policy to be somewhat critical toward them and to take such opportunities as we have to examine and test the answers they give us. In Chapters 12 and 13 we learned some techniques for coping with answers about which we are uncertain.

The Appeal to Popular Attitudes **(Ad Populum)**   The error based on the appeal to popular attitudes is closely related to the appeal to illegitimate authority. Some people are prone to be led by popular opinion. Their principle seems to be that if everybody is saying (or doing) it, it must be right. But, of course, truth does not always lie in numbers. We cannot uncritically accept popular attitudes as a reliable source of answers. Instead, care must be taken to examine what people are saying to see if there are reasons for going along with the crowd or not.

In our society we love to take polls and find out what people are thinking. There is nothing wrong with getting this information, but there is a temptation to think that once we know what the majority think we also know what is the truth. To give in to this temptation is likely to allow some unreliable answers into our inquiries.

The Appeal to Force (**Ad Baculum**)   In the case of the appeal to force, which also involves something like the appeal to illegitimate authority, we are tempted to accept answers to our questions simply because an individual or an institution holds some kind of power over us. It is easy to see that sometimes it may be necessary to adopt policies like

(∗) The boss is always right.

and

(∗∗) If the boss is wrong, see (∗).

However, as far as truth in inquiry is concerned, might does not make right. It can be necessary to listen to people who have power over us, but it is also necessary to examine whether the answers they give us hold up under scrutiny.

A Pause to Probe More Deeply   We could analyze appeals to illegitimate authority, to popular attitudes, and to force a little more completely by noting that, in a sense, people who make these appeals are *suppressing another question which needs asking.* In each case the question would be something like this: What is there about the authority, the majority, or the person in power that makes him or her a reliable oracle on the matters about which we are inquiring? If there are no good answers to this suppressed question, then there is no reason to admit answers from such an oracle into our inquiry.

The Appeal to Pity (**Ad Misericordiam**)   The appeal to pity also usually involves some kind of suppressed question. Suppose I am inquiring whether the grade of C that I gave a student in a course is appropriate. I might ask the student what he or she thinks, or (more likely) the student may come to tell me what he or she thinks. Perhaps the student says, "This is the last course I need to be able to graduate, and I must get a B to graduate." I might be inclined to believe that the information given is true. But it is clear that the student is also hoping that I will add another piece of information into my inquiry about whether the grade of C is appropriate or not. Wisely, the student usually does not explicitly draw attention to this other piece of information, but he or she is very much hoping that I will accept it into my inquiry.

We can express this suppressed question this way: Should a student's requirements for graduation be a factor in the instructor's decision about the student's grade in a course? As soon as this suppressed question is out in the open we see that the student's answer to my question about the appropriateness of the grade may not have been very relevant to the inquiry. It will be relevant only if requirements for graduation should be part of my decision on the grade.

The appeal to pity works on us in two ways. First, it keeps the key question about the relevance of some information suppressed, and, second, it plays on the human tendency to be sympathetic toward others. The hope is that feelings of pity or sympathy will keep the inquirer from examining the whole picture too closely. We, however, have learned that it is necessary to bring important suppressed questions to the surface. We should not proceed to a conclusion based on feelings of sympathy until we have examined whether those feelings are relevant to the inquiry.

It is important to notice that there *are* occasions when sympathy and emotions are relevant in important inquiries. You can find an interesting discussion of the role of sympathy in ethical inquiry in *The Conscience of Huckleberry Finn* by Jonathan Bennett (*Philosophy* 49[1974]: 123–134) and in *The Role of Emotion in Decisionmaking* by S. Callahan (*Hastings Center Report* 18, no. 3[1988]: 9–14).

What About You? (Tu Quoque)

What About You? **(Tu Quoque)**   This problem is often found in courts of law. The basic move looks like this:

ATTORNEY FOR THE DEFENSE: Mr. Gates, you have accused Mr. Doberly of embezzling $50,000 from the firm where you both worked?

MR. GATES: Yes.

ATTORNEY FOR THE DEFENSE: But you also have admitted embezzling a large sum from the firm, have you not?

MR. GATES: Yes.

ATTORNEY FOR THE DEFENSE: Can you explain why you expect us to believe your accusations against Mr. Doberly?

MR. GATES: . . . .

What will Mr. Gates say? More importantly, what should we think about this line of inquiry? The problem for us to decide is whether Mr. Gates's admission that he is guilty of the same crime discredits the answers he has given to questions about Mr. Doberly. In other words, the suppressed question has to do with assessing Mr. Gates's reliability as an oracle.

On the one hand, we will certainly be wise to be somewhat skeptical about Mr. Gates's reliability. But on the other hand, the fact that he is guilty of the same crime does not clearly indicate that he would be an unreliable source of information about Mr. Doberly. In a situation like this what is called for is a more careful examination of all the factors that might shed light on Mr. Gates's reliability. Here, some of the techniques we learned in Chapter 13 on testing the reliability of our oracles will come in handy.

The important point to notice is that it will not do simply to say "What about you? Didn't you do it too?" Instead, we must patiently examine how reliable our source of information may be.

Against the Person (Poisoning the Wells)

Against the Person (Poisoning the Wells)   A more general form of the "What About You?" problem involves all those occasions when our inquiry shifts from pursuing the truth to inaccurately or irrelevantly attacking one of the sources of answers for the inquiry—the opposite of the appeal to illegitimate authority. Here a legitimate source of answers is being undermined by inaccurate and/or irrelevant attacks on the answerer. It is a fact of human behavior that when we begin to be pushed toward some conclusion we do not like, we are tempted to take desperate measures to avoid the truth. One common desperate measure is to begin striking out wildly in an attempt to discredit the source of the answers that we find unpalatable.

Just as it is wise to be careful and critical about accepting answers from an authority, so it is wise to be careful and critical about refusing to accept answers. In the preceding example Mr. Gates may turn out to be a reliable and informative source of answers, despite his being a criminal. Facts about an individual's way of life, background, and character can be relevant to an attempt to assess how reliable that individual may be as an oracle. But other facts are relevant too, and we are warned here against the mistake of letting vigorous attacks on the individual mislead us about how reliable he or she may be in providing information.

This error is often popularly called the *ad hominem* fallacy. We thoroughly discussed the issues surrounding *ad hominem* errors in Chapter 13 (Section 13.4). The key confusion to avoid concerns the role of the person who is being criticized. If that person serves as an oracle for an inquiry, then facts about him or her may very well be relevant to the evaluation of his or her answers. But if the person is primarily constructing logical inferences for an inquiry, then it is an unmitigated fallacy to try to call the logical inferences into question by criticizing the arguer's character and personal characteristics.

Appeal to Ignorance **(Ad Ignorantium)**   Let us begin with an example: You and I are inquiring whether UFO reports really support the conclusion that our earth has been visited from time to time by intelligent aliens. We ask if there has ever been decisive proof that earth has never been visited. The answer seems to be "No, there has never been decisive proof that earth has never been visited by aliens." I then say, "Well, that decides it. Earth must have been visited at some time or other, and some of the UFO reports probably relate to these visits."

What do you think about my reasoning? I hope that by now you are well practiced in getting all the suppressed questions out or on (or, better yet, in) the table. My claim is that the lack of proof to the contrary shows that earth must have been visited. The suppressed question here is: What does the lack of proof show? The answer I am relying on is: The lack of proof for one possible answer shows that the opposite answer has been proved. But this suppressed question/answer step needs only to be made explicit for us to see what is wrong. The fact that I cannot prove that your mother *was not* born in Indiana does not prove that she *was* born there.

We learned back in Chapter 11 (Section 11.1) that a complex principal question often sets up more than one line of inquiry. In the example our complex principal question is "Was earth ever visited by aliens or not?" This requires one line of inquiry to test if earth has been visited, and another line to test if it has not. In either case it may turn out that we do not have enough information to get a conclusive answer. If this happens, then we must be content to recognize that we lack knowledge. The shortcut called "appeal to ignorance" will not solve our problems.

In everyday life and in business the fallacy of "appealing to ignorance" sometimes takes the form of asking "Why not?" When you are inquiring about a course of action, it is often better to ask "Why should I?" rather than "Why not?" In this way you will focus more closely on the contemplated action. Asking

"Why not?" may pose an appropriate difficulty for a critic of your proposal, but it will not likely help you develop your own argument.

Unreliable Answers About the Significance of Correlations Between Situations and Events (Post hoc ergo propter hoc)

The Latin sentence *Post hoc ergo propter hoc* gives an initial overview of the *"post hoc"* error. The sentence can be translated, "After this, therefore because of this." One of our most natural and powerful ways of questioning the world in which we live involves asking about connections between situations and events. We discussed some of the issues here in Chapter 19. If two events seem to correlate with each other—i.e., one follows upon the other with regularity—then we are right in asking whether there is some significant relationship between the two.

We may not, however, be right in thinking that answers to our questions about significant relationships are always reliable. There are a number of ways in which answers we thought were reliable turn out not to be so. One of the more obvious is that, if we have observed the correlation between two events or situations only a few times or perhaps just once, there is a good chance that any information we think we have about the significance of the correlation will not turn out to be reliable. If I have discovered that you are a student at Antarctic State and that you have studied Japanese, I may rightly ask whether Japanese receives special emphasis at Antarctic State. I would be foolish, however, to conclude that this emphasis existed, based only on what I have found out about you. Sometimes this is called the error of *hasty generalization*. We generalize a correlation before we have enough cases to make it seem significant.

In another version of this error we may find a high correlation between two events but, upon reflection, not find a significant relation between them. For instance, some have claimed that there is a high correlation between the long-term ups and downs of the stock market and the trend of ups and downs in the length of women's skirts. The simple fact of the correlation may make us ask whether there is some significant relationship between the two, but, by itself, the bare fact of the correlation is not likely to convince us that there is a significant connection. We would like to find further information that links the two phenomena.

In yet other versions of this error there may indeed be a significant relationship between two highly correlated events, but we may not get the right answer to the right question about the relationship. For example, suppose that we have noted a high correlation at a beach between the volume of ice cream sales at beach concessions and the number of swimmers who get into trouble. We might ask, "What is it about ice cream that causes people to have trouble in the water?" Or again, we might ask, "What is it about nearly drowning that makes people buy more ice cream?" But these are not perhaps as good questions as, "What is it that affects both ice cream sales and the number of swimmers?" The former questions seem to have no good, reliable answers. The latter question may lead to the simple answer that hot days bring a lot of people to the beach, more people are there to get into trouble in the water, and more are there to buy ice cream.

Our emphasis throughout the book has been on the importance of finding the right question that introduces the right individual into our reasoning. *Post hoc* problems result from inability or failure to ask the right questions.

Post hoc mistakes illustrate the difficulty of setting up general and exceptionless rules for inductive inference. Such rules are sometimes formulated in terms of the number of observed positive instances of the correlation or generalization. The *hasty generalization* form of the fallacy shows that this number may sometimes need to be larger than the inquirer imagined. Yet, in science, important generalizations are sometimes made on the basis of a minimal number of positive cases—for instance, on the basis of a couple of well-chosen experiments. See further Chapter 19.

The Gambler's Fallacy   The "gambler's fallacy" is the error of asking a wrong or somewhat vague question about what determines a given probability. Each time you flip a fair coin the odds are roughly 1/2 that you will get heads. The mathematics of probabilities tells us that the odds of getting heads five times in a row will be 1/32. We would be surprised to see five heads in succession very often.

Some people are misled, however, into thinking that after getting four heads in succession, the odds must somehow be very high against getting heads on the next flip of the coin. They have failed to note that different questions need to be asked. Prior to flipping any coins, we may ask what the odds are of getting five heads in a row. The answer is roughly 1/32. After we have got four in a row, however, the question is now what the odds are of getting heads on the next flip. The answer to that question remains roughly 1/2. People who make this error are confusing two different questions.

More generally, this error gets us thinking about the many ways mistakes can be made in the interpretation of probabilities and statistics. In Chapter 12 (Section 12.5) we commented on how rules for handling statistics might best be thought of as strategic rules which advise us as to when to accept (at least for the time being) certain answers that we are getting to our questions. This helps us remember that there are not many interesting, mechanical rules for statistical reasoning. Instead we find mainly strategic rules that help us assess the reliability of answers to our questions. This insight reminds us that we must remain masters of our statistical methods rather than hope that these methods will by themselves automatically lead to excellent results.

C.4   Puzzles, Problems, and Mistakes in Dialogues and Debates

We have been learning how to analyze, construct, and evaluate inquiries. For the most part this has meant studying inquiries in which the human participants are either cooperating in the research or, at least, are not actively competing with each other. At the end of Chapter 13 (Section 13.6), however, we briefly commented on dialogues and debates in which inquirers compete with each other. Most of the errors discussed in the preceding sections can be found in debate contexts. Several additional topics, however, which are traditionally treated under the heading of "fallacy" relate specifically to problems arising in the context of debates.

Red Herring

In a competitive debate context the goal for a debater may be not so much to establish some conclusion but to keep an opponent from establishing his or hers. One tactic in this context would be to tempt the opponent to start arguing about something that will not really lead toward the conclusion he or she is seeking.

Red herring names this tactic. The strange name comes from one of the ways dogs used to be trained to follow one scent and ignore others: The trail of the original scent was crossed with the different scent of herring. If the dog went after this new scent, it was driven back to the original.

In dialogical games in which your answers are used by your opponent as premises, the red herring tactic involves choosing answers which may lead your opponent onto a false argument track. This tactic can therefore be part of an overall strategy in such a context.

In a debate context it pays to be alert to ways in which an opponent might tempt us into an argument that takes us down a trail away from our main goal. Red herring refers to the tactic that tries to mislead in this way.

Shifting Ground

A debater who is in danger of losing a contest by having his or her position refuted may resort to the tactic of shifting ground. This tactic involves subtly changing the argument one has been defending so that one can claim that the refuted argument was not what one meant at all. This tactic is similar to red herring in that the intent is to throw an opponent off of what may be the winning trail. The term "shifting ground" reminds us to watch out for opponents who take this tack.

Straw Man

Another strategy in debate is to construct a fatally weakened version of the opponent's argument and to show triumphantly its fatal weakness. If this is done artfully enough, the audience and even the opponent may fail to notice that a "straw man" has been substituted for what could have been a much stronger argument.

Straw man names the strategy of presenting and defeating a defective version of the opponent's argument. Keeping the term in mind may help us be alert to those times when others are using the strategy against us or when we are tempted to use it against them.

The fallacies of shifting ground and straw man are normally violations of the definitory rules of dialogical games. Unfortunately these definitory rules often are not clearly formulated, and thus arguers can hope to get away with violating them. The widespread use of these tactics in competitive contexts illustrates the importance of being clear about what the rules of the debating games really are or ought to be. These fallacies are not recommended for anyone who wishes to win a debate in an honest and constructive manner.

Trivial Objections

In the strategy of trivial objections one hopes to give the appearance of victory by piling up so many objections that the audience and/or the opponent gets tired and gives up. Never mind whether the objections are very significant. The hope is that their sheer quantity will defeat the opponent.

Shifting the Burden of Proof

The following strategy is more sophisticated than most. In a debate context it is often the case that one side is given the task of establishing a particular conclusion while the other side is trying to show that the conclusion has not yet been established. If we are on the side that has the task of establishing the conclusion and we are running into serious trouble, we may try to get out of trouble by using a form of the appeal to ignorance. That is, we might claim that until our opponents show that the conclusion is false, we are satisfied that it is true. What we have done is try to get our opponents to take on the job of establishing something, that is, the opposite of the conclusion we were required to prove. This strategy is called "shifting the burden of proof."

It is not the case that in every debate context the burden of proof is clearly allocated to one side or the other. Sometimes, in a serious debate, it is an important matter to decide who precisely is supposed to be trying to establish what.

An old nationalistic joke among Europeans illustrates how allocation of the burden of proof might vary from context to context. It is said that in Britain what is not forbidden is permitted, but in Germany what is not permitted is forbidden. (The joke goes on to say that in Austria what is forbidden is permitted, and in Russia what is permitted is forbidden!)

The Exception That Proves the Rule

The following gem depends entirely on a shift in the meaning of the word "proves." Originally the phrase *the exception that proves the rule* made the obvious but important point that exceptions are "trials" or "tests" for a rule. They need to be dealt with or they threaten to overturn the rule. Modern uses of the word "prove," however, only rarely have the meaning of "trial" or "test." So there are people who think this phrase is supposed to mean that at least some exceptions to a rule can somehow *establish* or support it. In a debate context do not be misled by this misinterpretation of the word "prove."

C.5   Conclusion

There is no agreed list of errors that require naming. As Aristotle suggests, there are just too many ways for us to go wrong. What we have tried to do in this appendix is discuss a number of the most important errors that have been named over the centuries. And, more importantly, we have discussed these errors in light of the interrogative model of inquiry.

We believe that knowledge of and practice in the interrogative methods of analysis, construction, and evaluation will have equipped you to improve your reasoning and to detect errors—whether named or not. What you have learned by now has enabled you to be a careful and critical inquirer. If that task has been well accomplished, there should not be need here to unmask all of the many faces of error.

GLOSSARY

▼

Ad Hominem Fallacy: Both the older and more recent meanings of this error are discussed in Section 13.4. The more recent meaning involves clarifying an important distinction between the evaluation of the answers of an oracle which are particular steps in an argument and the evaluation of the logical structure of an argument. The *ad hominem* error is the mistake of evaluating the logical structure of a person's argument on the basis of an evaluation of his or her character. The error gains plausibility through being confused with the legitimate concern to evaluate an oracle's reliability.   13.4

Affirming the Consequent: See Invalid Inference Patterns.   9.4

Antecedent: In conditional ("if-then") statements the component statement to the left of the ⊃ is called the antecedent. In a typical conditional the antecedent is usually the statement that immediately follows the word "if." However, "only if" marks the statement which goes to the *right* of the ⊃ (the *consequent*).   6.3

Applying Formal Logic to English Statements: Formal logic was meant to show us many of the details of logical inference. From a practical standpoint it is not wise to spend a lot of time translating everyday English into formal representations. This is both extremely difficult and unnecessary. Instead, when you are working with a logical inference involving a complex English statement, ask yourself what the simpler statements are and how they are being joined by the main logical operator in the statement. You do not need to do any other translating, because once you have identified the simpler statements and the main logical operator in the statement, you will know which rule of logical inference to apply and how to apply it.   9.2–9.3

Argument Analysis: The process of discovering and listing the basic interrogative and logical inference steps found in a complex everyday inquiry. ("Analysis" is a word from the Greek language that originally meant "to take something apart.")

     3.1–3.6 (cf. also 1.9)

Argument Construction: The process of discovering and formulating the questions and logical inferences that create a rational inquiry. Skills in argument construction are closely related to skills in argument analysis. Argument construction involves three interrelated activities:

Step 1: Gathering argument materials.

Step 2: Using interrogative tables to analyze the information that has been gathered.

Step 3: Assembling the materials into one's own interrogative argument table.

The three steps can be repeated as needed until a satisfactory argument emerges.   4.1

Argument Evaluation: The process of checking an argument for definitory correctness, for strategic excellence, and for whether the argument table closes. Skills in argument evaluation are closely related to skills in argument analysis. The ability to analyze an argument provides a foundation for the evaluative tasks.   9.6

Argument Sketch: An oral or written report of a line of reasoning. Lines of reasoning are typically reported in a compressed, abbreviated form. (In the study of reasoning "argument" does not mean "quarrel.")   1.6–1.9

Aristotle: Aristotle (384–322 B.C.E.) came from Macedonia in northern Greece. At the age of seventeen he became a student in Plato's Academy in Athens. He stayed on for twenty years, becoming a teacher at the Academy. After Plato's death Aristotle traveled, pursued marine biological research, tutored Alexander of Macedon who came to be known as Alexander the Great, and eventually founded his own school, the Lyceum, in Athens. Sometimes he and his followers are called "peripatetics" (i.e., "walkers") because they are supposed to have conducted much of their reasoning while walking about in the school gardens. Aristotle, Plato, and Socrates are among the greatest philosophers in the Western tradition.   3.3

Authority, Fallacy of: In a truth-oriented inquiry the error of trusting uncritically an oracle's answers, when in fact that particular oracle is fallible. The error involves treating one particular oracle as an authority when it (he, she) does not deserve to be so treated. Such an error is a strategic mistake, not a violation of the definitory rules of the interrogative game.   13.3

Begging the Question: An interrogative fallacy involving an attempt to answer a big, principal question in an inquiry too soon. Since "too soon" is determined in part by our situation and purposes, this problem involves strategic considerations.   10.12

Conclusion: The statement of what has been derived from the premises. In deductive inferences conclusions are those statements which we are currently trying to imagine false while we imagine the related premises to be true.   5.8

Conclusive Answer: An answer which provides information that picks out the same item in every alternative situation left open by what the inquirer does not know.   10.2

Conditional: A complex statement formed with "if-then" or a related set of words. Conditionals are said to be false if the left component (antecedent) is true while the right component (consequent) is false. In the other three possible combinations the conditional is said to be true. A conditional treated in this way is sometimes called a "material conditional." In formal logic we represent the conditional by $\supset$.   6.3

Conjunction: A complex statement formed with "and" or a related word. Conjunctions are said to be true if and only if all components are true, and false if even one component is false. In formal logic we represent the conjunction by &.   6.3

Consequent: In conditional ("if-then") statements the component statement to the right of the $\supset$ is called the consequent. In a typical conditional the consequent often follows the word "then." The consequent is usually not the statement that immediately follows the word "if." However, "only if" *does* mark the statement which is the consequent.   6.3

Counterexample: An imaginable scenario in which the premise(s) all turn out to be true while the conclusion turns out to be false.   5.8–5.10 & 7.1–7.2

Deductive Logical Inference: An inference which introduces no new information and which is truth-preserving. The etymological meaning of the word suggests that we are "drawing out" and making explicit the information that is to be found in the premises of the inference.   5.3

Definitory Rules: The rules which define and describe how to play a game correctly.   2.3

DeMorgan's Equivalences: See Equivalence for Denial of a Conjunction and a Disjunction.
6.5

Denial (Negation): Denial (negation) of a true statement makes it false. Denial (negation) of a false statement makes the statement true. Denial reverses truth value. 6.2–6.3 & 9.3

Denying the Antecedent: See Invalid Inference Patterns. 9.4

Disjunction: A complex statement formed with "or" or a related word. Disjunctions are said to be true if even one component is true, and false if and only if all components are false. Disjunctions are thus treated as *inclusive* "or" rather than *exclusive* "or." An exclusive "or" is false whenever both components have the same truth value. In formal logic we represent the disjunction by $\vee$. 6.3

Disjunctive Syllogism: See Valid Inference Patterns. 9.4

Equivalence between Conditionals and Disjunctions: $(A \supset B)$ is equivalent to $-A \vee B$. 6.5

Equivalence for Denial of a Conjunction: $-(A \& B)$ is equivalent to $-A \vee -B$. 6.5

Equivalence for Denial of Conditionals: $-(A \supset B)$ is equivalent to $A \& -B$. 6.5

Equivalence for Denial of Disjunctions: $-(A \vee B)$ is equivalent to $-A \& -B$. 6.5

Exclusive "Or": See Disjunction.

Fallacy: A mistake in reasoning. Because reasoning involves both logical inference steps and interrogative steps, there can be *logical fallacies* and *interrogative fallacies*. Likewise, because there are definitory rules and strategic rules of reasoning, *definitory fallacies* and *strategic fallacies* can occur. 10.12 & Appendix C

Finished Tables: A table is finished when all of its paths are closed, or when the entire table is closed, or when the only unchecked lines in subtables lacking bridges are statement letters and denials of statement letters. 7.2

Hypothetical Syllogism: See Valid Inference Patterns. 9.4

Inclusive "Or": See Disjunction.

Inductive Inference: A nondeductive inference which introduces new information into an inquiry and thus may not be truth-preserving. Typically, inductive inferences proceed from premise statements about a number of particular cases to a general conclusion about all similar cases. Interrogative inquiry uses only *deductive* inferences. Inductive (and other nondeductive) inferences are replaced by carefully chosen interrogative and logical inference (deductive) moves. 5.4 & 19.6–19.7

Infer: To conclude something on the basis of information that is known or assumed to be true. 1.7

Inference: The process of inferring; something that is inferred; a conclusion; something derived from other information by reasoning. Note that an inference is not simply a statement but a statement that has been derived from other information by reasoning. Sometimes the word "inference" refers to the whole process of reasoning that led to the conclusion and sometimes the word simply refers to the conclusion itself. 1.7

Information: That which enables us to eliminate from our inquiry certain alternative situations that we otherwise might have thought possible. Information means the reduction of uncertainty. 1.6 & 10.1–10.3

Initial Premise(s): Explicitly acknowledged information that is available right at the beginning of an inquiry. In Chapter 1 (Section 1.7) we defined "premise" as "the information that serves as the basis for an inference step." Initial premise(s) are one source of material for future logical inference steps. 2.4

Inquirer: Our name for the person(s) pursuing a rational inquiry. 2.1

Inquiry: (1) The action of seeking for truth, knowledge, or information about something; search, research, investigation, examination. (2) The action of asking or questioning; interrogation. 1.2

Interrogative Approach to Inquiry: An approach that stresses the importance of questioning in rational inquiry.   1.2

Interrogative Game: A way to make an explicit description of the interrogative model of rational inquiry.   2.2

Interrogative Move: Another name for interrogative steps in reasoning. We also use the word "step," and sometimes we use the word "questioning" rather than "interrogative," as in "questioning move" or "questioning step."   2.4

Interrogative Step: A step in an inquiry which brings in new information. Another name is "interrogative *move*." Interrogative steps are not always phrased as questions but they can always be analyzed as though a question has been asked.   1.8

Invalid Inference: An inference in which it remains possible to imagine a way for the conclusion to be false while imagining all the premise(s) to be true.   5.9 & 7.2

Invalid Inference Patterns: Some of the more common invalid patterns of inference include   9.4

1. $P \supset Q$
Q
Therefore, P

Affirming the Consequent

2. $P \supset Q$
$-P$
Therefore, $-Q$

Denying the Antecedent

3. $P \supset Q$
Therefore, $Q \supset P$

Conversion

4. $P \vee Q$
P
Therefore, $-Q$

(No name; the problem involves the temptation to assume an exclusive *or.*)

Kant: The German philosopher Immanuel Kant (1724–1804), one of the most famous of relatively modern philosophers, was working at about the time of the American Revolution. He rarely traveled from his home, and he was so regular in his habits that people were said to set their clocks on the basis of his afternoon walks. Nevertheless, his mind ranged widely and powerfully over the most difficult problems in philosophy.

Kant gave us one of the most challenging accounts of how human beings know what they think they know. Both those who accept and those who reject Kant's account agree that it is very important to work through the insights he has left for us.   10.8

Logical Inference: An inference in which the conclusion cannot possibly be imagined to be false while the premises are all together imagined to be true. (The notion of "imagining" here is meant to be very wide-ranging. In testing whether an inference is a logical inference we are free to imagine situations that do not conform to the way things are in our actual world.)   1.7

Logical Inference Move: Another name for logical inference steps in reasoning. Also occasionally shortened to "inference move," "inference step," "logical move," or "logical step."   2.4

Logical Inference Step: A step which spells out some of the information that is already contained in previous steps of an inquiry. Another name is "logical inference *move*." Logical inference steps are sometimes phrased as questions, but if the step does not bring in new information, it should not be analyzed as an interrogative step. The basic test for a logical inference step is that it cannot possibly be imagined to be false while the previous steps on which it is based are imagined to be true.   1.8

Main Logical Operator: The primary logical concept in the statement, the one that must be dealt with first in logical inferences as we have formulated them. It is the one which, in a formal notation, would be enclosed in the smallest number of pairs of brackets or parentheses. There are no automatic, mechanical rules for determining the main operator of an English statement. The most important thing is to ask oneself what precisely is the meaning of the statement, how is it to be understood? What are the simpler statements and how are they being related to each other? Answers to these questions combined with an understanding of the meaning of the formal logical operators will usually show the way to arrive at correct logical inferences.
6.4 & 9.2–9.3

Many Questions: An interrogative fallacy which involves asking a question whose presupposition is not established. In this way more than one question is asked under the guise of asking only one. Because this error loads more than one question into what looks like a single question, another name that is often used is the fallacy or error of asking "loaded questions." The fallacy of many questions might also be called "jumping to a presupposition."   11.2–11.3

Modus Ponens: See Valid Inference Patterns.   9.4

Modus Tollens: See Valid Inference Patterns.   9.4

Necessary Conditions and Sufficient Conditions: The phrases "sufficient condition" and "necessary condition" provide another way to express conditional statements. "A is a sufficient condition for B" is represented by "If A then B." "A is a necessary condition for B" is expressed by "If B then A." In many cases the word "if" indicates a sufficient condition while the phrase "only if" indicates a necessary condition.   9.2

Negation: See Denial.

New Information: Information that was not previously available in any way for use in a given inquiry. New information will always be analyzed as coming into the inquiry by way of an interrogative step.   1.8 & 10.3

Open Path: In table analysis any path which is not closed is called an open path.   2.4

Operational Question: A question which forms the basis of one particular interrogative move in an inquiry. It provides part of the information needed to answer the principal question.   10.6

Oracle: Name for the source(s) of answers to questions asked in interrogative steps.   2.1

Partial Answer: An answer which provides information that does not necessarily pick out the same item in every alternative situation left open by what the inquirer does not know.   10.2

Path: A series of statements that always begins on the first line of the table and works down toward the bottom. There can be any number of paths on either side of the table.   7.2

Path Closure: (a) When two statements that cannot be imagined both together to be true occur in the same path on the left side of a table, the path in which they occur together is said to be closed and does not need to be considered any further. (b) When two statements that cannot be imagined both together to be false occur in the same path on the right side of a table, the path in which they occur together is said to be closed and does not need to be considered any further.   2.4

Plato: Plato (ca. 427–347 B.C.E.) was forty years younger than Socrates. As a young man he was profoundly influenced by Socrates's ways of inquiring about important questions in life. Plato was also deeply troubled by the events of the war between Athens and Sparta and by the trial and execution of Socrates. He devoted his life to philosophy, and he established the Academy, one of the first colleges or universities in Western history. Socrates left no written works, but Plato left a large number, and in his writings he tells us much about Socrates. Plato is the author of the *Meno,* and he makes Socrates the central character. The *Meno* is an extremely important early work in philosophy.   1.12

Premises: The information serving as the basis for an inference step. In deductive inferences premises are those statements currently imagined to be true.   1.7 & 5.8

Presuppositions of Questions: The asking of questions presupposes some possibilities. If the presupposition of a question is not true, the posing of the question can cause confusions and mistakes. The general form of the presupposition of a statement question is $(A \vee B \vee C \vee \ldots)$. The general form of the presupposition of a yes/no question is simply $(A \vee -A)$.   11.2

Previous Information: Information which was already available in some way in previous steps of the inquiry, but which may require a logical inference in order to show exactly what alternative situations are being eliminated. (Whenever a step spells out previously available information, the step will always be analyzed as a logical inference step.)   1.8

Principal Question: The question which sets up the goal or purpose of an inquiry. A conclusive answer to the principal question comes not in a single move, but through the whole inquiry, made up of a number of interrogative steps and logical inference steps.   10.6

Questions: A crucial part of reasoning. Having the imagination to ask the right questions is often the key to excellence in reasoning.   1.6

Rational Inquiry: Inquiry pursued with attention both to correct methods (definitory rules) and effective strategies in reasoning.   1.3

Socrates: Socrates (ca. 469–399 B.C.E.) was the first of the three most famous ancient Greek philosophers. (The other two are Plato and Aristotle.) He was a stonemason in Athens. During the early part of his life (469–430 B.C.E.) Athens was the foremost political, military, scientific, and cultural center in Greece. During the last part of Socrates's life (429–399 B.C.E.), Athens was engaged in a long and demoralizing war with the city of Sparta. Athens lost the war in 404 B.C.E., and in the aftermath of recriminations Socrates was found guilty of being some kind of religious innovator and of corrupting the youth. At the age of seventy he was executed by the Athenians.   1.12

Statement: A sentence which is being used to say something that is true or false. A statement usually serves to convey information to a hearer or reader. Another word sometimes used for such sentences is "proposition."   5.7

Statement Questions: Questions which pose alternative statements and ask which is the case. The simplest *statement* questions pose a statement and its denial and can be answered "yes" or "no."   11.2

Strategic Rules: The rules which give insight into how to play a game successfully and well.   2.3

Strategic Rules for Logical Inference: It is not possible to give completely general mechanical rules for the best strategies for logical inference. The most important advice concerns discovering which existentially quantified statements (on the left side) and/or which universally quantified statements (on the right side) to instantiate first. See Section 18.2. Some other quite modest strategic rules for logical inference are provided in Section 7.3.

Strategic Rules for Interrogative Moves: It is not possible to give completely general mechanical rules for making the best interrogative moves in inquiry. There are two different aims: to guide the inquiry to a desired conclusion and to guide it in such a way as to make the conclusion as reliable as possible. For the first aim the crucial advice concerns discovering which existentially quantified statement (on the left side) to use first as a presupposition of a "wh-" question. See Section 18.2. For the second aim the crucial advice involves strategies for evaluating answers and answerers. See Chapters 12 and 13.

Subtable: The pairing of open paths from the left (premise) side and right (conclusion) side of our tables. For a complete analysis each open path on the right side must be paired in a subtable with every open path on the left.   7.2

Sufficient Condition: See Necessary Conditions and Sufficient Conditions.

Syllogism (traditional): In Aristotelian logic a limited but powerful type of inference containing two premises of a specified form followed by a conclusion in similar form. Predicate logic provides much more powerful tools for analyzing these and many other types of inference.   14.10

Table: Construction for argument analysis, consisting of the premise information, questions, and left-side logical inferences on the left side and the conclusion information and right-side logical inferences on the right side.   2.4

Table Closure: Compare all open paths on the left side of the table with all open paths on the right side. If, for every pairing of left and right open paths, an identically matching whole line is found to occur in both paths, the entire table is said to be closed. Closure indicates that there is no way to imagine the conclusion false while imagining the lines on the left side of the table to be true.   2.4 & 7.1

Tautologies: Complex statements which cannot in any way be imagined false. A simple example is the formula $A \lor -A$.   8.3

Truth-functional Logic: Another name for statement logic (see Part 2). The truth values of the complicated statements are said to be functions of (to depend on) the truth values of the simpler statements.   6.3

Ultimate Conclusion: The goal of the inquiry, what the inquirer is trying to establish. In Chapter 1 (Section 1.7) we defined "conclusion" as "the statement of what has been derived from the premises." The ultimate conclusion is what the inquirer is hoping finally to derive from the entire inquiry.   2.4

Valid Inference: A deductive inference in which the relation between the premise(s) and the conclusion(s) is such that it is *impossible* to imagine the conclusion false while at the same time imagining all the premise(s) to be true.   5.9 & 7.1-7.2

Valid Inference Patterns: Five of the most basic valid argument patterns are   9.4

1. $P \lor Q$ **Disjunctive Syllogism**
   $-P$
   Therefore, Q

2. $P \supset Q$ **Modus Ponens**
   P
   Therefore, Q

3. $P \supset Q$ **Modus Tollens**
   $-Q$
   Therefore, $-P$

4. $P \supset Q$
 $Q \supset R$
 Therefore, $P \supset R$ **Hypothetical Syllogism**

5. $P \supset Q$
 Therefore, $-Q \supset -P$ **Transposition**

Validity and Invalidity Testing: If all paths on the left side in a finished table are closed, that is, have "x" at the bottom (Table Rule 7), or, if the entire table is closed (Table Rule 8), then the relationship of premises to conclusion is valid. Otherwise the finished table will produce a counterexample that shows the relationship of premises to conclusion to be invalid.   7.2

"Wh-" Questions: Questions which use words like "who" and "what." There are many different kinds of "wh-" questions; they make use of all the famous newspaper reporter words like "who," "what," "where," "when," "why," and "how." "How" can be used to ask a "wh-" question even though it is not literally a "wh-" word, but "whether" actually introduces statement questions.   11.2

▲
▼

Clues and Solutions
for Selected Exercises

Exercise 1-A

1. The second premise strongly suggests that "you helped the other side," but it does not completely eliminate the possibility of imagining that the person could protest "I have never helped the other side." If we add as a premise, "you helped the other side," then, when the premises are imagined true, it becomes impossible to imagine the conclusion false.

2. b. The last sentence is the conclusion. Not a logical inference.
   d. The first sentence is the conclusion. A logical inference if the last sentence is read as asserting that the car stopped suddenly.
   f. Conclusion is "no Christians are polytheists." Not a logical inference.
   h. Conclusion is last sentence. Not a logical inference. (The stated premises do not make it impossible to imagine that there might be noneven numbers which are still divisible by two. The fact that your knowledge of math tells you this is impossible needs to be made explicit in the premises before you claim there is a logical inference.)

    i. Conclusion is last sentence. A logical inference. (Give some careful thought to the difference between "only if" in the preceding exercise and "if" in this one.)

    j. Conclusion is "it's going to be a very good election." Not a logical inference but could easily be turned into one by adding the premise "If we have three people running, then it will be a very good election."

    l. Conclusion is "she will go." A logical inference. (Note the difference between "only" in the preceding exercise and "all" in this one.)

    n. Conclusion is "Vermicelli is fattening." Not a logical inference until we make explicit that vermicelli is a type of pasta.

Exercise 1-B

2. Interrogative move because there are ways to imagine the loss of jobs without rising unemployment. For example, immediately upon losing their jobs, people are hired by the government. Or it is the end of summer, and many students are both losing their jobs and leaving the job market.

4. Logical inference move.

6. Interrogative move.

8. Logical inference move.

Exercise 1-C

2. The conclusion seems to be that one should support Rep. Hardin for president. The fact that Rep. Hardin possesses needed traits suggests that Hardin *could* be supported but not that Hardin *should* be supported. The argument needs some more information. What kind of additional information is required to make the conclusion inescapable?

4. The last sentence is the conclusion.

6. The last sentence is the conclusion. Remember that when you analyze an argument you are looking for whether the information leads strongly to the conclusion. You do not have to agree with the information that the arguer is using to support the conclusion.

Exercise 2-A

1. Logical inference move. (You might imagine that "Mark" does not necessarily name a human person, and therefore it would not follow that "someone's in the kitchen with Dinah." This would defeat the claim that there is a logical inference. Here is an opportunity once again to consider how unspoken

information and our purposes and goals influence how we decide whether an inference is a logical inference or not.)

3. See Section 2.4 (p. 45) of this chapter for a discussion of inclusive and exclusive "or." Exclusive "or" would make this a logical inference move; inclusive "or" would not.

5. Logical inference move.

7. Not a logical inference move.

9. Not a logical inference move.

11. Logical inference move. Under the logicians' meaning of "if-then" the sentence can be a lie only if it is true that "I am a knight" and false that "I will tell you that I am." If we imagine that a knight speaks the sentence, it turns out to be true and all is well. If we try to imagine that a knave speaks it, the first part "I am a knight" will be false; and by the logicians' meaning of "if-then," the whole sentence will turn out to be true. So a knave, who always tells lies, cannot be speaking this sentence. The logicians' meaning of "if-then" will be explained in detail in Part 2 (Chapter 6, pp. 109–110).

because the knaves 'statement "I will tell you that I am" would not be a lie.

Exercise 2-D

On the right side we are trying to imagine each line false, so a logical inference will take place when it is impossible to imagine a line true when the preceding lines have been imagined false.

Exercise 2-E

1. This creature is an insect, and it has eight legs.

3. 1,000,000,000 is larger than 1,000,000.

5. Jack is a native of California.

Exercise 3-B
School Children and AIDS

Line 2 is an IM or an initial premise.
Line 4 is related to line 2, but an LI from 2 to 4 would involve the further information that medical precautions are needed only if the virus can be transmitted.
Line 6 is related to line 4 (and therefore also to line 2), but an LI from 4 to 6 relies on the unspoken information that these students pose a health threat to others only if special medical precautions need to be taken in relation to them.
Line 8 is an LI from 1, 6, and 7.

Greatness of a Work of Art

Line 2 appears to be a further specification of line 1. As is stands it is not an LI from line 1, but it also seems intended to be drawn out of line 1. Unspoken information involved in the step from line 1 to line 2 might include an assertion to the effect that because fellow artists are more sensitive to artistic value, a work's influence on other artists is more significant than its influence on the general public. This assertion, combined with line 1's claim that success in stimulating (influencing) others is a measure of a work's value, would then come close to establishing line 2.

Line 4 appears to come from line 3 along with a further "between the lines" assertion to the effect that subconscious or tacit influence is subtle and hard to detect.

Line 6 comes fairly directly from lines 2 and 5.

You should note that in Exercise 3-B there was important work for you to do in analysis even though you were not asked to discuss the reliability of the premise and interrogative information. The question of reliability of information is also important in assessing these arguments, but in Parts 1 and 2 of the book we are trying to develop your skills in discerning how information is connected into a logical whole designed to support a conclusion. We limit concerns about reliability of information to simply noting where the information may have come from, that is, who or what is serving as the oracle.

Exercise 3-C

1. In this "either-or" argument one alternative is eliminated so the other is concluded. You may have some difficulty seeing that the order of analysis is different from the order of the English sentences. Only the left side of the table is shown in what follows:

   1. Joe either escaped out the window or through the vent in the ceiling. Initial Premise or IM
   2. If he had escaped out the window, there would be footprints underneath it outside. IM
   3. No footprints could be found. IM
   4. Joe did not escape out the window. LI from 2 and 3.
   5. Joe escaped through the vent in the ceiling. LI from 1 and 4.

3. In this "either-or" argument both alternatives are pursued to the same conclusion that the president should be replaced. Sentence 2 develops one path of thought based on one alternative in sentence 1. Sentence 3 develops a path of thought based on the other alternative. Sentence 4 argues that both paths of thought lead to the judgment that she was neglectful. This LI is relying on "between the lines" information which would link both permitting unethical and illegal practices and being ignorant of important activities with neglect.

The last sentence is the ultimate conclusion, and it is an LI which relies on "between the lines" information linking the neglect in question with the decision to replace the president.

Exercise 3-E

1. The ultimate conclusion is that the continued prosperity of civilization is tied to zoos and botanical gardens. Think carefully about how the word "only" works in this exercise. What would happen if the word "only" were omitted from the argument?

2. The ultimate conclusion is that there are no moral absolutes. The difficulty in analyzing this argument lies in showing how the arguer thought it possible to get from the sentence "Who is to say which are wrong?" to a denial that "either the moral beliefs of our culture or the moral beliefs of other cultures must be mistaken." The arguer is relying on the highly implausible claims that no one can say that any culture's moral beliefs are mistaken and that this shows that neither our culture's moral beliefs nor the moral beliefs of other cultures are mistaken. The claim that "if there were moral absolutes, either our culture's beliefs or the beliefs of others must be mistaken" is also open to challenge. This is a good exercise for noting that in argument analysis we temporarily allow the implausible claims to be imagined true so that we can see what would be needed to make the logical inference steps go through.

Special note to exercise 8: Item 11 in the more complicated sketches found in the second group of sketches in Appendix A provides an occasion to address an issue that will be handled in more detail in Part 3. This item has as its ultimate conclusion the assertion that the present legal prohibitions against euthanasia ought to be lifted. The inquiry is sketched out in one paragraph, but it actually contains two independent lines of reasoning. The first three sentences provide introductory information. In sentences 4–6 one line of reasoning suggests that reflection upon humane treatment of ailing animals will provide an argument leading to the ultimate conclusion. Sentence 7 introduces an independent consideration of the implications of health care allocation problems for decisions about euthanasia. Sentence 8 sums up by saying that both lines of thought lead to the conclusion.

If you attempt to analyze this argument in one table, you should find that you will arrive at the ultimate conclusion before all the material has been handled. You may or may not be puzzled that you are tempted to proceed with more lines after the table closes. Once a table closes, however, you should not go on to write more lines. Instead, you should simply start a new table for the new line of reasoning that continues after analysis of the first line of reasoning produces a closed table.

In Part 3 you will learn in more detail about the significance of the interaction of independent lines of reasoning. Intuitively, however, you can recognize that a significant strategy for inquiry involves offering two or more independent lines of reasoning, each of which leads to the ultimate conclusion. This is an important way to provide stronger support for the ultimate conclusion.

Exercise 3-G

1. Sentences 2 and 4 are not relevant to the argument. The argument turns on the initial premise that something which is working should not be changed.

Exercise 4-A

1. A couple of sketches relating to this topic are provided at the end of Chapter 9.

Exercise 5-A

3. Some interesting questions arise here depending on how one does or does not incorporate our usual calendar conventions into the inference. Most people will treat it as deductive.
5. Nondeductive.
7. Deductive.

Exercise 5-B

See Exercise 1-C or 3-G.

Exercise 5-C

3. The conclusion is "The two-hour marathon is a feat which may not be accomplished in this century."
4. The conclusion is "We are destined to have less-than-great leaders."

Exercise 5-E

2. "Only if" causes problems here. A counterexample is possible because the first sentence makes honesty a necessary condition for reelection, but it does not make honesty a condition that is sufficient to guarantee the mayor should be reelected. You might concede the first and second sentences and nevertheless vote for someone else.
4. If you imagine the first sentence to be true, it is impossible to imagine that all of Tom's beliefs are true. Thus there is no counterexample.

5. Assuming that the puzzle is thinking about parties at which there are a finite number of people, you can see why a counterexample can never be constructed. If somebody at the party (call her Jane Doe) is a friend to everybody at the party, then everybody at the party will now have at least two friends; you must be a friend to yourself, and you must also have Jane as a friend. Now, if the total number of people at the party is n, Jane will have n friends, somebody can have two friends, but the other n-2 people at the party will each have to have a *different* number of friends drawn from the n-3 remaining available numbers. (1, 2, and n are not available.) This, however, is not possible. You could try then imagining that nobody has n friends, but this will leave you with n people who each need a *different* number of friends drawn from n-1 available numbers.

Exercise 5-F

Remember that the goal in argument analysis is to fill out the argument table in such a way that, if at all possible, all possible counterexamples are blocked. Sometimes, of course, this means bringing in between-the-lines information which you find far-fetched or implausible. This exercise is designed primarily to keep you aware of the connections between deductive logic and reasoning generally. We do not recommend devoting exhaustive effort to working out the analysis of each one.

Exercise 5-G

1. In clue b pay close attention to "exactly halfway." In clues c and d pay close attention to "exactly $20,000" and "exactly three times as much." You should find it impossible to imagine that Mrs. Jones is the brakeperson's nearest neighbor. Here we have a valid deductive logical inference.
2. To get an inescapable and complete conclusion to this puzzle, you will need to use common-sense knowledge about how mirrors work. Do not overlook the meaning of "teetotaler."

Exercise 6-A

2. The main statements are "Joshua sat at the lake" *and* "Joshua counted the fish as they jumped in front of him." Statement logic cannot capture the adverbial time indication of "as they jumped in front of him." One *could* divide the second statement into "Joshua counted the fish" *and* "The fish jumped in front of him," but "and" does not satisfactorily capture the meaning of "as."
4. We finished lunch, *and* we began to plan for the visit of the prime minister and her husband. Note that the "and" joining "the prime minister" and "her husband" is *not* the statement logic "and."

6. Bo Jackson is the most successful multisport athlete since Jim Thorpe, *and* Bo Jackson promises to eclipse even that great athlete's achievements.

7. *If* the readings of the Grand Wazoo are of use to you, *then* you are truly interested in the ways of wisdom and enlightenment. Note that the "and" joining "wisdom" and "enlightenment" is *not* the statement logic "and."

Exercise 6-B

2. *A & B*
4. *A & B*
6. *A & B*
7. *B ⊃ A*. Note that *A* represents the statement immediately following the words "only if" and ending with "enlightenment."

Exercise 6-C

1. ⊃
3. ∨
4. ∨
6. –, ∨
8. –, ⊃

Exercise 6-D

2. The most straightforward way to do this exercise is to keep Paul and Don together as the subject of the verbs and the navy and marines together as possible objects of "join." Then *A* can stand for "Paul and Don read the news," and *B* for "Paul and Don immediately decided to join either the navy or the marines." It is possible to make the picture more complicated by creating a greater number of complete statements such as: "Paul read the news," "Don read the news," "Paul decided to join the navy," "Paul decided to join the marines," etc. Then you could end up with (*A & B*) & [(*C ∨ D*) & (*E ∨ F*)].

4. There are two equivalent ways to capture "neither/nor":
   $$–(R ∨ S) ⊃ I$$
   $$(–R \ \& \ –S) ⊃ I$$
   It would be incorrect to write (*–R ∨ –S*) ⊃ *I* or to write
   $$–(R \ \& \ S) ⊃ I$$
   Remember that the upper-case letters stand for whole statements and not simply for Ruth or Susan.

6. There is possible confusion here about whether "or" or "and" is the main operator. Most likely $(A \lor B)$ & C is intended. Remember that the upper-case letters stand for whole statements and not simply for Smith, Jones, or Paulsen.

Exercise 6-E

1. John does not play tennis.
3. It is not easy to understand denials.
5. The stablemaster did not steal the horse.

Exercise 6-F

Note carefully that denials in complex statements are more complicated than might first appear. In item 2 choice a is the exact denial, but choice c may be very tempting for you. Both the original conjunction that is to be denied and choice 3 could be false, even though they cannot both be true together. For example, Elizabeth might live in Florida while Harold does not. Therefore, choice c is not an exact denial. Exact denial requires that the denial always have the opposite truth value from the statement which is being denied.

1. c
2. a
5. a
6. c

Exercise 7-A

2. a. Rule 5
    c. Rule 4
    d. Rule 4
    f. Rule 6
    h. Rule 6
3. a. Split table with $-(A \lor B)$ in one path and C & D in the other.
    c. Split table with A in one path and $(B$ & $C) \supset D$ in the other.
    d. Split table with $-(A$ & $B)$ in one path and C & D in the other.
    f. In the same path write $-(A \supset -B)$ & $-C$ as the equivalent.
    h. In the same path write A & $-(B \lor C)$.
4. In every case at least one of the lines can be further taken apart by application of one of the Table Rules 3 through 6.

Exercise 7-B

1.

Premises and Deductive Inferences				Conclusion
1. √	$P \supset -Q$		(prem)	4. $-P$
2. √	$-Q \supset -R$		(prem)	
3.	R		(prem)	
5. $-P$		$-Q$	(1 by 5)	
6. Bridge 5-4				
7. (Rule 8)		$--Q$ | $-R$	(2 by 5)	
8.		x | x	(5 & 7 by 7 and 3 & 7 by 7)	

2. Table cannot be made to close.

4. There are inconsistent premises.

Exercise 7-D

All five exercises are valid and lead to closed tables.

Exercise 8-B

Premises and Deductive Inferences	Conclusion and Right-Side Inferences	
Nothing needs to go on the left side of table. Line 1 is the conclusion to be proved. Lines 2 and 3 come from line 1 by Rule 4r. The path then closes by Rule 7, and that closes the whole table.	1. √ $A \vee -A$ 2. A 3. $-A$ x	

Exercise 8-D

1.

Premises and Deductive Inferences			Conclusion and Right-Side Inferences		
1. √	$-[A \supset (B \vee -C)]$	(prem)	2. √	$(A \supset -B) \& C$	
3. √	$A \& -(B \vee -C)$	(1 by 6)	10. √	$A \supset -B$ | C	(2 by 3r)
4.	A	(3 by 3)	11.	$-A$	(10 by 5r)
5. √	$-(B \vee -C)$	(3 by 3)	12.	$-B$	(10 by 5r)

6. √	−B & −−C	(5 by 6)
7.	−B	(6 by 3)
8. √	−−C	(6 by 3)
9.	C	(8 by 6)

Lines 7 and 12 provide a bridge for one subtable, and lines 9 and 10 provide a bridge for the other. The table is closed and this is a valid inference.

3. This generates a very complicated and messy table if you work it all out. Work on the conclusion side first. You will find that one open path will contain *D* while another contains −*D*. Because of Rule 7, any open path on the left side will not contain lines that can bridge both to *D* and to −*D*. If the premises are consistent, that is, there are open paths on the left side, then it will be impossible to close all the subtables. Invalid.

5. The conclusion has an open path with −*C* in it, but the premises require imagining that *C* is true. Thus, a subtable with −*C* on the conclusion side remains open. Invalid.

7. Invalid.

9. Valid.

Exercise 9-A

1 and 2. (The main operator is in bold face type.)

    b. −(John won the race) **&** John managed to finish the race.

    c. A decision has to be made as to who "she" is. **⊃**

    d. −(A visitor is allowed to step on the grass) **∨** (That visitor is accompanied by a member of the college).

    f. (Tom comes to Sue's party & Dick comes to Sue's party & Harry comes to Sue's party) **⊃** Sue is surprised.

    g. This statement cannot be further broken down by statement logic.

3.

    b. Rule 3

    c. Rule 5

    d. Rule 4

    e. The table is divided initially into two paths. "Sue is surprised" is put in the right path. In the left path we have "It is not the case that [(Tom comes to her party or Dick comes to her party) or Harry comes to her party]." Because of the equivalence for "not-or," we end up with the denial of each of the three alternatives included in the same left path—"Tom does not come to her party," "Dick does not . . . ," etc.

    f. Same as e except that the left path has "not-and" and the equivalence changes the complex statement to three simpler statements which are the denials of the originals now joined by "or." This will divide the original left path into three paths, each containing one of the denied alternatives.

g. No rule applies.

4.　　e. Same as 3e except that the path does not divide at first, but does divide in handling "not-or."

f. Same as 3f except that the path never divides.

Exercise 9-B

1.　　There is someone Jimmy cannot beat. ("Jimmy cannot beat anyone" would not be the appropriate denial because it is possible for both "Jimmy can beat anyone" and "Jimmy cannot beat anyone" to be false at the same time.)

3.　　There is someone Jimmy can beat.

5 and 7. The safest way is simply to say "It is not the case that. . . ." The problem is in specifying further what the denial means.

Exercise 10-A

2. b.

4. a. (a claims that one single person trusts everyone, while b only claims that for each person we can find someone who trusts that person.)

Exercise 10-B

1. How conclusive an answer is depends upon the background information that may or may not be available. Alternative a seems least conclusive, especially since the background information about who is the "best man" is likely to vary from person to person. Alternative d seems most conclusive, assuming that the name "George Bush" is likely to be reasonably well known to the questioner.

Exercise 10-G

1. A skier is likely to treat the question as an operational question to be answered by television or radio forecasts. The meteorologist is usually expected to be taking the question to be a principal question and to be answering it by structuring an inquiry based on the science of meteorology.

4. The question probably has widely differing consequences for the mentioned individuals. We would usually think that the question is far more important

to Sally and Sherman than to Sherman's roommate. The former are likely to give it much more thought, including some rational inquiry! It's hard to tell what Sally's father will think.

Exercise 11-A

1. Consider a legislator's reflections about whether or not to support a proposed piece of legislation. Persons arguing for and against the legislation are likely to develop arguments involving quite different tables. Or, consider a decision whether or not to smoke, or a decision whether or not to marry.

Exercise 11-C

3. statement
4. "wh-"
5. statement
6. "wh-"

Exercise 11-D

2 and 3. Bring it about that I know that your favorite play is *Hamlet* or I know that your favorite play is *Happy Birthday, Wanda June.*

4.   Bring it about that I know who your favorite author is.

5.   Bring it about that I know that you have a favorite author or I know that you do not have a favorite author.

6.   Bring it about that I know how you liked the play.

Exercise 11-E

1. The game is on TV and you will watch it, or the game is on TV and you will not watch it.
3. Mexico City is larger than Tokyo, or Tokyo is larger than Mexico City.
5. There is a president of France.

Exercise 11-F

1. a.   There is a present king of France and that person is bald, or there is a present king of France and that person is not bald. $(A \mathbin{\&} B) \vee (A \mathbin{\&} -B)$.

b. Nelson lives in an apartment or Nelson does not live in an apartment. $A \lor -A$. You might wonder whether you should indicate that the question presupposes there is a person named Nelson and there are such things as apartments. The main purpose of identifying presuppositions is to be able to ferret out and identify presuppositions which might cause trouble for an inquirer. In the usual context of a question like this, the presuppositions of Nelson's existence and of the existence of apartments are unproblematic. Consequently we treat the question as involving a simple yes/no alternation.

c. Most likely should be treated as assuming that Nelson lives in an apartment (statement A) and then asking luxury or not (statement L or $-L$). $(A \& L) \lor (A \& -L)$.

f. Mexico City is larger than Tokyo, or Tokyo is larger than Mexico City. $A \lor B$.

h. You have a favorite author or you do not have a favorite author. $A \lor -A$. The question of course assumes there are such things as authors and that a person could favor one over another, but in usual contexts these presuppositions are unproblematic and therefore do not require an exhaustive indication.

i. There are Jabberwocks of varying likability and you have a favorite Jabberwock, or there are Jabberwocks of varying likability and you do not have a favorite Jabberwock. $(A \& B) \lor (A \& -B)$. The assumption that there is such a thing as Jabberwocks and that you could favor one over another are much more problematic in our usual contexts than the assumption in item h about authors. Therefore the assumption is explicitly noted.

Exercise 11-G

The answer depends upon whether the question presupposes in addition to the opposed alternatives something that, in the context, could turn out to be false no matter whether the answer *yes* or *no* is given.

Exercise 11-H

1. a. The inquiry will have to establish that Leonard was here last night and was the last to leave.

Exercise 11-M

2. Ellen said that she would be here by seven. It was important to her that we see this film. Whenever something has come up in the past that kept her from meeting a commitment, she has let me know. I don't recall hearing anything about the traffic—no bad accident or traffic jam. The concluding sentence about car trouble also involves drawing upon tacit knowledge about possible explanations for lateness.

Exercise 12-A

Bracketing the first statement in the second clue makes it impossible to identify the murderer's profession and seating. Bracketing the second statement in that clue does not affect the solution of the puzzle, assuming you make careful use of the mirror information in the first statement.

Exercise 13-C

1. Item 52 in the last section of Appendix A begins on p. 400. Comment on what the author of the item was trying to suggest when he included Adolf Hitler among the people whose views are presented. Use your understanding of *ad hominem* reasoning to explain whether the reference to Hitler is legitimate or not. Presumably the author of this item is trying to call the conclusions of the various arguers into question. Is the author calling into question Hitler's character as an oracle or his character as a maker of inferences?

4. Items 18 and 19 on p. 381 of Appendix A raise a number of interesting questions about uncertainty of answers. For a more complicated case you might compare the interrogative moves concerning motives for the French and American revolutions and their pursuit of human rights in items 23 and 24 on p. 382 in Appendix A. Do the answers involved in the two items support each other or conflict with each other? What strategies could help bolster one or the other argument?

Exercise 14-A

1. Nonvariable names: "the cat," "the mat." Predicate: "_____ is on _____."
4. "Mabel" and "Harriet" are nonvariable names. "The news" and "the phone" could also be treated as nonvariable names, but they might be concealed in the predicates as follows: "_____ heard the news" and "_____ called _____ on the phone."
6. Nonvariable name: "Susan." Predicate: "_____ sings beautifully."

Exercise 14-B

1. Not identity.
3. Can be treated as an identity or as a predication.
4. Identity.

Exercise 14-C

1. a. *Lkm* & *Fkn* where *F* is the predicate "_____ imagines flying to _____."

   c. *Prsm* where *r* represents Reagan, *s* Sinatra, and *m* the medal of freedom.

   d. *Tmsn & Omg* where *m* represents Mike, *s* Susan, *n* Nancy, and *g* the gift.

2. a. Valid.

   b. The premises are inconsistent. Close every path on the left side with Table Rule 7.

Exercise 14-D

1. $\exists x\, \forall y\, xLy$ or, less likely, as for number 2.

2. $\forall y\, \exists x\, xLy$

5. $\forall y\, (Gy \supset Ey)$

7. $-\exists y\, (Gy\ \&\ Ay)$ or equivalently $\forall y\, (Gy \supset -Ay)$

11. $\forall y\, (My \supset \exists x\, Fxy)$ or equivalently $\forall y\, \exists x\, (My \supset Fxy)$

12. $\forall x\, [(Dx\ \&\ Fpx) \supset Bpx]$

Exercise 14-F

1. Valid.

2. The second premise produces an inconsistency. If you use only the first premise, can you get to the conclusion? Why not?

Exercise 14-G

2. Valid. Do the right-side conclusion instantiation first.

3.

Premises and Deductive Inferences		Conclusion and Right-Side Inferences
1. $\quad\quad \forall x\, \exists y\, xRy$ (prem)		4. $\checkmark\ \forall x\, \forall y(xRy \supset x{=}y)$
2. $\forall x\, \forall y[xRy \supset \forall z\, (xRz \supset y{=}z)]$ (prem)		(conclusion)
3. $\quad\quad \forall x\, xRx$ (prem)		5. $\checkmark\ \forall y(\alpha Ry \supset \alpha{=}y)$
7. $\quad\quad \alpha R\alpha$ (3 by 11)		(4 by 11r)
8. $\forall y[\alpha Ry \supset \forall z(\alpha Rz \supset y{=}z)]$ (2 by 11)		6. $\quad \alpha R\beta \supset \alpha{=}\beta$
9. $\checkmark\ \alpha R\alpha \supset \forall z\, (\alpha Rz \supset \alpha{=}z)]$ (8 by 11)		(5 by 11r)
10. $\quad -\alpha R\alpha$	11. $\forall z(\alpha Rz \supset \alpha{=}z)$	(9 by 5)
12. $\quad\quad$ x	13. $(\alpha R\beta \supset \alpha{=}\beta)$	
(7 & 10 by 7)	Bridge 13 to 6 – Rule 8	

Note that the first premise was not needed. It looks as though it might be helpful, but it will not be because of the restrictions on $\exists y$. The right-side instantiations must be done first because of the right-side restrictions on universal instantiation.

4. The table cannot be closed.

Exercise 14-H

1.

(*) Premises and Deductive Inferences			Conclusion and Right-Side Inferences
1.	$\forall x(Ax \supset -Bx)$	(prem)	3. $\exists x(Cx \ \& \ -Ax)$
2. $\surd$	$\exists x(Cx \ \& \ Bx)$	(prem)	(conclusion)
4. $\surd$	$C\alpha \ \& \ B\alpha$	(2 by 12)	10. $\surd$ $C\alpha \ \& \ -A\alpha$
5.	$C\alpha$	(4 by 3)	(3 by 12r)
6.	$B\alpha$	(4 by 3)	11. $C\alpha$ | $-A\alpha$
7. $\surd$	$A\alpha \supset -B\alpha$	(1 by 11)	(10 by 3r)
8.	$-A\alpha$ | 9. $-B\alpha$	(7 by 5)	Lines 5 & 8 provide
	x	(5 & 8 by 7)	bridges to both sides of 11.

(**) Premises and Deductive Inferences			Conclusion and Right-Side Inferences
1. $\surd$	$\exists x(Bx \ \& \ Ax)$	(prem)	3. $\exists x(Cx \ \& \ Ax)$
2.	$\forall x(Bx \supset -Cx)$	(prem)	(conclusion)
4. $\surd$	$B\alpha \ \& \ A\alpha$	(1 by 12)	10. $\surd$ $C\alpha \ \& \ A\alpha$
5.	$B\alpha$	(4 by 3)	(3 by 12r)
6.	$A\alpha$	(4 by 3)	11. $C\alpha$ | 12. $A\alpha$
7. $\surd$	$B\alpha \supset -C\alpha$	(1 by 11)	(10 by 3r)
8.	$-B\alpha$ | 9. $-C\alpha$	(7 by 5)	
	x(5 & 8 by 7)		

In this case it is not possible to find a bridge that will lead from the open path (line 9) on the left side to the first open path (line 11) on the right side. It is possible to construct a counterexample.

Exercise 15-A

1. Universal quantifier followed by denial, or denied existential quantifier.
2. Existential quantifier followed by denial, or denied universal quantifier.

5. Universal quantifier with denied consequent in an "if-then," or denied existential quantifier.

7. Existential quantifier.

10. Most likely the existential quantifier first.

Exercise 15-B

The main operator in the assumed premise is the universal quantifier.

2. Valid, even though this sentence makes a slightly different claim than the premise. Its main operator is "if-then," and both the antecedent and the consequent are existentially quantified.

3. The main operator in this sentence is "if-then." It will be possible to construct a counterexample. Perhaps you never passed Jane (or anybody else on the road), but Jane is still slower than you (she was simply too far in front). Nothing in the premise prevents imagining this situation.

Exercise 15-C

3. If this ring glitters, it is not gold. (How does this differ from "Not everything that glitters is gold"? Is there a difference in everyday use?)

4. If Shirley comes to the party, Sue will be pleased.

6. "If Jill comes to the party, she will be pleased." The most likely reading is to take "she" to refer back to the girl who comes to the party. In some contexts "she" might be referring to someone else. In either case the main operator would be a universal quantifier. In the first case "she" would be a variable name covered by the quantifier. In the other case "she" would be a nonvariable name referring to a particular individual.

Exercise 15-D

John Doe is a boy and Jane Roe is a girl and John was fooling Jane and kissed her, but Jane loved him.

Exercise 15-E

1. To make a valid argument a connection needs to be established between being a lover and x loving y. The English has to be taken as saying that "If there is a person who loves someone, then everyone loves that person." This will permit John's loving himself to fulfill the antecedent and the consequent will follow

with John as the person everyone loves. The usual understanding of the English, however, would more likely be "If there is a person who loves someone other than himself or herself, then everyone loves that person." In this case the conclusion will not follow.

3. Not valid. In predicate notation the premise is $\exists x \; Sx$ where S is "_____ can solve the problem." The conclusion is $\exists x \; (Sx \supset \forall y \; Sy)$. Surprisingly, this conclusion is a tautology. If you work only on the right side you can, with a little ingenuity, close the only path on that side by Rule 7, thus showing validity without even needing to refer to the premise. Why does this surprising result occur? Imagining this conclusion false requires simultaneously imagining that everyone can solve the problem and imagining that there is someone who cannot solve the problem. See Appendix C, pp. 415–417, for further reflection on this puzzle.

Exercise 15-F

1 and 2. a. This should be treated first as one existentially quantified statement. After instantiation there will be found two simpler statements joined by "and" and having the same individual as subject.

c. The main operator is "if-then" with two simpler statements. The antecedent statement will have a denied existential quantifier or a universal followed by a denial.

Exercise 15-G

3. b and d are the only candidates to be identities.

Exercise 16-A

Using a as the name for Wales and C as the predicate: "_____ is the capital of _____": The statement question becomes "Bring it about that I know that $\exists x \; xCa \lor$ I know that $-\exists x \; xCa$." The *wh-* question becomes "Bring it about that $\exists x$ such that I know xCa.

Exercise 16-B

a. The first premise is the presupposition for asking which individual is the one about which P and Q are true. If you get the answer $Pa \lor Qa$, then you have the presupposition to ask a statement question. If you get the answer Qa, the rest is easy.

b. If you treat both premises as presuppostions for questions, you can avoid having to work with dummy variables.

Exercise 17-A

1. The construction has to go back far enough with earlier generations (and in that way be made sufficiently complex) to show how the conclusion can be imagined false, even though the premises are imagined true. The formula 2^n is correct, but it does *not* guarantee 2^n *distinct* ancestors.

Exercise 17-C

3. See the discussion for 17-A.

Exercise 18-B

2. Without the new rules:

    1. $\forall y\ [aAy\ \&\ -\exists x\ (bAx\ \&\ xAc)]$ Premise
    2. bAa Premise
    3. $aAc\ \&\ -\exists x\ (bAx\ \&\ xAc)$ 1 by 11
    4. aAc 3 by 3
    5. $-\exists x\ (bAx\ \&\ xAc)$ 3 by 3
    6. $\forall x\ -(bAx\ \&\ xAc)$ 5 by 13
    7. $-(bAa\ \&\ aAc)$ 6 by 11
    8. $-bAa\ \lor\ -aAc$ 7 by 6

    Split table by Table Rule 4 from 8:
    9a. $-bAa$ 9b. $-aAc$
    Path through 9a closes by Table Rule 7 from lines 2 and 9a.
    Path through 9b closes by Table Rule 7 from lines 4 and 9b.

    Using the new existential generalization rule and conjunction rule made available by tautology introduction:

    Lines 3, 4, and 5 remain the same, but only two more lines are needed to show that everything closes by rule 7:

    6. $bAa\ \&\ aAc$ from lines 2 and 4 by conjunction creation
    7. $\exists x\ (bAx\ \&\ xAc)$ from 6 by existential generalization

    Now lines 5 and 7 close the table by Table Rule 7.

Exercise 19-A

1. A-answer
3. AE-answer, if mortal is defined as "there exists a time when a person dies."
    $\forall x \exists y\ (Hx \supset Dxy)$ where D represents "_____ dies at time _____."
5. A-answer

Exercise 20-A

Four weighings. First weigh 9 against 9 with 12 left out. If the heavier is in one of the groups of 9, that group will sink, otherwise the heavier is among the 12. If the heavier is in a group of 9, you will only need two more weighings; take the group of 9 that contains the heavier and weigh 3 against 3 with 3 left out. If the heavier is in one of the groups you weigh, that group will sink, otherwise the heavier is in the unweighed group. Take the group that has the heavier; weigh 1 against 1 with 1 left out. Either the heavier will sink, or it is the one left out.

But perhaps the heavier was in the group of 12. Weigh 4 against 4 with 4 left out. Then weigh 1 against 1 with 2 left out. You may find the heavier here, but you may also have to weigh the 2 left out for the fourth weighing.

If you have not been told whether the odd coin is heavier or lighter, separate the 30 into groups of 9, 9 and 12. Weigh 9 against 9. If they balance, the odd coin is among the 12. If the odd coin is among the 12, weigh 9 from the group of 12 against 9 that we know do not contain the odd coin. If they balance, you have isolated the odd coin in the 3 coins that have not yet been weighed. Weigh 1 against 1 with 1 left out for your third weighing. If they balance, the odd one is the 1 left out. Weigh it against any of the others to discover whether it is heavy or light. If the 1 against 1 do not balance, weigh the heavier against one of the others that is not odd. If it sinks, it is the odd one and is heavy. If the latest 2 balance, the other 1 is odd and is light.

But perhaps after the first weighing we discovered the odd coin was among the 12 and after the second weighing we found it among the 9 weighed against the 9 we knew weren't odd. In this case either the group with the odd coin was heavier or was lighter, so we know not only the 9 among which the coin is to be found but also whether the coin is heavier or lighter. Weigh 3 against 3 with 3 left out, and you can find which group of 3 has the odd coin. Weigh 1 against 1 with 1 left out and you will find which is odd, already knowing whether it is heavy or light.

But perhaps after the first weighing we knew the odd coin was not among the 12 but rather in one or the other of the first groups of 9, because the 9 against 9 did not balance. Weigh the heavier of the original groups of 9 against 9 from the group of 12 that must not be odd. If they balance, you know the other group of 9 contains the odd coin and it is lighter. If they don't balance, you know that the weighed group of 9 contains the odd coin and it is heavier. Now weigh 3 against 3 with 3 left out, and you can find which group of 3 has the odd coin. Finally weigh 1 against 1 with 1 left out and you will find which is odd, already knowing whether it is heavy or light. (We thank Katie Bachman for pointing us to pp. 367–373 of *With a Tangled Skein* by Piers Anthony [Ballantine Books, New York, 1985] where a related problem is part of a plot that foils Satan.)

Exercise 20-D

1. In both cases ask for further specification of "much older than."

Exercise 20-E

As soon as the argument is put in formal notation its invalidity can be seen:

1. $-(s = p)$
2. Mp
3. Therefore $-Ms$

Exercise 20-G

$-\forall x \forall y \{[(Hxy \ \& \ Wy) \ \& \ Lyx] \supset y = m\}$ or equivalently
$\exists x \exists y \{[(Hxy \ \& \ Wy) \ \& \ Lxy] \ \& \ -(y = m)\}$

Exercise 20-H

2. The definition for prime number is as follows:

   $\forall x \{Px \leftrightarrow -\exists y \exists z \ [x=yz \ \& \ (y \neq x \ \& \ z \neq x)]\}$ or alternatively
   $\forall x \{Px \leftrightarrow -\exists y \exists z \ [x=yz \ \& \ (y \neq 1 \ \& \ z \neq 1)]\}$
   The definition for "x is a power of some number" is:
   $\forall x \{[Px \leftrightarrow \exists y \exists z \ [x=y^z + (y>1+2>1)]\}$

Exercise 20-I

1. $\forall x \forall y \ [Gxy \leftrightarrow \exists z \ (Pxz \ \& \ Pzy)]$
2. $\forall x \forall y \ [Fxy \leftrightarrow (Pxy \ \& \ Mx)]$
    $\forall x \forall y \ [Oxy \leftrightarrow (Pxy \ \& \ -Mx)]$
    Definitions of Sxy, Cxy, and Bxy are given at the bottom of p. 351.
    $\forall x \forall y \ [Dxy \leftrightarrow (Pyx \ \& \ -Mx)]$
    $\forall x \forall y \ \{Uxy \leftrightarrow \exists z \exists w \ (Pzx \ \& \ Pwy \ \& \ Bzw \ \& \ -Bxy)\}$ In this case we used B, but
    B can be defined in terms of P as is shown on p. 351. So we could substitute
    that definition in each case where B appears in this definition. In this way
    specific reference to B can be eliminated.

Exercise 20-K

A pair of related models which can serve this purpose might be such that in both
of them Adam and Benjamin are brothers and Benjamin is the father of Chris and
Jan. In one model Chris is female and Jan male; in the other the other way around.

Exercise 20-L

1. The interrogative argument is as follows: since the conclusion $\forall x\,(Px \leftrightarrow -Rx)$ appears intact in one of the premises, begin by working on the premise side:

1. $\forall x\,(Px \leftrightarrow Px) \lor \forall x\,(Px \leftrightarrow -Rx)$		Premise
2. Pb		Premise
3. $-Rb$		Interrogative move

    4a. $\forall x\,(Px \leftrightarrow Rx)$ 4b. $\forall x\,(Px \leftrightarrow -Rx)$ 1 by Table Rule 4

    5a. $Pb \leftrightarrow Rb$ Table Rule 11   5b. Bridge to the Conclusion - Table Rule 8

    6aa. Pb 6ab. $-Pb$ (Biconditional

    7aa. Rb 7ab. $-Rb$ Rule from 5a.)

       x   x   Table Rule 7 in both cases.

    If the oracle's answer were Rb, the conclusion would be $\forall x\,(Px \leftrightarrow Rx)$.

2. Use Padua's method. The predicate R is the same in both of the interpreted models. In one of them P and R coincide, in the other P and $-R$ coincide. Both possibilities are permitted by the disjunction in theory T.

Exercise 20-M

In order to apply the identifying formula to a particular case b, we have to decide whether or not b is a descendant of f. If b is a descendant of f, this can be established by means of answers to questions of the form "Is c a parent of d?" On the other hand, if b is not a descendant of f, this too can be established by means of answers to the same form of question. You can trace back all the ancestral lines of b to a time before f. In this way you can establish that b is not a descendant of f. Note that your questions concerning parenthood must also include questions about birth dates if you are to discover ancestral lines trace back to a time before f.

▲ INDEX
▼